D0678879

Moving Toward
the Mainstream

Moving Toward the Mainstream

20th Century Change Among the
Brethren of Eastern Pennsylvania

DONALD R. FITZKEE
Foreword by Donald B. Kraybill

Good Books
Intercourse, PA 17534

To Becker, for urging me to be creative,
and not merely clever

Design by Dawn J. Ranck

MOVING TOWARD THE MAINSTREAM
Copyright © 1995 by Good Books, Intercourse, Pennsylvania 17534
International Standard Book Number: 1-56148-170-X
Library of Congress Catalog Card Number: 95-17793

Library of Congress Cataloging-in-Publication Data
Fitzkee, Donald R.
    Moving toward the mainstream : 20th century change among the Brethren
of eastern Pennsylvania / Donald R. Fitzkee.
        p. cm.
    Includes bibliographical references and index.
    ISBN 1-56148-170-X
    1. Church of the Brethren. Atlantic Northeast District—History. 2. Church of the
Brethren—Pennsylvania—History—20th century.
    I. Title.
BX7820.A75F57   1995
286'.5—dc20
                                                                    95-17793
                                                                         CIP

Table of Contents

Foreword

Wave upon wave of change has transformed American life in the 20th century. The pace and scope of that change have been astonishing. From cars and computers to television and laser surgery, technology has transfigured our way of life. Technology has spurred other developments as well—widespread industrialization and urbanization, centralized government, higher education, professional occupations, global communication, and growing mobility, to name a few.

A variety of ideas also surfaced on the tides of modernization: inclusiveness, ecumenism, tolerance, pluralism, diversity, gender equality, and individual rights. These and other values have slowly reshaped the consciousness of American culture.

The many changes threatened to erode the cultural boundaries that separated sectarian communities from the larger world. The plain-dressing religious groups of North America responded in different ways. The Old Orders resisted change and fortified their communities with cultural dikes of distinction. Other groups were more willing to adapt their ways to the new cultural patterns. The Church of the Brethren struggled with the changes but gradually flowed with the times.

Known as German Baptist Brethren at the turn of the 20th century, the Brethren were one of many separatist religious communities in eastern Pennsylvania. Brethren beliefs and practices set them apart from the larger religious mainstream; along with other Anabaptist groups, they often were tagged "nonresistant" and "plain." In fact, turn-of-the-century Brethren shared many beliefs and practices with their religious relatives, the Mennonites, Brethren in Christ, and Amish. Their common themes, among others, included nonresistance, nonconformity, distinctive dress, feetwashing, congregational discipline, adult baptism, simplicity, service to others, *a cappella* singing, and a lay ministry. There were some differences, despite the many similarities. The Brethren baptized by trine immersion and held a love feast with their communion services. Less obvious historical and theological differences also distinguished them from the Amish and Mennonites. The currents of modernization, however, soon dissolved many of the Brethren distinctives and carried them toward the religious mainstream.

In the following pages, Donald Fitzkee traces the story of the Brethren in eastern Pennsylvania from the late 19th century to the present. In this social history the Brethren struggle with participation in war, holding public office, membership in the National Council of Churches, dress practices, church architecture, professional pastors, and excommunication, to name a few issues. Fitzkee explores these changes and many others in lively prose. The story that he tells is significant because it goes beyond describing the many changes underway among the Brethren to addressing their consequences. Fitzkee traces the socio-religious trends, but he also confronts us with the questions of meaning and consequence. Where do these changes lead? Why do they matter? Are we better or worse off today? This is not a boring historical record, but a provocative account that surely will stir lively discussion.

The study of this particular Brethren community is important for several reasons. First, it formed the heart of Brethren life and culture for the immigrants who arrived in the 1720s and 1730s. A study of the oldest North American Brethren community charts the long-term trends of assimilation. Second, the Brethren of eastern Pennsylvania found themselves in the midst of an encroaching megalopolis as urbanization closed in on them in the 20th century. Fitzkee's study shows the variety of expressions that emerge when a rural religious community struggles to find its way in the crucible of urbanization. Finally, the setting of eastern Pennsylvania, with its sizable population of various Amish, Mennonites, and other Anabaptist descendants, provides a social laboratory of sorts to assess the outcomes of modernization. Some of the Anabaptist communities have drifted easily into the mainstream, while others have tried to swim against the currents of the times.

Fitzkee's lively style and creative analysis make this a stimulating venture into the pages of the past. Brethren will see themselves from new perspectives, and non-Brethren will recognize similarities with their own stories in many of the vignettes. Some will cheer this move toward the mainstream, while others will despair. Some will read the story as a liberation from cultural tradition. Others will read the same changes as signs of spiritual decay in a wayward drift toward worldliness. Regardless of how we interpret the signs, Donald Fitzkee prods us to ask what it means to be faithful to a religious heritage, while we struggle to respond to the changing currents of modern life. These are important questions for Brethren and non-Brethren alike.

—Donald B. Kraybill

Preface

This book tells the story of a people who were transformed from plain to Protestant. Once known as "Dunkers" and recognized for peculiar practices such as distinctive dress and trine immersion baptism, the Church of the Brethren during the 20th century traded many symbols of separation for mainstream cultural commitments. Along the way, this church that formerly shunned interaction with "other persuasions" became a leader in the ecumenical movement. A group that once worshipped in austere meetinghouses later erected magnificent churches with stately steeples. A people who universally rejected the use of force in personal and international relations saw nearly 80 percent of its young men march off to fight in World War II.

Why did such a radical transformation take place? How does a church evolve from plain to Protestant, from marginal to mainstream? What are the ramifications of such a radical reorientation for a people of faith? These are the questions with which this book wrestles. Although Brethren are scattered across the continental United States, this study focuses on a cluster of congregations centered in eastern Pennsylvania, east and north of the Susquehanna River. Known today as the Atlantic Northeast District of the Church of the Brethren, the region is a rich setting for a study of social change. Within its bounds lie the oldest Brethren congregations and some of the newest. It encompasses congregations who are traditional and progressive, urban and rural, theologically liberal and doctrinally conservative. In short, it is a microcosm of the larger Church of the Brethren.

This work builds upon Carl F. Bowman's groundbreaking narrative history of the Church of the Brethren, *Brethren Society: The Cultural Transformation of a "Peculiar People"* (Johns Hopkins University Press, 1995). His national study was an invaluable road map that pointed me to key topics for examination in district and congregational contexts. This book complements Bowman's seminal work by providing a case study that explores and expands many of his themes in a local context. Although this is the unique story of the Brethren of Atlantic Northeast District, it holds important implications for all Brethren and others seeking to understand the process of social change.

I am indebted to the many people who helped make this book possible. The Atlantic Northeast District Historical Committee initiated the project and provided financial and moral support at all stages of the work. Committee members— Wilma Albright, Patricia Bucher, Ann Carper, Elizabeth Funk, Ira Gibbel, Richard Groff, Naomi Keeney, J. Kenneth Kreider, Stephen L. Longenecker, Ernest Shenk, and Jay V. Wenger—reviewed portions of the manuscript at various stages and patiently waited when other endeavors distracted me from the task at hand.Carl F. Bowman, Donald F. Durnbaugh, Donald B. Kraybill, Stephen L. Longenecker, and Kermon Thomasson offered helpful critical reflections on all or parts of the manuscript. Many of their insights are reflected in the final work. Members of the Lancaster and White Oak congregations reviewed the final chapter on a tight deadline, and provided useful suggestions, as well.

The friendly staff at Elizabethtown College's High Library granted free access to Brethren heritage materials over an extended period of time, even bending rules on occasion to accommodate my needs. In addition, the High Library, the Brethren Historical Library and Archives, and *Messenger,* the latter two located in Elgin, Illinois, provided photographs that have greatly enhanced this work.

Allen Hansell, Linda Balsbaugh, and other members of the Atlantic Northeast District office staff lent indispensable support services, such as photocopying and mailing, always with a smile, and often on short notice. Pastors and other leaders furnished valuable information on an extensive survey conducted in 1989, and many congregations and individuals made available historical records and photographs. The more than 30 people who agreed to be interviewed added a much-needed personal touch to the story. Phyllis Pellman Good of Good Books provided excellent editorial support.

Donald B. Kraybill and Carl F. Bowman graciously granted

access to primary source materials that they had gathered, and Elizabethtown College's Young Center for the Study of Anabaptist and Pietist Groups provided a place in which to conduct interviews, as well as other support services. In addition, I saved countless hours by processing survey results with the Young Center's computer facilities.

Center director Donald B. Kraybill, my mentor and friend, has been my most ardent supporter throughout the project. During my undergraduate study at Elizabethtown College, Don piqued my interest in Brethren heritage and provided some of the analytical tools that were indispensable for this work. Throughout several years of research, writing, and rewriting, he spent many hours helping me to clarify convoluted prose and muddled thinking. I am deeply grateful for his sacrificial time commitment, wise counsel, and friendship over these several years.

It was truly a pleasure working with the many people who have been eager for this project to be completed. No one has been more eager than my patient wife, Carolyn, who supported me in periods of productivity and procrastination, offering many words of encouragement. All the while, without a hint of resentment, she kept us afloat financially so that I could do research and write.

—Donald R. Fitzkee

1.

Streams of Influence

When Mayno Hershey moved in 1929 from Ohio to Lancaster County, Pennsylvania, the Lititz Church of the Brethren refused to accept her as a member. The wife of a Brethren minister, and member in good standing in an Ohio congregation, she had always been active in the church. But Mayno had cut her hair and wore a fashionable hat, instead of the white mesh prayer covering that other sisters in Lititz wore. She owned a gold wedding ring, played cards, and dressed according to the fashions of her day. While the Ohio Brethren found none of these behaviors to be particularly objectionable, in eastern Pennsylvania they disqualified Hershey as a candidate for church membership.

Elders encouraged her to "come within the Order of the church," but Hershey resolutely refused to modify her actions. For eight years she worshipped in Lititz, but was denied the right to commune or hold office. Finally, in 1937, she was received as a member in good standing of the Lititz Church of the Brethren.[1]

Hershey's story is not unique. It is one of many that reveals the drama of a sectarian church grappling with modernity. Buffeted by relentless forces both outside and within the church, the Church of the Brethren during the 20th century experienced a wholesale transformation from plain to Protestant. This is the story of a group of congregations in eastern Pennsylvania who shed many of the peculiar trappings of their plain-sect heritage to plunge into the American Protestant mainstream.

Roots: Anabaptism and Pietism

"The best way to understand the early Brethren," says historian Donald F. Durnbaugh, "is to see them as a Radical Pietist group which appropriated an Anabaptist view of the church."[2] The group

(which deliberately remained nameless until 1836) was born in
1708 in Schwarzenau, a small town in central Germany's Wittgen-
stein territory, where a benevolent count offered refuge to religious
"separatists." Radical Pietists abandoned corrupt and spiritually
dead established churches, which they believed made a mockery
of genuine Christian discipleship.

As these diverse Schwarzenau Pietists discussed their faith, a
group of eight, under the leadership of Alexander Mack, concluded
that infant baptism was unscriptural. Obedience to Christ, they
agreed, required them to be baptized as believers. In late summer
1708, after circulating an open invitation for others to join them,
eight members of the Reformed and Lutheran churches were baptized by trine immersion (three times forward) in the Eder River,
launching the Brethren movement. A member, whose identity intentionally was obscured, baptized Mack, who then baptized the
others.[3]

Though the first Brethren were of Pietist stock, as they formed
themselves into community they strongly resembled their Anabaptist "cousins," particularly the Mennonites, with whom Mack and
the early Brethren interacted. Nourished by their Radical Pietist
and Anabaptist roots, the Brethren earnestly sought to emulate the
New Testament church. Reacting against the sterile creedal religion
of their day, they declared allegiance to "no creed but the New Testament."

From that "creed," Brethren determined that: 1) The church
should be a visible, gathered community, separate from the sinful
world; 2) joining the church required a conscious decision to follow
Christ. One could not be born into the church; 3) the true church
practiced strict discipline to restore errant members and maintain
the purity of Christ's body; 4) Christians rejected violence and
force; and 5) believers were called to lives of literal, radical obedience to Jesus's teachings.[4]

From Germany to Germantown

Spurred by religious and economic pressures and internal dissent, a group of Brethren under the leadership of Peter Becker
migrated to Pennsylvania in 1719. Alexander Mack led a second
contingent of about 120 in 1729, and a third group arrived in the
Philadelphia area in 1733. By the 1740s the Brethren, who peaked

Architect Joseph H. Hackman's concept of the first Brethren meetinghouse, built in Germantown in 1770. The building was altered in the late 1800s, and additions were constructed in 1896 and 1915. Elizabethtown College Archives.

at several hundred adherents in Europe, had virtually abandoned their homeland for the religious freedom and economic opportunities of the new world.[5] The early Brethren settled in Germantown, a village north of Philadelphia. Though they initially preferred to "meet from house to house in imitation of the primitive church," the growing Mother Church in Germantown in 1770 erected the first Brethren meetinghouse.[6] By then the Germantown church included 57 baptized members from about 30 families, according to Baptist historian Morgan Edwards.[7] In addition, early missionary forays by the Germantown congregation gave birth to four other churches, one as far west as Conestoga, Lancaster County. Each congregation called its own "free ministers," who served without formal education or salaries.

An Effective Growth Strategy

The 19th century was an era of growth, westward expansion, and organizational development. Following Germantown's lead, the setting of Brethren worship shifted from homes and barns to simple, rectangular meetinghouses during the early 1800s.[8] Initially, congregations drew members from large geographical areas, set off from other Brethren churches' territories by clear parish boundaries. The White Oak congregation, for example, covered much of Lancaster and Lebanon counties up until 1841, when the Lebanon territory was organized into the Tulpehocken congregation. To share the burden of travel over rough, country roads, congregations erected meetinghouses throughout their territories and alternated worship among several sites.

As congregations grew, they frequently divided to form new churches. This proved to be an effective growth strategy for the Brethren of eastern Pennsylvania. By 1915, 27 congregations in Lancaster, Lebanon, Dauphin, Berks, Schuylkill, and Northumberland counties traced their roots to the Conestoga congregation that had been established by Peter Becker in 1724.[9] From 1841 to 1938 the Tulpehocken congregation expanded into five churches, whose combined membership grew from 50 to 1,069 members.[10]

Germantown, Indian Creek, and Coventry—other early Brethren congregations—expanded in a similar fashion. (For a complete list of congregations and fellowships included in this study, see Appendix B.) In addition to the growth taking place within eastern Pennsylvania, Brethren eagerly joined the exodus toward the western

The Pricetown meetinghouse, built in 1777 northeast of Reading, is the oldest unaltered Brethren church building. Brethren Historical Library and Archives (BHLA), Local Church File.

Brethren gather in the P. H. Nyce building near Harleysville for a meal at the 1903 Eastern District Conference, hosted by the Indian Creek congregation. BHLA, *Brethren Encyclopedia* Collection.

frontier, establishing new colonies and congregations along the way. Brethren reached Kentucky, Tennessee, and Missouri by 1800, Iowa by 1844, and Oregon by 1850.[11]

Preserving Unity and Uniformity

As Brethren spread across the country, maintaining common understandings grew increasingly difficult. An "Annual Conference" evolved into the primary preserver of unity in the "Brotherhood" of congregations. A set of expectations for Brethren thought and behavior, built on Annual Conference minutes, became known as "the Order of the Brethren." Those who departed from common understandings and practices were declared "out of order." As the 19th century progressed,

> Unity of thought and practice and nonconformity to the World, which were previously ensured through informal channels. . . , could no longer be sustained on such a foundation. The Brethren responded to the new situation by codifying specific requirements for being Brethren, by sharpening and enforcing their once fuzzy Order.[12]

During the late 1800s, strict dress requirements were the heart of "the Order." By prohibiting such things as bells on meeting-houses, carpets, life insurance, lightning rods, likenesses (photographs), liquor, musical instruments, sleighbells, salaried ministers, secret societies, shows and fairs, tobacco, and wallpaper, Annual Conference hoped to further strengthen cultural fences to keep the encroaching world at bay.[13]

Annual Conference decrees were binding, and deviations from the Order were dealt with firmly.

> It was the rule of the Brotherhood. . . until 1848, when a church had trouble that could not be adjusted at home by the aid of adjoining (neighboring) elders, to take it to the "Big Meeting," and there if not always, at least often, it was taken up in open council and decided.[14]

But as the number of items brought to the "Big Meeting" increased, the church sought more efficient ways of handling business. In 1849 Conference began sending committees of elders to "adjust troubles" in congregations. These committees often found satisfactory solutions, but if they failed, the matter came before Annual Conference.[15]

The increasing volume of questions brought to Annual Conference for resolution, known as queries, led to an 1856 recommendation to establish districts of five or more congregations "to settle all questions of a local character." In 1866, Annual Conference gave district organizations new impetus and clarified relationships between congregations, district meetings, and Annual Conference.[16]

Eastern District: Mixing Plain with Fancy

When elders from eastern Pennsylvania met in the fall of 1866 to discuss organizing the churches east of the Susquehanna River into a district, some favored the creation of one district, while others called for two.

> Those favoring two were, as a rule, from the German churches, and the strongest pleas for one district came from the English. The arguments for two was [*sic*] the difference in language, and the laxity of discipline of some

churches on the matter of dress, while on the other side, it was argued, and that with tears, by some that by staying together, the influence of the plain churches might have a salutary effect on those dressy churches, by mingling together.[17]

In the end, the elders agreed unanimously to establish the Eastern District of Pennsylvania, composed of all 14 congregations east of the Susquehanna River. The first District Conference was held May 29, 1867, at the Chiques meetinghouse in Lancaster County.[18]

Forming all the churches east of the Susquehanna River into a single district curiously combined some of the Brotherhood's most conservative congregations in Lancaster and Lebanon counties with some of the most progressive churches in Philadelphia, where already by the 1860s Brethren were "following the road of 'popular Christianity' and abandoning elements of the self-denying Order."[19]

Largely having made the transition from the German language to English in the first half of the century, the Philadelphia-area churches were more open to mainstream cultural influences than their rural, German-speaking brothers and sisters. Philadelphia First church received visits from Annual Conference committees in 1865 and 1868 "to set them in order" in a number of areas.[20]

A committee of five elders appointed by Annual Conference again visited the Philadelphia Brethren in 1875 to calm congregational dissent. A minority in the congregation had complained that the majority, among other violations, had hired a pastor and set him above the home ministers, taken offerings during worship, conducted baptisms in a wooden pool in the meetinghouse, and included instrumental music in the Sunday school. The grieved minority concluded:

> They are in all the above new things in unison with the popular and fashionable religion, having abandoned the non-conformity testimonies and practices of the brotherhood.[21]

The Annual Conference committee, ruling with the minority on almost every charge, ordered the Philadelphia church to: 1) cease promoting J. P. Hetrick as their pastor to the detriment of the congregation's "free ministers"; 2) stop collecting offerings, baptizing in their indoor baptismal pool, and using musical instruments, all of which were off-limits for Brethren; and 3) "adhere to the doctrine of non-conformity to the world, in dress, in spirit, and in every way that that doctrine can be applied."[22] While many of the Philadelphia church's practices were taboo in the 1870s, a number of important innovations were gaining acceptance in the larger church—among

Philadelphia philanthropist Mary S. Geiger (1828-1916) championed Sunday schools and missions. The Geiger Memorial Church of the Brethren, her namesake, located at 26th and Lehigh Streets, Philadelphia, began as a Sunday school in 1896. Elizabethtown College Archives.

them Sunday schools, Brethren periodicals, higher education, foreign and home missions, and revival meetings. Along with these came agitation for a supported ministry and doubts about plain garb, which seemed to hinder evangelism.[23]

Sunday Schools: Seeds of Change

Sunday schools were discussed for the first time in 1838 when Annual Conference flatly ruled: "Considered most advisable to take no part in such things."[24] Many Brethren feared that Sunday schools, which were becoming popular in other denominations, would usurp the responsibility of parents to teach their children at home. Besides, nowhere in Scripture could they find a command to establish Sunday schools.

Despite the Annual Conference ruling, the first Brethren Sunday schools began popping up in the Eastern District. In 1845 Jonas Gibble and his wife organized a Sunday school in Lancaster County's White Oak District that flourished for several years before the Gibbles moved west.[25] When Henry Geiger was called to the ministry by Philadelphia First church in 1853, he accepted on condition that he be allowed to open a Sunday school. The congregation reluctantly agreed, and Geiger began a Sunday school at the Crown Street meetinghouse on June 4, 1856. Philadelphia served as a proving ground for this new evangelistic technique, and before long, more than 80 percent of the congregation's converts were Sunday school scholars.[26]

By 1857, when Annual Conference reconsidered Sunday schools, opposition had softened. The church decided: "We know of no scripture which condemns Sunday-schools, if conducted in gospel order."[27] Sunday schools were here to stay (although controversy would surround them for more than 30 years). By 1905, every congregation in Eastern District operated at least one Sunday school.[28]

Revivals and Missions: Reaching the Lost

Paralleling the rapid growth of Sunday schools among the Brethren was a blossoming interest in home and foreign missions. While in years past most Brethren had been content to let their pious and peculiar lifestyle witness silently, by 1860 some felt called to more intentional evangelism. Though resisted at first because of their

Elizabeth Gibbel McCann (1868-1944), an early missionary from the West Conestoga (Middle Creek) congregation. Middle Creek Congregational Archives.

reliance on emotionalism, "protracted meetings" and revivalistic preaching gained wide acceptance in the Brotherhood by the 1880s. The growing missionary sentiment resulted in the establishment of a Domestic and Foreign Mission Board in 1880 to further what came to be known as "the first great work of the church."[29]

Armed with two new evangelistic tools—the Sunday school and revival meetings—the Brethren of Eastern District turned their attention to spreading the gospel. More than 60 converts joined the Big Swatara congregation as a result of a single series of revival meetings in 1868.[30] The Philadelphia First church started two sister churches—Geiger Memorial (1896) and Bethany (1904)—by first establishing Sunday schools, which often were used to arouse interest for new fellowships.[31]

Missions were discussed at Eastern District Conference for the first time in 1871.[32] Two years later, the Eastern District Brethren sent two evangelists to Maine, but they soon returned with an un-

McCann (second from right) departed for India from New York harbor on October 31, 1897. Middle Creek Congregational Archives.

favorable report and the mission ended.[33] The district in 1878 established a two-member Missionary Board to fulfill requests for an evangelist, and detailed mission reports were soon a regular staple at District Conference. (Typically, evangelists were sent to areas where a few isolated Brethren lived beyond the bounds of the nearest congregation.) The board was increased to three members in 1879, and six in 1885 in response to a query urging the district to "not only fill calls, but seek openings," and to make a concerted effort to preach the gospel and build "plain houses of worship."[34]

The Mission Board eventually established churches as far south as the Peach Blossom (1881) and Ridgely (1884) congregations on the Eastern Shore of Maryland and went as far north as Montreal in Canada (1899). A mission started in Tower City in 1886 led to the creation of the Shamokin Church of the Brethren. In addition to its mission projects, the board provided ongoing aid to struggling congregations.[35]

Controversial Colleges

From the beginning, the mission fires in the larger church were fueled by the periodicals and schools that were springing up across the Brotherhood. Brethren publishing efforts began in 1851 with Henry Kurtz's *The Monthly Gospel-Visiter*, [sic] which eventually evolved into *The Gospel Messenger*, and then *Messenger*, the Church of the Brethren's official magazine. Begun as a private venture, the *Visiter* [sic] was permitted by Annual Conference in 1853. Promoted by Kurtz as a medium to preserve unity and provide instruction, its columns advocated many of the innovations sweeping the Brotherhood, including academies and colleges.[36] Brethren initiated 40 institutions of academy (high school) level or above between 1852 and 1923.[37] "From the beginning, the colleges were openly *progressive*" and closely linked with the missions movement, since overseas and urban missionaries required training that could be provided by the schools.[38] Conservative Brethren feared that colleges and missions would lead to an "unscriptural" salaried ministry. In time their fears would be realized.

The 1870 Eastern District Conference adopted and passed a statement to Annual Conference, stating, "We think unanimously that colleges and high schools should not be established among us." The query cited I Corinthians 1:21 and Matthew 11:25 as evidence of God's disapproval of higher learning.[39]

But over time, proponents of higher education prevailed. The Brethren's Normal School and Collegiate Institute opened its doors in 1876 in Huntingdon, changing its name in 1896 to Juniata College.[40] Progressive Brethren from the Philadelphia-area churches developed strong ties to Juniata, while conservatives could ignore an institution beyond the district boundaries. Before long, however, another new college would be impossible to overlook.

At the initiative of J. G. Francis, interested individuals met November 29, 1898, at the Reading meetinghouse to discuss founding a college *within* Eastern District. Though many Brethren still opposed higher education, Elizabethtown College was chartered September 23, 1899.[41] Strategically located in the conservative heartland of the district, the college soon became an agent of change.

Dunker Divisions

The innovations of the late 1800s sparked continual controversy at Annual Conference and called into question some basic Brethren assumptions about dress and nonconformity. Annual Conference responded to attacks on plain dress by codifying and strictly enforcing requirements. The 1887 Eastern District Conference asked for an Annual Conference committee to visit the Germantown, Coventry, and Philadelphia churches, whose fashionably dressed members were "more or less out of order." A query from the Hatfield congregation at the 1893 District Conference warned that Philadelphia-area congregations were still out of order and were contaminating neighboring congregations with their flouting of plain dress requirements. Similar concerns were expressed at the 1898 District Conference.[42]

These issues—missions, revival meetings, Sunday schools, higher education, dress—and others polarized the Brotherhood and led to a three-way split in the early 1880s. The traditionalist "Old Orders," who staunchly resisted most innovations, broke with the main body in 1881 to form the Old German Baptist Brethren Church. The "Progressives," who pushed for change at a more rapid rate, withdrew to form The Brethren Church in 1883. The main body, or "Conservatives," continued on as the German Baptist Brethren, the name Brethren had adopted in 1871. (In 1836 the group had taken the name Fraternity of German Baptists. Brethren also were known by less formal names such as "Dunkers" or "Dunkards," both references to the church's method of baptism.)

Though Eastern District included many congregations and elders who sympathized with the views of the Old Orders and a few who

---

Diagram 1.1
Three-Way Division in the 1880s

German
Baptist ——————————— 1881 Old German Baptist Brethren
Brethren   └─┬─ 1908 Church of the Brethren
                                   1883 The Brethren Church

Book collector and antiquarian Abraham Harley Cassel (1820-1908), ca. 1900, near Harleysville. Cassel preserved many rare historical materials, including the Sauer Bible on his lap. BHLA, Brethren Encyclopedia Collection.

leaned toward the Progressives, not a single congregation in the district withdrew from the main body.[43] Likewise, no eastern Pennsylvania congregations were "lost" to The Brethren Church at the time of the division, although trouble in the Philadelphia First German Baptist Brethren church led to the creation of Philadelphia First Brethren Church in 1887.[44]

Conflict Closer to Home[45]

Though Eastern District remained united through the divisions of the 1880s, by the turn of the century similar issues threatened to split the Pennsylvania Brethren. Differences were evident from Eastern District's creation in the fall of 1866. Representatives of plain, German-speaking churches, citing language differences and the laxity of discipline among Philadelphia-area Brethren, favored two districts. Those from the "English" churches held out for a united district, hoping that the "good" influence of the conservative churches might rub off on the others.[46] From the start, the marriage between progressive and plain was built on the premise that the two would learn to live together. Instead, lovers' quarrels festered into irreconcilable differences that could only be resolved by a painful divorce.

As members of progressive churches continued to lay aside the plain garb for the "gay fashions of the world"—with the tacit approval of their elders—the dress question loomed ever larger. The Annual Conference committee, appointed in 1887 to persuade the fancy Philadelphia-area churches to dress more in accord with the Order, and several similar committees labored at their task for the next 20 years but saw few gains. It was clear to the "fancy" churches that Scripture did not mandate uniform plain dress. "Plain" Brethren were equally convinced that the Order, which was based on Scripture, needed to be preserved at all cost.

Wrangling Over Representation

As skirmishes over dress persisted, other differences surfaced as well. An 1882 query to District Conference charged that the English-speaking churches were consistently under-represented on Standing Committee—the powerful judicial body that prepared the Annual Conference agenda and enforced the Order—because delegates nearly always were chosen from the district's German-speaking majority. Since they helped pay Standing Committee delegates' expenses, the "English" churches argued that they were being subjected to a sort of taxation without representation. Their pleas for a more just system, however, fell on deaf ears.[47]

After years of wrangling over representation, the 1904 District Conference finally approved a request from the Philadelphia First congregation that "at least every other year one member of [Standing Committee] be chosen from the churches now under the care of the Annual Meeting Committee" [the "English" churches].[48] While the "English" churches no doubt were pleased with the new arrangement, many in the district were not. It may have been true that under the old plan the "English" churches were under-represented on Standing Committee, but under the new one those same churches were greatly *over*-represented. Though only a half dozen elders served the "English" churches, compared to 40 or more in the rest of the district, over a two-year period a fourth of the district's Standing Committee delegates would be chosen from among those six elders.[49]

The 1907 District Conference appointed a "Committee on Territorial Division" to correct this imbalance, and, as a result of the committee's report the following year, the dividing line for choosing Standing Committee representatives was moved to the west, near Reading.[50] In the words of Carl F. Bowman:

> As a result, the eastern section came to include a number of plainer "German" congregations, and from that point on, whenever it was the easterners' turn to be represented, their delegate was chosen from the *German congregations* that had recently been shifted to their side of the line. This resulted from the fact that the plainer "German" elders constituted the bulk of the voting body, which enabled them to select, on alternating years, a "German" from the "English" side of the line. Frustrated at losing their Standing Committee representation in what seemed to be a clear case of Dunker gerrymandering, the progressive congregations withheld their annual financial assessments in protest.[51]

Progressives concluded that only the formation of a separate district could free them from the tyranny of the plain majority. Thus, many of the same churches that 40 years earlier had prevailed in their desire to form a single district now wanted out. Conversely, many conservative congregations, that in 1866 favored creating two districts, now opposed division.

Eleven congregations brought to the 1910 District Conference a petition to organize themselves into a new district, citing as reasons their under-representation on Standing Committee and their desire

Jacob T. Myers (1851-1915) was pastor and elder of several Philadelphia-area congregations. He advocated a division of Eastern District at the 1910 Annual Conference. Elizabethtown College Archives.

to engage in "more aggressive church work" in towns and cities. (The district's plain and rural-minded Home Missionary Board, the petitioners charged, had been reticent to dedicate time and resources to the cities. On the other hand, that all but one of the petitioning congregations were out of order likely heightened conservatives' reservations about urban ministry.)[52] Divided district elders forwarded the petition to the 1910 Annual Conference, where it prompted vigorous debate.

Prominent elder Jesse Ziegler pointed out that the paper came to Annual Conference as a "Christian courtesy" to the petitioners, not because the district supported it.[53] Those opposing the division raised several objections: 1) To divide a church district when not all parties were in harmony was highly irregular; 2) most of the seceding congregations had been out of order for years; 3) the proposed division was a "class line" rather than a geographical division; 4) a provision in the petition for other churches to "escape" into the lax new district would make it difficult for Eastern District to enforce Annual Conference decisions; and 5) the wording of the petition unfairly cast the district's plain majority in a negative light.[54]

Speaking on behalf of the seceding churches, Philadelphia pastor J. T. Myers reiterated grievances against the larger district and maintained that a division was the only solution. He concluded, ". . .I will go back to the East with a sore heart, and it won't end with me, if you, as an Annual Meeting, turn down this paper." Despite Brother Myers' assurances that "the kindest feelings prevail" among the churches of the district, it was evident that Eastern District had serious family differences.[55]

Annual Conference appointed a committee of three to investigate the matter, and at a September 21, 1910, special District Conference district leaders again discussed dividing. Although 12 speakers opposed the split and six favored it, by day's end a five-member committee was appointed to draw up an appropriate dividing line.[56] Their report was approved at the May 3 and 4, 1911, District Conference and passed on to the 1911 Annual Conference for ratification. At Annual Conference's end the former Eastern District was officially divided.

The plainer congregations to the west retained the Eastern District name, while the seceding congregations in the Philadelphia area became the "Southeastern District of Pennsylvania, New Jersey and

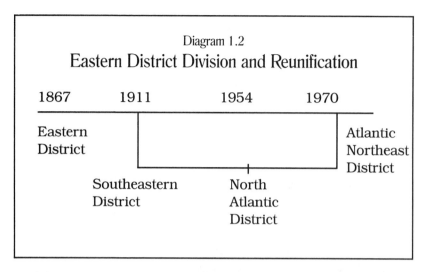

Diagram 1.2
Eastern District Division and Reunification

Eastern New York." The new district's already cumbersome name later was lengthened, before finally being simplified to North Atlantic District in 1954.[57] The two districts eventually would be reunited in 1970 to form Atlantic Northeast District.

Separating Plain from Fancy

The line separating Eastern District from the Southeastern District of Pennsylvania, New Jersey and Eastern New York was as complicated as the new district's name:

> Starting at Wilmington, Del., following the line of the Wilmington and Northern R.R. to Birdsboro, via Coatesville, thence on a line in a northeasterly direction to county line, one mile northeast of Pottstown, then line running parallel with Schuylkill river, one mile from the River, to point one mile east on Mingo Station, thence on a line northeast to North Wales, thence to New Hope on the Delaware River, then following Delaware River to New York State. The new district is to comprise the whole of the State of New Jersey, Greater New York City, Long Island and all the territory east of the proposed line.[58]

The convoluted line "was basically designed to achieve a *class* division by drawing *geographic* lines." Despite the committee's creative efforts to draw a line that separated "plain" from "fancy," the Norristown congregation, which better fit the "plain class" but fell on the "fancy" side of the new line, had to be listed as an exception: "The Norristown church is to represent in the old District."[59] (See Diagram 1.3.)

The new Southeastern District consisted of about 1,550 members in 12 congregations. Three of the 12 had more than 200 members; seven had 101 or less. The reconstituted Eastern District included about 6,000 members in 31 congregations. Fifteen congregations had over 200 members, while 11 had less than 100 members.[60] In short, the new district consisted mostly of small, urban and suburban congregations scattered around three larger congregations. Most large, rural congregations remained in Eastern District.

While the two districts agreed to jointly support the Brethren Home, Elizabethtown College, and the Children's Aid Society,[61] most other cooperation ceased in 1911. One woman who grew up

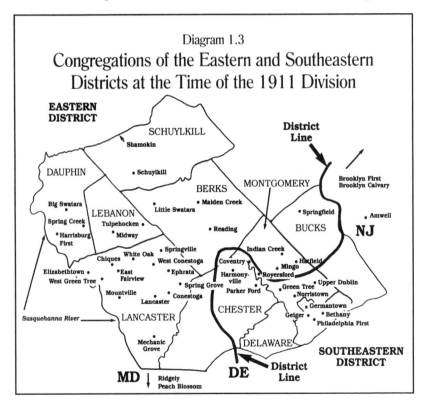

Diagram 1.3

Congregations of the Eastern and Southeastern Districts at the Time of the 1911 Division

in Eastern District's Mingo congregation recalls that during the 1920s and 1930s the district line might as well have been the Berlin Wall. Though Mingo was located just three miles from Southeastern District's Royersford church, the two congregations had little or no interaction. She recalls, "When I was a kid I don't even know if I knew there was a Church of the Brethren in Royersford. We were each in our own little world."[62]

While Mingo interacted with the nearby Indian Creek and Hatfield congregations, differences across the district line prevented association with Royersford. "The Jews had no relationship with the Samaritans," recalls a former pastor at Royersford. Only death broke down the dividing wall— Royersford members sometimes were buried in Mingo's cemetery.[63]

The Fundamentalist Controversy

By the time of the district division in 1911, an intramural theological battle between "modernists" and "fundamentalists" was raging within Protestantism. American cultural optimism and scientific progress in the decades before World War I had nurtured a new theology. Convinced of the inadequacy of traditional Christianity, liberal modernists argued that Christians needed to rediscover the essentials that would allow Christianity to speak to the present age.

Three core beliefs characterized modernist thought. First, they consciously adapted religious ideas to modern culture. Second, they believed that God not only revealed himself through Scripture, but was immanent in and could be known through human cultural development. Third, was the notion that human society was improving rapidly, moving toward the realization of the kingdom of God. Accompanying these core beliefs was a general optimism about the world's course, a downplaying of Christian distinctiveness, more emphasis on good works than doctrine, and a willingness to subject Scripture itself to scientific study.[64]

Rather than rediscovering essentials, conservative "fundamentalists" believed that modernists were leading Christians astray from the fundamentals of the faith. Missing from the new theology, conservatives believed, was a proper respect for the authority of Scripture, a biblical emphasis on personal salvation (which had been replaced by a "social gospel"), a realistic view of the depravity of humanity, and a zeal for the salvation of lost souls in worldwide missions.

The publication of *The Fundamentals,* 12 volumes published from 1910 to 1915, helped crystallize the fundamentalist opposition. Edited by Amzi C. Dixon and Reuben A. Torrey of Moody Bible Institute, these volumes attempted to set forth the clear essentials of the Christian faith. Fundamentalist voices were not confined to the Midwest, however. The World's Christian Fundamentals Association was organized in Philadelphia in 1919, and the presence of conservative institutions, such as Princeton Theological Seminary and the fundamentalist Philadelphia School of the Bible, helped establish the Greater Philadelphia Area as a center of fundamentalist thought during the late 1910s and early 1920s.[65]

As a people who emphasized the centrality of Scripture, orthodox doctrine, and living out one's faith, Brethren felt some affinity with both sides of the fundamentalist/modernist rift. They could appreciate the fundamentalists' literal interpretation of divinely inspired Scripture, while the modernists' emphasis on the kingdom of God, peace, and right living also meshed with the Brethren ethos. Separated by the "class line" that divided them, leaders of the two districts were further polarized by the ongoing debate.

Fundamental Brethren

Southeastern District Brethren clearly favored the fundamentalist side. Influential leaders in the district, C. C. Ellis and T. T. Myers, in 1918 established a School of Theology at Juniata College in Huntingdon, which during the 1920s was the leading voice for fundamentalist thought among the Brethren. Uneasy about the noncreedalism of the Brethren and their silence on key doctrinal issues, the founders of Juniata's School of Theology hoped to counter what they saw as a liberal leaning at rival Bethany Bible School in Chicago.[66]

The Juniata influence was evident at the 1922 Southeastern District Conference, where delegates approved a list of "Fundamentals" to be approved by new pastors entering the district:

> 1) The divine authority and the full and complete inspiration of the whole of the Old and the New Testament Scriptures; 2) The deity of our Lord Jesus Christ; 3) The doctrine of the Trinity; 4) The fall of man and his consequent depravity and atonement in His blood, which

was shed for sin, and His personal resurrection; 6) Justi-
fication by faith in our Lord Jesus Christ; 7) Regeneration
by the Holy Spirit; 8) The personality of the Holy Spirit,
and as the Divine Paraclete, the Comforter and Guide of all
the people of God; 9) Sanctification through the Word and
the Spirit; and 10) The personal and visible return of our
Lord Jesus Christ, the resurrection of the dead and the last
judgment.[67]

With the closing of the School of Theology at Juniata in 1925,
Brethren fundamentalists lost an articulate voice. But following
World War II, as the church's involvement in social ministries and
the ecumenical arena grew, it would become evident that some
churches of the district had maintained a distinctively fundamentalistic flavor.

Plain Liberals

Isolated geographically and intellectually from the ivory towers
of Protestantism, where much of the modernist/fundamentalist
battle was waged, the plain churches of Eastern District were generally less influenced by and less aware of the ongoing theological
debate. While Southeastern District during the early 1920s
churned out a list of doctrinal fundamentals, Eastern District leaders stressed Brethren distinctives more than theological purity.
Eastern District's Ministerial Board during the 1930s required
ministers to respond affirmatively to four questions before they
could assume pastorates:

1. Do you believe in the Bible as the inspired word of
God?

2. Do you accept in good faith the fundamental doctrines
of the atonement, the resurrection of the just and the
unjust, the second coming of Christ, and the final judgment?

3. Will you uphold, defend, and practice the specific
doctrines of the "Church of the Brethren" such as feet
washing, the Lord's supper, the communion, peace,

non-swearing, anti-secrecy, separation from the world, etc?

4. If called to this pastorate will you cooperate with the elders and ministers of the Eastern District of Pennsylvania in their effort to uphold, defend, and practice the decisions of the General Conference of the "Church of the Brethren"?[68]

While the questions touched on some of the same doctrinal issues as the Southeastern District statement, traditional Brethren practices such as *nonconformity* to the world seemed more important to Eastern District Brethren than *conformity* to any specific theological statement.

Some of those in Eastern District who were influenced by the ongoing modernist/fundamentalist theological debate tilted toward the modernists. Informed observers note that often beneath Eastern District elders' conservative plain dress lurked a surprisingly liberal set of theological views. Describing the paradoxical liberal theological bent of one respected leader in Eastern District, a close associate recalls, "Theologically, he wore a plain coat and that's all."[69] Some key leaders in the district listened regularly on the radio to Harry Emerson Fosdick, liberalism's premier preacher, during the 1930s and 1940s.[70]

Curiously, as Brethren peered across the district line, both sides perceived that those on the other side of the fence were more "liberal." The Dunkers of Eastern District, observing the stylish dress and fancy church buildings of the Philadelphia-area Brethren, could only frown at their "liberal" bent toward worldliness. The Philadelphia-area Brethren, on the other hand, standing firmly on the fundamentals of the faith, raised eyebrows at the "liberal" theology of some of their plain brothers and sisters.[71]

What's in a Name?

As Eastern District moved toward division in the first part of the century, the Brotherhood was debating another divisive question: What's in a name? As an informally organized fellowship, early Brethren were reluctant to adopt a formal group name. Out of necessity, the 1836 Annual Conference had decided that "Fraternity of German Baptists" was to be used in legal documents and other situations calling for a church name. This remained the legal name until 1871, when "German Baptist Brethren" was adopted.[72] But as "German Baptist Brethren" began taking the gospel to the cities and foreign mission fields—where most people were not "German"—some found their ethnic label hindered evangelism. Outsiders quite naturally assumed that German Baptist Brethren spoke and worshipped in German. A total of 14 papers concerning the church's name were brought to the 1888 Annual Conference, which decided to make no change.[73] The name question continued to agitate for the next 20 years.

Meanwhile, some Brethren had already begun to downplay their ethnicity. Members of the Harrisburg First church voted in 1897 to change the wording on their church sign to:

"German Baptist Brethren Church
Services in English"

In 1905 the Harrisburg Brethren dropped the German label altogether, referring to themselves simply as "Baptist Brethren."[74]

More traditional congregations, on the other hand, were satisfied with the "German Baptist Brethren" label, because that's what they were. Alarmed at the prospect of a name change, five Eastern District congregations sent queries to the 1905 Annual Conference, requesting that the name "German Baptist Brethren" be retained.[75] Instead, the name "Dunker Brethren" was suggested in 1905 and brought to a vote a year later, falling a mere 22 votes shy of the required two-thirds majority.[76] Finally, in 1908 the name was changed to "Church of the Brethren" by a vote of 289 to 103.[77] Having shed the limitations of their peculiar name, forward-looking Brethren were poised for ministry and outreach. The new name had the advantage of allowing the church "to carry its historical identity (of being 'brethren') into the future, without parading its peculiarity. It provided *continuity*, while downplaying *distinctiveness*."[78]

Growth and Decline

Following the 1908 name change and the district division of 1911, both districts experienced modest growth in membership, the number of congregations, and congregational size. (See Table

1.4.) Membership increased in the first half of the century as average congregational size grew and new congregations were formed by dividing existing churches. This method apportioned leadership, resources, and property between the old and new congregations, providing the new church with a ready-made meetingplace and a corps of leaders.

In addition to caring for the building and leadership needs of

Table 1.4

Congregations, Membership, Attendance, and Congregational Size in Atlantic Northeast District and Forerunner Districts

Year	Number of Congregations	Total Members	Avg. Size of Cong.	Avg. Attend.	Avg. Att. per Cong.
1911	37	7,545	204		
1916	49	8,384	171		
1920	52	9,665	186		
1925	57	10,297	181		
1930	57	11,627	204		
1935	59	13,068	221		
1940	61	14,419	236		
1945	59	15,006	254		
1950	60	15,962	266		
1955	62	17,300	279		
1960	64	18,310	286		
1965	67	18,810	281	12,709	190
1970	63	18,724	297	11,338	180
1975	61	18,488	303	11,295	185
1980	60	17,946	299	11,209	187
1985	61	16,845	276	10,930	179
1990	67	16,152	241	10,044	150
1993	72	16,016	222	11,154	155

Sources: (For years prior to 1930) *Church of the Brethren Yearbook; Minutes of the District Meetings of the Eastern District of Pennsylvania;* Elmer Q. Gleim (1975:35). Data for years prior to 1930 should be viewed as suggestive rather than definitive, since no standardized source of data is available. (From 1930 to present) *Church of the Brethren Yearbook and Church of the Brethren Statistics.*

new congregations, the traditional church planting pattern limited average congregational size. Thus, the church expanded in a way that preserved an intimate sense of community by keeping congregations from growing too large.

Two new arrivals in the early 1900s—automobiles and salaried pastors—began to change the way Brethren planted churches and their views on optimal congregational size. With improved transportation, scattered members could drive to a central building each week, instead of waiting for services to be held in the meetinghouse nearest them. At the same time, the need to provide financial support for pastors also fueled the trend toward larger congregations. Instead of meeting in multiple meetinghouses and dividing periodically, congregations closed meetinghouses and consolidated at a central meeting place.

While in 1905 the Eastern District consisted of 33 congregations meeting in 120 different buildings, by 1930, the number of active meetinghouses had declined to 104, and the number of congregations had grown to 57.[79] Extra houses gradually were phased out of service, so that by the mid-1960s most congregations met in a centralized building.[80] In a related trend, while the average congregational size in 1915 was a modest 171, by 1975 the figure had

Elmer Edris, a member of the Little Swatara congregation, in the late 1920s. Automobiles promoted a move from multiple preaching points to centralized places of worship. Esther Yenser Collection.

Construction of the Bareville meetinghouse in 1915. The Conestoga congregation at one time rotated meetings among five meetinghouses, before consolidating in Bareville. Conestoga Congregational Archives.

swelled to over 300. The profile of a typical Brethren congregation shifted from a small fellowship meeting in scattered meetinghouses, led by free ministers, to a larger congregation, meeting in a centralized "church," led by a salaried pastor. Congregations such as Palmyra—which extensively renovated and restyled its building in 1959 and 10 years later saw its membership eclipse the 1,000-member mark—became models for other congregations to emulate.[81]

But few congregations ever reached the numerical heights of Eastern District's Palmyra church. In fact, growth in Southeastern District had ebbed decades earlier. After nearly doubling in membership from 1,550 in 1911 to over 3,000 in 1930, Southeastern District membership leveled off at 3,633 in 1943 and then declined.[82] Membership in Eastern District grew modestly through the 1960s, peaking in 1968 at 15,749 members.[83] As churches struggled with declining membership, and the passage of time healed historical differences, steps toward reunification of eastern

Pennsylvania began in the 1960s. In 1970 North Atlantic and Eastern districts merged to form Atlantic Northeast District (AND). The combined membership of the two districts peaked in 1964 at 18,891. By 1990 AND membership had declined by 14 percent to 16,152.[84] In the denomination as a whole, membership peaked in 1963 at 202,257 members, but by 1990 had declined by more than 25 percent to about 150,000.

Denominational diagnosticians since the 1960s have mused on the Brethren membership malaise, citing loss of evangelistic fervor and distinctive identity, preoccupation with social witness, the gulf between denominational leaders and congregations, the demographic shift in the United States from the country to the cities, a lack of inclusiveness, and other factors as reasons for decline.[85] While many of these factors may be pertinent, numerical trends are best understood in light of the dramatic changes that have taken place since 1900 in leadership, organization, discipline, buildings and worship, and attitudes toward the ecumenical church and the world—topics with which the remainder of this book grapples.

2.

A Peculiar People

The Brotherhood-wide innovations of the late 1800s—publications, Sunday schools, revival meetings, colleges, overseas missions—had begun to nudge Brethren toward the religious and cultural mainstream. Alarmed by these trends, most Eastern District Brethren at the turn of the century tenaciously clung to the time-tested Order of the church.

Bent on preserving Dunker distinctives, conservatives combatted the raging wildfires of worldliness that were sweeping across the Brotherhood. The district's progressives, on the other hand, dismissed warnings that the church would be singed by harmful changes. Instead of dousing diabolical fires, they believed conservatives actually were quenching the Spirit that was leading backward Brethren into the world to save souls and spread the Gospel.

In time, progressives would carry the day. At the turn of the century, however, conservatives maintained the upper hand in eastern Pennsylvania. Eastern District Brethren were a peculiar people, dedicated to cardinal doctrines of nonconformity, nonresistance, and nonswearing. Their simple worship in plain meetinghouses; their reliance on a largely untrained, unpaid ministry; and their commitment to strict discipline all served to set them apart from the world and the "worldly churches." Forming the core of Brethren peculiarity was the doctrinal tripod of nonconformity, nonresistance, and nonswearing.

"Be Not Conformed"

The doctrine of nonconformity grew out of Scriptures such as Romans 12:2, which calls followers of Christ to "be not conformed to this world . . ." Brethren were required to forgo worldly amusements and pleasures; practice simplicity in speech, dress, and general conduct; remain honest, true, and pure; and practice temperance in

Samuel N. and Emma (Gibble) Becker family on their farmhouse porch near Mastersonville in 1906. The Beckers were members of the Chiques congregation. Floy Fitzkee Collection.

all things.[1] Nonconformity in dress was particularly important.

Brethren believed that outward appearance revealed one's inward spiritual condition. To them it was obvious that a meek and humble follower of Christ would spurn the world's vain fashions in favor of clothing more in accordance with Gospel plainness. Initially, this view was maintained through informal channels and common consent, but in the late 1800s Annual Conference adopted exacting requirements to combat the erosion of plain dress. "This issue of the 'garb' worn by Brethren probably took more time at Annual Meetings than any other topic between 1865 and 1910."[2] Ironically, the doctrine of nonconformity to the world called for a great deal of conformity to the Order of the Brethren. *Gospel Messenger* editor J. H. Moore provided rationale for uniformity in dress:

> If all Christian people would dress plainly, as directed
> by the Scriptures, and as taught by good common sense,
> the question of uniformity in dress would never need to

disturb us. But because of the ever-changing fashions, and the tendency of some of our own people to fall in with them, and thus be led away from Gospel plainness, it has been deemed proper, and wisely so, that we perpetuate the uniform style of attire that has come down to us, using it as an aid, or a means, of maintaining that plainness that should characterize the true people of the Lord. That plainness is most clearly taught in the New Testament must be admitted by all careful Bible students . . . The Brethren have reached the conclusion, that uniformity, or an established order in dress, is the very best known way of keeping members in the line of Gospel plainness.[3]

An 1893 Annual Conference decision spelled out some plain requirements for brothers and sisters:

By plainness of dress we mean the common order of giving shape to dress, as practiced by the old brethren and sisters generally, and by plainness of hair we mean the hair parted on the top of the head, or all combed back in a plain manner, or combed straight down all around the head, and not having the hair and beard trimmed according to the custom of the world.[4]

The 1898 Annual Conference elaborated further:

Gospel plainness requires that sisters attire themselves in plainly-made garments free from ornaments, ruffles and all unnecessary appendages. Plain bonnets and hoods are in harmony with Gospel plainness, and are adopted as the head dress for our sisters. The brethren likewise should dress themselves in plain attire, not wearing fashionable hats and neckties, gold for adornment or other superfluities.[5]

Though most Eastern District congregations were committed to uniform plain dress as spelled out by Annual Conference, several were failing to hold the line. Numerous visits from Annual Conference committees during the latter part of the 1800s had done little to restore order in these wayward churches. Deeply troubled by this, district elders in 1900 sent an impassioned plea for help to the Standing Committee of Annual Conference, which stated in part:

> We see no other way than to once more appeal to you for help—We are well aware that Committees have been appointed, and visit after visit have been made and that there are some improvements to a certain extent, yet as a whole with sorrow and regret we realize that our Spiritual Condition is gradually growing worse and church government is becoming more demoralized; officials receiving members into the church without any restrictions whatever concerning outward appearance, discarding the recognized head covering and bonnet. . . and instead substituting the hat. Under these conditions new churches are organized and the evil is spreading. . .

> We therefore prayerfully and conscientiously appeal to you, yea we insist for an immediate action. The Doctrine of Christ as believed and practiced by the Brethren Church must absolutely be executed in order that peace and union may prevail in the churches. We thus pray that the Spirit of the Lord may rest upon you and come to our rescue.[6]

Eight out-of-order congregations—Coventry, near Pottstown; Parker Ford; Royersford; Green Tree, in Oaks; Norristown; Upper Dublin (later Ambler); Sand Brook (New Jersey); and Philadelphia First—received visits in 1901 from an Annual Conference committee. The committee stressed the importance of "the Order and church unity in nonconformity to the world and committed them to the care of our Heavenly Father," but were unable to stem the tide of worldliness.[7] Even so, most leaders of the district remained committed to plain dress and other aspects of the nonconformity doctrine.

Much broader than the issue of physical appearance, the doctrine of nonconformity touched on many areas of life, including recreation and leisure activities, association with civic organizations, modes of transportation, the style of houses Brethren lived in, and more. A reading of the Council Meeting minutes of several congregations reveals that all of the following practices were frowned upon—at least by some Eastern District Brethren—at the turn of the century: bicycle riding; attending fairs, shows, mass meetings, conventions, the opera, and picnics (even other churches' Sunday school picnics); taking or displaying photographs; smoking and chewing tobacco; holding a life insurance policy; sleigh-bells; matting (carpet) in the aisles of the meetinghouse; playing checkers, dancing, drunkenness, and frequenting saloons; and holding membership in labor unions and secret societies.[8] In short, Brethren lived sober and self-controlled lives in their pursuit of gospel plainness.

"Turn the Other Cheek"

Closely tied to the doctrine of nonconformity were teachings on nonresistance and nonswearing. Scriptural injunctions to "resist not evil," "turn the other cheek," and "overcome evil with good" (Matthew 5:39; Romans 12:21) led Brethren to reject the use of force. They believed it was inconsistent for meek and humble followers of Christ to use force—even to achieve noble goals. Nonresistant Brethren would not participate in war, frowned on holding political office and using the law to prosecute claims, and sometimes refrained from voting in worldly elections.

Annual Conference statements issued during the Civil War, and still in force at the turn of the century, made participation in warfare a test of membership.[9] The church also prohibited its members from holding any political post "which requires them to administer an oath, or to use physical force, in performing the duties of the office."[10] Brethren were permitted to hold local offices that didn't violate "Gospel principles" but were strongly encouraged to "keep out of politics altogether."[11] Voting in "worldly elections," although not a test of fellowship, was frowned upon.[12]

Brethren also were slow to prosecute in civil courts, and would do so only after consulting with their local church. Sometimes the church, meeting in Council, recommended additional reconciliation efforts before a member went to court, and deacons were appointed to mediate. Those who neglected to consult the church before going to law were required to confess their fault before the church.[13]

"Let Your Yea Be Yea"

Nonswearing was the third leg of the Brethren doctrinal tripod. Based on Jesus's words in Matthew 5:33-37, Brethren refused to swear oaths, choosing instead to "let their yea be yea and their nay be nay." To Brethren, who believed a child of God always speaks the truth, oaths were superfluous.

Partly because of their belief in nonswearing, Brethren at the turn of the century—progressive and conservative alike—vehemently opposed oath-bound secret societies such as the Free Masons or the Grange. Speaking at a ministers meeting in 1895, progressive pastor J. T. Myers cited several reasons for Brethren to oppose secret societies: 1) They violate biblical principles by requiring initiates to swear oaths; 2) they are a threat to the home because they take the man away from his family; 3) they compete with the church for time and interest; 4) they pose as an alternative religion, but are without Christ; and 5) they violate scriptural teachings against secrecy.

At the same meeting, noted Brethren elder S. R. Zug stated: "I believe Secret Organizations are the worst thing in the world. I raised four boys, and I said to them, 'I will rather see you go into the grave than into the Secret Lodge.'"[14]

The 1870 Annual Conference required applicants for baptism to state whether they were members of a secret order.[15] Those who refused to renounce the lodge could not join the church.[16] In sum, the Brethren doctrines of nonconformity, nonresistance, and non-swearing effectively erected a barrier between God's peculiar people and the world around them.

"Other Persuasions"

Brethren at the turn of the century not only stood apart from the world, but also from "worldly churches." In fact, little distinction was made between "the world" and other churches, since it was abundantly clear to the Brethren that they were the one, true, scriptural church.

A brother preaching at Elizabethtown College in 1904 stated "that there are 366 churches in the world, but only one [is] right . . . [T]he time will come when God will say to the 365 churches, 'Depart from me, ye workers of iniquity.'"[17]

Though Brethren affirmed the core of historic Christian beliefs, they emphasized practices that set them apart, such as their distinctive mode of baptism. Brethren at the turn of the century insisted that trine immersion (baptizing three times forward) was the Christian mode of baptism.[18] Further, to be valid, baptism had to be administered by a German Baptist Brethren minister in good standing, and "if it be reasonably convenient," in running water.[19] Thus, new members coming from other denominations—even denominations who practiced trine immersion—were rebaptized.

Separateness also was maintained at love feast, the three-part

Noted Lancaster County elder Samuel Ruhl Zug (1832-1926). Zug and other Brethren staunchly opposed secret oath-bound organizations.
Elizabethtown College Archives.

communion service, which was open only to correctly baptized Brethren who were within the Order of the church. Brethren believed that "one of the essentials to profitable communion is union. There should be love, harmony, peace, union; as far as possible unity in faith." Participation in the love feast was equivalent to declaring that one was in complete harmony with Brethren doctrines and practices, and with all brothers and sisters gathered at the Lord's table. Such an understanding ruled out participation by non-Brethren.[20]

For similar reasons, Annual Conference ruled in 1849 that Brethren

> cannot, consistently with the views we entertain of the Gospel order, commune with other societies. And if any of our members should do so, they ought to be tenderly admonished, and given to understand that the Brethren cannot hold them in fellowship, if they continue to do so.[21]

Minutes from an 1899 Council Meeting at the Lancaster congregation report that a couple

> had gone to the Moravian Church and participated with them in their Lovefeast. They now consider it a violation; are sorry for it and ask the church to forgive them. The church forgave them and [they] were admonished to be more careful in the future.[22]

When members left "to unite with another persuasion" they were unceremoniously dropped from the Brethren membership roll. Polite transfers of membership were unthinkable. One either was or was not a member of the church.

Brethren at the turn of the century were cautious about inviting non-Brethren to speak in their services, even on topics dear to the Brethren such as temperance. The Chiques congregation until the early 1920s refused to allow a representative from the Anti-Saloon League to speak, even though the congregation sympathized with the league's concerns.[23] The Mountville congregation in 1906 was admonished "not to call in ministers of other denominations to preach the main sermon on funeral occasions."[24]

When non-Brethren were present, they were greeted with the right hand of fellowship, but not the holy kiss. The kiss was reserved for fellow Brethren in good standing, thus reinforcing the outsider status of others.[25] And while members of the fellowship called each other "brother" and "sister," "Mr." and "Mrs." were used for nonmembers.[26]

Distinctive dress also served as a visible boundary marker. The White Oak congregation's Elder Hiram Gibble, speaking at the turn of the century on the prayer covering, described this function of plain dress:

> I and another brother once came into a family where there were three sisters that had no covering on. After we left I said, "I suppose these are religious professors too, and I presume they belong to such a church."
>
> "O," he replied, "they are all members of our fraternity."
>
> "Well," I said, "if they would have the sign I would have recognized them as members. But so I did not know it."[27]

To be Brethren was to be separate, distinctive, plain, peculiar. At the same time, being Brethren required living in peace and harmony with brothers and sisters of like precious faith. A member who transgressed the Order disrupted the unity of the church and was dealt with accordingly. In a word, the Brethren view of the church as a nonconforming community demanded congregational discipline.

"If Thy Brother Shall Trespass Against Thee"

Matthew 18, more than any other scripture, epitomized Brethren at the turn of the century. This text was the foundation and blueprint for resolving conflicts and practicing congregational discipline:

> Moreover if thy brother shall trespass against thee, go and tell him his fault between thee and him alone: if he shall hear thee, thou hast gained thy brother. But if he

will not hear thee, then take with thee one or two more, that in the mouth of two or three witnesses every word may be established. And if he shall neglect to hear them, tell it unto the church: but if he neglect to hear the church, let him be unto thee as a heathen man and a publican. Verily I say unto you, Whatsoever ye shall bind on earth shall be bound in heaven; and whatsoever ye shall loose on earth shall be loosed in heaven. (Matthew 18:15-18, KJV)

The groundwork for effective church discipline was laid well before prospective members joined the church. Applicants for baptism first were visited by two or three brethren who examined "their convictions, their faith in Christ and their agreement with the *doctrines of the church* as taught in the Scriptures, such as the ordinances, as we practice them, non-resistance, non-swearing, non-conformity and the avoiding of secret, oath-bound societies."[28] Provided that the investigation unveiled nothing objectionable, the congregation would approve the candidate for baptism.

Prior to the baptism, Matthew 18:10-22 was read "as a rule for the government of [the applicants'] lives and dealing with each other after becoming members of the church. . . ," and additional comments were offered on the meaning of church membership. Elder Jacob H. Longenecker, who oversaw the Spring Creek congregation in Hershey during the early 1900s, addressed these topics in his baptismal instructions: 1) Whether the applicant was at peace; 2) nonswearing; 3) "noncombativeness"; 4) nonresistance; 5) nonconformity, which was broken down into specific instructions on one's Christian walk, dress, hair, jewelry, shows, fairs, theaters, photographs, and "spending money extravagantly"; 6) the importance of family worship ("family altar") and attending services and Council Meetings; 7) avoiding secret societies and life insurance; 8) divorce and remarriage; and 9) tobacco use.[29] Only those who accepted such a definition of membership were baptized.[30]

Disciplinary matters dominated congregational Council Meetings at the turn of the century.[31] Having promised to do so prior to baptism, members were expected to confront each other and work

Applicants for baptism in the Little Swatara congregation, ca. 1920. Sandra Kauffman Collection.

out differences as they arose. Cases that could not be settled by the parties involved came before Council Meeting for resolution by the entire church.

The language used in Council Meetings was analogous to a courtroom. Council dealt with the *case* of so-and-so, who was *charged* with an offense. If the charge was *sustained,* the offender would need to confess before the church. Discipline, at its best, was practiced out of a dual concern for the purity of the church and the spiritual welfare of the offending member. Even in cases where members were disowned from the church, the ultimate goal was restoration.

Frequently, lesser offenses—such as slight variations in dress—resulted in an admonition from the congregation's elder, instructing members to come within the Order. Admonitions were given on a wide range of topics, as these turn of the century examples show:

> An admonition to members who are not in the order of the brethren, such as wearing mustache, in their clothes, too proud, and talking while others are engaged in prayer.[32]

An admonition that brothers shall not wear their hats according to the fashion of the world with a broken crown in the middle. And also sisters shall not go without aprons or capes.[33]

An admonition, Brethen shall not use Tobacco in our houses of worship in time of meeting. Neither any other time.[34]

An admonition that Brethren shall stay at home with their families and not spend their Evenings at Hotels and stores and such places.[35]

Admonition for parents not to dress their children after the gaudy fashions of the world.[36]

Admonition for parents to be more careful in allowing their children to attend spelling bees held at public places.[37]

When admonitions proved futile, deacons or "visiting brethren," as they were called, were dispatched to convince offenders of their error. Only after admonitions and visits failed and members had been given ample time to come within the Order were they called to appear before the church. New members, particularly, seem to have been given time to adjust to church dress standards. The idea was that when Jesus came into a person's life, prideful and worldly appendages, such as neckties and puffed sleeves, gradually would "drop off." A 1906 Elizabethtown Council Meeting minute, suggesting that the congregation require "more to drop off before baptism," indicated that old habits sometimes died hard.[38]

When offenses were serious, sinners were invited to confess their wrongs to the church. Drunkenness; using the power of the law without the church's permission; attending forbidden events such as shows, fairs, and picnics; and fornication were some of the most commonly confessed sins.

Having heard the confession, in most cases the congregation voted to forgive, often with an admonition for the offender to be more careful in the future. Sexual sins—fornication and adultery—resulted in automatic disowning. Those who remarried while a previous partner still lived were considered to be living in adultery and could not be members. In many cases those who committed sexual sins asked to be disowned, and later confessed and were received back into fellowship.

Some members expressed deep regret for besmirching their Lord and the church, as in this letter of resignation submitted by a sister in the Lancaster congregation in 1901:

> I take this method to express my sad, sad regrets for my unfaithfulness and lack of chastity, having been overtaken in an ungarded [sic] moment, and for the maintainance [sic] of the churches [sic] purity and her rules, I feel my unworthyness [sic] of church member-ship and therefore tender you my resignation as a mem-ber and desire that you pray God, the author of my being, for a full pardon for my guilt.[39]

Of course, some members who were forced to confess diplomati-cally expressed regret that the church had taken offense, without actually admitting any wrongdoing.

Congregations seldom acted arbitrarily when the one invited to confess failed to appear, but instead extended additional invita-tions, sometimes over a period of several months to a year. Members who would not confess their wrongdoing were "dealt with according to Matthew 18" and disowned from the church. Fre-quently minutes report disowning for a certain behavior and "failing to hear the church." Failure to hear the church represented a clear breach of the promises made prior to baptism to uphold the Order and submit to the church's counsel.

Disowned members were restored to membership only if they confessed their error. These times of reclaiming members were joyous occasions, as members filed past wayward sheep and extended the right hand of fellowship and kiss of charity to welcome them back into the fold.

How closely a congregation enforced Annual Conference deci-sions through church discipline depended to a large degree on the will of the congregation's elected leaders, particularly the elder-in-charge.

Homegrown Preachers and Deacons

During the Church of the Brethren's first 150 years, congregations were served exclusively by nonsalaried "free ministers" and deacons, who were called from within the congregation they were to serve. As in other matters, Brethren searched the Scriptures for their leadership patterns. They found no biblical evidence of preachers receiving salaries, but they did find a comparison of "hireling" shepherds with the Good Shepherd (John 10), which seemed to them an apt metaphor for paid preachers and dedicated free ministers.

The Brethren ministry was divided into three levels. First degree ministers were permitted to preach or conduct an entire worship service if no senior ministers were present. After a period of testing, first degree ministers were advanced to the second degree, which allowed them to schedule services, baptize, perform weddings, and do most of the tasks of an elder, if no elder was present. Typically, a minister served at least 10 years before being considered for the eldership, the highest degree of ministry. Elders (occasionally called bishops) presided over Council Meetings and love feasts and

Bearded elders (left to right) D. L. Miller, S. R. Zug, and George N. Falkenstein in the early 1900s. Earl and Vivian Ziegler Collection.

Ministers of the Midway congregation gathered on August 13, 1923, the day of Alvin F. Brightbill's (1903-1976) ordination. Pictured are elder-in-charge Nathan Martin (left foreground), Aaron Heisey (against porch post), William Forry, Samuel K. Wenger, elder Martin Heisey (partially obscured), Brightbill (standing), and his college roommate Francis Barr (seated on porch). Brightbill went on to become a professor of church music and popular music leader. Midway Congregational Archives.

provided oversight for congregations. Age and experience commanded respect: Senior ministers usually entered the meetinghouse first according to a peculiar pecking order based on length of service that determined where each minister and deacon sat.

While several elders may have resided in a single church, each congregation elected a presiding elder or elder-in-charge, who assumed primary leadership. Popular presiding elders often oversaw several congregations at one time. Though free ministers received no salaries, some congregations did provide their elders and ministers with gifts and an allowance for expenses. Visiting evangelists who conducted revival meetings received reimbursement for expenses plus a small fee.[40]

Congregations also called deacons, who annually visited every member, normally prior to the spring love feast; cared for the poor in the church; visited members who were not within the Order;

made preparations for the love feast and baptisms; solicited funds from members for particular causes; and assisted ministers in worship by reading Scripture, leading prayer, or "bearing testimony" to the words of the preachers.[41]

Both ministers and deacons were called from within the membership of the congregation to serve for life. When leaders felt additional ministers or deacons were needed, neutral "adjoining elders" from neighboring congregations were summoned to Council Meeting to conduct an election. Members were notified of the upcoming election and instructed to be in prayer.

Following the reading of appropriate Scripture passages (1 Timothy 3:1-7, Titus 1:4-9, and 2 Timothy 2:1-15 for ministers; 1 Timothy 3:8-13 for deacons), the adjoining elders retired to an anteroom where members, both men and women, filed by and stated the name of the person they felt God was calling. The new minister or deacon was chosen by plurality vote and immediately installed into office. In some instances, two members would receive a large number of votes, and both were called. At other times the votes were scattered, and no one was called.[42]

Most free ministers were self-educated, with eight years of formal education or less. The topic of an educated ministry was controversial in the district at the turn of the century. Traditional voices favored prayer and Bible study as the best forms of education for a minister, while progressives advocated a formally educated ministry to reach the unsaved on urban and overseas mission fields. At an Eastern District Ministerial Meeting in 1896 participants debated the question, "Is a College Education a Necessity for Preaching the Gospel Through the Power of the Holy Spirit?" and several ministers aired these views:

> J. H. Price—No! No! NO! . . . The ministry should be a Holy Ghost work from the start. A minister should be a man of wisdom—a different wisdom from a college education . . . The secret closet is the best college for a minister.

> Isaac Taylor— . . . A college education is not necessary, but a great advantage. Sometimes the Holy Ghost is crowded out through a college education . . . I would

rather have the power of the Holy Ghost than all the education in the world. Going to church is done too much to be entertained and not enough to be instructed. A college education entertains best . . .

J. T. Myers—To this question I say both no and yes. Men of very little education have been successful in preaching Christ; but to preach the Gospel in India or Armenia one must study that language. To preach the doctrine of the resurrection or baptism, we, like Paul, must have education. In the history of our Church the very ablest men, men of books, like R. H. Miller and James Quinter, were selected to defend our doctrine.

H. E. Light—We have men who preach the Gospel effectively without a college education, and we have men with a college education who preach without effect.[43]

Some free ministers, it appears, *were* a little rough around the edges. At an 1895 Ministerial Meeting, ministers shared pointers for proper pulpit conduct. Educated pastor J. T. Myers noted, "It is bad to blow the nose in the pulpit, or to spit over it." Others cautioned against the use of awkward gestures, repeating what previous speakers just said, and telling the congregation, "I have nothing to say." "Making apologies is not the proper thing to do," said Jacob Conner. "The congregation will find out soon enough when there is necessity for them."[44]

The Council Meeting and Official Board were the central organizational entities in Brethren congregations. Decision-making authority rested with all church members meeting in Council. Even routine matters such as when to hold a love feast and whom to schedule as a revival speaker were decided by a "committee of the whole." The primary tasks of the board, composed of ministers and deacons, were preparing items for Council and providing spiritual oversight.

Even though important issues were deliberated by the entire church, the wise counsel of elders carried considerable weight. Authority earned through years of sacrificial service compensated for a lack of formal power, enabling these patriarchs of the church to guide the democratic process.

In addition to the Official Board, most congregations had Sunday schools, headed by a superintendent, who often was a deacon or minister. While the Official Board was comprised only of men, women assumed active leadership roles in the Sunday school, particularly as teachers. Elected trustees cared for church property in some congregations.

Peculiar Worship

Their unaffected style of worship set Brethren apart from fashionable and worldly churches. Services began with an unaccompanied congregational hymn. At times, the song leader, who was often one of the ministers, would "line" the hymn, reading a few lines at a time, which the congregation then would sing. Following the hymn, the congregation knelt for a lengthy, extemporaneous opening prayer, which a second minister concluded with the Lord's Prayer. Men and women were seated on separate sides of the meetinghouse throughout the service.

After the reading of a Scripture text by a minister or deacon, two sermons were preached, the second one shorter than the first. Other ministers and deacons could then "bear testimony" to what the main speakers said, offering comments as they felt led. The service concluded with a hymn, kneeling prayer, the Lord's Prayer, and announcements of the times and sites of future meetings.[45]

The language of worship in Eastern District congregations at the turn of the century included English, German, and Pennsylvania Dutch. Many congregations were in the midst of a language transition. Some held German services one week and English services the next. (The singing and Scripture reading were in German, while the preaching was in the Pennsylvania Dutch dialect.) Others featured the main sermon in one language and the short sermon in another. At a 1903 revival meeting in Lancaster County's West Conestoga church, the evangelist preached English and German alternately throughout the week to cater to the divided church.[46] Requests for more German or more English preaching frequently came to Council Meetings, as congregations picked their way through the transitional period.[47]

Worship was changing in other respects as well. By 1900 congregations with paid pastors usually omitted the second sermon and bearing of testimony.[48] Other innovations had crept into Brethren worship as well, particularly in urban congregations. The Philadelphia First church, for instance, had been censured by an 1875 Annual Conference committee, among other things, for using instrumental music in Sunday school and taking "basket collections" during their services.[49]

Generally, however, Brethren were careful to avoid worldly worship practices, such as instrumental music, vain "special music" performed by soloists or small groups, pronouncing benedictions, and lifting offerings.[50] Most congregations relied on deacons to collect a "church income tax" in the course of the annual visit. Some churches also maintained collection boxes for the poor and sent deacons to solicit funds for special causes.

In addition to Sunday morning services, the church schedule included weekly Sunday school, held either in the morning or afternoon; Sunday evening services; midweek prayer meetings; quarterly Council Meetings (with others scheduled as needed); annual or semi-annual love feasts; and periodic "protracted meetings" (revival meetings).

Brethren called the buildings where they worshipped "meetinghouses," not churches. (They understood the "church" to be the *people*, the body of believers.) Most meetinghouses were simple, rectangular structures, free of adornment inside and out. Steeples, stained-glass windows, bell towers, and the like, may have been common in fashionable, worldly churches, but were off-limits for simple Brethren. Some Brethren even thought it inappropriate to put the name of the church on the meetinghouse, perhaps because they desired to maintain a clear distinction between the church and the building.[51]

Meetinghouses were functional for regular worship and love feasts. Worshippers entered directly into the auditorium through two doors—one for men and one for women. Arranged along a horizontal axis (in contrast to the long, narrow sanctuaries of worldly churches), Brethren auditoriums communicated community and equality. Ministers sat in the front of the room (the long side), behind a long preachers table on the same level as the congregation. Altars, raised pulpits, and worship centers, were conspicuously absent. Rows of benches faced the preachers table in the center; benches along the sides faced across the meetinghouse so that those sitting on the right could look directly across

Interior (top) and exterior (bottom) of the Middle Creek meetinghouse, ca. 1915. Built in 1874, the building included a basement kitchen and hinged benches that were converted to tables at love feast occasions. Side benches were raised for visibility, and the "preachers table" (right) was elevated one step. Middle Creek Congregational Archives.

the house at those seated on the left. These side benches often were elevated to improve visibility. This peculiar seating pattern shifted the focus from altars and preachers to the gathered community.[52] (See Diagram 2.1 below.)

A single congregation frequently met alternately at several meeting-houses to spread the burden of horse and wagon travel. Larger "love feast houses" were equipped with crude kitchen facilities and benches that could be converted to tables at love feast times.

Spiritual Highs: Love Feasts and Revivals

Spring and fall love feasts were social and spiritual highlights. These two-day events, usually held at midweek, attracted Brethren and non-Brethren from miles around, including hucksters who came to market their wares to the crowds that gathered. Members of the host congregation saw to it that Brethren arriving by train or trolley were picked up at the stations and delivered to the services. When enough people had arrived, usually by mid-morning, the love feast began with a preaching service, followed by a noon meal. Often visiting ministers—as many as a dozen—would attend, and each would be given opportunity to speak during the two-hour morning

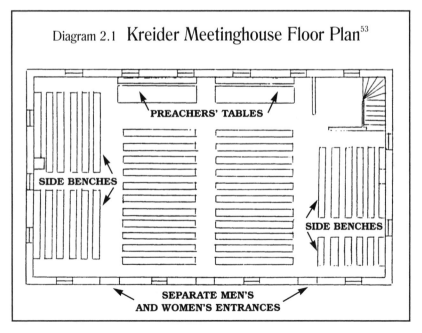

Diagram 2.1   **Kreider Meetinghouse Floor Plan**[53]

PREACHERS' TABLES

SIDE BENCHES

SIDE BENCHES

SEPARATE MEN'S
AND WOMEN'S ENTRANCES

service. The "self-examination service" convened after lunch. After the reading of 1 Corinthians 11, ministers encouraged members to examine themselves and not partake of the bread and cup unworthily.[54]

Following a late afternoon intermission, during which final preparations were made and the children were fed, Brethren surrounded the tables (which had been created from the benches they earlier had sat on) in the meetinghouse auditorium for the evening love feast service. The service imitated as nearly as possible the events that took place in the upper room on the eve of Jesus's crucifixion. The ordinance of feetwashing came first, with brothers washing the feet of brothers and sisters the feet of sisters. (As in all worship services, men and women were seated separately.)[55]

Next came the Lord's Supper—a full meal simultaneously patterned after the Last Supper and looking forward to the great marriage supper of the Lamb that would take place when Christ returned to claim his bride (Revelation 19:7-9). As many as four people ate sop (usually a beef, broth, and bread mixture) from a

Meeting Brethren at the Salford Station, Lower Salford Township, Montgomery County, in 1903. BHLA, *Brethren Encyclopedia* Collection.

"Love Feast of Manheim Dunkers," drawn by Alice Barber Stevens in 1897, depicts a Lancaster County Brethren love feast. The drawing appeared in the Ladies Home Journal *in 1918.* BHLA, *Brethren Encyclopedia* Collection.

common bowl, as Christ and his disciples did. In some congregations, leftovers were eaten by the non-member children, who were seated in the aisles during the service.[56] Following the meal, participants passed a holy kiss from person to person, uniting the entire group.

Finally, the officiating elder, who typically had been invited from a neighboring congregation to lead the service, guided the communicants through the communion service. Two ministers carried unleavened bread, baked in strips about two-inches-by-18-inches, from table to table. One man broke off a piece of the bread and passed it to the next man. When that strip became too short, the minister provided a new piece to continue the process. On the women's side, the minister broke bread for each woman, since no women communed with Christ in the upper room.[57]

Two common cups—one for men and one for women—were passed through the entire group and refilled as needed. Again, men passed the cup on their own, but a minister served the cup to each woman.[58] With the communion service concluded, the communicants sang a song and went out into the night. Those who had travelled from a distance slept in the attic of the meetinghouse or in nearby homes. All gathered the next morning for a concluding preaching service and noon meal.[59]

If love feast was the spiritual highlight of the Brethren year, revival meetings (or "protracted meetings," as they were sometimes called) were a close second. By 1900 revival meetings had become the main avenue for new members to join the church. Typically, a guest evangelist conducted a series of meetings in late fall or winter, after the harvest was gathered. Meetings ran each evening for two weeks or more. Usually only the starting date was publicized so services could continue as long as the Spirit seemed to be moving.

Revival meetings were simple preaching services, after which an invitation was extended for those not yet saved to come forward and join the church. Sometimes the work of a good evangelist coupled with the prompting of the Holy Spirit brought dramatic results. Within a six-week period in 1898, the Chiques congregation baptized 50 new converts, most of whom came forward at revival meetings held at the congregation's two meetinghouses.[60]

Following instruction, applicants were baptized in a nearby stream, often in the dead of winter. Stories abound of Brethren who could be baptized only after a hole was cut through the ice on the stream. Some argued that willingness to be baptized in frigid stream water demonstrated the sincerity of one's commitment.[61]

Poised for Change

Those who were baptized around 1900 covenanted to live according to the cardinal doctrines of nonconformity, nonresistance, and nonswearing. At the time of their baptisms, they consented to live as a peculiar people, separate and nonconformed to the world. In a word, they promised to follow the Brethren understanding of what it meant to be Christian. But even as converts emerged from the chilly baptismal waters in 1900, a radically redefined Brethren identity was emerging to replace traditional emphases. Little did those converts know that within a few decades their church would undergo a sweeping transformation.

3.

From Free to Salaried Ministry

As Brethren involvement in church planting, foreign missions, and higher education expanded at the turn of the century, some questioned whether the church's 200-year-old system of leadership was equal to the demands of a new age. The free ministry, they argued, had served well in its day, but now was out of tune with the times.

But what began as tinkering with an old tune eventually led the church to a whole new score. Proponents of change were heartened as the free ministry (those who were nonsalaried and "called out" by the congregation) was replaced with a more modern system of paid, professional leaders. If the church was to be successful, they argued—in the city, on the mission fields, and elsewhere in the increasingly complex 20th century—bearded elders, cow-milking ministers, and plain-dressed deacons would have to give way to a new generation of educated professionals, who could dedicate themselves fully to the Lord's work.

Others wondered why the church was so eager to sing a new song when the free ministry served them just fine. While recognizing that free ministry had its share of limitations, they pointed out that the sophisticated new practice was out of tune with the rest of the simple Dunker repertoire. And they grew increasingly concerned over the direction in which the professional ministry would lead the church.

Few changes impinged upon the Church of the Brethren as forcefully as the transition from the plural, nonsalaried (free) ministry to salaried professionals.[1] As interest in church planting (home missions) and foreign missions grew during the late 1800s, it became apparent that the free ministry system was ill-suited for striking out into new territory. As long as Brethren had started new

Brethren spearing tobacco on a Lancaster County farm in 1918. The case for salaried pastors was less compelling in rural congregations, where farmer-preachers had flexible work schedules. J. Becker and Vera Ginder Collection.

churches by colonization or dividing existing congregations, the free ministry had sufficed. But to participate in the modern missions movement, Brethren evangelists and missionaries needed to be paid by the church, since this work left them no time to earn a livelihood otherwise.[2]

The Salary Question

Brethren had always believed it was biblical and proper to give informal financial support to their ministers, but a set salary was a different matter. The 1866 Annual Conference had ruled that it is "Not wrong to support the ministry, where it is needed. 1 Tim. 5:18; Luke 10:7. But we do not approve of paying a stated salary."[3] As Brethren saw it, ministry and money did not mix. Preachers preached because the Holy Ghost called them, not to make a living.

Though Eastern District also opposed salaries for ministers, the 1892 District Conference granted the Missionary Committee permission to pay "compensation to missionaries for time, if in the judgment of the committee they deserve it."[4] With the precedent of paying ministers established in mission churches, a few congregations in the district by the turn of the century had hired professional pastors. Finally, in approving a 1912 ministry report, Annual Conference *de facto* accepted the validity of salaried ministers.[5]

From Cultural Hubs to Hinterlands

As with many innovations in the district, paid pastors appeared first in city churches. The Philadelphia First church reportedly paid a pastor from private contributions as early as the 1860s, and it was there that Tobias T. Myers became the first full-time, salaried pastor in the Brotherhood in 1891.[6] As many as nine other congregations in the district—most located in the Greater Philadelphia Area—paid a "pastor" by the turn of the century.[7] (See Table 3.1.)

While city and mission churches readily adopted the salaried pastoral system, small town and rural congregations—where the merits of salaried ministry were perhaps less clear—were more cautious. In some congregations, the decision to hire a pastor stretched out over several years from the time the matter was first broached. In the Spring Creek congregation in Hershey, for example, 10 years passed from the time pastoral ministry was first dis-

Philadelphia First church's Tobias T. Myers (1865-1929), on the left, became the first full-time, salaried pastor in the Brotherhood in 1891. He is pictured with Brethren missionary Wilbur B. Stover (1866-1930), who pastored the Germantown congregation in the early 1890s, before departing for the India mission field. BHLA, *Brethren Encyclopedia* Collection.

Free ministers of the East Fairview congregation near Manheim, ca. 1944. (Left to right) J. Stanley Earhart, J. Norman Weaver, Allen G. Becker, Harry G. Fahnestock, Henry L. Hess, and Howard A. Merkey. East Fairview hired a salaried pastor during the 1960s, as did a number of other rural congregations. J. Stanley Earhart Collection.

cussed until a full-time pastor was hired in 1934.[8] Many congregations first hired part-time pastors as a transitional step toward full-time, salaried ministry.[9]

Paid pastors came first to the cities, then to small towns in the shadow of Philadelphia, and finally to other small towns and rural areas. By 1930, Southeastern District churches were served exclusively by paid pastors, while the transition in Eastern District was only beginning. Not surprisingly, in 1930, of the 21 meetinghouses in the Southeastern District, 15 (71 percent) were located in cities or small towns, with only six in rural areas. Of the 82 meetinghouses in Eastern District, 46 were rural, 29 were located in small towns, and only seven in cities.[10]

A tidal wave of transition swept through Eastern District in 1930, claiming 11 churches for paid pastoral ministry. Nearly all were small town congregations or new churches. During the 1940s and 1950s the trend toward paid pastoral ministry continued, with most of the remaining town churches and the first rural churches making the switch. By 1945 all Southeastern District churches and

Table 3.1

Number of Congregations Served by Paid* Pastors in Atlantic Northeast District and Forerunners

	Eastern District				North Atlantic District			
Year	Congs.	FT Pastors	PT Pastors	Total Pastors	Congs.	FT Pastors	PT Pastors	Total Pastors
1900	28			10				
1905	33			12				
1910	37			16				
1915**	34			4	15			13
1920	36			5	16			13
1925	40			6	17			16
1930	39	4	0	4	18	11	5	16
1935	41	4	9	13	18	9	7	16
1940	42	6	9	15	19	10	8	18
1945	40	10	10	20	19	12	7	19
1950	41	14	3	17	19	11	7	18
1955	42	13	6	19	20	11	7	18
1960	44	18	5	23	20	11	8	19
1965	46	21	6	27	21	11	9	20
1970	45	26	4	30	18	11	7	18

Atlantic Northeast District***			
1975	61	37	12	49
1980	60	44	9	53
1985	61	47	8	55
1990	67	53	8	61
1993	72	45	21	66

Sources: 1920-1985 *Church of the Brethren Yearbook*. Data for the years 1900-1915 obtained from *The Brethren Almanac,* district and congregational histories, district directories, and the *Congregational Profile*, should be viewed as suggestive of the general trends, rather than authoritative, since definitions of "independent congregation" and "pastor" are unclear. The year refers to the year of the yearbook or other source. Caution should be exercised in determining the number of free ministry congregations from these statistics since some congregations served by pastoral ministry may not be listed as having pastors due to temporary vacancies.

*The term "paid" is used rather than "salaried" because the terms of payment, particularly in early years, are not clear. Statistics reveal the number of congregations who report having "pastors," however they define the term.

**In 1911, Eastern District was divided to form (what would become) the North Atlantic District.

***In 1970, the Eastern and North Atlantic Districts were reunited to form the Atlantic Northeast District.

half of Eastern District churches were served by paid full- or part-time pastors.[11]

A second wave in the 1960s and early 1970s carried most of the remaining rural churches into salaried, professional ministry. The Mohler congregation, near Ephrata, in 1980 was the most recent free ministry congregation to hire a pastor. By the late 1980s, only six congregations—all rural—maintained plural, nonsalaried ministry,[12] and no new free ministry congregations had been formed since 1959, when the Springville (now Mohler) and Cocalico churches separated into independent free ministry congregations.

Hiring Pastors: Common Patterns

According to Carl F. Bowman:

> The earliest salaried ministers attended progressive Brethren colleges, received additional training at non-Brethren seminaries, and were then placed into urban "mission churches." . . . Thus, higher education, non-Brethren institutions, and domestic and foreign missions were the early bridges that carried Dunker preachers toward full-time pastoral support.[13]

All of these factors came into play as the first Eastern District churches hired pastors at the turn of the century. Among the first to employ leaders were urban mission churches—Geiger Memorial, in Philadelphia, and Harrisburg First. Early pastors in Philadelphia-area churches frequently came from a Brethren college to attend one of the region's many theological schools—Yale, Princeton, Eastern Baptist, Temple, Crozer—while pastoring churches.

Early pastors included missionary Wilbur Stover, who served at Germantown while attending Temple; Daniel Webster Kurtz, who came from Ohio to Juniata College, and then went on to Yale and the University of Pennsylvania while pastoring the Philadelphia First congregation; and Tobias Timothy Myers, who attended Mount Morris (Ill.) College and then pastored the Germantown and Philadelphia First congregations while studying at Temple and Crozer.[14]

For urban Brethren congregations, surrounded by Presbyterian, Baptist, and Lutheran neighbors, the salaried professional ministry was an idea whose time had come. Free ministry, it seemed to them, may have sufficed in rural churches where self-employed farmer/preachers were free to lead the flock, but the situation in the city posed problems. Urban ministers who worked full-time day jobs lacked the flexibility of self-employed, rural ministers who set their own hours and could take time off for church functions. Not only did the urban ministers have less time to give, but the urgent needs of the city constantly clamored for their attention. With leadership squeezed by time constraints, it seemed prudent to hire a pastor who could minister full-time.

It seemed especially prudent to progressive Brethren, eager to replace embarrassing Dunker peculiarities with more widely accepted Protestant practices. While the more traditional Brethren in the country could compare themselves to their free ministry-led Mennonite and Amish "cousins" and not feel out of place, urban Brethren were much more likely to emulate their mainline neighbors, who were led by educated, salaried pastors.[15] Thus, a dual desire to be more prudent and less peculiar tilted urban congregations toward professional preachers.

With an alternative model established, other congregations struggled to maintain the free ministry. In earlier days, congregations worked through leadership difficulties out of necessity, because no acceptable options existed. If they were dissatisfied with their free ministers, they learned to live with their dissatisfaction and make the best of it because that was the only system they practiced. But as professional pastors claimed the cities, onlookers in the hinterlands considered whether a full-time professional might also be a panacea for their problems.[16]

The rise of salaried professionals presented other challenges for free ministry congregations. Some called ministers to serve at home, only to see them go off to seminary and become pastors.[17] Other capable free ministers were tapped by the District Mission Board to lead new fellowships.[18] In short, some congregations' ablest leaders went with the wave of the future, leaving their home churches high and dry in their quest for qualified free ministers.

Other churches hesitated to call new ministers, either because they saw no qualified candidates and feared that those who were qualified would refuse the call, or that, once called, they would leave the congregation to become paid pastors elsewhere.[19] Some con-

A popular elder, Frank S. Carper (1893-1975) evolved from free minister to part-time pastor in the Palmyra congregation, paving the way for the congregation's first full-time, salaried pastor in 1961. Elizabethtown College Archives.

gregations began to feel that calling individuals to the ministry was an imposition. While in earlier days the voice of the church was considered synonymous to the voice of God, the concept of the church telling individuals what to do with their lives became untenable, as Brethren accepted the individualism of the wider society. One free minister, who had been called to the ministry in 1941, explains why his congregation later stopped calling leaders:

> I don't think they really saw anyone in the congregation that felt they would *want to* take up that position.
>
> Q: But that wasn't a consideration when they called you. They didn't ask.
>
> No, that wasn't a consideration then, but later on it was.[20]

As a result, in some congregations the number of ministers dwindled to three, two, or even one. At the same time, aging free ministers in rural and small town congregations found themselves less free to serve. While urban ministers had faced the employment quandary years earlier, as small town and rural ministers moved from farm to factory during the 1930s and 1940s, they, too, began to feel the pinch.[21] Consequently, free ministry became less effective in some congregations because the number of ministers was decreasing, the age of ministers was increasing, and the availability of the ministers was reduced due to their having less flexible employment.

An Educated Laity: Rising Expectations

As the quantity and availability of free ministers decreased, the educational level and expectations of Brethren in the pews were rising. In tandem with the consolidation of public schools during the 1940s and 1950s, increasing numbers of Brethren young people completed high school and continued on to college.

While free ministry churches often called their brightest and best to ministry, at times less capable ministers also served. In addition, most free ministers before 1950 had eight years of formal education or less. As Brethren laity advanced further in education, ". . . the deep reverence they once had for the Dunker preacher who expounded to them on Sunday mornings was gone."[22]

> When. . . the ministering brethren continued to use plural verbs with singular nouns and plural subjects with singular verbs, the irreverent giggles from the back benches of the meetinghouse became audible and dismay and dissatisfaction spread . . . We must have an "educated ministry," became the slogan.[23]

While in earlier days ambitious brethren may have secretly aspired to the venerated position of free minister, as educational levels and professionalism increased in the larger society, free ministry became less attractive. Professions—including pastoral ministry—offered respectability, opportunity, and a salary. Free ministry did not.

Not only were the brightest and best from free ministry congregations no longer interested in becoming free ministers, they also were demanding a more professional ministry to serve them. They wanted better preaching and administration, more availability for pastoral counseling and hospital care, and more work with youth.[24] It soon became evident that a full-time, professional pastor could better provide the services that many Brethren sought.

In most free-ministry congregations, the aging free ministers, handicapped by a lack of formal education and time, struggled to keep up with the demands of the church. In a few congregations, however, the exceptional qualifications of an elder-in-charge also spelled the end to the nonsalaried, plural model. In these congregations a capable, progressive elder gradually took on more church work until he *de facto* became "pastor."

Some congregations consciously crowned their longtime elder as pastor, while others found that when longtime leaders passed away, they had not groomed younger ministers to fill the void. To maintain the high level of leadership which they desired, they looked outside the congregation.[25] Asked at the 1931 Eastern District Ministerial Meeting why congregations were not electing more ministers, Elder J. H. Longenecker responded: "The transition through which we are going may account for it. Folks are looking toward the Pastorate."[26]

Another group of congregations likely could have maintained free ministry but saw no need to buck the trend toward paid pastors. Eager to shed Dunker peculiarities, they cast their lot with the mainstream model.[27]

In sum, factors fueling the trend toward salaried, professional ministry varied from church to church. Congregations seem to have been seeking more—more sophisticated leaders, more visiting, more professional counseling, more youth work. Churches seeking vigorous programming and consistent administration generally found that a pastor was better able to deliver the goods than the free ministry. But there were some things that pastors could not do.

From Calling to Career

Much more than a simple, pragmatic shift, the introduction of salaried, professional pastors radically redefined leadership requirements, reflected a new set of values and priorities, and permanently altered congregational dynamics. (See Table 3.2 for a comparison of characteristics of the free ministry and salaried professional models.)

Traditionally, Brethren had viewed ministry as a calling from God that came through the voice of the church. Those chosen from within the congregation usually had demonstrated leadership ability in their families, the church, and the working world. "It was very rare to see an unsuccessful farmer elected to the ministry. It was the successful farmer or school teacher who was called by the church."[28] Character, rather than specialized ministry skills, was the main criterion for selection. God, it was thought, would provide those who were called with the necessary gifts for ministry.

But according to the professional model, ministry was a career chosen by an individual (whose call from God was affirmed by the church). Proper educational and professional credentials replaced character as the chief qualification for ministry. In fact, as congregations hired pastors based upon references and resumes, they had relatively little personal contact to assess realistically the character of their potential pastor. An educated pastor and respected church leader noted in the 1940s that "under the former system of

---

Table 3.2

Comparative Characteristics of Ministry Models

Free Ministry	Salaried, Professional
Plural leaders	Single leader
Token support	Set salary
Calling	Career
Church initiative—calling	Individual initiative— volunteering
Calling from within	Hiring from without
Character	Credentials
Age, Experience, Stability	Youth, Energy, Change
Tradition	Future
Primacy of people	Primacy of program, staff, facilities
Peer Counseling	Professional Counseling
Lifelong service	Renewable contracts
Informal expectations	Formal evaluations/ job descriptions
Egalitarianism ("Brother")	Elevation ("Reverend")
Meetinghouse	Church plant
Pulpit freedom	Pulpit prudence
Sacred/Ordinary harmonization	Sacred/Ordinary dichotomy

the church's calling. . . the possibilities for selecting the wrong man for the ministry were far less than under the latter system."[29]

The professional ministry also reflected a new set of values. While free ministry churches sought to preserve the faith of their fathers, the coming of pastors shifted attention to programs, staff, and facilities to meet the needs of future generations. Congregations looked to pastors who were young, energetic, and open to change. Free ministry congregations valued wisdom, experience, and the stability afforded by a system in which change occurred incrementally as one generation of leaders naturally replaced another. The quality and quantity of program and facilities took a back seat to "being the church."

The simple meetinghouse, where several "brothers" preached from a "preachers table" located on the same level as the rest of the congregation, epitomized free ministry. The sprawling "church plant," with an elevated pulpit from which the "reverend" expounded, re-

As Brethren made the transition to professional ministry, they sought pastors who were young, energetic, and open to change. Youthful pastor Nevin Zuck (center) is pictured at the 100th anniversary candlelight service in the Ambler church, October 27, 1940. Ambler Congregational Archives.

flected the values of the new professional model of ministry.[30]

Free ministers and deacons, who provided a sympathetic ear and commonsense counsel during times of need, were replaced by professional pastors who had studied psychology and counseling techniques. While paid pastors had the benefit of proper training and skills, free ministers shared years of common life experiences with those they counseled.

Observing the trend toward professional ministry, an advocate of the free ministry sharpened the difference in a 1938 *Gospel Messenger* article:

> We realize that the professional pastor can do some things that the free minister did not have time and training to do. But, after all, of what value are sympathy and sociability when they have to be paid for?[31]

Paid pastors scheduled appointments with parishioners during office hours; free ministers interacted daily with the congregation in the course of their work routines. While pastors could more easily separate church work from their private life, the free minister's conduct on the job, with his family, and in the church were all parts of his calling and service. Free ministry effectively synthesized the ordinary and the sacred, demonstrating that for the Christian all of life is holy.[32]

Free ministers served a lifetime, so long as they met generally understood informal expectations. With guaranteed "job security" (and minimal financial support) they were free to preach from the heart, even if it meant tramping on toes. Pastors, on the other hand, looking toward the next formal performance evaluation and salary review, had good reason to exercise prudence before addressing controversial topics. At the same time, free ministers, faced with competing time commitments and little performance account- ability, were more prone to neglect aspects of church work than the salaried professional, who was expected to earn his keep by in- creasing membership and attendance (demonstrated by carefully tabulated statistics), carrying out regular visitation, and effectively initiating and administering vital programs.

In short, free ministry and professional ministry represented alternative views of the church, its values, and the primary qualifications of ministers. For that reason, the shift toward paid professionals in Brethren leadership was more complicated than simply replacing one style with another. The addition of salaried pastors necessitated replacing some old practices and understandings and adapting others to fit.

"Don't Call Us, We'll Call You"

One of the first practices to be adjusted was the church's 200-year-old method of selecting ministers. Convinced that the call of God came through the voice of the church, the Brethren attitude toward those who claimed an individual call to ministry had always been, "Don't call us, we'll call you." But salaried professionals clearly couldn't be called in the traditional manner.

After indirectly affirming salaried pastors, the 1912 Annual Conference appointed a five-member committee to investigate carefully "the whole ministerial question, including election, qualifications, instructions, distribution and management" and report back to the next Annual Conference, or as soon as possible.[33] As it turned out, the committee's controversial task dragged out over the next four years.

In the meantime, Eastern District ministers discussed a version of the evolving report at their annual Ministerial Meeting in November 1915. The sections of the report on educational requirements and electing ministers drew the most fire. Specifically, the paper would have required ministers to have "a literary course equivalent at least to a high school course and to two years Bible course followed by two years' reading course . . ."

Elder Samuel H. Hertzler's thoughts on these requirements seemed to speak for many of those attending the Ministerial Meeting. "I think we are all agreed that some of us have felt the need of better qualifications for some of our ministers," said Hertzler, but "I think we all feel that this asks too much." Observing that three-fourths of Eastern District's ministers would be considered unqualified by the proposed standard, Hertzler concluded that ". . . the standard here is set a little higher than we ought to go."

Elder John Herr voiced even stronger opposition to the paper's provisions for choosing ministers. While the report affirmed the traditional way of electing by majority or plurality vote, it also provided an additional path into the ministry—affirming *volunteers* by a two-thirds majority vote. Herr observed:

Prominent Lebanon County elder John Herr (1848-1931), pictured above with his wife, Annie, and Lancaster County elder Samuel H. Hertzler (1853-1936), with his wife, Annie (below), opposed those persons who claimed an individual call to ministry. Myerstown Congregational Archives and BHLA, *Brethren Encyclopedia Collection.*

Churches under pastoral care seldom if ever hold an election. They are not contented with beginners in the ministry. They want to have them ready made, manufactured preachers, fresh from the college or from such place. Under our present system over two hundred years the church has prospered and we believe the churches in holding elections. . . are making choice of the very best talent that they have . . . If this is adopted it. . . revolutionizes the whole system of church government relative to elections . . .

Building on Herr's comments, elder Jesse Ziegler warned that accepting volunteers to the ministry would "open the way for those who feel they are called to preach and feel that they are able to preach." Allowing such self-promotion, Ziegler cautioned, circumvented the Holy Spirit working through the church and increased the likelihood of approving ministers who had not been called by God.[34]

The five-part report—minus provisions for specific educational requirements—came before the 1917 Annual Conference where, again, the section on methods of electing ministers sparked the most debate. Representing Eastern District, elder Samuel H. Hertzler stated his opposition to the provision for multiple paths to the ministry: "I don't know that there is any Scripture precedent for more than one method [of calling]."[35] As Hertzler and the traditional free ministry Brethren understood the one scriptural method, it was God, speaking through the church, who called. But after two centuries of unanimity on calling, delegates voted in 1917 to accept volunteers, whose call to ministry came directly from God rather than through the church.

Congregations with paid pastors quickly adopted the new way of calling. Volunteers were readily accepted and "calling" as previously practiced all but vanished. Free ministry churches were less eager to tamper with the traditional terms of calling, which continued to serve their needs. Some even refused to recognize the validity of an individual's call.

Thus, as part of a denomination that accepted volunteers, but of congregations that did not, some young men who felt an individual call found themselves in an awkward position. One minister recalls his experience in 1933:

I felt a definite call, but when I asked the Annville congregation to license me they said they could not do that because they felt that this was an evidence of self-centeredness, and I should wait for the church to call me to the ministry.[36]

Another minister summed up the attitude of the more traditional churches toward volunteers for ministry:

They said that we don't get ministers that way. "If God wants you to be a minister, he'll let us know, and we'll vote for you in Council Meeting." [37]

Instead of waiting, the young Elizabethtown College student transferred his membership from Annville to the Elizabethtown congregation, which had no qualms about licensing volunteers. Six years later, in 1939, another young man volunteered for the ministry at Annville and was accepted.

Similarly, a volunteer in the East Fairview congregation near Manheim, in 1940 was instructed by the Official Board to wait. Two years later he volunteered again and was accepted.[38]Some free ministry congregations gradually accepted the validity of the individual call, particularly if the volunteer intended to go into full-time pastoral ministry elsewhere, but most free ministry congregations continued to call their home ministers in the traditional way. Of the six remaining free ministry congregations in Atlantic Northeast District (AND), only one had accepted volunteers to the ministry between 1960 and 1989.[39]

Is Anybody Calling?

While Annual Conference likely never intended it, over time, volunteering all but replaced the traditional method of calling. As churches hired salaried pastors from outside the congregation, the incentive for calling ministers from within withered. The hiring of a pastor frequently marked the end of active congregational calling. Of 54 AND congregations reporting in 1989, 32 had not initiated a call to ministry for 30 years. Another 16 had called one or two.[40] Only the six remaining free ministry congregations have called out three or more ministers since 1960.[41]

Volunteers to the ministry have not taken up the slack. Of 65 AND congregations reporting in 1989, 49 had licensed three or fewer ministers (volunteers and those called out by the congregation) in the previous 30 years. Congregations "produced" an average of about 2.5 ministers from 1960 to 1989, far less than the number of pastors "consumed" by most churches during the same period.[42]

Ironically, when the church was served by multiple, nonsalaried ministers, ministerial supply generally met demand. But having converted to professional ministry, which required only one minister per congregation, the church almost immediately was faced with a leadership shortage. By 1987, denominational ministry staff were asking, "Is anyone in the church calling?" They lamented:

> When congregations had to find their ministers within their own ranks, calling was taken quite seriously. Now, congregations frequently assume their responsibilities for calling are completed when they call a pastor, thus relying on a ready-made pool of called leaders to draw from . . . As a result, we have too great a dependence on persons who volunteer or promote themselves, with or without qualifications.[43]

"Let the Pastor Do It"

In some congregations, the hiring of a pastor was accompanied by a loss of community and collegiality. Brethren theologian Dale Brown points out that while the debate over free versus salaried ministry often focused elsewhere—on calling, salary, education—more foundational and less justifiable was the shift from multiple leaders to a single pastor.[44] The introduction of a salaried pastor often marked the end of shared leadership and fueled a decline in the congregation's sense of community and fellowship.[45]

In free ministry congregations, where members called leaders to serve, those who did the calling felt obliged to work with their ministers and deacons. There was a feeling of, "We're in this together." The arrival of a pastor sometimes altered these dynamics, and congregations that had hired pastors to *lead* them in ministry, gradually accepted the notion that the pastor was paid to *do* most of the ministry himself. The spirit of shared responsibility for the work of the church gave way to feelings of "let the pastor do it."

Expanding Pastoral Staffs

Over time, congregations learned that it was unrealistic to expect a single pastor to carry out the tasks formerly handled by up to a dozen or more ministers and deacons. Beginning in the 1950s, larger churches hired additional pastoral staff to meet congregational needs. The trend toward multiple staff accelerated dramatically in recent years. A total of 10 congregations reported hiring second staff in the three decades prior to 1980, with nine adding additional staff during the 1980s. A few larger congregations employed more than two salaried staff.[46] At the same time, some pastors in recent years placed renewed emphasis on activating and training laity for leadership. A few congregations experimented with calling individuals from within the congregation to perform specific ministries under the guidance of a salaried pastor.[47]

The move toward multiple staff helped open the door for women to assume pastoral roles in some congregations. Since the mid-1970s, the number of female pastoral leaders has increased modestly. All told, 19 congregations licensed or ordained at least one woman to the ministry at some time during their history. Nine congregations actually hired a woman as a pastor or co-pastor, while seven employed a female associate or assistant pastor. Only one congregation hired female pastoral staff prior to 1974.

In 1989, out of 66 congregations, five were served by female co-pastors, but none employed a woman as the lone head pastor. No free ministry congregation has licensed, ordained, or been served by a female minister. Asked "Do you think your congregation would accept a qualified woman pastor?" 30 percent (20) of the 66 congregations responded yes, 38 percent (25) no, with the additional 32 percent (21) unsure.[48] In sum, while the number of women in ministry increased during the 1970s and 1980s, less than one-third of the district's congregations had overcome reservations toward women in ministry. There seemed to be less resistance toward women serving as associates or assistants to the head pastor.

While the dominant trend prior to 1980 was to replace multiple ministers with a single salaried pastor, in recent years congregations have been moving back toward the ideal of shared leadership among multiple salaried staff. The old free ministry model called only men to be ministers, while churches adding additional staff sometimes include women on their leadership teams.

The move toward multiple staff in recent years has provided opportunities for women to assume pastoral roles in some congregations. Members of Harrisburg First church's pastoral staff in 1993: (from left) Co-pastors Irvin and Nancy Heishman; Rafael Rivas, Hispanic ministries; and Gerald Rhoades, community ministries. Messenger Collection, photo by Bob Balsbaugh.

Only the Beginning

The move from free ministers to paid professionals was only the beginning of a series of significant organizational changes. As pastors became the central players on the Brethren leadership scene, other once respected leaders—such as elders and deacons—seemed more or less expendable. As these "outdated" relics were phased out, modern, bureaucratic congregational and district structures took their place. These and other organizational issues are the subjects of the next chapter.

4.

Burgeoning Bureaucracy

Learning the ins and outs of Brethren organization at the turn of the century was relatively simple. Authoritative leadership by elders, ministers, and deacons; democratic decisionmaking; and structural simplicity were "in." Lay leadership; delegated decision making by special boards and committees; complexity and bureaucracy were "out."

As the century progressed, however, the ins and outs of Brethren organization gradually were reversed—first at the denominational level, then at the district level, and finally in congregations. By the late 1960s, Brethren organizational patterns and values had shifted so dramatically that deacons and elders—who occupied the seats of honor in the old system—no longer could find places at the leadership table. In their stead were professional pastors; an array of boards, commissions, and committees; and a new class of salaried staff.

Three-Tiered Simplicity

Brethren organization as it had evolved by 1900 was a system of three-tiered simplicity. *Congregations* made decisions in Council Meetings, whose agenda were prepared by the ministers and deacons of the Official Board. *Districts* made decisions at District Conferences, whose agenda were set by the District Elders Body. The *Brotherhood* was guided by the decisions of Annual Conference, the highest human authority in the church. Annual Conference's agenda were set by the Standing Committee, which was composed of elders from across the entire Brotherhood.

Elders were key players at all three levels. In the congregation the elder-in-charge handled "general oversight" and discipline, presided over Official Board meetings and Council Meetings, administered the ordinances, preached, and served as the central spiritual leader of the congregation.[1]

The District Elders Body presided over elections and installations of deacons and ministers in congregations; decided when ministers could be advanced to the eldership; served as arbiters of congregational disputes; disciplined fellow ministers and elders; and prepared business items for District Conference.[2]

At the Annual Conference level, elders served on Standing Committee and prepared business items; elected the Annual Conference moderator and other officers from their ranks; and served on specially appointed committees to adjust irregularities in congregations.

Business items flowed in both directions among the three tiers. Items originated in congregations and were channeled to District Conference. Items of a local nature were settled there, but larger issues were forwarded to Annual Conference. Conference decisions then were carried back to districts and congregations, where they were scrupulously observed.[3]

Transformation at the Top

Already by 1900 a new organizational entity—a task-oriented board—threatened the three-tiered simplicity of Brethren organization. The Domestic and Foreign Missions Board (1880) was the first of these executive agencies, formed to carry out ministries on behalf of the Annual Conference. Similar boards and committees gradually were added over the next few decades.[4]

By 1923, when the church published its first pastor's manual, the denominational organization included four boards: the General Mission Board, to guide mission and publishing work; the General Sunday School Board, to address Christian education concerns; the General Educational Board, to keep tabs on the Brethren academies and colleges; and the General Ministerial Board, largely to handle the growing need for pastoral placement services. In addition, nine committees dealt with other concerns, and a Council of Promotion, formed in 1923 from a representative of each board and committee, coordinated the efforts of the various groups.[5]

Before long, the growing number of boards and committees altered the way Brethren did business. While traditionally congre-

Members of the Church of the Brethren General Mission Board in 1920, one of many denominational boards and committees that came into being around the turn of the century. BHLA, *Brethren Encyclopedia* Collection.

gations fed business items to Annual Conference (through District Conferences), the agencies that had been created to carry out Annual Conference directives increasingly shaped the Conference agenda. The 1923 Pastor's Manual noted that, "The chief sources of business for the [Annual] Conference are the local churches *and the General Boards.*"[6]

Clearing the Organizational Air

By the mid-1940s, the number of autonomous boards, departments, and committees reporting to Annual Conference had grown to a cumbersome, confusing, and sometimes competing 17.[7] The denomination was so blanketed by bureaucratic haze that Annual Conference appointed a committee in 1943 to clear the organizational air. In 1945, Conference expanded the committee to a "Commission of Fifteen," and charged it with devising a plan "which will provide a minimum amount of organizational machinery and a maximum efficiency."[8]

Conference approved part one of the Commission's report at the 1946 meeting. The new plan reorganized the former boards and committees into a single General Brotherhood Board, which, in turn, was divided into five commissions—Foreign Missions, Ministry and Home Missions, Christian Education, Christian Service, and Finance. The new 25-member board—comprised of elders, ministers, and lay members—was officially incorporated March 1, 1947, and began its work.[9] The following year, Conference approved the remainder of the Commission of Fifteen's work, which dealt with the three tiers of Annual Conference, districts, and congregations, and formally added a fourth tier—the region. While the report seemed to be aimed at efficiency and coordination, it struck another target as well—the authority of elders.[10]

At the Annual Conference level, elders lost their exclusive power base in the Standing Committee, which was opened to other ministers and laity. Further, Annual Conference moderators, who formerly had been chosen by the elders of Standing Committee from their own ranks, now would be elected by the Conference delegates and could be selected from among elders and other ordained ministers.

In districts, the report called for the creation of District Boards to oversee most program matters. The District Elders Body's functions were to be limited to advising, monitoring spiritual welfare of churches, approving ordinations, and carrying out discipline. In addition, the district moderator position was opened to any ordained minister, and the District Elders Body was now to include in their meetings ministers and lay members who served as moderators of congregations.

In congregations, the report recommended a Church Board composed of "men, women and youth" to plan, supervise, and coordinate the work of the church—functions previously carried by the Official Board. The Official Board was to retain "general oversight of the church's spiritual welfare and church discipline." In addition, laymen could be called to serve as "moderators" of congregations, in place of an elder-in-charge.[11]

The approval of the 1946 and 1947 Annual Conference reports on organization marked a radical departure from the past and opened the doors to unprecedented participation of the laity in the leadership of the church. At the same time, it hastened the erosion of the authority of elders. During the next 20 years, the provisions of these reports were phased into the lives of districts and congregations, while the role of the elder was phased out.

By the mid-1960s, new organizational issues had emerged. Concerns about overlap of responsibilities and general confusion about the names and functions of the various General Brotherhood Board commissions prompted a 1968 Annual Conference action to shorten the name of the General Brotherhood Board to "General Board" and to reduce the number of commissions from five to three—Parish Ministries, to undergird and strengthen congregations; World Ministries, to spearhead peace, justice, and mission programs; and General Services, to support the other two commissions.[12]

While much of the direction for organizational change originated from Annual Conference, the drama was largely played out in districts and congregations, each of which lent its own interpretation to the structural script.

As in the rest of the Brotherhood, new church agencies sprouted in Eastern Pennsylvania District, beginning with a three-member Missionary Board in 1880. In 1897, with the district's approval, the Brethren Home for the elderly, located near Manheim, opened its doors.[13] In 1911, Eastern and Southeastern districts organized a Children's Aid Society, and the following year a Home for Orphan and Friendless Children opened at Neffsville in conjunction with the relocated Brethren Home.[14] Interested Brethren started Elizabethtown College in 1899, and by action of the 1917 District

The first Brethren Home, located on Hernley Road north of Manheim, was founded in 1897. The home moved to Neffsville in 1907. Earl and Vivian Ziegler Collection.

(Top) The Home for Orphan and Friendless Children, in Neffsville, housed nearly 1,000 children and young people from 1914 to 1962. The building is now part of the Brethren Village retirement community campus. (Bottom) Children at the home in 1945, along with houseparents John and Elva Mae Hevener. Earl and Vivian Ziegler collection and Elizabethtown College Archives.

Conference, ownership and control of the college were transferred to Eastern District.[15]

To coordinate and encourage the growing Sunday school movement a District Sunday School Board was authorized by the 1920 District Conference. In 1932, this board merged with the District Welfare Board to form the District Board of Religious Education.[16] Other committees and boards formed during the early part of the century were the Temperance Committee (1911); a committee to publish an annual district directory (1914); a Sister's Aid Society (1919); a Welfare Board to address issues of temperance and purity, dress, and peace (1926); and a Men's Work committee (1939).[17]

Key Players: Authoritative Elders

Of all the new boards and committees, none exerted more influence than the District Ministerial Board. Recommended by the 1917 Annual Conference,[18] District Ministerial Boards were to aid in pastoral placement and ministerial distribution; "the initial idea being that they would only *encourage* ministeral [*sic*] elections and *recommend* pastoral placements, being careful not to encroach upon the supervisory role of district elders over congregational ministerial matters."[19]

However, citing the need for "more efficiently supervised pastoral care," the Brotherhood's General Ministerial Board brought a report to the 1927 Annual Conference, recommending expansion of District Ministerial Boards' scope. In addition to previous responsibilities for making reports and "distributing ministers" (pastoral placement), the new, more powerful ministerial boards were to examine, license, ordain and install ministers (with the approval of the District Elders Body), and to "assist churches in the adjustment of difficulties arising from or affecting the ministry."[20]

Speaking from the floor, Eastern District elder Samuel H. Hertzler opposed expanding the power of these boards at the expense of District Elders Bodies. He observed, "We are vesting the authority of what was formerly the duty of the elders in a very limited number, just in this particular board, the District Ministerial Board."[21]

While Hertzler was correct that a strengthened District Ministerial Board would undercut the authority of the District Elders Body, in Eastern District the move enhanced the influence of a small

Young people, ages 20 to 30, at the Sixth Young People's Conference, August 20-25, 1934. Such conferences at Elizabethtown College during the early 1930s eventually led to the founding of Camp Swatara in 1943 near Bethel, Berks County. Elizabethtown College Archives.

group of elders—including Hertzler—who served on the Ministerial Board. During the late 1910s and 1920s, the elders serving on this board ruled the roost in Eastern District. One informant recalls:

> The district was democratically organized under the autocratic supervision of some powerful elders. They had a strong clutch on Eastern Pennsylvania as long as they lived. They were good men, and they were respected, highly respected. But they kept things in order![22]

Elders Isaac W. Taylor, Jacob H. Longenecker, Samuel H. Hertzler, and Henry K. Ober dominated the Ministerial Board for most of the 1920s and into the early 1930s. Taylor, Longenecker, and Hertzler were so well-known that at times they were simply referred to as "the triumvirate."[23] In addition to serving on the Ministerial Board, Longenecker and Taylor took turns moderating District Conference. Taylor moderated the odd years, beginning in 1913 and ending in 1929—missing only 1927 (when Ober was moderator). Longenecker handled the even years from 1914 to 1922.[24] Ober moderated in 1932 and 1934. The District

Conference moderator also headed the District Elders Body Meeting.[25]

One longtime church leader, the son of a Lebanon County elder, recalls how his father looked up to Longenecker, Taylor, and others:

> When they spoke, it was really almost the same as God speaking. They had an authority that was earned and respected within the government of the church. I can recall my dad getting a little concerned about [a controversy] at a District Meeting. I don't remember what the problem was, but I remember [my father] saying, "J. H. Longenecker spoke up and the boat stopped rolling and rocking."[26]

In addition to counseling and settling disputes in congregations, Ministerial Board members were "present at all elections, ordinations, and installations of elders, moderators, ministers, pastors, and deacons in the District."[27] In effect, the District Ministerial Board functioned as an executive committee that "sought to represent the Elders Body," handling ministerial matters and discipline on an ongoing basis.[28]

By the 1940s, the district organization, with its scattered committees and boards, had begun to create confusion. Eastern District formed a Promotion Committee in 1943 to coordinate the various bodies, but things grew more complex the following year when the district—already overseeing a retirement home, a Children's Aid Society, and a college—authorized the Board of Religious Education to purchase property for a church camp. By-laws and a charter for Camp Swatara, located in Berks County near Bethel, were approved by the 1949 District Conference.[29]

Meanwhile, Southeastern District also grew rapidly after the 1911 district division. Immediately following the split, the new district formed a Temperance Committee, a Sunday School Commission, and Mission Board. A Peace and Service Committee was added in 1917, followed by a three-member Board of Religious Education in 1921, and a committee to strengthen ties between the district and Juniata College in 1922. In 1925, a Council of Promotion, responsible for Christian education, temperance, purity, and ministerial supply, replaced the Board of Religious

Education. The Mission Board, the district's other main organizational entity, spearheaded church planting and home mission projects.[30]

A three-member Advisory Committee of Elders, with major responsibilities in the areas of pastoral placement and discipline replaced the Council of Promotion in 1929. Among the new Council's responsibilities was:

> To take the place and function in the capacity of the Adjoining Elders of former days in being a committee to whom local churches may appeal for counsel and advice in matters which cannot be amicably adjusted by the local congregation.[31]

To pick up the Christian Education work formerly carried by the Board of Religious Education, a new Board of Christian Education was formed in 1933, and in 1934 the Advisory Board of Elders was renamed the District Ministerial Board.[32]

In 1939, the district launched a camping program with the creation of Camp Stardust, near Collegeville. The camp at that site closed in 1943, after peaking at 168 campers. After several years of searching for a permanent campsite, the Southeastern District Conference in 1949 voted to cooperate with Eastern District's new Camp Swatara. The district in 1948 instituted a Council of Boards to coordinate the various boards and committees, and in 1954 they adopted the name "North Atlantic District."[33]

Adding an Organizational Tier

Despite the mishmash of committees and boards at the denominational and district levels, some thought districts still were insufficiently equipped for their growing responsibilities, particularly in pastoral placement. Seeing this need for increased district services and for closer ties between Brotherhood and district structures, Annual Conference in 1947 recommended a fourth tier of organization—the Region.[34] On September 1, 1947, the new Eastern Regional organization began its work, with an office located in Lemoyne. The new region was composed of the five Pennsylvania districts. A Regional Council—consisting of two elected members from each district, the presidents of Elizabethtown and Juniata colleges, and any members of the General Brotherhood Board residing in the region—was formed to oversee the work of new regional secretary Levi K. Ziegler, an assistant regional secretary, and an office secretary.[35] Before long, the regional office developed its own cadre of committees and councils to carry out its work.

In a 1953 report Ziegler summarized the function of the Regional Council as "promotion, stimulation, counseling, and administration in certain situations only when no other provision has been made for necessary administration."[36]Pastoral placement, in cooperation with District Ministerial Boards, was a central function of the regional secretary. Thus, responsibilities once carried solely by the District Elders Body and later in concert with the District Ministerial Board now were to be shared with a salaried regional secretary.

Eliminating the Office of Elder

Elders not only lost sway to salaried staff and new bureaucratic structures, but surrendered responsibilities to the laity, as well. As a result of a 1955 Annual Conference decision, the "presiding officer" of a congregation was to be known as "moderator," regardless of whether he was an elder, minister, or layman. Further, congregational moderators were to serve no longer than six successive years.[37]At the district level, the District Elders Body was to be renamed the "District Elders and Moderators Council," and the 1947 directive that this body be opened to lay moderators was re-emphasized.

Eastern District in 1957 formed an "Elders, Pastors, and Moderators Council," as Annual Conference had instructed. The group met in two sessions, the first open only to elders and the second open to the entire council.[38] In North Atlantic District, where the Elders Body was small and perhaps less influential, lay members attended Elders Body meetings by 1948.[39]

While the regional program provided additional services, it did little to simplify and coordinate the many district boards and committees. In 1958, both districts implemented new plans of organization, replacing most existing structures with a 25-member Board of Administration.[40] The new board was divided into five commissions—Christian Education, Ministry and Evangelism,

Missions and Church Extension, Social Education and Action, and Stewardship and Finance.[41]

In addition to simplifying and centralizing district structures, the new board sounded the death knell for elders. Most elders' responsibilities, including preparing the District Conference agenda, were assigned to the Ministry and Evangelism Commission, which included elders, ministers, and laity.[42] For all practical purposes, only discipline remained under the purview of elders. Ten years later, the 1967 Annual Conference terminated the office of elder. Citing the historic erosion of elders' responsibilities, Conference recommended that ordination of elders cease and that District Elders bodies surrender their few remaining functions to the district boards.[43]

The Conference decision to eliminate elders was unpopular among traditional Brethren in Eastern District. Many felt that the Elders Body still filled a need. Others were glad to oust the outdated relics of an earlier era so that the church could move ahead. The age of the elder in Eastern District unceremoniously ended at the October 1967 District Conference, when delegates, some eagerly, some reluctantly, voted to comply with the Annual Conference decision.[44]

Moving Toward Merger

Though the creation of District Boards of Administration had helped eliminate organizational confusion, some felt that employed field staff could more efficiently carry out the district's work. While the denomination, and later regions, employed executives, districts, hindered by the economics of scale, continued to rely on volunteers. Most districts simply could not afford to hire staff.[45]

Prompted by Annual Conference, Pennsylvania districts explored a cooperative solution to the staffing problem. A 1960 Conference Study of District and Regional Organization and Realignment called for reducing the denomination's 58 existing districts to 18 within 10 years. The report specifically recommended that Eastern Pennsylvania, Southern Pennsylvania, and North Atlantic Districts merge and employ a chief executive officer called the "district executive secretary." The report urged "functional cooperation" among the three districts as a step toward eventual merger.[46]

The 1960 district conferences approved establishing a Tri-District program with a salaried Christian education staffperson. The new Tri-District Program of Christian Education was formally organized January 14, 1961, with a nine-member steering committee (three from each district) overseeing the paid staff.[47]

By 1963, two districts of the Eastern Region (Middle and Western Pennsylvania) employed full-time executive secretaries, and the remaining three districts cooperatively employed a staffperson. Thus, demand for services from the Regional Office waned. At the recommendation of the Eastern Regional Board, the district conferences voted in 1963 to discontinue the regional program as of September 1, 1964.[48] In its place, participants in the Tri-District program would hire a Tri-District executive secretary to service the districts. Joseph M. Long began work as the first Tri-District executive secretary on September 1, 1964, setting up shop at the United Church Center in Harrisburg.[49]

After evaluating the Tri-District program and available alternatives, the Tri-District Steering Committee in May 1966 recommended that the three districts merge by 1968. With their historical differences largely healed by the passage of time, North Atlantic and Eastern Districts favored the merger, but Southern District had reservations.

At a joint meeting of the Tri-District Committee and the three district boards on September 10, 1966, the group agreed to present merger plans to district conferences, despite concerns raised by Southern Pennsylvania representatives about "the centralization of administration and loss of local autonomy" that the merged district might bring.

Among the benefits cited for the proposed merger were simplifying schedules of field staff, who found it difficult to relate to the many commissions of the various district boards; more effective specialization of district staff; and strengthening the smaller North Atlantic District. Disadvantages cited were unwieldy size, greater distance (geographically and organizationally) between staff and congregations, "the stifling influence of centralization of administration," and the "present wide divergence of thinking by the boards."[50]

Eastern and North Atlantic District conferences voted in 1966 to continue merger conversations; Southern District urged continuation of the Tri-District program. After further conversation, in April 1968 the merger matter was put to a vote at a special Southern District Conference. The tally was 49-39 in favor of merger, short of the required two-thirds vote. Southern District was out of the merger picture.[51]

A special District Conference, held April 4, 1970, elected a new district board, and at a joint District Conference, held October 10-11, 1970, at the Lititz Church of the Brethren, North Atlantic and Eastern Districts formally merged to form the Atlantic Northeast District (AND). The Tri-District arrangement officially ended August 31, 1970, and the former Tri-District staff became staff for the new district.[52]

The new District Board was comprised of four commissions—Ministry, Nurture, Stewardship, and Witness.[53] By the mid-1980s, however, it was evident that the Witness Commission's responsibilities were too broad. The district by-laws were amended by the 1986 District Conference to expand the District Board to 36 members and create a fifth commission—the Church Development Commission—to assume responsibility for planting new churches.[54]

An Authority Vacuum

By the mid-1970s, it was evident that the new, more efficient district organization, with its boards, commissions, and executives, was seriously flawed. It lacked a body that could effectively settle congregational conflicts. The 1976 Annual Conference urged districts to form Discipleship and Reconciliation Committees to fill the void. While the more polite term "discipleship" was used in place of "discipline," these new committees essentially were to pick up where elders had left off.[55]

The Atlantic Northeast District Board reported to the 1980 District Conference formation of a District Reconciliation Committee "to deal with conflict resolution when needed."[56] A key difference between the elders of old and the Reconciliation Committee of the 1980s was authority. While the elders had authority to settle conflicts, the new committee could do little more than help the disputing parties hear each other. The new committee "doesn't quite have the clout" to carry out its task, says one longtime district leader.[57] "We're just floundering now

The Official Board and wives in the Spring Creek congregation, Hershey, during the 1940s. Spring Creek Congregational Archives.

when it comes to discipline," says another.[58] Former elder Nevin Zuck sharpens the difference:

> There was a lot of tenderness and a lot of love in the Elders Body, but when something needed to be done, it was done . . . So some of us, as we look back now, are a little bit concerned about what we did when we got rid of the Elders Body. I don't want to be rough. I don't want to be tough. But in love there is a time to say, "This is it. Let's move." I know we could have saved a lot of trouble.[59]

The Brethren of the 1980s, however, were much less disposed to such shows of authority. While discipleship and reconciliation seemed like admirable goals, Brethren had come to believe that discipline as formerly practiced by elders was authoritarian and unloving. Zuck disagrees:

> They were as loving as we are now. But they also had the concept that for the unity of the church there are times we need to act and we need to move into a situation and not wait until it festers and becomes a real difficult situation.[60]

To clear up confusion and improve the committee's perform-ance, the District Board in 1990 approved a set of procedures and guidelines to be used when the services of the Discipleship and Reconciliation Committee were needed.[61] District leadership was still in search of some mechanism or body that could discipline as effectively as the elders had more than 20 years earlier. In many respects, elders had become expendable. Respecting discipline, they have thus far proved irreplaceable.

Revamping Congregational Structures

Congregational decisionmaking at the turn of the century was centered in the church Council Meeting, where all major items were decided by a committee of the whole. The church, meeting in Council, called ministers and deacons from within the congregation to lead. Together ministers and deacons formed the Official Board, which prepared the Council Meeting agenda and guided the church. The presiding elder, or elder-in-charge, led Council and Official Board meetings, serving as the congregation's spiritual and administrative head.

While the Council Meeting was purely democratic, the church frequently followed the course charted by the "official Brethren." When highly respected elders, ministers, or deacons spoke in Council Meeting debate, their opinions frequently figured largely in the final decision. No one wielded more authority than the presiding elder, who by his very presence set the tone for congregational life. Thinking back to the days of authoritative elders, one member recalls:

> There was a continuity of spiritual leadership. The elder was there. He was the spiritual father of the congregation. He had respect as well as clout. We didn't consider what the elder said as domination; it was wisdom![62]

The office of deacon, too, was a high calling. Deacons were called to serve for a lifetime. In addition to serving on the Official Board, they played meaningful roles in visiting, discipline, and finance. Deacon responsibilities included caring for the poor, conducting an annual visit of each member, investigating and resolving conflicts and violations of church expectations, visiting the sick, and preparing for the love feast and baptisms. In addition, deacons assisted ministers in leading worship, if needed, and, in the absence of a minister, deacons were authorized to preach.[63]

A longtime elder recalls,

> The office of deacon was very important in those days. I remember being at Council Meetings where deacons were elected. They felt so sensitive to the call that they would shed tears, that the church had called them to serve in this office.[64]

By mid-century, with shifting organizational patterns and values, many deacons would "shed tears" for different reasons, as they were demoted and dismissed from central leadership roles.

Already by 1900, many congregations' organizational trees were sprouting new committees and boards. As bureaucracy burgeoned at the denominational and district levels, congregations followed suit.[65] By 1920, the Spring Creek congregation in Hershey was served by a Missionary Committee, a *Messenger* Distributing Committee, a Temperance Committee, a Sunday School Lookout Committee, and a Sisters' Aid Society, along with the Official Board and Sunday school organization.[66]

Members of the Lititz congregation's Sisters' Aid Society during the 1920s. Lititz Congregational Archives.

During the 1920s and 1930s, many congregations organized "Young People's Societies" or "Brethren Young People's Departments" (BYPDs)—the first youth groups[67]—and in the 1930s and 1940s, Boards of Christian Education were coming into vogue.[68] In short, the early decades of the century were marked by organizational growth as new structures grew alongside the Official Board and Council Meeting.

But despite the growing number of committees, deacons, ministers, and elders remained the heart of the organization. Overall, the traditional organization pattern stood firm—until the arrival of a salaried pastor.

Salaried Pastors: Incompatible Parts?

While congregations initially may have expected pastors to function effectively within the traditional organizational pattern, the new pastoral component proved to be incompatible with parts of the traditional model. Instead of simply fitting a new part into the organizational machinery, the machinery itself needed to be rebuilt from the bottom up to accommodate paid pastors.

The incompatibilities were both functional and philosophical. An obvious functional conflict was between pastors and free ministers. Pastors were hired to preach. Sometimes free ministers continued to teach and fill the pulpit when needed, but, for the most part, the hiring of a pastor rendered them obsolete. Similarly, deacons surrendered their traditional visiting responsibilities to pastors. In many cases, congregations cited the desire for more visiting as a reason for hiring a pastor in the first place.[69] Often even the traditional annual deacon visit—a primary means of accountability—was discontinued shortly after the arrival of a pastor.[70]

As pastors became the chief spiritual leaders, the Official Board became the last bastion of power for otherwise deactivated free ministers and deacons. Before long, however, even this final refuge was under siege. While in earlier days the board provided administrative *and* spiritual leadership, the Official Board in many congregations increasingly was perceived as just an administrative body—a stubbornly conservative administrative body. Energetic, young pastors assumed the helm of some congregations, eager to sail off in new directions. They sensed that the laity were eager to embark, but conservative ministers and deacons refused to go along. The pastor looked to the board to provide wind for the congregational sails, but board members understood their role more in terms of an anchor.

A pastor recalls his association with a deacon-dominated Official Board in the 1950s: "Yes, we had a Deacon Board—I don't mind talking about them—who were opposed to everything that you wanted to propose that was a little different."[71]

A longtime leader in the Harrisburg First congregation recalls, "We had some pretty hide-bound members on that [Official] Board . . . So it was decided that we better get some younger blood into the board."[72]

Board Transfusions: Adding New Blood

Adding younger blood to the board meant one of two things: expanding the size of the board or getting rid of some old blood to make room for the new. Prior to the 1950s, congregations mostly worked at the problem by expanding the Official Board. The Elizabethtown congregation, for instance, voted in 1944 to add the Sunday school superintendent, heads of other boards, and a youth representative to their Official Board.[73]

But the problem of "entrenched power" in the hands of lifetime ministers and deacons persisted.[74] Seeing that they "just didn't have the cutting edge of the congregation in the Official Board,"[75] congregations, with the encouragement of pastors, reorganized, replacing the deacons and ministers of the Official Board with a Board of Administration, largely composed of lay members. The new board was divided into functional groups, called commissions, modeled after the pattern of the General Brotherhood Board. Board members were elected from the entire congregation for specific terms of service, and lifetime ministers and deacons, who previously had "dominated" decisionmaking, were confined to a separate commission or board, on the margins of power.[76]

Pastors and others promoting such changes extolled the virtue of opening leadership positions to younger lay members and sharing power among a wider spectrum of church members. One pastor argued that the new form of organization would benefit "overworked" deacons by narrowing their responsibilities.[77] Another pastor saw the move as a way "to free the deacons to do what they were really called to do." He argued that deacons should be spiritual leaders instead of managing program and finance.[78]

Demoting the Deacons

In most congregations, deacons hadn't requested lighter work-loads. Most were wise enough to see that the new plan of organization would bring their influence to an end. Like tailfins on a 1990 automobile, it was evident that deacons—as their role was traditionally understood—were anachronistic holdovers from an earlier era. Beginning in the mid-1950s, congregations in eastern Pennsylvania reorganized—10 during the 1950s, 21 more during the 1960s, and 14 others during the 1970s and 1980s. In 1989, three-quarters of the district's congregations were served by Boards of Administration, comprised of various commissions. The remaining free ministry congregations, and a few others, maintained the traditional Official Board.[79]

In many congregations, the transition from the Official Board to the Board of Administration was painful, as longtime leaders felt the sting of rejection. A pastor who promoted the change in his congregation recalls,

> We went through the agony and hurt of really saying, "You lifetime deacons, we won't take your office from you, but you have no power anymore." And that's a tough one. You once were guiding the destiny of this congregation, and now you are no longer . . . And I had real problems with some of them, because they would contend with me that the church is being unfair . . . So some of it was painful. It wasn't all easy, but it had to be done . . . The larger concerns of the church had to take precedence.[80]

While the reorganization was promoted as a means to share decisionmaking with a broader spectrum of people, in fact, the opposite took place in some congregations. While Official Boards had exerted a great deal of influence, under the old system major decisions still were hashed out by the whole congregation meeting in Council. Speeches of board members often guided the decisions, but it was the congregation that ultimately cast the votes.

With the creation of Boards of Administration, congregations

Lifetime deacons and deaconesses of the Elizabethtown Church of the Brethren in 1953. Several years later the congregation began electing term deacons and replaced the Official Board with a Board of Administration. Elizabethtown College Archives.

increasingly delegated decisionmaking to the board, and members perceived Council Meeting as little more than a rubber stamp. Rather than debating and deciding real issues, Council Meeting attendees heard the pastor's report and ratified board decisions. "Council don't amount to much anymore," says a longtime minister. "The board and the pastor run the show."[81] As a result, Council Meeting attendance in many congregations has plummeted.[82]

Thus, an organizational shift promoted as being more democratic, in some cases actually eroded purely democratic decisionmaking. "The individual had more part in the work of the congregation then [in the days of the Official Board] than they do now, more direct," observed a retired minister.[83] Rather than sharing power with the whole congregation, reorganization mostly transferred authority from conservative, lifetime deacons and ministers to more progressive pastors and lay leaders.

The most immediate effect, however, was that deacons were out of a job. Having lost spiritual nurture and visiting responsibilities to pastors, they now were forced to yield administrative responsibilities to the laity. Little remained for deacons to do, other than preparing for love feasts and assisting with baptisms.

Seeing the erosion of the deacon office, some congregations attempted to redefine that role by initiating Undershepherd Programs, where deacons would maintain contact with a particular "flock" of families throughout the year. While deacons of old often were perceived as intrusive inquisitors who knocked on members' doors once a year to see if they were keeping the faith, new deacons were to be friendlier, less formal, and more nurturing.[84]

Some saw this new style of deacon ministry as a big improvement over the annual visit:

> The annual visit wasn't all that it was cracked up to be. It was very perfunctory. It was stiff. It did not have the nurturing, discipling aspect to it, at least as I remember it . . . It had some good points to it, but it also had a kind of dullness.[85]

But demoted and demoralized deacons, accustomed to their traditional role, were slow to grasp the new role that was offered them. Frustrated by lifetime "deacons who didn't deac," congregations in the late 1950s first began to elect deacons for specific terms of service instead of for life.[86]

But rather than strengthening the deacon ministry, the reduction of the office from lifetime calling to a three-year term contributed to the deacons' demise. While congregations were *saying* deacons were important, their *action* to reduce the position from a lifetime calling to a three-year term communicated the opposite. Between the late 1950s and 1989, a total of 31 congregations elected term deacons. Most of the conversions took place during the 1960s and 1970s, but congregations continued to change from lifetime deacons to term deacons throughout the 1980s.[87]

By then, congregations were beginning to see that deacons could fill a needed spiritual role, and efforts began to revitalize the office. At the denominational level, a new deacon manual was published in 1987, and a part-time denominational staff member gave impetus to the deacon revival.[88] Several congregations gave renewed emphasis to Undershepherd Programs, every-member visitation plans, and a few returned to lifetime deacons after trying term deacons.[89] A congregation begun in 1990 defined the deacon role along traditional terms, listing among deacons' duties an annual visit and occasional preaching.[90] After decades of downgrading deacons, by the 1980s, efforts were underway to restore respect to the office.

Who's in Charge Here?

The trend to hand over the reins from ordained lifetime leadership to lay leaders also had an impact on the role of the elder-in-charge. In many congregations, a shift from ordained elders-in-charge (or moderators) to lay moderators accompanied the move from an Official Board to a Board of Administration. At the recommendation of Annual Conference, beginning in the late 1950s, a few congregations traded in their elders for lay moderators. The transition accelerated during the 1960s and 1970s, and by 1989 more than half of the district's 66 churches were served by lay moderators.[91] Others relied on a minister or pastor from a neighboring congregation to fill this role, while the free ministry churches continued to define the position more in terms of the old elder-in-charge.

In the days prior to professional ministry, the elder-in-charge had served as the spiritual and administrative head of the church. But along with pastors came role confusion. Who was the spiritual head of the church—the elder or the pastor? Sometimes when a pastor entered a congregation led by a strong elder-in-charge, a tug-of-war ensued as both vied to be spiritual head. Some congregations resolved the tension by electing their pastor to serve as elder, too, but that wasn't always possible.

To clarify ambiguous lines of authority, the role of elder-in-charge was redefined in administrative terms, and the name was changed to "moderator."[92] According to these new definitions, the pastor would be the spiritual leader, and the moderator would serve as administrative head. But the new pattern of organization also introduced a third key leader into the mix—a Church Board chair.

While the roles of moderator, board chair, and spiritual leader formerly were embodied in one elder-in-charge, three people now shared these responsibilities. The intent was to involve more people in leadership and to move beyond authoritative (understood as authoritarian) models of the past. "We had some very good elders-in-charge," says a former elder, "but we also had elders-in-charge who were dictatorial. . . and really threw their weight around."[93]

The new system reduced the risk of dictatorial leadership but brought drawbacks of its own.

One by-product of decentralized authority has been role confusion. A former church executive explains:

> There are three people in charge of the congregation these days—the moderator, the Church Board chair, and the pastor. We have a three-headed monster which isn't working well, because who is in charge? But I guess, strictly speaking, the moderator is.[94]

Another former church executive disagrees: "I think the pastor is more the head than the moderator in churches that have a pastor."[95]

The shift from an authoritative, longtime elder-in-charge to a short-term lay moderator introduced confusion in other ways, as well. One informant laments:

> We got rid of the eldership and started putting in anybody for moderator, and we have lost that spiritual authority which is so important to the growth and development of the church.[96]

Pastors, he continues, have been unable to fill the void:

> A pastor can be as dedicated and as deeply spiritual as he wants to be, but he leaves in five years and the church is lost. *We knew what we believed when we had an elder who was with us through a lifetime.* But now each pastor comes with a different style. Just about the time we get to thinking we understand what his spiritual values are, why he packs up and leaves, or else we decide we don't like him and tell him he should leave.[97]

Every change involves trade-offs. Beginning in the 1950s, congregations and pastors eager to move ahead of their conservative elders and Official Boards opted for new organizational patterns, which allowed them to chart their own course without the "domination" of elders and deacons. In many congregations, reorganization unplugged a decisionmaking bottleneck, and a flood of significant changes followed soon after the new board assumed power. Congregations that for years had struggled with building questions, for example, embarked on ambitious building projects shortly after new boards took over.[98] Congregations eager to move "ahead" were able to move. But the price they paid in some instances was a loss of continuity in leadership, the decline of Council Meeting, a blurring of identity and purpose, and loss of clear lines of authority.

Congregations that stayed with more traditional models have also faced trade-offs. They have been more bound by tradition, less able to spawn new ministries, and at times inefficient. But they have maintained a stronger sense of identity and purpose, clearer lines of authority, and have more effectively preserved the ideal of democratic decision making by the entire congregation.

A Wholesale Changing of the Guard

By 1990 it was no longer a simple matter to learn the ins and outs of Brethren organization. Most of the "ins" of earlier days were "out." And the new set of "ins" was no longer simple. The Brethren organization of three-tiered simplicity had grown increasingly complex at the denominational level and in districts and congregations.

During the course of 90 years the church witnessed a wholesale changing of the guard as professional pastors, educated lay leaders, and district and denominational staff unseated elders, free ministers, and deacons from their seats of honor. In tandem with the new players and patterns, new values—professionalism, rationalism, and efficiency— replaced Dunker virtues of simplicity and democracy.

5.

The Crumbling Wall of Separation

Prior to the turn of the century, Brethren placed a premium on peculiarity. Their doctrines of nonconformity, nonresistance, and nonswearing formed an imposing wall of separation between them and their neighbors. Clad in distinctive garb, aloof from "worldly" politics and organizations, and united in their stand against participation in war and violence, Brethren viewed separation from the world as an integral component of Christian faith. To be Christian, in the Brethren mind, was to "come out from among them and be separate" (2 Corinthians 6:17).

By 1900, the Brethren barricade of separation was beginning to crack as an insidious mix of internal and external forces eroded the sectarian mortar joints. Reactions to the tottering wall varied. Some leaders, convinced that separation was an eternal mandate for the church, scrambled furiously to shore up the sagging rampart. If the wall were to fall, they believed, the forces of worldliness surely would wreak havoc in the church. Others sought to eliminate the cultural obstruction that, they believed, impeded the church in its ministry to the larger world. As the century unfolded, the forces bent on destroying the wall would overwhelm those trying to defend it, and the Brethren would enter the cultural mainstream.

Breaking the Language Barrier

Brethren separateness before 1900 had been bolstered by cultural and geographical isolation. Their use of the German language and propensity to settle in rural areas segregated many Brethren from the surrounding society. As a result, they were better able to maintain doctrinal distinctives. But by the turn of the century, sweeping changes in American society began to exact their toll on the cultural and geographic fences that had protected Brethren identity. The transition from the German to the English language and the later acceptance of technological innovations—automobiles, electricity, radio, and, eventually, television—made it increasingly difficult for Brethren to remain culturally and geographically insulated. New technologies in communication and transportation not only brought the world to Brethren, but carried them beyond the boundaries of their cultural enclaves. Bombarded by factors such as these, congregations began to surrender historic practices of nonconformity, nonresistance, and nonswearing.

A. L. B. Martin (1866-1935), clean-shaven, English-speaking pastor of the Harrisburg First church from 1901 to 1911. Elizabethtown College Archives.

Use of the German language was a cultural fence that fell early
to the forces of modernity. Already by the 1860s, Brethren churches
in the Philadelphia area were known as "English" churches and
were not as plain as rural, German-speaking churches.[1] Founded
in 1893, the Royersford congregation, located in a small town west
of Philadelphia, never worshipped in German.[2] By 1915, German
had disappeared in the Green Tree church near Oaks.[3]

To the west, the Reading congregation, organized in 1898, initially conducted services in German in the morning and in English in the evening. By 1915, German sermons had become rare.[4]
The rural Hatfield church, located northwest of Philadelphia but
within the bounds of conservative Eastern District, discontinued
German language worship in 1918.[5] By then, anti-German sentiments swirling around World War I had further accelerated the
Brethren shift to English.[6]

During the early 1900s, many Eastern District congregations
were in the midst of a language transition. The quandary faced by
Harrisburg First church's English-speaking pastor A. L. B. Martin
around 1906 illustrates the unevenness of the shift. Martin readily
accepted an invitation from a Lebanon County elder to preach at a
two-week-long revival meeting, but, upon his arrival at the rural
church, he received a shock:

> When I came there, I was asked if I could speak German.
> I spoke no German, but a little Pennsylvania Dutch. I was
> told that these were German people and that I would have
> to preach in German. "But," I said, "I am speaking English,
> working with English people. I can't do that." Then the
> reply, "You will have to do it. You are the first English
> evangelist that has entered this house."
>
> I was told to do my best. He introduced me. The first
> thing I did was to announce a German hymn . . . I read
> the text in English, then in German. Then I preached
> English and part Pennsylvania Dutch, where I could fit
> it in. It suited fine.

But the conservative German-speaking elder of the congregation
still objected to Martin's use of English. Martin continued:

> We were visiting one day and I spoke German to the fathers and mothers and English to the children, but Brother Wengert said I wasn't to do that. A dog came up to me and I spoke to it in English. Brother Wengert said in Dutch, "He didn't understand a word that you said."[7]

In Lancaster, Lebanon, and Berks counties, the German language lingered into the 1920s,[8] although by then, German preaching was dropped from the annual Ministers Meetings.[9]

A few congregations—including Schuylkill, Annville, and Conewago—continued occasional German preaching into the 1930s.[10] The Indian Creek congregation, nestled in the Pennsylvania Dutch country around Harleysville, was likely the last to use German in worship.[11] German services were held six times a year at Indian Creek during the 1940s, later reduced to two a year, and finally discontinued in 1953. Occasional German singing persisted into the 1960s.[12] Thus, nearly 100 years elapsed from the time the first eastern Pennsylvania Brethren had abandoned German until it totally disappeared.

Worshipping in German was a powerful symbol of separation from the dominant culture. As Brethren adopted the "foreign" language of the mainstream culture, they began to feel more at home in the world and less like aliens and strangers. In short, those congregations that were first to use English were also the first to discard other symbols of separation, such as plain dress. Congregations that continued to use German in worship also preserved plainness.

Automobiles: Accelerated Assimilation

Unlike the language transition, Brethren quickly accepted automobiles. When cars first arrived, some Brethren expressed reservations. The Midway congregation, for instance, voted in 1908 to forbid automobiles on church property.[13] The West Conestoga (later Middle Creek) congregation in 1910 agreed to formulate a query for Annual Conference regarding owning and riding in automobiles.[14] Other congregations evidently had fewer qualms about cars. A 1909 Mountville church Council Meeting query asked, "Is it objectionable for members to have automobiles providing they are plain?" The answer was, "No objection."[15]

The Annville meetinghouse and horse shed were rebuilt following a cyclone in 1915. A few years later the automobile (foreground) would render the horse shed obsolete and help transform Brethren life. Annville Congregational Archives.

While automobiles initially had been pretentious playthings for the rich, ownership by middle-class people became increasingly common when Henry Ford began assembly-line production in 1913. Ford's declaration that "any customer can have a car painted any color that he wants so long as it is black" surely met with approval from the plain Brethren.[16]

Brethren automobile owners were common enough in 1915 that the Chiques church appointed someone to "take care of automobiles" at a district-wide gathering hosted by the congregation.[17] By the late 1910s, the number of Brethren car owners was growing. The Mechanic Grove congregation, with 86 members in 1918, reportedly had eight families with cars.[18] Three years later, the Spring Creek congregation in Hershey removed hitching posts from the meetinghouse grounds, signaling the triumph of the horseless carriage.[19]

In Palmyra, Elder Frank Carper was one of the first to purchase a car. He defended his 1913 Ford as a necessity to keep up with his hectic church schedule.[20] A deacon in the Conestoga congregation offered a similar argument around 1911. A longtime member recalls:

The first car in the Conestoga congregation was about
in 1911. It was a 1911 model and at that time the car issue
came to the Council Meeting, and some people spouted off.
Then finally a young deacon got up and he said that he
thought this car wasn't all that bad . . . The deacon said
that there is a wheel there that you turn and the car goes
wherever you want it to go. It will go to church or it will go
to the movies, or to anywhere. It is not the car, he said, it
is you. He thinks he can use this car to good advantage.
The Council Meeting allowed him to have it.[21]

A Sunday school teacher in the Lititz congregation around 1920
made good use of his car. While the rest of the congregation's teachers competed for students' attention in the crowded meetinghouse,
Landis Stehman taught in the quietness of his Packard automobile.[22]

Although Brethren eagerly welcomed the benefits of the automobile, acceptance of autos was later viewed as a key factor in the
demise of nonconformity. Cars improved mobility and increased
interaction with the world. As Brethren became conspicuous con-
sumers of expensive, and sometimes stylish, cars, the case for
plainness and simplicity in other areas of life seemed less compelling. Brethren historian Floyd Mallott facetiously noted: "The Dunker elder bought an automobile and stepped on the gas; out the
window went his broad brim, followed by his wife's bonnet, followed by his whiskers."[23] Stepping on the gas not only boosted
personal mobility, but also accelerated the rate of social change in
the church.

Plugging into the Pulse of Society

Brethren also were quick to accept electricity and radio as these
innovations emerged. Thomas Edison patented his electric light
bulb in 1880 and, before long, electric lighting replaced kerosene
and gas in city homes and streets. The expense of constructing
public utility lines, however, slowed the flow of electrical current to
the country. With government agencies providing the impetus,
power lines spanned the countryside during the 1930s, and, by the
mid-1940s, most rural areas in eastern Pennsylvania had access
to electricity.[24]

The path of electric power into Brethren communities can be traced by noting when meetinghouses were wired. In 1897, the question of electric lighting in the Elizabethtown meetinghouse sparked a Council Meeting debate. A motion to install electricity failed by a 74-50 vote, but three years later electric lights were approved 66-46.[25]Electric lights followed in other urban and small-town meetinghouses. Philadelphia First church added electricity in 1905, Palmyra in 1906, Mountville in 1911, and Coventry in 1916.[26] By the late 1920s and early 1930s, rural Brethren were plugging in, as well.[27]

Radio followed electrical lines. Only three radio stations existed in the U.S. in 1920. By 1923, the number had mushroomed to 600, and, by the late 1920s, many Brethren were listening to new voices that entered their homes via radio.[28] As with automobiles and electricity, Brethren welcomed the radio, evidently giving little thought to its impact on nonconformity. Some Brethren even viewed the radio as an opportunity to speak to the outside world. As early as 1923, the Pottstown congregation was broadcasting worship services over station WFI in Philadelphia.[29] Lancaster's first radio station, WGAL, began broadcasting in 1922,[30] and, by the mid-1930s, radios had found their way even into the homes of rural Lancaster County Brethren.[31]

Oddly enough, although nonconforming Brethren at the turn of the century had taken great pains to shield themselves from the mainstream culture, they now readily plugged into the pulse of the society around them. Radios piped the world's values and ideas into Brethren homes, while automobiles afforded freedom to see new places and try new things without the fear of conservative elders peering over one's shoulders.[32] By the 1950s, many Brethren also were watching television.[33] Influenced from the outside by technological factors and propelled from within by a growing missionary and evangelistic zeal, Brethren began to question their principles of nonconformity.

A Call for Leniency

By the first decade of the 20th century, variations in dress standards across the Brotherhood continually exacerbated tensions within the church. Seeking clarity on a topic that long had tormented the Brethren corporate soul, the 1909 Annual Conference appointed a committee of "seven faithful, intelligent, conservative brethren" to re-examine the Scriptures, the teachings of the early church, and Brethren Annual Conference minutes on plain dress "with a view of giving us a clear, concise restatement of our position on this vexed question, so that all may understand alike and be unified and dwell together as becometh children of the family of God—in love and peace and harmony."[34]

After thoroughly researching the issue, the committee concluded in 1910 that the Brethren dress code "is quite consistent with all New Testament principles." The report affirmed previous dress decisions as "the best interpretation and application of the Scriptures on nonconformity to the world in dress" and recommended that these decisions remain in force.

Although Annual Conference approved the report, it did little to simplify the numerous dress decisions of previous decades. Nor did it satisfy progressive voices in the church who were eager to dress for success in evangelism and missions. So the 1910 Annual Conference appointed a new committee to formulate "a restatement reducing all the teachings of the Conference on Christian attire to *one plain and concise minute.*"[35]

Carl F. Bowman notes, "The composition of the new committee contrasted conspicuously with that of the old." Instead of older elders, the new committee was made up of younger, more progressive brethren who were involved in pastoral ministry and home and foreign missions.[36] The committee presented its "plain and concise minute" to the 1911 Annual Conference in St. Joseph, Missouri.

The first eight points of this landmark report reaffirmed plain dress as traditionally understood by Brethren: men were to wear plain clothing, including the coat with standing collar (especially ministers and deacons), and were to wear their hair and beard in a plain and sanitary manner. The mustache alone was forbidden. Women were to dress in plainly-made garments, free from "ornaments and unnecessary appendages." Plain bonnets or hoods (a form of bonnet) were to be worn (as opposed to hats), and the prayer covering was required. Gold and jewelry were taboo for both sexes. Only those who dressed according to the Order could serve as District and Annual Conference delegates or be considered for the offices of minister and deacon.

While the report reaffirmed traditional Brethren views on plain dress, it *failed* to make proper dress a test of fellowship. Instead, section 9 of the report stated:

> That those who do not fully conform to the methods herein set forth but who manifest no inclination to follow the unbecoming fashions, and whose life and conduct is becoming a follower of Christ, *be dealt with in love and forbearance;* and that every effort be made to save all to the church until they see the beauty of making a larger sacrifice for Christ and the church. But if, after every effort has been made, they, in an arbitrary spirit, refuse to conform to said methods, and follow the foolish fashions of the world, they *may* be dealt with as disorderly members.[37]

This new call for leniency toward dress offenders prompted vigorous debate, but, in the end, the report passed. While dress vio-

Members of the Ambler congregation, pictured in front of the Upper Dublin meetinghouse, ca. 1922. Southeastern District Brethren dressed more fashionably than their plain brothers and sisters in Eastern District. Ambler Congregational Archives.

lators *could* be disciplined or disowned, the decision to do so now would rest with congregations and districts. Annual Conference no longer mandated discipline for dress violators.[38]

The 1911 report affected Eastern and Southeastern Pennsylvania districts in dramatically different ways. In the newly formed Southeastern District, where committees had labored unsuccessfully for decades to bring congregations in line with Annual Conference standards, the dress issue finally was laid to rest. District Conference and Elders Body minutes from Southeastern Pennsylvania were virtually silent on dress after 1911. After years of artificial life support, plainness was finally allowed to die a natural death.[39] Eastern Pennsylvania elders, on the other hand, continued to enforce the traditional Order.[40]

Distraught with the 1911 decision, Eastern District sent a query to the 1912 Annual Conference in York, asking that the 1911 decision be amended to *require* plain dress across the entire Brotherhood.[41] The meeting was held in traditional Brethren territory, and more than half of the delegates in 1912 favored mandatory plain dress, but the vote fell short of the necessary two-thirds majority. The 1911 decision stood.[42] If plain dress were to persist in Eastern District, elders and congregations would have to enforce it themselves, without the clout of Annual Conference to back them.

But all was not lost. Annual Conference *had affirmed* plainness. And the exodus of the more worldly Southeastern Pennsylvania congregations from Eastern District in the split of 1911 left a strong consensus for plainness among most of the remaining churches. Eastern District was far from ready to capitulate to the forces of worldliness, as struggles over the next 20 years would demonstrate. But even as Eastern District elders dug in their heels and formed their lines of defense, a new menace was already infiltrating the churches of the district—the stylish and worldly hat.

The Hat Question

Stylish hats had yet to make inroads among Brethren at the turn of the century, as indicated by a 1903 *Gospel Messenger* editorial recounting an editor's exasperating experience in a non-Brethren church service one evening:

Anna M. Brunner and Amanda R. Kratz, members of the Ambler congregation, 1922. Prohibited in Eastern District, women's hats were common in South-eastern District during the 1920s. Ambler Congregational Archives.

> A number were in front of us, and among them a lady with a hat trimmed up to date. The hat and feathers combined formed quite an obstruction to our view . . . We bent first to the right and then to the left and more frequently bent low so as to see through under the hat and feathers . . . And so we passed the evening, getting what little we could out of the meeting.

After marveling at the folly of feathery hats, he concluded, "We wonder if the time will ever come when such attire will be seen among our people."[43]

He didn't need to wonder for long. By 1911, women in Eastern District had begun to test the disciplinary waters by donning hats like those worn by women in worldly churches. Three sisters in the Harrisburg congregation in 1911 received visits from deacons and chose to be disowned, rather than surrender their hats. Five years later, a sister who confessed and promised to put away her hat was received back into fellowship.[44] Other congregations dealt with hat-wearers in a similar manner during the 1910s.[45]

Despite the district elders' best efforts, by the late 1910s, the hat situation had come to a head in the Springfield congregation located outside Coopersburg, near the fancier congregations of Southeastern Pennsylvania. Responding to reports that Springfield leaders were accepting women who wore hats, the district elders in 1919 dispatched a committee to set things in order.[46]

(Top) Members of the Coventry congregation, near Pottstown, wore fake beards and prayer coverings for a November 7, 1924, 200th anniversary pageant. The costumes worn by the Coventry members approximated the actual dress in some Eastern District churches. (Bottom) Coventry members in their normal dress the following day. Coventry Congregational Archives.

In the meantime, the elders penned a resolution to stem the "tide of worldliness" that was engulfing Springfield and other churches. The 1920 District Conference approved the following resolution from the elders:

> Since there is a constantly increasing tide of worldliness making encroachments upon the Church, such as sisters wearing hats and members affiliating with oath-bound secret societies, and wearing jewelry:

> We, the Elders of Eastern Pennsylvania, assembled in District Meeting April 29th, 1920, in the Schuylkill Congregation, resolve to stand by the dress decision of 1911 in the interpretation that we do not receive into fellowship by baptism or letter, sisters who refuse to wear the plain bonnet or hood . . . and we further resolve that members who refuse to be governed by the above mentioned rule deprive themselves of the right to commune . . .[47]

Backed by this firm statement, the committee of elders laboring with the Springfield congregation brought its report to the 1921 District Conference:

Report of Committee to Springfield Congregation

> . . . After laboring with the congregation for nearly two years by meeting with them in services and love feasts and council meetings, and visiting in the homes of those directly concerned, we submit the following as our final report.

> 1st. OUR FINDINGS. We found about twenty-nine sisters wearing hats. Some wearing jewelry for adornment. In our first visit in their homes we were kindly received by nearly all. Some manifested a teachable disposition, others were quite determined in their opinions.

> 2nd. THE CAUSES for the existing irregularities are numerous. Some of long standing. It is the opinion of the

Committee however that the main reason lies in poorly organized methods of church activities and government. In this the Elder-in-charge and the official body are largely at fault . . .

3rd. THE REMEDY. In the beginning of our work we had reason to hope for changes for the better, but after a second visit from house to house our expectations and sincere desires were not realized, evidenced by the fact that a majority of those involved are not willing to conform to the simple life in the order of dress as defined in 1911. . . and reaffirmed by. . . District Meeting of 1920.

In light of the facts herein set forth, and with the hope of saving the erring members and the future welfare of the Springfield Church: we decide that in order to enjoy the fostering care, fellowship and communion of the Church, sisters shall cease wearing hats and all members who may be wearing gold for adornment shall likewise put away the forbidden things . . .

A failure to comply with the above named conditions will be construed to mean forfeiture of church membership . . .[48]

The report was approved.

Unsatisfied with the district's hardline approach, the Springfield congregation appealed to Annual Conference. The 1924 Annual Conference sent its own committee to investigate the Springfield situation and, without consulting district leaders, overturned their decision and restored to fellowship the out-of-order members. Not only was Annual Conference no longer supporting districts that enforced plain dress, but, in this case, the national committee subverted the district's authority to set its own standards. The 1925 District Conference responded to Annual Conference with an indignant letter of protest.[49]

With little hope of reconciling Eastern District and the Springfield congregation, the Annual Conference committee in 1926 recommended that Springfield transfer to the more lenient

Southeastern District. Eastern District initially objected, but in 1926 the transfer was completed. The Springfield women could keep their hats and Eastern District its dress standards.

By the time the Springfield situation was resolved, the Harrisburg congregation was embroiled in yet another hat controversy. With four sisters reportedly wearing hats in April 1920, the congregation agreed "to make every effort to win them and hold them in fellowship." But after nearly three years of discussion and pleas for the sisters to appear before Council, the congregation finally took action in January 1923, voting 47-3 to disown three women who continued to wear hats.

In February 1924, the three sisters brought a petition to a Special Council Meeting, asking the church to reconsider.

> To the Harrisburg Church of the Brethren:
>
> We, the undersigned sisters expelled by action of the Church on January 30th, 1923, hereby declare that we maintain our faith in Christ as our Savior in accordance with our baptismal vows; And further:
>
> We represent that we are in full accord with the *vital doctrines* of the Church and we affirm our devotion to the Master's cause and the welfare of the Church. Therefore,
>
> We respectfully ask that we be restored to the fellowship which was disrupted by the said action, so that our spiritual life may be conserved and that we may be under the care and guidance of the Church.[50]

The church, however, disagreed with the sisters' definition of "vital doctrines" and stood firm. The sisters then appealed to the District Elders, who, after hearing both sides of the case at a Special Council Meeting in May 1924, sustained the congregation's decision.

In the meantime, 52 Brethren from "Harrisburg and vicinity" petitioned Annual Conference through Standing Committee to investigate the situation. The petitioners maintained that the disowned sisters were "persons of excellent character and fine Christian spirit—the charge alone being that they wear hats." Further, a letter of support for the sisters noted that they had "caught the present spirit and trend of the Church of the Brethren and they are interested in its various activities and its welfare." The precedent-setting disowning of these women, the letter writer argued, impeded "progress" in the church.[51] In its reply, Standing Committee expressed sympathy for the petitioners but urged them to adjust to conditions as they were in Harrisburg.[52] The ruling of the Harrisburg First church and Eastern District stood firm.

But the turmoil wasn't over. By the mid-1920s, the hat controversy had reached crisis stage. In 1927, mission churches in Lake Ridge, New York, and Peach Blossom, Maryland, reportedly had accepted women wearing hats.[53] The following year at the annual Ministers Meeting, the question was put directly to the conservative Eastern District Ministerial Board:

> What constructive program does our Ministerial Board have to suggest for handling the hat question in this immediate pressure for solution which can no longer be deferred?

The reply from elders I. W. Taylor, J. H. Longenecker, and S. H. Hertzler reaffirmed the district's hardline position:

> The answer depends on what is meant by constructive. If it means a more devoted, consecrated, separate from the world membership, the answer would be for every Elder and Minister of the district to whole-heartedly stand by the 1920 decision of our State District, which is based on what the Annual Meeting decided should be the sisters' attire, including the head dress.

> The fact that the practice of the brotherhood in general is out of harmony with this decision is *no good reason for our district to follow suit.* Some churches have also ignored other decisions of conference. The following violations might be named:

"The triumvirate," influential Eastern District elders during the 1920s: (from left) Isaac W. Taylor (1856-1938), Samuel H. Hertzler (1853-1936), and Jacob H. Longenecker (1852-1938). The man in "worldly" dress is not identified. Elizabethtown College Archives.

Holding in fellowship lodge members, Ku Kluxers, Legionnaires, sisters with bobbed hair, and some of these ministers. Members indulging in different forms of worldliness, such as dancing, card playing, wearing jewelry, attending movies, theaters, etc. Members communing with other denominations and without washing feet.

If following the lead of the general brotherhood in violating the decisions of conference is justifiable on the dress question, it is equally so on the other deviations. *Not only so, but it is the inevitable result.* We do not think our district is ready for such a condition.

If, on the other hand, by constructive is meant an increase of membership in some of our churches regardless of the spiritual welfare of its members, with the chance of losing hundreds of our most devoted members to the Church, then all we as ministers need to do is to let things go as they will. Therefore, our answer is for all of our ministers to faithfully stand by the conference decision of 1911 as interpreted by our district.[54]

The District Ministerial Board was sure that yielding on the hat question would lead to other concessions. In fact, in much of the denomination, it already had. Eastern District was not ready to follow the broad path toward the mainstream taken by the rest of the church.

The Ministerial Board's response to the hat question, along with the 1920 District Conference decision on dress, was printed and distributed to all ministers in the district. The former was brought to the 1929 District Conference for endorsement. Rather than approve it, delegates voted to "spread the query on the minutes" until Annual Conference dealt with a related issue—the certificate question. By tabling the matter, delegates may have hoped to encourage discussion and move the church toward consensus.

As the church became more diverse, transferring a certificate of membership from one congregation to another had grown increasingly complex. At times, a member in good standing in a progressive congregation could not transfer to another church because he or she failed to meet its stricter requirements. The decision on the certificate question—of who was to define a member in good standing—had the potential to make binding dress requirements at the district level obsolete by allowing each congregation to set its own standards.[55]

As Annual Conference debated the certificate question for the next two years, district elders hesitated to hold the line on hats. The Harrisburg congregation in October 1930 reinstated the three women who were disowned in 1923, and the district elders took no action.[56]

When three sisters in Lebanon County's Annville congregation donned hats around 1930, the church, at first, barred them from communing. But in March 1931, with members of the District Ministerial Board present, the congregation reversed this decision "even though it was explained that it is contrary to the decision of the Eastern District of Pa."[57]

The certificate question was settled by the 1931 Annual Conference. In essence, delegates decided that *each* congregation would determine its *own* membership requirements. When the District Ministerial Board's strong condemnation of hats, on hold since 1929, came before the 1932 District Conference, it was considered a moot question. District Conference ruled:

> Since we have the 1931 decision of the Annual Conference on the Certificate Question, making our churches largely congregational in applying methods of procedure and practice, we decide that we consider this question answered and reaffirm our loyalty to the brotherhood in annual conference decisions.[58]

The era of authoritative district elders enforcing plain dress in recalcitrant congregations had ended.

The Dunkard Brethren Division

Dissatisfaction with the church's eroding dress standards during the 1920s extended beyond Eastern District. B. E. Kesler, a Brethren elder from Missouri, in 1923 founded *The Bible Monitor* to counteract the church's softening standards on dress and secret societies, and the rise of a salaried, professional ministry. A group of conservative Brethren—mostly from outside Eastern District—coalesced around this new publication.

When Kesler was refused a seat at the 1923 Annual Conference because of his writings, the *"Monitor* family" held its own meetings over the next three years—including two within the bounds of Eastern District in northern Lebanon County—to discuss the church's sorry state.[59] By the 1926 Annual Conference in Lincoln, Nebraska, the *Monitor* group appeared ready to leave the church.

Adding to the tension at Lincoln was a strongly worded query from Eastern District, expressing concerns that were virtually identical to the *Monitor* group's agenda. The Eastern District petition noted that the church "has been and now is rapidly passing through a remarkable period of transition," which many view as "a departure from the faith." Specifically, the petition protested sending out-of-order missionaries to foreign mission fields; receiving into fellowship members of secret societies; ignoring Scripture and Annual Conference rulings on dress, as evidenced by sisters cutting their hair, discarding the prayer veil, wearing jewelry and "apparel

B. E. Kesler (1861-1952) (left) edited The Bible Monitor *and was instrumental in the formation of the Dunkard Brethren Church in 1926.* BHLA, *Brethren Encyclopedia* Collection.

in quality and style that borders on indecency and shamelessness"; and more.

Noting that the direction of the church was "causing many honest souls to place a question mark in all seriousness on the propriety of supporting church work and missionary activities," the query asked Annual Conference to enact specific sanctions "to regain unanimity of faith and practice in the church, that confidence and quiet may be restored."[60]

To some it appeared that the future of Eastern District depended on Conference's response to the query. If delegates ignored conservative concerns, many Eastern District Brethren could join hands with the *Monitor* group. If a division were to occur—which seemed likely—thousands of committed Brethren could be lost to the Mother Church. On the other hand, delegates were unlikely to pass the strongly worded recommendations sought by Eastern District.

Sensing what was at stake, Manchester (Indiana) College president Otho Winger, who shared a mutual respect for conservative eastern Brethren, carefully crafted a substitute motion, reaffirming the church's opposition to the trends to which Eastern District objected, without advocating any means of enforcement.[61]

Passage of the substitute motion placated Pennsylvania Brethren,[62] but was not strong enough for Kesler and his supporters. At a meeting in Plevna, Illinois, in June 1926, a week after the Lincoln Conference, the *Monitor* group seceded and formed the Dunkard Brethren Church.[63]

Though they agreed with the Dunkard Brethren diagnosis of the church's ills, experienced Eastern District elders rejected division as an effective remedy. Armed with an affirmation of their concerns by the 1926 Annual Conference, the influential members of the Eastern District Ministerial Board steered the churches in their charge away from schism. Upon learning of the Dunkard split, the board sent a letter to the elder-in-charge of each church in the district:

> Dear Brother _____,
>
> We are told that a group of our dear brethren and sisters have about decided to withdraw their fellowship from the Church of the Brethren . . . We would indeed deeply deplore a step of this kind. It would bring back again as from the grave all the dark record, the painful experiences, and horrors of things that happened some forty years ago [the Progressive and Old Order splits of the 1880s] . . .
>
> Experience has taught us that division was no cure then. We have no reason to believe it will mean a cure now. Above all there is no assurance that it would meet the approval of the Father of mercies . . . Scripture has no plain case where God countenances division.
>
> . . . Some of us who felt there was just cause for complaint were greatly encouraged at our last Annual Conference by the attitude of our church leaders. We therefore think it would indeed be very unfortunate to agitate or disturb the church with a spirit of division at a time when there is hope of a check to the worldly trend in the main body of the church.

While we are not unmindful of the many problems with which the faithful are confronted in these last days, . . . we, however, do not think that our people in eastern Pennsylvania would be ready for another break in the Brotherhood.

We take this opportunity. . . to earnestly plead with our dear brethren and sisters, to be cautious and move slow in an issue fraught with such grave and tremendous responsibilities.

> Ministerial Board of Eastern Pennsylvania:
> I. W. Taylor
> J. H. Longenecker
> Samuel H. Hertzler[64]

Having lived through the Dunker divisions of the 1880s and the district division of 1911, the Ministerial Board firmly cast its lot with the Church of the Brethren, despite their dissatisfaction with its growing worldliness. Had they opted for the Dunkard Brethren, much of Eastern District may have followed.[65]

A Double Standard for Men

Even as Eastern District elders contended for plainness at Annual Meetings during the first decades of the 1900s, dress standards within the district were slowly shifting. For men, a double standard had developed by the turn of the century.[66] The 1911 Annual Conference dress decision recognized this double standard by emphasizing that "especially ministers and deacons" should wear traditional garb, and only plain-dressed brothers should be installed into office.[67] Thus, beards, plain suits with standing collars (and without neckties), and broad brim hats—the distinguishing features of Eastern District men—were mandatory for ministers, but less stringently enforced for laymen. By the turn of the century, beards evidently had become marks of leadership status.[68]

Fashion-conscious laymen soon challenged the church's resolve by wearing neckties. While they initially met opposition—particularly for flashy ties—seldom did tie infractions evoke more than an admonition. A 1902 Mountville Council Meeting ruled that men shouldn't crease their hats or wear neckties. In 1910, a Mountville brother wearing a "fashionable necktie promised to put it away if the others do," and the congregation approved a motion "to have all neckties not for comfort or health put away till next council."[69]

Neckties met similar opposition in the Chiques congregation. Admonitions against neckties were given in 1904 and 1906, and again in 1910 and 1911. Chiques brethren in 1911 were admonished for going without the "brethren's suits." By 1912, an admonition against neckties was qualified to "fashionable neckties," and a 1923 admonition specified that "long or fashionable neckties" should be avoided.[70]

As laymen laid aside the garb, some congregations required distinctive dress for officeholders. The Official Board of the Harrisburg First church was admonished in 1906 not to nominate for office any persons who were out of order.[71] Some congregations continued such policies into the 1920s. The Hanoverdale Sunday school, several miles north of Hershey, closed for several weeks during the 1920s until a newly elected Sunday school superintendent received a plain coat from the tailor.[72]

By the late 1930s, up to three-fourths of Eastern District men likely had traded plain clothes for suits and ties. Ministers and deacons continued as the primary standard-bearers for distinctive dress.[73]

A Close Shave for Ministers

Dress standards in Eastern District, even among ministers and deacons, were evolving prior to the 1920s. At the turn of the century, ministers were called and licensed to the first degree of ministry. After a test period, usually of one year, a minister could be advanced to the second degree. Among requirements for advancement was growing a beard.

When the Harrisburg First congregation sought to advance a minister to the second degree in 1901, officiating elders balked. A kind elder took the young minister aside and explained the situation:

> I was told that because my beard was too short, they didn't want to advance me. He said they may pass me,

they may not. "Don't worry," I said. "I will preach the gospel of Christ the best way I can, whether I am advanced to the second degree or not."

In the end, the elders asked the congregation whether they wanted to advance their minister to the second degree without a proper beard. "Someone said, 'He couldn't raise one if he tried to.' They advanced me to the second degree in the ministry."[74]

The brother in the Harrisburg congregation was an exception, however. In 1913, another minister was refused advancement because he *would* not grow a beard. After a three-year struggle, this one brother was advanced in 1916, but the District Elders reaffirmed their beard requirement.

Elders discussed the beard matter the following year and decided they would not *ordain* without a beard. Ministers generally were *advanced* to the second degree and *ordained* to the eldership, so the 1917 decision evidently was a concession. Beards now were required for *elders* only.

Before long, this rule, too, was challenged. Elders refused for several years to ordain Henry R. Gibbel, a beardless minister in the Lititz congregation. Finally, in 1926 the elders relented, but Gibbel died and was buried on the very day he was to have been ordained. Nevertheless, precedent had been set.[75] A short time later beardless Frank Carper was ordained an elder in the Palmyra congregation. Carper's daughter recalls that a kindly elder explained to her baby-faced father, "The Lord doesn't expect us to do what we can't do."[76]

By the early 1930s, a new class of beardless elders was emerging in Eastern District. Ralph W. Schlosser, an Elizabethtown College professor and respected churchman, was one of the first. Writing to Carper in 1929 to accept an invitation to preach in Palmyra, Schlosser made specific mention of his chin:

> I now belong to the "beardless" eldership, but I suppose that will not interfere with my coming. I felt there was nothing to be gained here [at graduate school in New York] by wearing it, and besides it would have made me the target of much unnecessary jesting and unpleasantness as it did the other time I was here. And I believe that

there are many more at home even who will give me credit for it than will criticize me for it.[77]

Ties That Bind

Having broken the beard barrier, ministers soon exchanged plain garb for worldly suits and ties. By the 1930s, a younger generation of ministers chafed under the stiff coat collars that separated them from the world. Longtime minister Harry Enders recalls:

> I didn't like the separateness of the church from the community . . . The church when I was a kid was pretty much an isolated island of self-righteousness, and out there was that wicked world . . . Plainness was separating the church from its ministry.[78]

Another minister remembers that as a youth he "was beginning to feel awkward" without a necktie. "For me, it wasn't a religious conviction; it was something kind of handed down." While he agreed Christians should be different, he believed distinctive convictions and principles were more important than distinctive dress. "I came to realize," he said, "different for the right reasons."[79]

Such convictions led some newly elected ministers to keep their ties when they were called to the ministry. Harry Enders readily accepted the Mountville congregation's call to ministry in 1933. The church relicensed him in 1934 and 1935 but refused to advance him to the second degree because of his necktie. Enders recalls:

> That was when I declined any further relicensing because it became apparent it was a standoff, that I wasn't about to wear the plain suit and the church was not about to ordain a minister that didn't wear the plain suit.
>
> Q: Why wouldn't you wear a plain suit?
>
> Well, because to me it was hypocritical. I could not support something that I did not believe in. Preachers were preaching sermons on why you should wear plain

Four ministers in the East Fairview congregation near Manheim, ca. 1953, illustrate the evolution of men's dress: Henry L. Hess (second from left), plain suit; Howard A. Merkey (left), standard suit with plain vest; J. Norman Weaver (second from right), standard suit with bow tie; and Robert Turner (right), standard suit with necktie. Ernest and Marian Shenk Collection.

suits. I just couldn't find the background to preach a sermon on that.[80]

Finally, in 1944 the congregation relicensed Enders with the understanding that plainness would not be required. He could keep the tie that disqualified him nine years earlier.

A growing number of congregations began to accept young ministers with neckties during the late 1930s and early 1940s. In some cases young ministers heeded requests to remove their neckties. A more common concession was wearing a "plain vest" with a regular shirt and tie. This plain vest was a way for young ministers to "live in both worlds," satisfying the congregation's desire for plainness and their own yen to dress more according to the style of the day.[81]

Other ministers—particularly those associated with Elizabethtown College—found other ways of living in both worlds. College leaders

A. C. Baugher and Ralph W. Schlosser during the 1930s were notorious for alternating between plain and fancy dress. One former Elizabethtown student recalls:

> They would start out at Elizabethtown not wearing a [plain] vest and stop along the road and put it on. That's the story. That's the legend that went with it. And I think it was probably true.[82]

Another minister, who was a student at Elizabethtown during the 1930s, recalls that Baugher came out to the conservative Annville congregation one evening to ask for a contribution to the college: "Oh, he was plain as midnight, you know, plain garb and all that. The next day I saw him with a tie. And everybody knew that [he did that]."[83]

The college from its beginning had a reputation for being soft on dress.[84] Over time the contagion grew worse. Brethren young people eager to ditch distinctive dress often found that college offered them freedom to do so. By the late 1920s, faculty continued to dress plainly, but most students did not. By the 1930s, even some key faculty and administrators had permanently traded their plain clothes for more fashionable attire.

When Harold Bomberger was called to the ministry in the late 1930s, a conservative deacon in the Annville congregation suggested that he should dress plainly. Bomberger recounts:

> I said, "Well, I don't really feel that strongly about it, but if it's a burden to you people, I'm willing when I come over here to teach or preach to take off my tie and buy a straight coat. But when I go to school [at Elizabethtown] and do other things, I'll put a tie on." And I still remember him, a good old guy. He said, "Well, brother, I'd sooner have you be consistent."[85]

For Bomberger, and a growing number of young ministers, being consistent meant wearing a tie.

By the 1950s, most Eastern District ministers still wore plain coats, but congregations continued to accept young ministers with neckties. The acceptance, in some instances, was less than unani-

Table 5.1

Pattern of Disappearing Plain Dress
Among Eastern District Men

1900s-1910s Beards and plain dress required for *all* ministers. Laymen begin wearing neckties but receive frequent admonitions from elders.

1910s-1920s As neckties become common for laymen, some congregations require officeholders to wear plain coats. Beards required for elders only.

1920s-1930s Most laymen wear neckties. Ministers and deacons continue as standard-bearers for plainness. Beardless elders emerge.

1930s-1940s Young ministers keep neckties when called to the ministry. Some wear "plain vests" in deference to their congregations. College leaders dress plain in some situations, fancy in others.

1940s-1950s Neckties become acceptable for ministers, but most continue to dress plainly. Some wear beards.

1950s-1960s Plain dress fades even among ministers. Elders preserve plainness.

1960s-1980s Distinctive male dress disappears except in a few conservative congregations.

mous. When the Chiques congregation called Robert O. Hess to preach in the mid-1940s, members tried without success to persuade him to remove his tie. When Hess preached, one member closed his eyes rather than view the offense.[86]

Most of the district's elders continued to dress plainly into the 1960s, but as the older generation passed on, so did plain dress for men in Eastern District.[87] (See Table 5.1 for a summary of Disappearing Plain Dress Among Eastern District Men.)

Backsliding Sisters

As men traded beards and plain suits for smooth faces and neckties, sisters also donned the world's fashions. In the Mountville church, the transition began with a shrinking prayer covering and ended with few vestiges of plainness some 90 years later.

As early as 1902, sisters in the Mountville congregation were admonished to "wear the right covering."[88] A few months later, sisters were reminded to avoid ribbons on bonnets and "watch guards" on their capes. A few sisters had begun to abandon the

Three sisters from the Schuylkill congregation, Pine Grove, ca. 1912. Seated in front of a massive chestnut tree on the Jacob Morgan farm are (from left) Rebecca (Zerbe) Kintzel, Alice (Kintzel) Zerbe, and Ellen Zerbe.
Schuylkill Congregational Archives.

cape dress in favor of "coats which expose their entire form." Fed up with deviations in dress, the church in 1905 gave members who were testing the church's resolve four weeks to come within the Order or appear before the Council Meeting. The ultimatum apparently was taken to heart. Few dress concerns were voiced at Council Meetings for the next several years.

In 1910, sisters again were warned "not to have such small caps."

Two generations of sisters in the Spring Creek congregation in Hershey during the 1940s show the evolution of dress for Brethren women. Spring Creek Congregational Archives.

Young women's Sunday school class members in the Conestoga congregation, May 6, 1946. (Seated from left) Ethel Myer, assistant teacher; Mary Hess, teacher; Ellen Hess; Floy Wenger; Evelyn Good. (Standing) Ruth Graybill, Naomi Martin. Conestoga Congregational Archives.

Similar admonitions were given in 1912 and 1913. By 1913, not only were coverings shrinking, some sisters were wearing "short sleeve and low neck dresses." In 1915, a lengthy admonition advised members "not to have caps so small and *without strings,* [not to] leave off the cape and apron, [and to put away] tight skirts, and low neck dresses." By December 1915, the situation was out of hand. Five separate admonitions were leveled at fashionable sisters:

> Admonition to sisters not to comb their hair so as to look so much like the world and thereby hide the sacred covering which the Apostle Paul has set forth that should be worn by all professing godliness.

> Admonition to sisters not to wear immodest dresses as some are doing, low necked, short sleeves, tight fitting skirts till all modesty is gone. I Tim. 2:9-10 tells how.

Why is it that some of our sisters who had been wearing the cape and apron are now laying them aside? Because the love of many wax cold.

Admonition to sisters not to part their hair at the side so as to look like the world.

Admonition to sisters to put away those rosettes from their bonnet strings.[89]

Mountville in 1917 barred sisters wearing low neck dresses from communion, and admonitions were registered during the 1920s against "unbecoming head dress," parting the hair on the side, and improper coverings. More than one sister was reported "having gone worldly" and asking to be disowned from the church.

The congregation reached a turning point in 1928 when Council "decided to be charitable but firmly *request* the transformed life be exemplified" by those who were out of order.[90] A September 1935 query "requesting that the church take a stand against worldliness, especially the wearing of hats by sisters, and that sisters wearing hats be asked not to commune," was lost. By 1939, women were cutting their hair, and in 1943 a member objected to sisters wearing "garments which pertaineth to a man."[91]

By the mid-1940s, women's dress was no longer debated at Mountville Council Meetings, and the wearing of the prayer covering was beginning to fade. By 1989, one or two women wore a covering to Sunday morning services. More women— about a fourth—donned prayer veils for semi-annual love feasts.[92] This pattern of disappearing plainness for women was repeated in congregations throughout Eastern District. (See Table 5.2.)

In general, the erosion began with a shrinking prayer covering in the first decade of the century. Before long, younger sisters removed cap strings from their veils. By the 1920s, younger women had begun to "drop their bonnets," and "gay" dresses replaced modest cape dresses. Some young women in the 1920s and 1930s bristled at the thought of wearing a peculiar prayer covering in public. A girl in the Lititz congregation in the 1920s delayed joining the church because she feared her covering and bonnet would elicit ridicule from classmates:

Table 5.2
Pattern of Disappearing Plain Dress
Among Eastern District Women

1900s-1910s   Young women wear smaller prayer veils, some without strings. A few trade cape dresses for "gay dresses."

1910s-1920s   Young women "drop bonnets," begin to wear gay dresses with short sleeves, lower necklines, add decorative lace. A few test the church's resolve with hats and are disowned.

1920s-1930s   Older women and wives of ministers and deacons maintain cape dresses and two-piece coverings with strings, while the younger generation wears smaller coverings and gay dresses. Some younger women part hair on the side and style it around shrinking coverings.

1930s-1940s   Young women begin cutting their hair and wearing coverings to church services only. Hats gain acceptance in some churches. A few women begin wearing make-up and slacks. Few are disciplined for dress infractions.

1940s-1980s   Wearing of the prayer covering gradually fades and women dress according to the styles of the day, including shorts, slacks, and skirts. Jewelry and make-up become acceptable in most churches.

1990   A few congregations continue to require prayer coverings for worship, but most have few coverings at regular services. Coverings remain common at semi-annual love feasts.

> I would have been interested in joining the church a
> couple years earlier than I did because every night when
> I went to bed I was afraid I was going to die and go to
> hell. The reason I put it off so long was I was determined
> I wasn't going to wear a bonnet and I wasn't going to wear
> a covering to school.[93]

The sister, beset by fear of eternal damnation, joined the church in 1926 at age 13. After a year of wearing her covering to school, she decided to wear it only to church services. Before long, other schoolgirls in the congregation followed her lead.

In many congregations, wearing the prayer covering gradually faded, with no official decisions to end the practice. Elsewhere, a key woman in the church, such as the pastor's wife, stopped wearing the covering, and others quickly followed suit. A few passed official policies. The Middle Creek congregation, for example, in 1985 made the covering optional, but encouraged sisters to wear it while teaching or leading in worship, and required it for love feast and baptism.[94]

A handful of congregations in the Atlantic Northeast District in 1989 continued to urge women to wear the prayer covering seven days a week, and in others many women wore coverings to worship services. Nearly 20 percent (12 congregations) of congregations reported that 75 percent or more of women members wore prayer coverings to regular services. Of those, six congregations reported that all women wore coverings to services. On the other hand, 60 percent of the congregations stated that five percent or fewer women wore coverings to services. Seventeen congregations reported no coverings at all.[95]

Ironically, even in congregations where regular use of prayer coverings faded four decades ago, coverings were common at love feast in the late 1980s. A full third (22) of congregations reported that all women members wore the prayer covering at love feast. Thirteen others said that 75 percent or more of women wore coverings to the communion service. In sum, a large majority of women wore coverings to love feast in more than half the congregations of the district in 1989.[96] Remarkably, even in the historically progressive Philadelphia First congregation which discarded plain dress in the early 1900s, all women in 1989 continued to wear coverings at love feast.[97]

Matters of the Heart

The Church of the Brethren's historic preoccupation with dress is incomprehensible to modern Brethren. For many, plain dress symbolizes all that was wrong with the "legalistic" church of the past, a church that dwelled on minor matters, such as dress, while pressing world issues clamored for its attention. Modern Brethren blush at the thought that their ancestors combatted the evil of women's hats while thousands in Europe were dying in real combat in the early years of World War I.

Moderns argue that external appearance is irrelevant to faith. After all, a pure heart is what matters to God. What right does the church have to tell individuals what to wear? Yet many moderns willingly clothe themselves in the garb of corporate employers who require particular styles of suits and ties. As corporate America recognizes, outward appearance shapes inward identity. The employee wearing the garb of IBM also embraces the goals and values of the corporation. Similarly, distinctive dress powerfully symbolized separation and group identity for Brethren. It served as a visible sign of inner commitments to separation, simplicity, equality, and humility.[98]

Not surprisingly, as Brethren dressed more like the world, they paid increasing attention to its affairs. The passing of plain dress corresponded with shifting attitudes toward political participation, war and peace, and involvement in social issues and civic organizations. At the same time, as Brethren dressed more like the world, their entertainment and leisure activities, moral decisions, and the style of their meetinghouses and worship reflected a move toward the mainstream. Things once declared off-limits gradually became acceptable, and a church that traditionally had exercised strict discipline grew increasingly reluctant to regulate its members' lives.

6.

The Decline of Corporate Discipline

While plain dress was the keystone of the Brethren wall of separation at the turn of the century, Brethren stood apart from the world in other ways, as well. Their shunning of "sinful amusements," such as cards, dancing, and movies; unyielding opposition to secret organizations, life insurance, and labor unions; and enforcement of strict sexual standards increased the height and breadth of the Brethren barrier. Solidifying the wall was the mortar of church discipline. In time, however, both wall and mortar would crumble, and inclusivity would replace accountability as a cardinal virtue.

1900-1910: Accent on Accountability

During the first decade of the new century, discipline was as central to church life in eastern Pennsylvania as prayer and preaching. Cases of admonition, confession, or disowning often dominated congregational Council Meetings, and impulses to love the things of the world were checked by the likelihood of being called to account.

Churches laid the foundation for effective discipline even before prospective members joined the church. Applicants for baptism were first visited by two or three brethren who explained the church's unique doctrinal positions and practices. Prior to baptism, verses from Matthew 18 were read, and applicants agreed to follow this scriptural prescription for mutual correction.

Ritualized reminders helped members to keep their commitments. In a special afternoon service before each love feast, members were challenged to examine their relationship with God and with brothers and sisters in the church. Similarly, during an annual visit, deacons posed three questions to every member: 1) Are you still in the Faith of the Gospel as you declared when you were baptized? 2) Are you, as far as you know, in peace and union with the Church? and 3) Will you continue to labor with the Brethren for an increase of holiness, both in yourself and others?

Despite these regular check-ups, some members still strayed from the faith. In such cases, the church employed the rites of redemption—admonition, confession, disowning, and reclaiming—to restore sinners and preserve the church's purity. Transgressors were confronted and asked to confess before the church. Those who confessed nearly always were forgiven and retained in full fellowship.[1] Those who refused, however, were disfellowshipped.[2] (The Brethren tended not to use the word "excommunication" because they felt it implied both the use of force and a sacramental theology.) When wandering sheep did confess, they received a warm welcome back into the fold "by hand and a kiss according to the regular custom of the brethren."[3]

Clear geographical boundaries between congregations, a requirement that Brethren hold membership in their congregations of residence, and a prohibition against transferring out-of-order members from one congregation to another made it virtually impossible to escape church discipline.

"The Heart of Fools Is in the House of Mirth"

Annual Conference minutes and congregational Council Meeting minutes at the turn of the century are rife with examples of the church's unyielding stance on worldliness. Conference ruled in 1892 that cards and games of any kind were "unquestionably wrong" and in 1906 prohibited Brethren merchants from selling cards, dice, dominos, diamonds, gold rings, and gold watches. From the 1850s on, attending state and county fairs, patronizing the theater or opera, dancing, and similar frivolities also were off-limits for Brethren.[4]

Gospel Messenger editor J. H. Moore denounced the values of pleasure-seeking Christians:

> [They] think more about the theater than they think
> about the house of God. Not a few are more interested

in the card table than the Lord's table, and are more gifted in shuffling cards than in turning the leaves of the Sacred Volume . . .

Well may it be said of this generation, as it was said of a generation in the ages gone by: "The heart of the wise is in the house of mourning; but the heart of fools is in the house of mirth" (Eccles. 7:4). What else are the theater, the dance-hall, the billiard-hall, the card-room, and many of the places of entertainments, but houses of mirth?[5]

Eastern District congregations at the turn of the century kept close watch over members lest they be led astray by frivolous entertainment. In a 1901 case, Lancaster Council Meeting minutes reported,

Before the evening services in presence of the members present Bro.____ confessed to having gone to the Opera-house for which wrong he is sorry and asks the pardon of the church promising to be more guarded in the future. Upon consideration it was decided to forgive him and admonish him to be more careful here-after.[6]

At a 1903 Council Meeting in the rural Chiques congregation the question was raised: "Is it becoming for our members to have such games as checkers, croquet, and others of like character allowed in their homes, where quite a number of young and even married men are indulging in the same on Sundays?" The emphatic answer was no.[7] The Elizabethtown church prohibited baseball and shooting matches in 1906 and attending "theatoriums" in 1909.[8] Chiques ruled in March 1911 that "the whole church is unanimous that having ball matches in the homes of the brethren is wrong on Sundays" and warned, a few months later, that those attending baseball matches "on Sunday or any other day" will "fall into the judgment of the church."[9] A sister in Elizabethtown in 1910 confessed attending a dance, and the following year a general admonition was issued against "attending theatoriums, pool rooms, bowling alleys, dances, clubs, etc."[10]

Lodges, Life Insurance, and the Law

Brethren also adamantly opposed using the law, purchasing life insurance, and joining secret societies. The 1891 Annual Conference required Brethren to consult the congregation before using the law, and Eastern District members regularly asked permission or confessed their fault in not having done so.[11] Annual Conference decisions in 1902, 1904, and 1908 reaffirmed the church's historic opposition to life insurance, labor unions, and secret societies, respectively.[12] An 1897 Eastern District petition to Annual Conference urged stricter opposition to life insurance for several reasons:

1. Because Life Insurance is selfish in that it gives no benefit to the really poor and needy.

2. Because it robs the church of true Christian charity.

3. Because it is a childish savings bank, and thus kills the ability to properly take care of means.

"Old Joe Price," a member of the Indian Creek congregation, fishing near Harleysville, ca. 1910. Fishing was a permissible leisure activity for Brethren. BHLA, *Brethren Encyclopedia* Collection.

4. Because many who take part in Life Insurance experience Jer. 17:11 [which likens a man who gains wealth by unjust means to a partridge that hatches eggs it did not lay].

5. Because it is a lottery—all expect more than they give.

6. Because it is an incentive to covetousness and murder.[13]

The 1904 Annual Conference stated:

Labor unions as now conducted often lead to violence, and sometimes to riot and bloodshed, and as these are contrary to the spirit and teaching of the Gospel of Jesus Christ, we cannot allow our members to unite with or belong to them.

A 1908 ruling opposed secret and oathbound organizations and labor unions in the same breath.[14]

Eastern District churches rigorously enforced Conference positions, as illustrated by several cases in the Lancaster church. Lancaster disowned a man in 1900 for joining a lodge and heard a confession the following year from a brother who had joined a labor union. In 1903, the church disowned another man who had joined a labor union and, a few years later, disowned two members for having their lives insured. In 1911, the congregation ruled that members "who are connected with Life Insurance or beneficiary societies" be given three months to be reconciled to the church.[15]

"Waiting Too Long to Get Married"

While Brethren in the early 1900s disciplined for a variety of transgressions, they reserved harshest judgment for sexual sinners. An 1898 Annual Conference action reaffirmed that divorced and remarried persons were adulterers who could not be church members unless the divorce was obtained due to unfaithfulness by the other partner. Similarly, fornication—sometimes delicately described in Council Meeting minutes as "waiting too long to get married"—brought automatic disowning. After a period of separation from the church, the transgressor could confess and be reinstated.

Members of the Upper Dublin (later Ambler) congregation, September 1915.
Ambler Congregational Archives.

Congregational minutes vividly portray the church's no-non-sense approach to sexual sin. In 1906 in Mountville a sister who had "two husbands living at present" withdrew her membership, and another was disowned for marrying a divorced man. A year later the second sister was reinstated, but only after separating from her second husband.[16]

Disowning and reclaiming fornicators also was a familiar ritual. At a single Mountville Council Meeting in 1910, two men and one woman were disowned for fornication, while two women and one man who had been disowned at an earlier time repented and were reclaimed, the one sister "with the understanding that she has no correspondence in any way or even speak to him without any witness."[17]

In short, Annual Conference decisions prior to 1911 generally upheld the time-tested Order of the church and bolstered those congregations seeking to preserve peculiarity. Standing firm on Annual Conference decisions, most Eastern District congregations deployed strict discipline against encroaching worldliness.

There were exceptions, however. The Philadelphia First and Ambler churches, for example, evidently practiced little discipline from the late 1800s on.[18] While such congregations were rare in eastern Pennsylvania, by the 1910s, progressives throughout the denomination were nudging the church toward tolerance. Typically, advocates of change stretched or ignored a Conference ruling until the church was forced to issue a new statement, more in line with the practice of progressive congregations. Conservative churches, who remained intensely loyal to Conference, then grudgingly acquiesced to the more lenient rulings.[19]

"Violating No Gospel Principle"

After the 1911 district division, Southeastern District churches downplayed discipline, but Eastern District continued to toe the line. A perplexing problem for the Mountville church was members sneaking across the Susquehanna River to the York Fair. A 1902 Council Meeting minute reported that a sister was "at the fair and while there was dancing." Other members confessed succumbing to the fair's allure in 1904, 1910, and 1917. At a 1910 Council Meeting, no less than 14 members acknowledged attending the fair.[20]

By the mid-1910s, Annual Conference was ready to reconsider fairs. A 1914 paper attempted to distinguish between beneficial "exhibitions and educational features" and "positively harmful and demoralizing" entertainment found at fairs. In essence, the report approved of fairs where the good features outweighed the bad. However, conservatives, including Eastern District's J. H. Longenecker, objected, and the paper was returned to a committee for more work.[21]

A brief 1916 Conference report took a different tack. While it "strongly advised" church members to "avoid any fair or other gathering, at which they. . . may be thrown into evil associations," it left the matter of disciplining fairgoers to congregations. The report passed without any debate.[22] By 1920, fairs were seldom mentioned in eastern Pennsylvania congregational minutes.

During the 1910s, Brethren also softened their stand on sexual sin. Two queries to the 1915 Annual Conference asked the church to reconsider its ruling that all fornicators—even repentant ones—be automatically disowned. The petitioners noted that some congregations already retained those who confessed, and, in others, the time between disowning and reclaiming was so brief as to be meaningless.[23] In the end, the 1915 Conference agreed that only unrepentant fornicators deserved to be disowned. Eastern Pennsylvania congregations gradually adopted the more lenient ruling.[24]

Also in 1915, Annual Conference qualified its opposition to labor unions. Although a 1912 report had declared joining unions to be "unwise and exceedingly dangerous," delegates in 1915, in deference to urban Brethren seeking work in union- dominated trades, ruled, "Members may belong to Labor Unions. . . when, by doing so, they violate no gospel principle."[25]

The trend toward relaxing ancient Annual Conference writs reached new heights in 1920. Applying the same logic to life insurance, the 1920 Conference permitted life insurance "where the taking of such policies violates no Gospel principle." Individuals and congregations could decide just when a Gospel principle was imperiled.[26]

Another 1920 Annual Conference statement equivocated on the question of law. In surprisingly positive language, the paper noted, "'A legal process, when properly conducted, is a search for truth,' and an instrument of justice." Brethren were to continue to consult

A concession stand staffed by the Annville congregation at the 1949 Pennsylvania State Farm Show in Harrisburg. Until the 1920s, Brethren were discouraged from attending fairs. Annville Congregational Archives.

their congregations before going to court, but the statement explicitly permitted bringing suit and the practice of law by Brethren.[27]

The notion of a Dunker attorney was too much for Eastern District elder J. H. Longenecker, who rose to speak against the paper:

> I am at an age where it goes very hard with me to see this change come to our church, when our members will open law offices. I wish they would open mission offices, to aid in carrying the Gospel that shall regulate our lives, instead of opening offices to regulate our lives by law . . . My prediction is that if this report carries. . . the church will have more trouble with the lawyers inside of the church than they had when we went to lawyers for counsel outside of the church.[28]

Despite such objections, the statement passed.

Another 1920 Conference paper, titled "Difference of Practice and Teaching," generated even more discussion than the law decision. The paper came in response to a plea from conservatives for the church to crack down on Brethren who accepted civil offices, affiliated with secret lodges, used musical instruments in worship, engaged in "worldly games manifestly sinful," and wore worldly apparel.

Instead of tightening restrictions, however, the 1920 Conference loosened standards even further. While reaffirming the Brethren opposition to all worldliness, the paper permitted the holding of civil offices "when by so doing no Gospel principle is compromised" and allowed musical instruments in churches where it would not disturb the peace. On amusements, the paper ruled that "all games manifestly sinful be forbidden" but left it to *individuals* or *congregations* to decide exactly which games were sinful. The report opposed membership in secret lodges, but only when it "would require the individual to violate Gospel principles." Earlier decisions on hats, neckties, and gold were reaffirmed.[29] In short, Annual Conference in 1920 backpedaled on one issue after another, seeking to accommodate an increasingly diverse church.

From Coercion to Persuasion

No longer able to rely on firm Annual Conference statements, Eastern District leaders began to yield on issues such as sinful amusements. By the 1920s, confessions or disownings for participating in amusements were rare. When such issues were broached, it was usually in the form of a toothless admonition. The Lititz church, for example, in 1923 approved a recommendation from the Official Board "that our members be *requested* to keep away from carnivals and Sunday Base Ball." Lititz elder J. W. G. Hershey in 1927 "*admonished strongly* against attending and participating in questionable worldly amusements," arguing, "We should have no desire to go, for it kills the desire for church services."[30] Similarly, the Mountville church in 1933, speaking against the opera and moving pictures, stated: "The church *desires* to use all her *influence* in having members abstain from every appearance of evil and *desires* that members keep away from worldly places."[31]

Changing views on sports provided further evidence of a cultural shift. Elizabethtown College's board of trustees had ruled in 1904 that "baseball and football are not in accord with Christian virtue and true education," and some churches during the 1910s had denounced Brethren ballplayers. In 1928, however, college trustees

Elizabethtown College trustees in 1928 sanctioned intercollegiate athletics, overturning an earlier ruling that "modern match games . . . are not in accord with Christian virtue." (Left to right) Trustees H. K. Ober, S. H. Hertzler, John Miller, Rufus Bucher, Aaron Baugher, Michael Kurtz, Rufus Royer, Frank Carper, and C. R. Oellig. Elizabethtown College Archives.

The 1929 Elizabethtown College girls basketball team. The college had informal athletic teams as early as 1905, but only after 1928 did they compete with college approval against teams from other schools. Elizabethtown College Archives.

endorsed intercollegiate athletics.[32] Southeastern District's Pottstown congregation in 1935 initiated church-related baseball and basketball clubs.[33] By 1930, most congregational minutes were virtually silent on sinful amusements.[34]

Of course, not all forms of entertainment were acceptable by then, but the battle had shifted from coercive Council actions to the persuasion of pen and pulpit. The District Welfare Board reported to the 1928 District Conference that it was defending the simple life by "teaching against worldliness as commercialized by the amusement interests: the theatre, dance, swimming pool and kindred evils."[35]

Elder Carl Zeigler recalled:

> I heard sermons [during the 1920s] on such subjects as, "Can you imagine the Apostle Paul playing baseball or basketball. . . ?" In my own home there were absolutely no games—checkers, parcheesi, none of those games—they were simply not allowed.[36]

Zeigler himself penned a pamphlet during the 1920s titled "Baneful Effects of Worldly Amusements," in which he specifically mentioned cards, dancing, and movies as hindrances to spiritual life. He pointed out,

> Jane Adams [sic] of Chicago Hull House fame says, "eighty-five per cent of the fallen girls cite the Dance as the beginning of their decline." Many a criminal has cited the card table as his first downward step . . . Uncontrolled card playing inevitably leads to Gambling . . . The fruitage of movies is equally alarming.[37]

A girl growing up in a rural Lebanon County congregation during the 1940s recalls,

> Oh my Lord, the sermons we got against going to the movies. When you went you couldn't even enjoy it because you knew the roof was going to fall in on your head. You were told that.[38]

Cards, dancing, and movies continued to be frowned upon into the middle decades of the century, but seldom was anyone disciplined. A *Gospel Messenger* writer from Elizabethtown in 1938 summed up the change as he saw it:

> The idea of being different is not popular today, and so many of us have fallen into drifting with the world . . . There are some in our ranks who go to the theater on Saturday night and on Sunday morning stand before a class and attempt to teach the way of Christ . . . There are some who go to the dance hall on Saturday night and partake of the holy communion on Sunday night. O church member, thinkest thou Christ is pleased with such conduct?

> Worldly allurements such as the dance hall, the theater, commercial amusements all are the instruments of Satan to send poor lost souls to hell and to destroy the witness of Christians.[39]

Ongoing Discipline in the 1920s

While Eastern District Brethren during the 1920s relented on amusements, they stood firm on weightier matters. Churches continued to monitor members' use of the law, as shown by a 1923 case in the Mountville church in which a woman who had used the law without permission was instructed "to always seek and take the advice of the church."[40]

The historic opposition to secret societies also remained strong. In fact, many congregations during the 1920s not only opposed affiliation with *secret* organizations, but with *any* organization outside the church. The Chiques church in 1922 was admonished against "going to community meetings and taking part in them." Similarly, Mountville in 1922, considering the propriety of members joining farm bureaus, decided that it was "unwise to be members of any organization outside the church . . ."[41] The Elizabethtown church, located in strong Mason territory, reaffirmed in 1928 that "oathbound brothers" could not commune and disowned lodge members in January 1929 and May 1933.[42]

In progressive Southeastern District, views on secret lodges were mixed. Asked "whether it is in keeping with the church to invite secret orders to our church services?" Southeastern District elders in April 1925 ruled "that all pastors should under all circumstances uphold the present position of our Brotherhood." But three years later the Royersford church asked for an opinion on Brethren lodge members, and elders recommended "that forbearance be exercised with continued upholding of the New Testament teaching and the ruling of Annual Conference."[43] Thus, Southeastern District elders advocated opposition of lodges, but tolerance for Brethren lodge members.

Meanwhile, an important Annual Conference debate during the 1920s and early 1930s threatened to erode church discipline even further.

The Certificate Question[44]

As Annual Conference during the 1910s and 1920s granted more leeway to individual congregations, the once simple matter of transferring memberships grew complex. A 1907 Conference ruling had delineated proper transfer procedures: A member moving from one parish to another was to obtain a certificate of membership from the home congregation to present to the new congregation. No church was to grant or accept certificates of out-of-order members.[45]

But by the 1920s, membership standards varied widely. Thus, while most congregations in Eastern District continued to enforce plain dress and uphold other traditional teachings, churches in Southeastern District, and in much of the Brotherhood, did not. A member in good standing in a progressive church would present a certificate to a conservative congregation and be rejected.

Similarly, an out-of-order member who moved into a more progressive congregation often was denied a certificate by his home church. Such members found themselves in a catch-22—unacceptable in their old church and unable to join the new for lack of a letter. Conservatives vehemently objected when progressive churches "illegally" accepted such out-of-order members.

Further complicating the picture was the Brethren's geographic definition of congregations, whereby each church had a monopoly on Brethren within its boundaries. Thus, moving from one congregation's territory to another's necessitated moving membership, even if the move was only a few miles down the road.[46]

Such concerns led to the appointment of a committee by the 1923 Annual Conference to "obviate the confusion" around transferring certificates. Far from a trivial technical matter, the "certificate question" was intricately tied to the ability of congregations to set their own membership standards.

After rejecting a proposed solution in 1924, Conference surprisingly gave near unanimous approval to a new report in 1926, which affirmed two "Basic Principles":

> 1. Since the local congregations are the units that constitute the general Brotherhood, to hold membership in a local congregation is to have membership in the general body. The New Testament is the basis of membership . . .

> 2. The requirements for membership are the requirements for transfer of membership. Both are the same. Therefore, the requirements for the transfer of membership must not be greater than the requirements for membership.[47]

Both conservatives and progressives could affirm these general principles. To conservatives, the paper appeared to affirm a traditional understanding of church unity, where all congregations would uphold Annual Conference standards. Progressives, on the other hand, believed the paper guaranteed them membership in any congregation, since to be a member of one congregation was to be a member of the general body.[48] The certificate question appeared to be solved.

Before long, however, conservatives recognized their error in approving the 1926 report. A 1929 query from Eastern District's Big Swatara church asked Conference to turn the clock back to 1907 when Conference had ruled: "Churches shall not grant letters of membership to, nor accept letters of membership from, members who are living in violation of the Gospel as defined by Annual Meeting."

Elizabethtown elder Samuel H. Hertzler explained at length on the Conference floor the shortcomings of the 1926 decision. Citing the paper's principle that membership in a congregation is paramount to membership in the general body, Hertzler argued:

> Work that out to its logical conclusion, and it would mean that if you have membership in any local church it gives you a right to have membership in any other local church in the Brotherhood . . . *It would tend to make every church in the Brotherhood as liberal as the most liberal.*

> I wish the fact was not in existence, but some of you know we have some very liberal churches that receive into fellowship not only sisters wearing hats. . . but brethren who belong to oath-bound secret societies, who belong to The American Legion, who belong to the Ku Klux Klan.

According to the 1926 report, conservative congregations were obligated to accept such members.

Hertzler also objected to a more specific directive that congregations grant letters to out-of-order members. According to the 1926 report, if a congregation could not bring a transferring member in line with its standards, the elder was to scrawl an "exception" on the back of the certificate and forward it anyway. Hertzler recounted an episode in Elizabethtown:

> A young brother of ours left our church, moved out into the state of Missouri, was gone four years. He came back wearing a Masonic badge and asked for his letter of membership. Of course, we didn't grant it . . . I didn't believe I had the privilege or anybody else had the privilege to grant a certificate and write on the back of it that he was just out of line a little bit, that he belonged to the Masonic lodge . . .

> The outcome of it was that we disfellowshiped the young man, after making every effort to make him see his mistake and withdraw from the lodge. He said, "I talked with an old elder in another State where I am now residing, . . . and this old elder said you had no business to withhold my certificate. All you needed to do was write on the back what your objection was."

> Well now, what does become of our decision on a war question, peace doctrine, or the oath question, if any subject may just be stated on the back of the certificate?

Hertzler summed up:

> . . . this kind of a minute gives a local church the right to vote out all our distinctive doctrines, if they wish, on any subject. You say you could hardly conceive of a local church doing a thing like that. Yes, I conceive it. Some of you will say, "Bro. Hertzler, are you not seeing things?" Yes, I am seeing a lot of things that I don't like to see, that I have to see.[49]

As Hertzler saw it, the 1926 decision was unacceptable.

In response to Eastern District pleas, Conference appointed Hertzler to a new committee, which proposed yet another certificate solution in 1930. This time progressives cried foul. On the surface the report appeared to be neutral. Each congregation could decide whether or not to grant or accept any certificate it pleased. But progressives quickly detected that they would be held hostage by conservative churches. While conservatives could join or leave any congregation, those who belonged to a lodge or dressed fashionably would be denied entry into and exit from conservative churches. Delegates referred the paper back to the committee for more work.

The committee in 1931 proposed a new solution that finally satisfied progressives and conservatives: Each congregation could accept or reject any member, with or without a letter. Conservatives were free to refuse anyone, and progressives could welcome anyone, even those who were denied a certificate by another congregation.[50]

The 1931 certificate solution permanently reshaped discipline in the Church of the Brethren. Once the authoritative voice in the church, Annual Conference had ceded power to *districts* during the 1910s and 1920s. The 1931 decision further transferred authority to *congregations*, who were freed to discipline as much or as little as they pleased. It also made it easier for members to "escape" to more forgiving congregations, presaging the day when *individuals* would become their own final arbiters of truth.

The Blurring of Congregational Boundaries

The erosion of parish lines in eastern Pennsylvania further encouraged flight from more strict churches. Although the 1931 Conference report reaffirmed boundaries, it also allowed Brethren to "hold their membership in congregations where they do not reside" when both congregations approved. In actual practice, it had been common for several years for members who did not meet Eastern District standards to hold membership in more lenient urban churches.

Two couples from Elizabethtown, for example, joined Philadelphia First church in the early 1930s because the men's Masonic Lodge affiliation disqualified them from membership and communion in Elizabethtown. They continued to worship in Elizabethtown, but communed in Philadelphia. Similarly, several Harrisburg women during the 1920s joined Baltimore First church rather than surrender worldly hats.[51]

Southeastern District's Ambler church, located near several

conservative Eastern District churches, agreed in 1928 to accept members from Hatfield and Indian Creek without letters of transfer. As a result, dissatisfied members of these conservative churches—including many youth—sought refuge at Ambler.[52]

At times, Eastern District Elders were summoned to settle boundary disputes. When the Midway church divided in 1933 to form the Lebanon church, a dozen or so members who fell within the bounds of the city church refused to hold their membership there. The Elders Body advised that members be allowed to choose which congregation to join, with the consent of both congregations.[53] A pastor in Lebanon during the 1930s recalls,

> We had people who wanted a little more progressive program coming to us, and some people who wanted a more conservative program were going to Midway. You see, it wasn't all bad. There was something for everybody.[54]

An even more ticklish case in 1936 involved congregations on both sides of the district border. The Springfield church, located in Southeastern District, wanted to license a member of Eastern District's Hatfield church to the ministry, but Hatfield considered him out-of-order and refused to transfer his membership. Finally, the two districts negotiated a deal. Following the 1931 Conference policy, Hatfield dropped the man from their membership list, and Springfield accepted him and licensed him to the ministry. In the end, a man who was not considered fit for membership in one church was licensed to the ministry several miles up the road.[55]

By the 1940s, congregational boundaries were largely ignored, and Brethren could join—or flee from—any church they chose. While individual Brethren at the turn of the century counted the cost of joining the church, by 1940 it was *churches* who counted the cost of potential membership loss before asking too much of their members. By then a pattern was emerging. Churches would discipline less and less, eventually delegating the responsibility to the church board and, finally, the pastor. As discipline decreased, churches were faced with growing lists of inactive members. Not surprisingly, inactives surfaced first in the "lax" congregations of Southeastern District.[56]

(Top) Groundbreaking for the Ambler church, May 28, 1922, and (below) the new building. During the late 1920s, some members of strict Eastern District congregations "escaped" to the more lenient Ambler church. Ambler Congregational Archives.

The Philadelphia First church had grown to 460 members by fall 1945, but, during one eight-week period, average worship attendance dipped to 114. To determine why people did not attend, the deacon board mailed a questionnaire to all members, but the response was so small that the survey was considered useless.[57] By the 1930s, inactives were emerging in the city and town churches of Eastern District, as well. Harrisburg First, Mountville, Lititz, Elizabethtown, and Spring Creek all saw discipline decline and inactivity emerge by 1940.[58]

Reconsidering Remarriage

Though discipline was waning by the 1930s—particularly in congregations in towns and cities—many churches still held sexual sinners accountable. Confessions of fornication continued—especially in rural churches—and a 1907 Annual Conference statement, barring divorced and remarried people from joining the church while a former companion was alive, remained in force.[59]

But in a 1932 study, sociologist Frederick Dove found that some Brethren were ignoring the Conference ruling on remarriage. "The problem has not been reconsidered," Dove noted, "but the divorcees have not been excommunicated."[60] With some congregations running ahead of Conference, and others growing uncomfortable with the church's uncompromising approach, delegates in 1932 appointed a committee to "consider the whole question of divorce and remarriage."

The committee's 1933 report essentially reaffirmed the church's traditional view, except for the final section, titled "Dealing With Exceptions." Divorced and remarried persons could be held in full fellowship, the paper stated, "if there seems to be evidence of repentance from sin and a desire to live as nearly right as possible thereafter . . ." Such members were restricted to the laity, however, and ministers were not to perform marriages for divorcees.

Explaining the relaxation of standards, the paper's final paragraph noted,

> In receiving or retaining such persons as members,
> the church is not ignoring the Christian ideal of marriage
> but is making an exception for the truly repentant, giving

them the advantages of church membership and commending them to the mercy, love and grace of God . . .[61]

Gradually, Eastern District congregations adopted the new policy.[62] The Lititz church, for example, in September 1937, accepted its first divorced and remarried member. The official action affirmed the sanctity of marriage and spoke against remarriage, but nonetheless recommended:

> (a) That the responsibility of this union be left between Bro. ____ and God. (b) That the church bear with the situation, and permit him to remain and work with the church in the laity.[63]

Remarriage, once flatly prohibited by no less an authority than Annual Conference, had become an individual matter.

"Lax and Uncertain" Statements

Other Annual Conference statements during the 1930s and 1940s reflected and promoted the ongoing relaxation of church discipline. A 1935 query, noting that Brethren had become "lax, vague, and uncertain," asked for a restatement of Brethren disciplinary policies. The 1937 Conference response, at first glance, seemed to affirm traditional understandings. It stated that discipline is necessary for the sake of the wrongdoer and the purity of the church and reaffirmed Matthew 18 as the blueprint for mutual correction.

But rather than disowning those who failed to hear the church, the paper recommended more amorphous "disciplinary measures." Further, the paper distinguished between two types of sins—sins of *nonspirituality* and sins of *immorality*. Only the latter merited discipline. Although at first glance it appeared to affirm traditional understandings, the 1937 report actually justified less stringent disciplinary methods.[64]

If any doubt remained that Brethren were losing their desire to discipline, a 1938 Conference statement on military service removed it. While recognizing that Brethren soldiers were "not in full accord with the faith and practice of the general brotherhood," the paper advocated "brotherly love and forbearance," rather than disowning. Even an act as antithetical to the Brethren faith as enlisting in the military would now be tolerated.[65]

By the mid-1940s, eroding standards necessitated a revision of certificates of membership. While certificates traditionally had testified that the transferee was a *member in good standing,* the 1944 Annual Conference approved a new form which stated simply that the transferee was a *member.* "Member in good standing" had become an obsolete category.[66]

Indicative of changing attitudes was a 1947 Conference polity statement on "counseling and discipline" which introduced some new terminology. First, the addition of "counseling" reflected a move from public discipline toward private pastoral counseling. Even more interesting were the background Scriptures cited. Alongside Matthew 18 stood 1 Corinthians 13, commonly known as "the love chapter." Obviously implying that traditional discipline practices sometimes lacked love, which is "patient, kind, and keeps no record of wrongs," the paper urged that transgressors be approached "in the spirit of Matt. 18 and 1 Cor. 13."[67]

A 1954 Conference statement on secret societies illustrated discipline according to 1 Corinthians 13. While calling membership in such groups "a compromise with secular standards that is unworthy of a consecrated Christian," the report nonetheless urged holding lodge members "in *loving* fellowship."[68] By the 1950s, secret organizations were a dead issue in many eastern Pennsylvania congregations.

Outmoded Accountability Mechanisms

By the middle decades of the century, traditional accountability mechanisms such as the reading of Matthew 18 before baptism, the annual deacon visit, and the love feast self-examination service were becoming anachronistic in churches that seldom disciplined. One observer estimated that in the 1940s about one-fifth of Brethren congregations nationwide had substituted other scriptures for Matthew 18 at the time of baptism.[69] The deacon visit also was in decline.

Originally conducted before the love feast to assure that sufficient peace and harmony existed within the congregation, the visit annually reminded members of their commitments to the church. But as congregations downplayed discipline, the visit shrank in significance. After all, why ask three probing questions to members when the church no longer acted on negative responses? Further, as inactive lists grew, some members refused to cooperate with deacons. Burdened by the volume of visits, deacons were haunted by suspicions that they were making liars of members who seldom darkened church doors, but nonetheless declared they were still in the faith.

With congregations already questioning the visit's value, the arrival of a paid pastor often clinched its demise.[70] Friendly, nurturing pastoral visits gradually replaced the deacon visit, and private pastoral counseling supplanted public confession. In general, the deacon visit faded first in those congregations that hired professional pastors first.[71]

The Lititz congregation illustrates the point. Founded in 1914, the church decided in 1923 that members who failed to answer the deacon questions "in a satisfactory manner" for two consecutive years would "fall into the judgment of the church."[72] But a decade later, the deacon visit at Lititz was in jeopardy. As one longtime deacon put it, "Some of the folks would say, 'Yes, we're in the faith, we're in the faith.' But we knew that they weren't anyhow. They weren't exactly telling the truth."[73]

The congregation's first full-time pastor arrived in 1935. The following year two deacons refused to visit, and, in 1937, deacons were late in completing the visit. After normal visiting in 1938 and 1939, deacons requested that the practice be discontinued. The congregation decisively rejected their request. The deacons in March 1940 reported that they were "unable to agree to make the annual visit." The church passed a strong motion, instructing deacons to "fulfill their duty," but they refused.[74]

Similar scenarios played out in other congregations. By the late 1980s, only 14 percent of congregations conducted a traditional deacon visit.[75] More than half of those who ended the practice did so during the 1950s and 1960s.[76]

The traditional self-examination service prior to love feast declined in similar fashion. Typically, attendance at the afternoon service dwindled until mostly deacons and ministers attended. By 1989, 11 percent of congregations held special self-examination services. Most continued to incorporate self-examination into the Sunday morning service prior to the feast or during an abbreviated time of reflection immediately preceding the service, but others replaced the theme of self-examination with a more inclusive invitation for all to come to the Lord's table.[77]

"Expanding the Ministry of Forgiveness"

By the 1950s, some Brethren again were uncomfortable with the church's position on divorce and remarriage, particularly the 1933 prohibition against pastors remarrying divorcees. Carl W. Zeigler, who pastored the Lebanon church, recalled that in a single evening around 1950 he declined three weddings because one partner was divorced in each couple:

> I was troubled and felt badly. I wanted to win people into the life of the church and here I couldn't give the blessing of the church. I felt that the Official Board was in my way. I would at that time personally have been able to marry them . . . I felt that we needed to be redemptive in these situations.[78]

By the early 1960s, as divorce became more common within and outside the church, many pastors did remarry divorcees, despite Conference's prohibition.[79] Spurred by this reality and a desire to be more "redemptive," Annual Conference in 1962 appointed a committee to study divorce and remarriage yet again. Advocating an "evangelical rather than a legalistic approach to the problems of divorce," the committee's 1963 report focused almost entirely on the church's obligation to forgive those who divorced. The committee asserted that "the church *owes* the sinner. . . her counsel and her message of forgiveness," and recommended that pastors perform marriages for repentant divorcees. Delegates recommitted the report to an expanded committee.[80]

The revised 1964 report allowed pastors to remarry divorcees, but was clear that "no minister. . . , against his own conscience, is obliged to marry a couple of which one or both persons have been divorced." Noting that "the church is entrusted with a ministry of reconciliation," the statement recommended an "expansion of the church's ministry of forgiveness, redemption, and reconciliation" for persons with the "special experience" of divorce. In some cases, the paper asserted, "this redemptive approach may include divorce. . . and the freedom to enter a new marriage with the guidance and blessing of the church." The statement was approved by a two-thirds majority vote.[81]

Some Second Thoughts

As the flight from traditional forms of discipline continued, some Brethren began to raise questions. Theologian Dale Brown in a 1963 article observed:

> I have been a member of four congregations among the Brethren, and I have yet to sit in a council meeting in which we have even considered throwing someone out of the fraternity for wearing a tie or a hat. Yet I have participated in Brethren discussion groups again and again in which we have deplored these very sins. Let us declare a moratorium on confessing the sins of our grandfathers! Our sin today is not that we have an authoritarian type of discipline; it is that we have so little.[82]

Leading denominational thinkers gathered in 1964 at Bethany Theological Seminary for a study conference on "The Meaning of Membership in the Body of Christ." Summarizing the mood, the writer of the meeting's official report noted:

> One could sense at Oak Brook a persistent concern over the permissiveness of Church of the Brethren congregations. It was proper, some were saying, to give up the legalistic intolerance that gave the church a hard and unlovely image. The trouble is that the baby was thrown out with the bath. Having done away with deacons' visits and strict adherence to Matthew 18, contemporary congregations have very nearly given up all sense of discipline . . .
>
> Few of the conference participants were happy with conditions in the local congregations they knew . . . But neither were the majority of delegates committed to going back to former patterns of church authority even should such an option be possible.[83]

Congregations, too, struggled to find their way. The Elizabethtown church exercised corporate discipline regularly into the late 1930s. Finally, in March 1938, the congregation agreed that confessions would be made privately to a committee appointed by the church board.[84] The deacon visit was discontinued in 1942, and, by the mid-1940s, little evidence of church discipline appears in the minutes. In 1952, the absence of discipline prompted a Council Meeting confession of sorts from the Elizabethtown elder. Minutes report:

> The Elder stated that there are a number of serious discipline problems within the church . . . [He] stressed the need for patience with those members to whom the Apostle Paul referred as "poor" members. The elder assured council that. . . the official board is putting forth every effort and exerting every influence to. . . correct conditions that are not in keeping with the standards and requirements of the church.[85]

The board during the 1950s did handle a few disciplinary matters. In a 1953 case a church member asked "permission to use the law, if necessary, against another *brother* in the Church." At the board's recommendation, Council appointed a committee to resolve the dispute, but conceded that, if the brothers insist, the church would grant permission for them to fight it out in the courts.[86]

By the early 1960s, the congregation had initiated a voluntary covenant through which members promised to attend worship, "exercise Christian care and watchfulness over others," live by the Golden Rule, maintain personal and family devotions, and support the church with time and substance. But no disciplinary steps were taken against anyone who failed to live up to the covenant.

In a June 1963 congregational newsletter, four Elizabethtown members reflected on the topic of membership requirements. Referring to the church covenant, one writer concluded, "I have made *my* covenant and *I* will need to answer to *my* God. *For me,* church membership does have requirements." Another reasoned,

> Church membership ought to denote full and complete dedication of one's life to Christ. This involves a kind of discipline that must be an *inner experience.* Yes,

Church membership is made too easy. The blame, however, rests not necessarily with the leadership of the Church, but with the *individual's response* to Christ's claim.

A third writer argued that "the Church must light the Way (to God) by continuing to place the greatest emphasis on *spiritual development*—as revealed in the Holy Scriptures— *rather than adding more requirements for membership.*" The final person wrote more favorably of membership requirements: "I definitely would favor some requirements for church membership. Shouldn't we at least be required to attend services now and then?"[87]

While they seemed to recognize that church membership often was taken too lightly, the Elizabethtown Brethren rejected corporate discipline. Instead, they redefined discipline as inward, personal, and spiritual. By the 1970s, the Elizabethtown church still hadn't found a solution to church discipline. In 1976, the church board attempted to reinstitute the annual visit, along with the traditional questions, but too few people volunteered to visit the church's 440 families, and the idea died.[88]

Having abandoned corporate discipline in the 1940s, the congregation struggled for the next 30 years to find an appropriate corrective. In the end, it could do no better than declare that discipline is a personal matter between individual members and God. The church's role was to welcome and include all, leaving it to God to separate the wheat from the chaff. The disciplined, visible church of Anabaptism had yielded to the invisible church of mainstream Protestantism, where the manner of church members' living was scarcely distinguishable from persons of the surrounding society.

Repudiating the Past

By the 1970s, Annual Conference statements repudiated traditional understandings of discipline. A 1976 paper on "discipleship and reconciliation" officially purged the word "discipline" from the Brethren vocabulary. Written as an update of the 1947 polity on "counseling and discipline," the 1976 statement rejected these traditional terms in favor of "biblical and positive words"—discipleship and reconciliation. Stating overtly what many Brethren had been feeling, the writers noted:

> The word *discipline* carries widely varying meanings and has become associated frequently with negative, unloving, and punitive overtones. *Counseling,* as traditionally used in this context, often implies "pressuring" and "advice giving . . .

New words—brokenness, healing, reconciliation, loving acceptance, *self*-discipline, openness, caring, understanding—replaced the traditional language of discipline—words like sin, offense, admonish, confess, disown. But most remarkable was the paper's reinterpretation of Matthew 18, the keystone of traditional disciplinary practices:

> The biblical teaching of Matthew 18, traditionally practiced in the Church of the Brethren, can be misinterpreted. It can be insensitively and hastily employed. However, when verse seventeen, ". . . let him be to you as a Gentile and a tax collector" (RSV), is understood within the context of the *total* chapter, it reflects the openness and unending compassion of Jesus. Gentiles and tax collectors. . . were the focus of his compassion and forgiveness.[89]

In the words of Carl F. Bowman,

> In a few simple sentences, Annual Conference thus rejected its historic grounds for corporate discipline, making Matthew 18 instead the grounds for "openness and unending compassion" toward the oppressed. The same scripture that had been cited so confidently and consistently throughout Brethren history as the Biblical foundation for *church purity and separation from sin,* was now being invoked as the basis for *unconditional forgiveness and inclusion.*[90]

The following year Conference applied the new philosophy of reconciliation to the topic of divorce and remarriage. By 1964, the church had accepted divorced and remarried persons as members, and allowed pastors to perform remarriages, but divorced pastors, themselves, could not remarry. A 1977 Annual Conference statement officially removed this final barrier. "Divorce," the paper stated, "as a tragedy is not to be judged, but is to be seen with sorrow and compassion . . ." It urged Brethren "to be loving rather than judgmental with regard to remarriage, *both of the laity and the clergy*."[91]

Summarizing the statement's tone, Carl F. Bowman observes:

> Acceptance, support, and redemptive love are presented as the appropriate responses of modern-day Brethren to this formerly reprehensible moral violation. Parties to divorce and remarriage are portrayed as victims of brokenness who require healing therapy, not moral condemnation. In fact, to the extent that moral censure is detectable, it seems to be directed more against the modern "sin" of judgment than against the traditional ones of divorce and remarriage.[92]

Atlantic Northeast District churches didn't immediately embrace this new philosophy. In most cases during the 1970s and 1980s, churches were slow to forgive when pastors divorced, regardless of whether remarriage was involved. While most congregations tolerated divorce and remarriage among the laity, pastors who divorced almost always resigned or were forced to resign their posts. Between 1970 and 1981, 10 ministers—including two associate district executives—divorced, and in 1981 only two continued to serve in the district.[93] Not until 1989 did a congregation call a divorced and remarried pastor to serve, and even then at least one family left the church over the issue.[94]

While many Brethren by then agreed with the need to deal redemptively with divorced lay members, most would not accept divorced pastors. A few congregations—five of 66—continued to bar divorced and remarried people from *church membership*. Several others had explicit policies restricting divorced and remarried members to the laity, and nearly all balked at hiring a divorced pastor.

Even so, the views of eastern Pennsylvania Brethren had evolved significantly. In many congregations, a member could separate, divorce, and later remarry without any official action from the church. While in earlier years the congregation would have disowned or at least required a confession, by the 1990s, cases of divorce—as well as other disciplinary issues—were left to the pastor, who could grant absolution, counsel, or simply look the other way. Remarriage had evolved from an issue acted upon by the corporate body to an individual matter addressed, if at all, in the privacy of a pastor's study.

Contemporary Views

By 1989, corporate discipline was virtually extinct in eastern Pennsylvania. Nearly two-thirds of the churches (41 of 66) had no membership requirements other than general baptismal vows. The most common "requirement" was simply attending a membership course, with only a handful of churches mandating specific behavioral expectations. Well over half of the district's churches could imagine no behavior for which a member would be disfellowshipped. Asked whether members actually had been disfellowshipped since 1960, nearly 90 percent could cite no such cases.[95]

In short, while Brethren at the turn of the century regularly heard confessions and disowned when necessary, in 1989 members could engage in almost any behavior without forfeiting church membership. The only "sin" likely to result in removal from the roll was prolonged inactivity.

A longtime minister in the Mountville congregation, who had been denied ordination because he wore a necktie, applauds the relaxation of discipline:

> There was something within me that rebelled against [discipline and public confessions] . . . It's this old idea of the woman taken in adultery. He who is without sin cast the first stone . . . Somehow or another there was always this feeling of superiority, that here was this person grovelling in the dust before us and we were the holy ones passing judgment.
>
> In the old excommunication concept we pushed them out and didn't support them in any redemptive way . . . And once they came to their senses and were

willing to confess. . . then we'd give them another try . . . I think now we have moved in the direction of a redemptive fellowship, supporting people in their rehabilitation.[96]

On the other hand, an elder who once downplayed corporate discipline later had "some real reservations":

I sometimes put it like this—I think there was a time when we were entirely too negative, but I think now we've moved into the direction [where] everything is accepted . . . I think there are still times when it would be perfectly in order for a member of the Church of the Brethren to appear before the congregation and say, "I have sinned, brethren and sisters. I want to be forgiven."[97]

But even those few churches that continue corporate discipline find it difficult to maintain. The White Oak congregation, which still disciplines—mostly sexual indiscretions—has seen a marked decline in public confessions in recent years. A White Oak minister comments:

The incidence of confessions has dropped in my time quite a bit at White Oak . . . I've been a little troubled by it. I don't believe that it means our people are living more holy lives.[98]

As older patterns of church discipline near extinction, a few congregations have attempted to develop new methods. A 1985 Annual Conference report on church membership encouraged mutual accountability and urged periodic renewal of baptismal vows, either through a deacon visit or some other means.[99] The most common method has been a "congregational covenant." From its beginning in 1986, the innovative ACTS Covenant congregation in Lancaster has required "covenant members" to pledge fidelity to Christ and the church each year. Another new church, Stevens Hill Community, begun in 1990, also requires members to sign a covenant. Deacons visit each member annually to review and renew commitments.[100]

The Lititz church, in 1990, instituted an annual "Service of Covenant Renewal," during which members were asked to sign a card stating, "I reaffirm my belief in Jesus Christ as my Lord and Savior, and renew my promises to live out that commitment as a faithful member of the [church]." Members who did not sign a card for three consecutive years were to be visited, with the possibility of being placed on a "separated members" list.[101]

A Hospital for Sinners

Clearly, the radical decline of corporate discipline represents a metamorphosis of the Brethren psyche. While discipline traditionally had been understood as tough love, necessary to preserve the purity of the church and guard the spiritual condition of members, as Brethren moved into the cultural mainstream they redefined love. A new generation perceived public confessions and disownings as heavy-handed power plays, unnecessary intrusions into the private lives of individuals, even as acts of vindictiveness and unloving judgment. Love and judgment, once considered allies, more and more were viewed as enemies.

The traditional concept of the church as a disciplined, nonconforming community has virtually disappeared. In place of a "pure and holy city set on a hill" is a new vision of the church as an inclusive "hospital for sinners," where "all have sinned and fallen short of the glory of God."

7.

Responsible Christian Citizenship

The shedding of distinctive dress was a highly visible outward sign of important inward changes taking place among the Brethren in the early years of the century.[1] Their growing penchant to *dress* like the world indicated that Brethren had begun to *think* like the world, as well. Buoyed by the optimism of an age of technological advances and progressive social theories, Brethren were reconsidering their understanding of Christian citizenship.

Taking their cue from Romans 13, Brethren historically had shown respect for government leaders and conscientiously obeyed the laws of the land, so long as such obedience did not conflict with God's higher law. They willingly paid taxes and offered earnest prayers for those in power.

But along with respect for government, Brethren harbored a deep conviction that earthly rulers were part of a wicked world in which God's people were but "aliens and strangers." Their beginnings as dissenters from established state churches and their subsequent experiences of persecution— especially during times of war—had reinforced the conviction that governments, though ordained of God, were part of an inherently evil world system.

Few Brethren prior to the turn of the century dreamed of transforming sinful societal structures. They believed in sharing God's love by being a pure and holy city set on a hill, not by soiling themselves in the swill of the world's politics. Jesus said, "My kingdom is not of this world" (John 18:36). Thus, the primary responsibility of meek and humble followers of Christ was to "come out from among them and be separate" (2 Corinthians 6:17).

Convictions such as these, which sprung naturally from their doctrines of nonconformity and nonresistance, prevented most Brethren from voting, campaigning for candidates, holding political offices, joining civic organizations, using the law to prosecute claims, displaying national flags, and participating in warfare. In general, preserving purity took precedence over political participation.

By the early 1900s, however, some Brethren borrowed other biblical imagery to describe how residents of God's kingdom should relate to the kingdoms of this world. Not only were Christians to be a "city set on a hill," but also salt and light. To let their distinctive Christian flavor season the surrounding society, Brethren would have to jettison their separatist shaker. According to proponents of this emerging activist view, participation in political and social issues was part and parcel of responsible Christian citizenship in a democratic society.

As they pondered political involvement, Brethren wondered: Was it enough merely to model the way of Christ by remaining pure and passive in the face of the great moral issues of the day? Or did God call his people to roll up their sleeves and courageously cure the ills of an ailing world? Were Brethren to avoid evil or to transform it into good? How, and how much, were citizens of God's kingdom to participate in the affairs of this world?

The Influence of Alcohol

While social and cultural ferment prior to the turn of the century had set such questions to brewing among Brethren, it was *brewing* of another sort that brought the debate to a head. The great American crusade against alcohol gradually enticed the Brethren from political passivism toward an activist conception of responsible Christian citizenship.

As part of a wave of evangelical social reforms in the United States during the first half of the 19th century, Christians summoned their forces to battle the evil of distilled liquors. The Temperance Movement ebbed for a time during the Civil War, but picked up steam with the founding of the Prohibition Party (1869), the Women's Christian Temperance Union (1874), and the Anti-Saloon League (1893). While temperance advocates initially promoted individual abstinence, by the latter part of the century emphasis was shifting toward outlawing the manufacture and sale of distilled liquors, wines, and beers.[2]

Though early Brethren were far from teetotalers, by the mid-1800s, many sympathized with the temperance cause. At issue was how best to combat this obvious evil. Certainly members of the church should abstain, but was God calling Brethren to do more? As responsible Christian citizens, should they make common cause with other temperance groups? Could they vote and lobby for Prohibition?

Prior to 1900, Annual Conference consistently cautioned against political participation and cooperation with other temperance groups. An 1884 ruling advised that it was "best not to petition Congress (to enact a law to prevent the manufacture of ardent spirits), but we should continue to labor earnestly *in the church* against this and all other evils."[3] An 1889 statement reaffirmed the Brethren stance "against the use or toleration of intoxicants," but "advised against taking part in the public agitation of the subject."[4]

A 1900 query to Annual Conference asked the church to soften its stand against political participation. While the delegates' response recognized that "it was the duty of the Christian church to mould temperance sentiment, without which no law can become operative," it advocated prayer for civil rulers, rather than direct political action.[5]

A 1903 *Gospel Messenger* columnist explained why Brethren should avoid groups such as the WCTU:

1. The church is a temperance society of the purest brand; . . . to join a second temperance society virtually says that the first society, the church, was defective . . . Hence for Christian women in the Brethren church to hold membership in the W.C.T.U. is superfluous.

2. All the good done in the W.C.T.U. should be done in the church; to do otherwise is robbing God and dishonoring Christ.

3. The Lord's work is not done on the department plan; with its temperance work in one society, its missionary in another, etc. It is complete within itself without any appendages or sub-organizations.[6]

Brethren had few doubts that alcohol consumption was an immense evil, but they advocated prayer and personal purity among the saints as the proper responses. Political action and cooperation with other groups remained off-limits.

Inching Toward Activism

Progressive Brethren continued to advocate active involvement in the larger temperance movement. A 1908 Annual Conference action to form a "permanent temperance committee" cautiously inched the church toward the activist camp. In sharp contrast to the church's previous passive position, the opening paragraph of the 1908 proposal maintained that "it is the duty of Christians to endeavor to suppress all forms of evil that imperil the morality of the people, as well as the sacred interests of the visible church . . ."[7]

The new three-member committee was to educate Brethren "against this evil" by publishing tracts, helping congregations and districts organize temperance meetings, and planning a temperance program at every Annual Conference. Most significantly, the committee was authorized to procure information from the larger temperance movement and distribute it to Brethren "as may be helpful in creating a more concerted action in dealing with the temperance question."[8] The proposal sparked vigorous debate. Conservatives argued forcefully that maintaining purity *within the church* was the best defense against the evils of alcohol. Progressives, on the other hand, implored the church to take the offensive with like-minded Christians who were voicing their views directly to government leaders.[9]

Despite objections, the paper passed, but only after its most controversial provision was removed. Deleted was a section authorizing the committee to represent Brethren views on temperance to state and national government leaders so that Brethren "may know that they have liberty and authority to work in the interests of this great cause . . ."[10]

Brethren views of responsible Christian citizenship were changing. The 1908 plan nudged the church toward cooperation with other groups and indicated a new openness to reforming the larger society. Even so, the church was reticent to advocate outright political action.[11]

The denomination's Temperance Committee for the next several years continued to advise against entanglement with non-Brethren organizations. The committee's 1912 report said, in part:

> After . . . seriously considering . . . the many organizations at work in the temperance cause and our federation with them, we feel constrained to say that in our judgment the greatest care should be exercised in linking arms with these organizations if, indeed, it be ever advisable to do so.
>
> Our work is the salvation of souls and the extension of God's kingdom in the world rather than aid in organizing forces to drive the enemy from the face of the earth, even if such a thing were possible . . .
>
> We therefore urge our own beloved people to fully consecrate themselves in this great work instead of inviting speakers of organized bodies into our pulpits, causing our money to be used by organizations foreign to the church . . .[12]

Chief among conservative Brethren's objections toward other temperance groups was the emphasis they placed on the ballot box. Thus, the 1912 Annual Conference in York, re-examined the question of whether Brethren should vote. In a pattern that was becoming common for the increasingly diverse Brethren, the 1912 report reaffirmed the church's traditional position, but allowed dissenters to do as they wished:

> 1. It is evident that the governments of this world are ordained of God, and that it is our duty to pray for them and in all things to render unto them their dues (Matt. 22:21; Rom. 13:1-7).
>
> 2. However, the church of Jesus Christ is no part of this world system. The child of God is to be in the world but of the church, furthering her interests, raising her standards and enlarging her borders (John 17:15, 16; 18:36).
>
> 3. His citizenship being in heaven (Philipp. 3:20, R. V.), the child of God sustains the attitude of a pilgrim (1 Peter 2:11) to the affairs of state. Though subject under

God to the man-made laws of the country (Rom. 13:1), yet, with love and holy zeal, he presses on others the requirements of the law of God. He aims at individual regeneration (Rom. 12:1, 2) by the grace of God, rather than at civic reformation through legislation and enforcement of law. He pleads for that reformation which is the result of regeneration (2 Peter 1:5, 6) and not for an enforced reformation while the hearts of men remain untouched by the grace and Spirit of God (John 17:9).

4. We, therefore, urge the brethren not to allow themselves to become entangled in politics, nor even interested in a way that would lessen their zeal for the salvation of souls, or in a way that might militate against their usefulness in the church (2 Tim. 2:3, 4).

5. We advise that brethren neither vote nor accept an office of any kind *unless they are convinced that by so doing they can more completely fill their mission in the world relative to themselves, to their fellow-men and to God.*

6. We urge that the brethren shall accept no office, the performance of the duties of which would require the use of physical force or which might compromise, in any way, the nonresistent [sic] principles of the Gospel of Christ (Matt. 5:38, 39; John 18:36).[13]

In its effort to placate progressives and conservatives alike, the committee drew fire from both sides. Conservatives were perturbed by the permissiveness of Section Five of the report. As advocates of the two-kingdom theology of Sections Two and Three, they argued that Brethren had no business meddling in the world's corrupt politics. Instead, the church should focus on preaching the gospel and reaching the hearts of individuals.

Progressives, on the other hand, wanted the church to fully sanction voting as a valid expression of Christian faith. Philadelphia First church's progressive pastor D. W. Kurtz bristled at the report's "outdated" theology:

> I am opposed to adopting this report as it stands . . . The
> theology in Sections 2 and 3 is the kind of thing I do not
> believe in . . . I do not like to be told that a thing is all wrong,
> but, if you can't help yourself, you may have permission to
> vote once in a while. I would like to have Sections 2 and 3
> knocked out of the report . . .[14]

Despite objections from both sides, the report was approved.
Annual Conference would continue officially to oppose voting and
holding political office, but would tolerate individual aberrations.
At the same time, the report urged Brethren to exert their influence
through the church's Temperance Committee, rather than through
outside groups.

Just as they had diverged on dress, Eastern and Southeastern
Pennsylvania Brethren also disagreed on how best to advance the
temperance cause. Both districts formed Temperance Committees
and passed resolutions favoring temperance legislation. But while

*D. W. Kurtz (1879-1949) urged Brethren at the 1912 Annual Conference not
only to tolerate, but to encourage, voting in government elections. Kurtz,
who pastored the Philadelphia First church from 1910 to 1914, was a
leader in the organization of the new Southeastern District in 1911. He is
pictured here as a young student at Juniata College.* Juniata College Archives.

Southeastern District Brethren during the 1910s generally favored voting, direct political participation, and cooperating with other groups, their "plainer" brothers and sisters in Eastern District continued to balance a concern for temperance with a desire to remain separate from the world.

Although Annual Conference in 1866 had declined to make voting a test of fellowship, few Brethren voted prior to 1900. By then, however, some Brethren—particularly those in the more progressive congregations of the Greater Philadelphia Area—were taking interest in local and national politics and exercising their right to vote.[15] By the 1910s, voting was gaining wider acceptance in Southeastern District, while ministers in Eastern District continued to preach against political participation.[16]

But even in Eastern District, opposition to political participation was softening. Both districts during the 1910s began to use the political process to promote temperance. Eastern District in 1914 passed a resolution "heartily (endorsing) the Proposed Amendment to the Constitution . . . looking forward to the Prohibition of the manufacture, sale and importation of alcoholic beverages."[17] Meanwhile, the ministers of Southeastern Pennsylvania applied more direct political pressure. The district's ministerium agreed in 1915 to circulate petitions among their congregations and present them to "our legislature urging them to grant a Local Option Law in Pennsylvania."[18] Progressives and conservatives alike rejoiced in the passage of the 18th Amendment to the Constitution in 1919.

A League of Their Own

As Brethren concentrated more on the political scene, the question of whether to join hands with groups such as the Anti-Saloon League surfaced repeatedly. By the late 1910s, some congregations were cooperating. A speaker from the Anti-Saloon League addressed the members of the Philadelphia First congregation in 1917.[19] The Lake Ridge congregation, near Ludlowville, New York, reported to *Gospel Messenger* readers in 1918 that their congregation had hosted the "Township W.C.T.U Institute," where a number of outside speakers provided instruction.[20] The Lebanon congregation's *Gospel Messenger* correspondent in 1918 proudly proclaimed that "The Anti-Saloon League has found it can always depend on the Brethren in Lebanon."[21]

Some churches remained cautious. The Chiques congregation in 1916 denied a request from the Anti-Saloon League to have a speaker "come into the Chickies congregation and explain the method of its work." The church decided that its own temperance committee should continue as before.[22]

Sometimes interaction with outside groups caused commotion. The Harrisburg First congregation invited an Anti-Saloon League speaker to the church in 1922. A very able speaker from Pittsburgh arrived, but "from outward appearance, he did not look like a 'brother.'" The fact that he wore a wedding ring so offended the non-conforming Harrisburg Brethren—who viewed the wearing of jewelry as ostentatious worldliness—that the congregation resolved henceforth to invite only *Brethren* Anti-Saloon League representatives to speak.

Three years later the League sent a Brethren speaker to Harrisburg First, but "he happened to be a man who was rather progressively minded and had been allied to a group that was interested in easing the 'dress problem' . . . This again was repulsive to our church fathers." Thus, in 1926 the congregation decided not to invite Anti-Saloon League speakers in the future.[23] Despite the potential for controversy, Annual Conference's Temperance and Purity Department in 1926 encouraged cooperation with the Anti-Saloon League, even to the point of inviting its representatives to speak in Brethren meetinghouses.[24]

Presidential Politics and Prohibition

As the 1920s progressed, more Pennsylvania Brethren were voting, lobbying, and cooperating with other groups to ensure that the 18th Amendment remained the law of the land. As the 1928 presidential election approached, the fate of Prohibition hung in the balance. Heading the Democratic ticket was New York Governor Alfred E. Smith, a Roman Catholic who, since 1920, had advocated "repeal of the national amendment which prohibited the sale of intoxicating beverages." In his letter accepting the Democratic nomination, Smith made plain his intention to work for repeal. In contrast, Republican nominee Herbert Hoover was an avowed "dry" on the liquor issue. "The Republicans could hardly have picked a better candidate than Herbert Hoover to symbolize tranquility, prosperity, and purity."[25]

Faced with a clear choice between a "dry" Republican and a woefully "wet," Roman Catholic Democrat, Brethren who thus far had resisted the temptation to vote found it difficult to shun the ballot box yet another time. While just 20 years earlier Annual Conference had strongly discouraged voting, by 1928, the church's *Gospel Messenger* editors were exhorting Brethren to do their Christian duty by voting against Smith. A barrage of editorials leading up to the election berated Smith for his anti-Prohibition position. An October 27 editorial cautioned that the election of Smith "would be a great triumph for the liquor forces." The writer stated unequivocally: "He is wet, soaking wet, dripping wet, and all the world knows it . . . As for Governor Smith, or any candidate of like views on the liquor issue, the *Messenger* is against him."[26] A final entry before the November election left little doubt about the responsible Christian course:

> As for the great national contest to be staged next Tuesday, our advice is: Go quietly to the polls and cast your ballot in the fear of God . . . The saloon . . . is engaged in a titanic struggle to come back. Don't let it. Record your vote against it.[27]

Pennsylvania Brethren evidently took the advice to heart. By Council action, the Richland congregation gave explicit permission for its members to vote in the 1928 election.[28] A number of Eastern District informants recall 1928 as the year that they or their parents voted for the first time in a presidential contest.[29] By the 1930s, a majority of Eastern District Brethren conscientiously cast their ballots at the presidential polls.[30]

Thus, within a 20-year period, Brethren had turned their definition of responsible Christian citizenship on its head. Whereas, previously, voting Brethren were looked on with suspicion, by the 1930s, in some circles, nonvoters were accused of shirking Christian responsibilities. A November 1939 note in the bulletin of Southeastern District's Ambler church no doubt expressed a growing sentiment in the churches of eastern Pennsylvania:

> Tuesday will be election day in our state. Every Christian should feel it is his duty to go to the polls and cast

his vote for those he believes most worthy to hold offices in civic government. Church people can do much to maintain high standards of government by their support of honest and trustworthy candidates.[31]

While Brethren of both districts during the 1910s and 1920s had begun to accept voting and some forms of political action, they remained divided on the question of holding public offices. It followed logically that if Brethren could work for the good of God's kingdom at the polls, they could do even more good by electing their own members to political offices. Yet, Eastern District Brethren were acutely aware of the corrupting influence of political power.

Eastern District elders in 1909 (prior to the district division) revealed how deeply opposed they were to Brethren officeholders, when the Lancaster congregation proposed a "letter carrier" as a candidate for the ministry. After some discussion, the elders voted against ordaining the brother "because of the political influence surrounding his position, and the Sunday labor that is involved."[32] Just five years later, many of these elders who took pause at the political influence of a letter carrier would be scandalized when a Brethren minister would be elected governor of Pennsylvania.

Brumbaugh: Idol or Infidel? [33]

Martin Grove Brumbaugh was a Dunker ahead of his time. Born in 1862 in Huntingdon County, he began a distinguished academic career at (what would become) Juniata College, a Brethren school in Huntingdon. After additional study at Millersville State Normal School and Harvard University, he earned his Ph.D. from the University of Pennsylvania in 1895. The first holder of a Ph.D. among the Brethren, he was later awarded seven additional honorary degrees.

Having served concurrently as president of Juniata College and professor of pedagogy at the University of Pennsylvania, Brumbaugh in 1900 was tapped by President McKinley to become the first commissioner of education for Puerto Rico. His duties included organizing the educational system, serving as acting president of the Puerto Rican Senate, and participating in the island's civil administration. He returned to Juniata and the University of Pennsylvania in 1902, and four years later was appointed superin-

Brethren governor Martin Grove Brumbaugh (1862-1930) pictured in front of
the governor's mansion in Harrisburg, April 6, 1915. BHLA, Brethren Encyclopedia
Collection.

tendent of Philadelphia schools. During his eight-year tenure as
superintendent he solidified his reputation as an effective educator
and leader.[34]

With the support of key players in the Philadelphia Republican
machine, Brumbaugh won the governor's election of 1914 by a
margin of nearly a half-million votes. In a solidly Republican state,
he ran on a progressive platform that included the franchise for
women and local option legislation to allow municipalities to prohibit the sale of alcohol. At his January 1915 inauguration, Brumbaugh, in deference to his nonswearing Brethren heritage, *affirmed*
his dedication to his duties, rather than swearing the oath of office.[35]
In Carl F. Bowman's words, "With these accomplishments, he became the first, genuine, Dunker dignitary, and the rest of the church
watched in amazement."[36]

Though Brethren universally were amazed by the extraordinary
accomplishments of their governor, not all were pleased. While

some considered Brumbaugh a Brethren idol to emulate, others saw him more as an infidel who was blatantly disloyal to the principles of his church. He generally was appreciated more in progressive Southeastern Pennsylvania than in Eastern Pennsylvania.

Brumbaugh had been active in the Philadelphia First church after 1902 and brought his certificate of membership there in 1912. As a minister in the second degree, he preached occasionally to the Philadelphia Brethren prior to his election, and he continued to make frequent appearances at Philadelphia First during his tenure as governor. In addition, Brumbaugh was a popular speaker at building dedication ceremonies and other special events throughout Southeastern District.[37]

Progressives pointed to Brumbaugh as a prime example of what the church could accomplish if only it would unload the baggage of its separatist heritage. Many Eastern District Brethren, on the other hand, still staunchly opposed a Brethren minister holding such an office. To some it seemed obvious that Brumbaugh was thumbing his nose at the church in his pursuit of political power. After all, while not totally forbidding holding political offices, the 1912 Annual Conference "Statement on Voting and Politics" *had* strongly discouraged "accepting an office of any kind," particularly those that could lead to compromising the church's nonresistance principles.

With Brumbaugh settled in the governor's mansion, Brethren continued to debate their relationship to government. The June 1915 Annual Conference in Hershey, not far from the state capital, passed a resolution lauding Brumbaugh and his administration for "the high ground he has taken upon all moral issues," particularly on temperance. Delegates expressed hope that Brumbaugh might be "an instrument in the hands of the Master in giving to the people of this great State a clean, capable and righteous administration of its public affairs."[38]

Eastern District remained circumspect. Without mentioning the governor's name, the April 1915 Eastern District Conference, held after Brumbaugh's inauguration but before Annual Conference, officially endorsed an April 17, 1915, *Gospel Messenger* editorial on "The Church and Civil Government." The statement expressed some openness to political participation, even to the point of holding offices that do "not call for the violation of any New Testament requirement," and went on to affirm that "We may in every manner consistent with the Gospel influence the governments along right lines." But in what may have been intended as a rebuff to Brumbaugh, the statement concluded with strong words of caution:

> Here is where the danger threatens our people . . . Our policy has been for Brethren to accept no office in a government, State, county, township or city, the duties of which will conflict with any of the requirements of the New Testament. *Upon the part of some there is a disposition to set this policy aside, and accept any civil office within their reach.* This leads to the threatened danger . . . In attempting to make ourselves a power in the world for good, our members cannot afford to mix with the unrighteous in politics. An endeavor to purify the political atmosphere by becoming a party in the conflict, simply means the loss of power for good on our part. If we would be regarded as efficient in the saving of souls, and thereby improve the condition of the masses, *let us stand by our profession and not lose our identity in a mixture with the world.*[39]

As World War I approached, Governor Brumbaugh became painfully aware of the compromises that his position could require. With the entrance of the United States into the war, Brumbaugh, as commander-in-chief, was obligated to call the Pennsylvania militia to arms. To conservative Eastern District skeptics, the spectacle of a nonresistant Brethren minister calling out the militia was the final proof that Brumbaugh had lost his "identity in a mixture with the world."[40] Though Brumbaugh's Harrisburg executive mansion was within the bounds of Eastern District, seldom was he invited to preach in local churches. In the eyes of Eastern District Brethren, Brumbaugh was suspect at best, disloyal at worst. An Eastern District elder recalled how Brumbaugh was viewed:

> The rumor is, and it's only a rumor, that the only way any person could be elected Governor of Pennsylvania is that he belong to the Masonic Order. And there are those that are absolutely sure that M. G. Brumbaugh was a

Mason . . . And, you see, he was governor during World War I when he had to call out the state militia. He was really criticized . . .

Brother Brumbaugh wasn't one of the Brethren idols in those days. They would have felt he was disloyal to his ministry and disloyal to the church. He was not used very much in [Eastern] District circles, or even in local congregations.

I heard him speak at the Annual Conference at Hershey. I can remember him coming there in a big white limousine, and personally, as a boy, I was thrilled that this man was a member of the Church of the Brethren. I remember my parents said, "Well now, don't be too proud of that fact." They didn't rejoice too much.[41]

Martin Grove Brumbaugh clearly was a Dunker ahead of his time. Some Brethren gazed with awe upon the accomplishments of their governor. Others pitied him for the compromises the duties of his office forced upon him. Still others viewed him with scorn for his infidelity to the time-tested principles of the church. In general, Brethren saw in Brumbaugh what they wanted to see. Reform-

Brethren held Annual Conference every three years from 1915 to 1936 at the Hershey Auditorium (pictured here in 1918). Marlin Buck Collection.

minded progressives, eager to engage society's ills, saw in their Brethren governor much to idolize. Cautious conservatives, still committed to purity and separation from the world, perceived their governor more as an infidel than an idol.

Brethren Politicians

While many Eastern District Brethren had frowned on Brumbaugh's entanglement in state politics, by the 1930s, the number of Brethren holding *local* offices was growing. A brother in the Annville congregation was a township supervisor, while a member of the Conewago congregation served as Dauphin County Commissioner during the 1930s.[42] Popular elder Rufus Bucher ran for school board and was actively involved in local politics during the 1930s and beyond.[43] Local offices such as these, which generally did not compromise Brethren nonresistance principles, were acceptable and created little controversy in the church.

But political involvement beyond the local level—particularly by Brethren preachers—continued to draw criticism. Henry K. Ober (1878-1939), a popular Lancaster County educator, churchman, and former president of Elizabethtown College, in April 1932 ran in the Republican primary for the Seventeenth District's (consisting of most of Lancaster and Lebanon counties) State Senate seat. Despite his popularity in church circles, Ober lost by a margin of nearly three to one.[44]

The following month he was called before the Elizabethtown church's Council Meeting to request "forgiveness for allowing his name to be used in a recent election."[45] Elder Carl W. Zeigler recalled, "He was severely criticized by his colleagues in the district" for his run for office.[46] Despite the criticism, Ober evidently remained popular among Eastern District Brethren. Just two days after his loss in the Senate race, he was elected to moderate the church's District Conference.[47]

While Ober's congressional bid failed, a decade later another Eastern District man succeeded. Samuel G. Kurtz, a member of the Lebanon congregation, was elected to the Pennsylvania House of Representatives in 1944, and reelected in 1946. An insurance broker, Kurtz's resume included involvements with the Chamber of Commerce, the YMCA, the Kiwanis Club, the Knights Templar, the Country Club, and various gunning organizations.[48] Kurtz was a prime example of the new breed of Brethren, who during the 1930s and 1940s were becoming community and business leaders.

A Grand, Old Flag?

As Brethren such as Kurtz assumed leadership in the mainstream American society, they also began to adopt some of the pertinent cultural symbols, among them the American flag. Carl Zeigler, who pastored the Lebanon congregation during the 1940s and 1950s, recalled:

> Sam Kurtz caused me all kinds of problems. I came to church one Sunday morning [about 1945] and here was the American flag in the church, and he hadn't gotten permission. And finally we had to go to Council Meeting, and Council agreed he could leave the flag there if he put up a Christian flag.[49]

The Christian flag was purchased, and both remained in the Lebanon church into the 1990s.

What would have seemed preposterous at the turn of the century to Lebanon Brethren—the displaying of a national flag in the church—now seemed to reflect who they were. No longer were they aliens and strangers passing through a hostile world. Instead, they were responsible, American, Christian citizens, who perceived little conflict between their nation and their faith.

The Lebanon church was by no means the first Brethren congregation in Eastern and Southeastern Pennsylvania districts to fly the American flag. As early as 1918, the Green Tree congregation, near Oaks, displayed the American flag in their meetinghouse. A sister explains:

> The reason for that is that there's a flag factory just down the road. At one time the owner of the flag factory came to Green Tree and a lot of people from Green Tree worked in the flag factory. I believe he donated the flag and donated money to the church. But [today] you wouldn't dare to take the flag out of the church.[50]

A 200th anniversary celebration at the Amwell meetinghouse, Sergeantsville, New Jersey, on September 17, 1933, included a prominent display of the American flag. Elizabethtown College Archives.

Whereas, in 1900, Brethren wouldn't have dared to place a flag *in* the church, 90 years later, a few congregations wouldn't dare to take it *out.* Even so, displaying American flags in churches has yet to become a universal practice among Atlantic Northeast District Brethren. In 1989, nine out of 66 congregations reported American flags in their sanctuaries, with a total of 18 displaying flags somewhere in the church building, often for use by church-sponsored Scouting troops.[51]

Brethren Boy Scouts

Participation in the Scouting movement serves as another barometer of the Brethren move into the American mainstream. Founded in 1910, the Boy Scouts of America and Camp Fire Girls initially were opposed by Brethren. Southeastern Pennsylvania ministers discussed the Scouting movement at a November 1912 meeting and concluded that, while in Europe the Scouting movement generally lacked a "military element," it "contains much of it in America."[52] Annual Conference in 1926 also advised against affiliation with the Boy Scouts and Camp Fire Girls programs, because neither was church-centered, and "because in addition the Boy Scout program, contrary to the stated purpose of the organization, fosters attitudes and actions which are militaristic."[53]

The Philadelphia First church, evidently unimpressed with Annual Conference cautions, organized a local Scouting troop in 1928 and honored them during a May 5, 1929, church service.[54] Other

Scouting in the Spring Creek congregation during the 1940s was further evidence of the Brethren move toward the cultural mainstream. Spring Creek Congregational Archives.

urban-oriented congregations followed suit during the 1930s, establishing Scouting as part of their youth programs.[55]

By the 1940s, a few congregations in Eastern District joined the growing movement. The Spring Creek congregation in Hershey established Boy Scout, Girl Scout, Brownie, and Cub Scout troops around 1940.[56] Though the Elizabethtown church in 1916 had declared the Scouting movement off-limits, by the mid-1940s, the congregation was ready to reconsider. The Elizabethtown Brethren organized their first Cub Scout pack in 1947. By 1950, Girl Scouts were given equal time in the church basement.

Pastor Nevin Zuck reported to Council Meeting in 1962 that one of the congregation's own members had earned the "God and Country award" in Scouting. The Elizabethtown church in 1964 hosted an evening program in honor of the "50th Anniversary of Scouting in Elizabethtown." The evening's festivities got off to a rousing start with the singing of the national anthem and included an address from British Consul General Thomas Stuart Tull. Having sung of the "rockets' red glare and bombs bursting in air," the group, in deference to the speaker, rendered the British National Anthem, as well.[57]

"Substantial and Respectable Citizens"

By the late 1950s, many urban and small-town congregations were involved in Scouting. *Gospel Messenger* reported that, at the end of 1957, 127 Brethren congregations across the country sponsored Scout troops, and 37 Brethren boys had received God and Country Awards during the year.[58] The writer of a 250th anniversary history of the Coventry congregation, located near Pottstown, in 1974 summed up the value of that congregation's longstanding Scouting program with these words: "Yes—Good Scouting is conducive to the development of good, loyal, substantial and respectable citizens."[59]

While the Brethren at the turn of the century trained their young people to shun the "world" and be loyal to the church, by the 1970s, some congregations considered molding "citizens" loyal to their country to be part of their mission. The age-old tension between the kingdom of God and the kingdoms of this world, in some congregations was considered resolved. Being good Christians and good citizens were one and the same.

8.

Making Peace with War

As Brethren moved from their separatist past toward a new conception of responsible Christian citizenship, their views on war and peace shifted as well. For nearly 200 years, the Church of the Brethren had preached the concept of nonresistance to its members. Based on scriptural injunctions to "resist not evil," "turn the other cheek," "love enemies," and "do good to those who hate you," this doctrine required Brethren to follow the example of Jesus, who accepted death on a cross rather than using violence.

During the Civil War, Annual Conference had ruled unequivocally against Brethren joining the military:

> Can a brother be held as a member of the church who
> will, when put into the army, take up arms and aim to
> shed the blood of his fellow-man? Answer: He can not.[1]

The Brethren aversion to voting also stemmed from the doctrine of nonresistance. The government official who called out the troops, they believed, was no more a sinner than those who elected him in the first place. Further, if Brethren helped choose government leaders, what right had they to refuse when those leaders issued the call to arms? In short, abstention from politics and conscientious objection to war were two halves of a single doctrine.

World War I: Time of Transition[2]

As World War I approached, however, Brethren had been abandoning parts of their nonresistance doctrine in favor of a more activist view of Christian citizenship. Spurred on by their interest in temperance, more Brethren were participating in the political process. In fact, Brother Brumbaugh resided in the governor's mansion in Harrisburg and regularly signed bills into law.

With the church in transition and war brewing in Europe, Brethren wondered whether they should do more than sit on the sidelines. In wars past, nonresistant Dunkers knew instinctively and stated officially that, as aliens and strangers, they had no part in the world's sinful wars. But by the 1910s, the emerging paradigm of responsible Christian citizenship led some to reconsider the claims of Uncle Sam. Annual Conference actions reflected changing sentiments.

After more than 20 years of silence on war and peace, Annual Conference encouraged "the entire membership to activity in the cause of peace" in 1910,[3] and a year later appointed a Peace Committee, whose duties included:

> First: to propagate and aid in the distribution of such literature as may be helpful in the better understanding as to the sinfulness and folly of resorting to arms in the settlement of differences;

> Second: to use every lawful gospel means in bringing about peaceful settlements of difficulties when such may arise between governments or societies;

> Third: to keep the Brotherhood informed, from time to time, through our publications, as to the true status of the peace movement.[4]

As with temperance, Brethren were beginning to rethink their responsibilities on peace. While the church previously had been content merely to prevent members of the church from going to war, by 1911, Annual Conference sought to help "governments and societies" reconcile their differences.

With the war in Europe already underway, Annual Conference in 1916 unanimously passed a strongly worded resolution against warfare and militarism, serving notice of the church's intent to seek conscientious objector status for its young men, should the United States enter the war. Eastern District's I. W. Taylor was part of the three-member committee that drafted the resolution and delivered it to President Wilson in July 1916. It stated in part:

> The church reaffirms its position in favor of peace even
> at the cost of suffering wrongfully, if need be, and its
> unalterable opposition to war and bloodshed under any
> conditions of provocation, and all preparation for war as
> one of its primal teachings . . .[5]

In Eastern District, elders continued to stand firmly against
Brethren participation in the military. When a member of the
Lancaster congregation enlisted in the Navy in 1915, pastor T. F.
Imler came to his colleagues for advice. The District Elders Body

> decided that it is the unanimous opinion of the Elders
> that the course taken by the young Brother is inconsis-
> tent with the Doctrines of the Bible and the rules of the
> church and should not be held as a Brother in the church
> while in such services.[6]

Reaffirming the traditional Brethren stand, the elders declared that
enlisting in the military resulted in forfeiture of church membership.
But the fact that the Lancaster pastor consulted his peers on what
always had been a cut-and-dried question suggests that the church's
changing conception of citizenship was fostering uncertainty.

The situation became even murkier when the United States
declared war against Germany on April 6, 1917, and enacted a
draft law the following month. While the law exempted from
combatant duty members of "any well recognized religious sect or
organization. . . whose existing creed or principles forbid its
members to participate in war in any form," *noncombatant* duty
was to be defined later by the president.[7]

"Constructive Patriotism"

In response, the 1917 Annual Conference approved a lengthy
resolution, expressing appreciation to government authorities for
the "exemption from militant, combative service" and articulating
the new Brethren vision of Christian citizenship. The resolution
stated in part:

> Averring our loyalty to civil authorities, and desiring
> to serve our country in the peaceable arts and productive

industries, we commit ourselves to a *constructive patriotism* and *loyal citizenship* of real service.

Therefore, we resolve. . . to be *patriotic* and *loyal* in the highest sense to our beloved country to which our forefathers fled for religious liberty. We resolve to invest our lives and all our energies for the conservation and promotion of all that is true, good and noble . . .

We believe in constructive patriotism, therefore, we dedicate ourselves anew. . . to the great and fundamental interests of the church and state, namely, the cause of the Sunday-school, missions and Christian education. We would lay upon the conscience of every member of the church, the solemn obligation of making sacrifices commensurate with the sacrifices made by those who are not exempted from military service . . .[8]

Thus, by the early months of U.S. participation in the war, Brethren had expressed opposition to war, appreciation for exemption from combatant duty, and a commitment to "constructive patriotism." But they had failed to spell out specifically how Brethren should respond to the draft. Adding to the confusion was President Wilson's delay in declaring what forms of service would be categorized as noncombatant. Not until March 23, 1918, did Wilson define noncombatant service.[9]

In the meantime, Brethren were drafted and reported to training camps. While most understood that their church did not want them to fight, they were unsure just how much they should cooperate. Could peace-loving Brethren wear military uniforms? Could they shoulder rifles and do military drills? Should they perform noncombatant duties within the army, or was that, too, an unchristlike contribution to the war effort? Faced with such quandaries, conscientious Brethren draftees clamored for clarity from church leaders. But clarity was a commodity in short supply.

Southeastern Pennsylvania District in 1917 appointed a Peace and Service Committee to relate to boys in training camps. Leaders from Eastern and Southeastern districts visited camps regularly to counsel, preach, and conduct love feasts,[10] but the advice the boys received from one visiting delegation seldom squared with advice from another.

Some urged Brethren young men to respectfully refuse to drill, wear the uniform, or render service of any kind, while others instructed Brethren boys to cooperate as fully as possible with the authorities. Eastern District elders I. W. Taylor and H. K. Ober visited 27 draftees from Brethren, Mennonite, Brethren in Christ, and Friends churches at Camp Meade, in Admiral, Maryland, during the summer of 1917. Taylor reported the visit in a *Gospel Messenger* article:

> They are all of the class who will not accept any service, combatant or noncombatant, under the military arm of the Government. They are not uniformed, and do not receive any training apart from a daily walk . . . The status of these men is yet to be determined by the War Department . . .
>
> The attending officer kindly extended to us the liberty of addressing the party . . . We are sorry that several newspapers misinterpreted some remarks made by Bro. Ober,—in substance, that if President Wilson so decrees, our Brethren will enter the army and navy and fight. The thought of Bro. Ober was that as nonresistant Christians, they would abide by what President Wilson might ask of them.[11]

Ober and others argued that the government had been gracious in granting exemption from combatant duties and, therefore, Brethren boys should cooperate as fully as possible, without actually taking up arms. Eastern District in 1918 passed a resolution, collectively expressing "appreciation to the national government for recognizing our distinctive peace doctrines and. . . permitting non-combatant work for our brethren."[12]

How many Brethren from Eastern and Southeastern districts were in training camps is difficult to determine. Many young men from rural Eastern District received agricultural exemptions.[13] In fact, one longtime elder recalled, "I know some Brethren were criticized for bringing their sons back to the farm to escape military service."[14] Not all Eastern District men escaped the draft, however. Members of the Lititz congregation remember a few men from their ranks reporting to military camps.[15]

In the urban Southeastern District, more men entered the military. The Philadelphia First congregation's *Gospel Messenger* correspondent in May 1918 mentioned "our boys who have gone away from us to Training Camps," but failed to give numbers.[16] The Bethany congregation, also in Philadelphia, in 1917 "entertained a group of United States sailors from the Philadelphia Navy yard at church services and in the homes of members."[17] By September 1918, a total of 24 Bethany men had been drafted and reported to training camp.[18]

Lacking clear direction from the church, Brethren draftees relied on their own consciences to determine how much to cooperate. Rufus D. Bowman, author of the most complete history of the Brethren and war, maintained that nationwide most Brethren served as noncombatants. A much smaller number refused all service and were kept in detention camps, furloughed to do farmwork, or imprisoned. A few others served as combatants.[19]

To quell the confusion surrounding the war, a special denomi-

Brothers in a cornfield on a Lancaster County farm in 1918. Many rural Brethren received agricultural exemptions from military service during World War I. J. Becker and Vera Ginder Collection.

national General Conference was held January 9, 1918, at the Goshen City (Indiana) church. After months of uncertainty, the church finally spoke with clarity. In a comprehensive statement reaffirming the church's nonresistant position the Conference declared, in part:

> I. We believe that war or any participation in war is wrong and entirely incompatible with the spirit, example, and teachings of Jesus Christ.

> II. That we cannot conscientiously engage in any activity or perform any function, contributing to the destruction of human life.

After providing scriptural backing for these assertions, the statement concluded with the clearest instructions yet for Brethren draftees:

> We further urge our brethren not to enlist in any service which would, in any way, compromise our time-honored position in relation to war; also that they refrain from wearing the military uniform. The tenets of the church forbid military drilling, or learning the art or arts of war, or doing anything which contributes to the destruction of human life or property.[20]

The authoritative Goshen Statement was distributed among Brethren draftees and, before long, came to the attention of military officers. On July 18, 1918, church leaders, including Eastern District's I. W. Taylor, were summoned to Washington for an emergency meeting. If the church did not withdraw the "treasonous" section of the Goshen Statement advising Brethren not to drill or wear uniforms, they were told, the officers of the Goshen Conference would be prosecuted and imprisoned. Rather than face prosecution, the church withdrew the statement.[21]

Though the Goshen Statement had spoken with clarity and authority against participation in warfare, by the time it was released, many Brethren had already accepted noncombatant duties *within* the military. With the statement's subsequent recall,

The 1924 Annual Conference, meeting in Hershey, passed a comprehensive statement on "Our Relation to War and Peace." BHLA, Annual Conference File.

Brethren continued to accept such duties. For the first time in over 200 years, Dunkers donned uniforms and entered the armed forces, albeit mostly as noncombatants.

Between the Wars

Chastened by their failure to uphold the church's nonresistant principles, Brethren following the war were determined not to be caught unprepared again. Led by men such as M. R. Zigler, Dan West, and Rufus Bowman, Brethren launched educational programs, issued clear statements, and worked cooperatively with Mennonites and Friends to lay the legal groundwork for alternative service, should the United States go to war again.[22]

"Practically every Annual Conference between the world wars made a strong declaration on peace."[23] Annual Conference in 1919 voiced opposition to universal military training,[24] and Eastern District followed suit in 1920 with a similar resolution.[25] In response to a request from the Harmonyville congregation, near Pottstown, the 1924 Annual Conference adopted a comprehensive statement on "Our Relation to War and Peace." Reviving some of the language of the withdrawn Goshen Statement (1918), the paper declared that "war or any participation in war is wrong" and that "the follower of the Lord Jesus should not engage in war or learn the arts thereof."[26] Churches in Eastern District continued to disown those who enlisted in the military.[27]

While the language of nonresistance persisted in statements between the wars, the emphasis of the Brethren peace position was shifting. Having seen the carnage of modern warfare, after World War I the church increasingly aimed to prevent *wars in general*, rather than merely preventing church members from participating.[28] Annual Conference resolutions in 1931 urged the government to reduce armament expenditures, condemned aggressive foreign policy, and opposed universal conscription in peacetime.[29]

Eastern District Brethren also were voicing their concern for peace to government leaders. The Lititz and Elizabethtown congregations, in 1924, expressed disapproval of the upcoming "Mobilization Day." In a letter to President Calvin Coolidge, Lititz leaders J. W. G. Hershey and Henry R. Gibbel wrote:

> As patriotic citizens of our beloved country and as devoted subjects of the United States for peace and good will, we the members of the Church of the Brethren do humbly desire to register our conviction against the proposed program of Mobilization Day September 12, 1924. We feel I) That the spirit of peace and good will should be promoted in all our domestic and international relations and that such a military display might be easily misunderstood as a threat or provocation to other nations; II) That our display will have the psychological effect of instilling militarism into the youth of the land . . .[30]

As World War II loomed on the horizon, the 1935 Annual Conference restated the church's peace position. The new document, which was printed and circulated as the official position of the church, directed strong words to church members and government leaders alike:

> We believe that all war is sin; that it is wrong for Christians to support or to engage in it; and that war is incompatible with the spirit, example and teachings of Jesus. We believe that war is not inevitable. Those beliefs. . . arise from our application of Christian stand-

ards to all human relations, whether individual, group, class, or national. To settle conflicts in any of these relationships by war is not efficient, not constructive, not permanent, and certainly not Christian . . .[31]

Peace wasn't just for Brethren anymore. Governments, too, were to pursue the things that make for peace. While the statement affirmed the church's historic opposition to war, the negative language of nonresistance was replaced with a positive message of peacemaking.

Early Relief Efforts

Coupled with growing Brethren concern to prevent wars was an interest in aiding those who suffered the ill effects of warfare. Brethren received their first taste of relief and reconstruction work in the years immediately following World War I. From 1918 to 1921, the church donated about $267,000 for relief in Armenia, where Christians were suffering at the hands of the Turks. This early relief effort expanded Brethren horizons and whetted their appetites for serving the world.[32] While Brethren formerly had taken care of their own, for the first time they had engaged in a large-scale effort to relieve the suffering of people *outside* the church.

Eastern and Southeastern districts endorsed a new Brethren relief effort in 1936 and 1937, respectively, when they adopted resolutions in favor of "Spanish Neutral Relief." Brethren Dan West and others in late 1936 had joined with the American Friends Service Committee to provide relief for sufferers on both sides of the Spanish Civil War. The Brethren in 1939 formed the Brethren Service Committee (later known as the Brethren Service Commission, BSC) to facilitate additional relief work.[33]

Between the wars, Brethren, in cooperation with Mennonites and Quakers, also laid the groundwork for alternative service for conscientious objectors in case a draft was reinstated. The Selective Service and Training Act—the first peacetime conscription law in American history—was passed in September 1940. Peace churches initially opposed the law, but when its passage seemed inevitable, they worked for provisions to keep conscientious objectors out of the military. Under the law, pacifists could serve as noncombatants within the military or do "work of national importance under civilian direction." The program to direct this latter type of work became known as Civilian Public Service (CPS).[34]

At the urging of the Brethren Service Commission, the Standing Committee of Annual Conference held a special meeting in December 1940 to consider the CPS plan. Eastern District followed suit with a Special District Meeting on February 22, 1941, at Elizabethtown College to discuss how the churches of the district could support CPS.

Past Annual Conference moderator Rufus Bowman explained that this "new type of service is intended to keep our boys from coming into contact with the army camp. It is also intended to be a peace testimony which we can bring to the world." According to the plan, special CPS camps would be provided for conscientious objectors, with the peace churches shouldering the cost. District delegates enthusiastically endorsed the plan and appointed Henry G. Bucher to garner financial support from the churches for the camps.[35]

World War II: Dunker GIs

When the United States entered World War II, the church appeared to be ready. During the previous 20 years it had issued numerous statements, clearly articulating its opposition to warfare. Leaders such as M. R. Zigler and Dan West had traveled far and wide among the churches of the Brotherhood, preaching peace and good will. Further, unlike World War I when the confused Brethren had no clear alternative, this time around the Civilian Public Service program was firmly in place. Yet when the call to arms came, an estimated 80 percent of Brethren accepted *full, combatant military* duties. Another 10 percent entered the military as noncombatants, with less than 10 percent choosing alternative service through CPS.[36]

In Southeastern District, where most Brethren had shed Dunker distinctives in favor of the cultural mainstream, the percentage of Dunker GIs probably was even higher than the nationwide figure. The Ambler, Royersford, Philadelphia Calvary, Parker Ford, and Philadelphia First congregations produced virtually all soldiers.[37]

While in previous wars, fighting Brethren would have been disciplined or disowned, a number of Southeastern Pennsylvania congregations openly revered Brethren soldiers for their valor. The

Bethany congregation in Philadelphia dedicated an honor roll, listing those rendering military service.[38] The Quakertown congregation in 1945 organized a fellowship meal "to honor its returning servicemen,"[39] and a number of churches placed banners in their church buildings "celebrating those who had been in the war."[40]

A 1944 Royersford church newsletter prominently featured photos of 15 uniformed members. In the newsletter, pastor Caleb Bucher assured his congregation's military men and women that they would be warmly received at war's end. Acknowledging that the Church of the Brethren is "an 'historic peace' church," Bucher argued for mutual understanding between pacifists and military Brethren:

> Each group [pacifists and soldiers] is contributing to the national security according to the best understanding each has regarding its duty to its country. After the war is ended, I feel certain that these two groups may again be assimilated into one solid fellowship. By the very essence of our doctrine we must be sympathetic toward one another and go forward as Brethren.[41]

While most Southeastern Pennsylvania Brethren entered the military, percentages of Eastern District Brethren going to war varied widely from congregation to congregation. In general, the district's urban and small-town congregations tended to produce mostly soldiers, while plainer, rural congregations turned out more conscientious objectors.

A CPSer from the Palmyra congregation recalls doing an informal tally at war's end and being shocked that, of about 130 draftees from the congregation, only four chose CPS.[42] Similarly, the Harrisburg First and Lebanon congregations had few conscientious objectors.[43]

On the other end of the spectrum were a number of congregations in which well over half of those drafted chose CPS. A young man growing up in the East Fairview congregation west of Manheim estimates that 80 percent chose CPS.[44] Few or no draftees from the White Oak and Indian Creek congregations entered the military during World War II.[45]

Other congregations filled out the center of the spectrum.[46] All told, Eastern District appears to have had a greater percentage of conscientious objectors than the Church of the Brethren as a whole. Yet even in Eastern District, more than half of those drafted likely entered the military.

Postmortem on a Peace Position

Several factors contributed to the diversity of decisions across the two districts. Chief among them was the church's changing view of the world. While the church had been preaching peace in the years leading up to the war, its members were becoming business and civic leaders. Rather than shunning an evil world, these Brethren were reaping the fruits of participating in mainstream society. Immersed in the dominant culture, some Brethren felt obligated to defend its interests, despite the church's teaching.[47]

On the other hand, those congregations that maintained some semblance of separation from the world generally had more young men lining up with the church's peace position. A free minister in the White Oak congregation explained his church's ability to hold the line against military service:

> I think the twin doctrines of nonresistance and nonconformity for the Anabaptist groups have a pretty strong connection. White Oak has tried to maintain a pretty strong emphasis of separation from the world . . . One of our former ministers was in the war before he was a Christian, and. . . he would at times share bits and pieces of his experience. You know, the whole thing was presented as war is something in the world and not part of the Christian's experience.[48]

Prior to World War I, Brethren viewed themselves as separate from an evil world. Since the world was evil, members of Christ's kingdom had no business becoming entangled in its affairs—especially its wars. Nonconformity buttressed nonresistance. But as they accepted responsibility for combatting society's ills, as they voted and became community leaders, Brethren undercut their traditional rationale for shunning participation in warfare. Evil was not simply something to avoid; Christians were called to contest it.

Faced with an evil foe such as Hitler, many Brethren decided to make peace with war.[49]

Longtime pastor Carl W. Zeigler remembered counseling young men on the question of military participation. Many, Zeigler recalled, felt that they had to lead an exemplary Christian life to be worthy of conscientious objection:

> When I was pastor at Lebanon, this was the position again and again—"We're just not worthy of this." And, "Where would we be if we hadn't fought in the Revolutionary War and the Civil War?" . . .
>
> I always presented the biblical foundation and. . . the importance of loving one's enemies . . . And again and again I heard the statement, "This is idealistic, but it isn't practical" . . .
>
> Some of these young men said, "We've been praying about this, and we feel a sense of loyalty here, and our

A February 22, 1944, Men's Fellowship gathering at the Lebanon church featured American flags and an honor roll for the congregation's fighting Brethren. Elizabethtown College Archives.

conscience tells us to. . . join the army. This is a part of
our civil responsibility. This is a part of being law-abiding." That term "law-abiding" just came up again and
again. And when I quoted the New Testament they always
said, "Well, that's alright in theory, but—"[50]

In most congregations, young men were free to follow their
consciences without fear of discipline. Though Annual Conference
had spoken strongly against participation in war, a 1938 statement
also had urged tolerance. In response to a query asking how to deal
with Brethren *enlisting* in the military, the statement recommended
"brotherly love and forbearance" and efforts to "restore him to full
accord as long as he expresses his desire to continue membership"
in the church.[51]

Thus, with the church exerting little pressure against fighting, and
with peers and propagandists exerting great pressure to fight, most
Brethren entered the military. By war's end, the church's peace
convictions were listed among the casualties. The traditional doctrine
of nonresistance, which had suffered self-inflicted wounds before the
war, was finally left to die on the battlefield. The church saved from
the fray only a greatly compromised "peace position," that had been
severed from the traditional doctrinal moorings of nonconformity and
nonresistance.

Expanded Relief Efforts

But while Dunker GIs fought, Brethren on the home front prayed
and, in some instances, paid for peace. Before and during the war
both districts frequently adopted resolutions urging peace and
calling on congregations to support Brethren Service efforts. At
first, relief work was centered in Philadelphia, where the American
Friends Service Committee provided space for Brethren to process
materials.

Philadelphia First church's Florence F. Murphy served on the
Brethren Service Committee from 1938 to 1945 and was liaison
between Brethren and Friends. With Murphy at the heart of
Brethren relief efforts, the churches of Southeastern District
rallied around the cause. The district formed a Brethren Service
Committee of its own in 1941 to network with the denomination's efforts.[52]

Congregations in both districts helped shoulder the burden of administering the CPS program, which by war's end had cost Brethren $1,300,000.[53] Meanwhile, Brethren CPSers provided useful services in forestry and soil conservation projects, as mental hospital workers, as subjects for medical experiments, in agriculture, and more.

The organization known today as Heifer Project International was begun by Brethren Dan West at the end of World War II. (Above) Members of the Spring Creek congregation and "heifers for relief" earmarked for Europe. (Below) Recipients of a heifer from the Spring Creek congregation. Spring Creek Congregational Archives.

Women from eastern Pennsylvania folding clothing at the Brethren Service Center in new Windsor, Maryland. The center was established in 1944 to accommodate rapidly expanding Brethren material aid efforts. BHLA, *Brethren Service File.*

As the end of the war neared, congregations—especially women—redoubled material aid efforts. The Women's Fellowship of the Philadelphia First congregation, using sewing machines and quilt racks in the church basement, produced more than a ton of relief materials for Europe during 1945.[54] The denomination in 1944 established the Brethren Service Center in New Windsor, Maryland, to accommodate the church's rapidly expanding material aid efforts.[55]

Brethren from both districts also generously supported a creative effort initially known as "Heifers for Relief." At the initiative of Dan West, who had seen firsthand the inadequacy of traditional handout approaches to relief during a stint in Spain in the mid-1930s, Brethren began to explore the idea of shipping live animals overseas. A committee was formed in 1942, and the first heifer was donated in 1943. Within a year, Brethren across the U.S. donated a thousand or more cattle, but logistical problems stymied shipping them to war-torn Europe.

Brethren Service Commission executive secretary M. R. Zigler began to explore shipping options with the United Nations Relief and Rehabilitation Administration (UNRRA) during the early 1940s and called on the Mountville congregation's Benjamin Bushong to work with UNRRA on a cattle-breeding project in Greece. A dairy farmer in fertile Lancaster County, Bushong was ideally situated to circulate among Brethren farmers and to maintain contacts with agencies in New York City, Washington, D.C., and New Windsor.

A major breakthrough came in June 1945, when UNRRA obtained seven boats to ship donated cows to Europe, if Brethren could provide handlers to accompany the shipment. Bushong scrambled over the next few months to coordinate the shipment and find the first "sea-going cowboys," as those accompanying the cattle came to be known. By 1951, more than 350 Brethren and others had made one or more trips abroad with cattle shipments.[56] Brethren in Eastern and Southeastern districts eagerly supported the new Heifer Project. Congregations that had sent soldiers to Europe during the war later sent heifers and "sea-going cowboys."

The Church of the Brethren in 1948 established a peacetime volunteer program known as Brethren Volunteer Service (BVS), which sent a new wave of volunteers to aid in the rebuilding of Europe. By July 1950, 15 young people from Eastern and Southeastern districts had entered BVS.[57] Also growing out of the destruction of World War II was a refugee resettlement program, centered in New Windsor.

While at first glance, World War II had appeared to sound the death knell for the Brethren peace position, in the war's aftermath it became evident that in some ways the church was more actively engaged in peacemaking than ever before. Seeds of active service and peacemaking programs sprouted from the rubble of post-World War II Europe, and Brethren tangibly demonstrated a renewed commitment to the things that make for peace. On the other hand, in subsequent conflicts, Brethren young men would continue to fight.

Conscientious Objection in the Cold War

Brethren entering the military after World War II continued to outnumber those choosing alternative service. In the Palmyra congregation, where during World War II nearly all of its drafted members entered the military, a higher percentage of members after 1950 chose alternative service.[58] A partial listing of Coventry

The Eastern District Men's Work organization sent 100 harnesses to Poland in the summer of 1947. (Top) H. M. Frantz (right) and assistant Ira W. Gibbel in the H. M. Frantz Harness Shop in Elizabethtown. (Bottom) Gibbel and harness recipient Jan Glab. Martha Gibbel Collection, photos by J. Henry Long.

Church of the Brethren members in the period after World War II included 32 men in the military and 13 in alternative service programs.[59] A survey conducted by Eastern District's Social Education and Action Commission in 1963 reported that *"recently 43.1% of our youth have gone into B.V.S. or Alternative Service, and 56.9% into the Armed Forces."*[60]

Though many Brethren men took up arms in Vietnam and were supported by Brethren back home, the church's official statements at the district and denominational level consistently voiced opposition to the war. The 1967 Eastern District Conference approved publication of the following newspaper advertisement:

A Plea for Peace

We, as members of the Church of the Brethren of Eastern Pennsylvania, meeting in District Conference in Lancaster on November 4, 1967, plead with all parties concerned with the Vietnam war to take the following steps toward achieving peace.

I. Stop the bombing of North Vietnam and seek an immediate cease fire, even at some sacrifice of military advantage.

II. Suspend additional troop movements to Vietnam.

III. Request all parties involved in the war to negotiate in good faith.

And to the public, our plea is that all persons be actively committed to peacemaking efforts.[61]

Some Brethren of Atlantic Northeast District, in concert with the church's statements, openly opposed the war. In April 1967, about 100 veterans of various forms of alternative service gathered at the Elizabethtown church to form the Brethren Peace Fellowship (BPF).[62] The following year, BPF initiated a monthly newsletter edited by pastor C. Wayne Zunkel. The newsletter maintained a consistent witness against the war, and many BPF members participated in demonstrations and other acts of witness.

In a 1966 *Messenger* article, Lancaster Church of the Brethren member and BPF supporter Inez Long described her participation in a peace march in Washington and chided the Brethren for the "parochialism" that prevented them from embracing the larger peace movement. Long lamented that "less than a hundred Brethren" from across the country had marched with her.[63]

Nevin Zuck, pastor of the Elizabethtown congregation, in 1967 presented a statement on the war to his congregation and the media. According to a *Messenger* writer, "The statement was in response to arch-critics who from outside and within the community attacked the loyalty of the denomination and of local members." It said in part:

> There are many people who oppose the present war in Vietnam and who do so out of a love for their country which they feel is presently cast in an indefensible role . . . We would affirm that one of the basic reasons for the existence of the Christian church is that it should be the conscience of the community and the nation . . .[64]

Brethren participate in a June 25, 1962, peace demonstration in Washington, D.C. BHLA, *Brethren Encyclopedia* Collection.

While he pastored the Harrisburg First congregation in 1968, Wayne Zunkel's outspokenness on peace issues caught the attention of "a group of religious, civil rights, and peace and labor people, concerned about peace," who asked Zunkel to allow his name to appear on a primary ballot for the Democratic National Convention. By a 29-23 vote, Harrisburg members expressed their support for this "worthy means of bearing witness to Christian concern for peace . . ."[65]

About the same time, Elizabethtown College became a lightning rod for anti-war activism. During the late 1960s, Elizabethtown and other Brethren colleges permitted military recruiters on campus, along with other potential employers. In an updated statement on war, Annual Conference in 1970 declared, "While recognizing the necessity of preserving academic freedom, we find recruitment by the armed forces on Brethren college campuses inconsistent with the church's position."[66]

In October 1970, the Atlantic Northeast District Board unanimously requested Elizabethtown College trustees to review their policy on military recruiters, but the college made no change. College spokesmen argued that the military needed to be presented as a valid career option, and that it was inappropriate for an "educational institution" to withhold diverse points of view from students. James Yeingst, executive assistant to the college president, added, "I believe that the presence of college trained leaders in our military structure is important to preserving the traditional concepts of American military service."[67]

In an August 1971 letter to the editor in *Messenger*, Elizabethtown faculty member J. Kenneth Kreider refuted the administration's arguments. Kreider affirmed having pro-military voices on campus in settings of discussion and debate, but categorically opposed military recruiters on the campus of a "peace church's" college. Kreider wrote:

> When the college announces the coming of a "recruiter" with other "prospective employers," however, it is endorsing that particular profession as a legitimate way to put to use the knowledge which has been acquired at college . . .

> To provide a room and time to listen to diverse ideas does not imply agreement. To allow a recruiter for the military. . . to be scheduled through the placement office signifies endorsement. The issue, therefore, is not academic freedom or freedom of speech. The issue is whether colleges are being true to their reason for existence or are being used as willing tools of the military.[68]

The October 1971 District Conference asked Elizabethtown "to change the current policy to show by their actions that they do not believe in the usage of, training for, or profession of violence, by no longer scheduling military recruiters through the Placement Offices . . ."[69] The issue was resolved the following year when the college yielded to the letter of the request, if not the intent. The college reported to the 1972 District Conference that the placement office would continue to provide students with information on the military, and those students desiring more details would be referred to an off-campus recruiting office.[70]

In April 1972, the college again appeared to support the military when it hosted a concert by the Air Force Band and Singing Sergeants. A dozen BPF members and college students handed out leaflets at the concert, welcoming the military men but adding "we raise our voices in the strongest possible protest to the job these men are assigned to do which is promoted tonight."[71]

Much peace activism in Atlantic Northeast District centered around the college faculty and a few large churches where BPF members served as catalysts. Elsewhere, attitudes ranged from confusion to indifference to active support for the war.

Reacting to an anti-war *Messenger* editorial, David C. Ogren of Lancaster believed atrocities committed by the Vietcong justified the U.S. war effort. He wrote:

> In your editorial you said, ". . . we need more expressions of concern from Christians who realize that moral issues are involved."
>
> My Christian faith heartily concurs! We need to cry out against the Viet Cong violations of human decency and personal atrocities . . ."[72]

Ogren concluded by insinuating that Brethren who questioned the war effort were "ignorant, uninformed, or disloyal."

Toward Militant Pacifism

Although individual Brethren and congregations sometimes objected, official denominational statements during the 1960s and 1970s gradually moved the church toward a more militant pacifism. While statements prior to World War I had primarily urged nonparticipation, during the world wars, church position papers increasingly advocated positive peacemaking efforts. Official statements during the Vietnam era took the Brethren one step further: Not only were Brethren to promote peace; increasingly the church called on its members to actively oppose the war in Vietnam. As Brethren during the late 1960s and early 1970s broached controversial topics such as war tax resistance and noncooperation with the draft, the radicalization of the peace position disturbed the peace within the church.

Annual Conference in 1948 had approved a comprehensive statement on war that reaffirmed the church's conviction that "all war is sin," urged its young men to choose alternative service rather than enter the military, and called on its members to be responsible Christian citizens. At the same time, the paper advocated tolerance toward those who did participate in the military.[73]

In response to a concern that the church's peace position was eroding, the 1948 statement was reexamined and revised in 1957. The new "Statement of the Church of the Brethren on War" included an expanded section on "The Church and Citizenship," instructions to members to "study international relations and foreign policy," and some general foreign policy advice directed toward government leaders.[74]

Competing conceptions of Christian citizenship vied for supremacy in the church during the 1960s and 1970s. As the Vietnam War dragged on, some Brethren resisted U.S. policy through civil disobedience, noncooperation with the draft, and tax resistance. Others, citing Romans 13 and Jesus's admonition to "render unto Caesar," believed such means of protest violated clear scriptural teachings.

A 1967 Annual Conference statement, "The Church, the State, and Christian Citizenship," left room for those who chose a more adversarial stance toward government. Recognizing that "the church will at times find itself in conflict with the state," the paper urged Christians to speak out against unjust government actions. "Such expressions," it added, "may include disobedience to the state." Churches were urged to "respect the right of individual conscience" and support those who would choose more controversial courses.[75]

The following year, a revised form of the church's general statement on war was again before the delegate body. A key addition was a section on payment of taxes for war purposes. Due to the controversial nature of this topic, the statement could do little more than recognize that Brethren were divided on the issue and urge further study.[76]

The 1969 Conference dealt directly with civil disobedience. Prompted by discussions on citizenship in 1967, the 1969 position paper, "Obedience to God and Civil Disobedience: A Word is Needed," provided a strong historical and theological case for civil disobedience. Delegates approved the paper by a vote of 607 to 294, slightly more than the required two-thirds majority.[77]

The following year the church approved yet another revision of its general statement on war. At issue in 1970 was a new section, sanctioning noncooperation with the draft. The revised paper passed by a vote of 754 to 103, but the church's support for noncooperation continued to engender strong feelings of opposition.[78] Recognizing the ongoing dissatisfaction generated by the church's official approval of noncooperation, the 1971 Conference appointed a committee to serve as a reconciling agent in the church.[79] The committee over the next two years listened to various voices in the denomination, interpreted the intent of the statement, and sought to increase understanding.[80]

Debates over Draft Cards

While the church's official statements roused those on both sides of the noncooperation issue, much of the debate in Atlantic Northeast District focused on Ted Glick. A young man from the Lancaster congregation, Glick burned his draft card in an act of civil disobedience during a panel debate on stage at the 1969 Annual Conference.[81] Glick's action was thoroughly discussed in the "readers write" section of *Messenger* during the next several months.

An irate sister from Harrisburg voiced disapproval for "the shameful act of civil disobedience which I personally witnessed. . . at the Annual Conference of our church . . ." She described how she felt as Glick burned his draft card:

> I couldn't believe what I was hearing or seeing. My first reaction was: "I can't sit and watch this shameful act"; so I got up and left. My next reaction was to cry for all the boys that gave their lives so that all youth could grow up in a free land.[82]

A writer from Elizabethtown countered the following month:

> It seems tragic to me that so many Brethren become so much more indignant over the burning of a part of a piece of paper in front of Annual conference than over the burning of human beings in Vietnam and elsewhere.[83]

A public demonstration supporting Ted Glick during a Vietnam-era Annual Conference. Glick (front left) burned his draft card on stage at the 1969 Annual Conference. BHLA.

Another writer, from Mount Joy, suggested that Jesus himself broke laws and mused, "I wonder if he [Jesus] would not be burning his draft card, too."[84]

A Manheim writer countered that Jesus broke religious laws but did not directly confront civil authorities. He argued, "We can change society only by changing men's hearts . . . This we do in service to man, not in demonstration or acts of civil disobedience."[85]

Glick became even more of a lightning rod for criticism when he was arrested in Rochester, New York, in September 1970 for alleged draft file destruction and was then placed in federal prison. He was later indicted as one of the "Harrisburg Eight," a group charged with conspiracy to kidnap Henry Kissinger, to blow up the heating system in Washington, D.C., and to destroy government files and property.[86]

As Glick's trial approached in January 1972, Brethren Peace Fellowship members Wayne Zunkel and John R. Gibbel drafted a statement of concern for Glick and the others that eventually was signed by more than 300 Brethren, including denominational and district leaders. The statement commended Glick "for his spirit of humility, goodwill and loving concern for the dignity of humanity in his struggles to remain obedient" and declared that the signers "stand with him and with the others of the Harrisburg Seven [the number changed when Glick was tried separately] in their struggle of conscience against war." Further, the paper challenged Christians to strongly oppose the war:

> We do not all agree about all of the methods they [the Harrisburg Seven] have chosen for their witness. But, with our voices and our lives we join them in crying out against a way in which, this past year alone, more bombs were dropped by our nation than were dropped in all of World War II on three continents . . . As members of the Church of the Brethren we are called to follow the teachings of Christ in opposing war in all forms.[87]

In sum, during the Vietnam years, Brethren peace statements showed increasing openness to more radical forms of witness—with some Brethren even supporting acts as drastic as Ted

Glick's alleged offenses. While Brethren prior to World War I had mostly aimed to keep their youth out of wars, and Brethren between the wars began to more actively promote peace, by the 1970s, Annual Conference statements sanctioned active opposition to government policies, even through civil disobedience and noncooperation with the draft. Brethren from Atlantic Northeast District remained divided on these issues.

Bidding for Unity

While the district was divided on how to respond to the Vietnam War, a new method of relief work begun by youth during the divisive Vietnam era gradually grew into a major unifying force. During the late 1960s, the Eastern District Youth Cabinet organized a small District Youth Auction at Root's Country Market south of Manheim. Selling mostly household furnishings, the auction raised nearly $5,000 for several charitable causes. The youth project continued several years longer before being dropped.

The auction idea was revived in 1977, when James C. Gibbel, Jacob H. Ruhl, and Jay M. Witman sought sponsorship from the Atlantic Northeast District. The 1977 auction netted about $11,000 for disaster relief projects from the sale of donated home furnishings, antiques, and household goods. In ensuing years, a quilt sale, a livestock auction, arts and crafts exhibits, and other innovative moneymaking projects were added.

During the late 1980s, auction proceeds mushroomed. Year after year the relief sale caught the imagination of the churches, who united around a worthy cause. Earnings in 1986 eclipsed the $200,000 mark for the first time.[88] Three years later, Southern Pennsylvania congregations joined the auction as partners, and proceeds climbed over $300,000.[89] All told, by 1990, more than $2 million had been raised through the auction for the Church of the Brethren Emergency Disaster Fund (EDF). By then, the auction annually produced nearly half of all monies channeled through the EDF to help victims of disaster.[90]

Who's Irresponsible?

The Brethren reinterpretation of responsible Christian citizenship and its impact on the church's peace position is fraught with ironies and questions. What does it mean to be responsible Christian citizens in a world of evil? Brethren at the turn of the century believed separation from the world was the best course. The duties of responsible Christian citizens were to pray for leaders, obey the laws of the land (except when they clearly violated God's higher laws), and stand apart as a paragon of goodness in a sinful world. Yet, today's Brethren call their "separatist" forebears irresponsible for ignoring the world's needs and idly looking on while nations moved toward war.

On the other hand, as the church began to work for peace through protest and political action, it increasingly accepted the methods of the very structures it sought to shape. While the church preached peace to the world, its own members marched off to war. The Brethren of old would call their pacifist progeny irresponsible for abandoning the doctrinal moorings of nonconformity and nonresistance that for two centuries had preserved the integrity of the church's peace witness.

Clearly, the church's peace position has changed. Whereas Brethren at the turn of the century sought to preserve the purity of the church by shunning the world's evil wars, 90 years later, many Brethren had accepted *peacemaking* as their Christian responsibility. But as an historic peace church moved toward the mainstream, many of its members made peace with war.

9.

The Divisiveness of Unity

Most Brethren at the turn of the century considered their church to be the only true Christian body. While other denominations professed to be Christians, it was evident to the Brethren that they were mere *pretenders*, rather than *contenders* for the faith. Brethren shied away from "other persuasions" in order to maintain true Christian unity within their own ranks.

Today's Brethren, on the other hand, while recognizing their denomination's unique heritage, view themselves as one member of the larger body of Christ. Unity means minimizing differences, emphasizing common goals, and cooperating with other churches. Ironically, church unity became a major source of divisiveness as Brethren moved from the former view to the latter.[1]

Avoiding "Other Persuasions"

Eastern District Brethren in 1900 shunned interaction with other Christians. They would neither commune with nor recognize the baptisms of non-Brethren, and they seldom invited outsiders to speak at their gatherings. In a 1906 column arguing against non-Brethren speakers in Brethren services, a *Gospel Messenger* writer sharpened the difference between Brethren and others:

> We have not only come out from among the unbelievers so as to be a separate people, but we have in like manner come out from the other denominations. We teach the portions of the Scriptures which others teach, and the rest besides. Our claim takes in the whole Gospel, and this is what cuts us off from other denominations.[2]

A Lancaster County minister born in 1913 recalls, "When I was a kid I used to pity these other people, like the Lutherans and Reformed, who didn't have the Brethren heritage because they were lost."[3]

Church Council Meeting minutes at the turn of the century depict a strictly separate church. The Middle Creek congregation in 1903 admonished a member to stay away from Salvation Army and Young Men's Christian Association (YMCA) meetings.[4] A member of the Mountville congregation, who was teaching in a nearby Mennonite Sunday school and thus "showing a disposition adverse to the doctrine of the brethren," was disowned in 1908.[5]

Brethren extended the cold shoulder not only to mainstream Protestant groups—disparagingly referred to as the "fashionable and worldly churches"—but also to other Anabaptists, such as the Mennonites. Brethren given the opportunity to preach in the presence of Mennonites were notorious for speaking on the mode of baptism, the one area where the two groups disagreed. Carl W. Zeigler told of a popular Brethren minister in Lebanon County who frequently preached at non-Brethren funerals. Zeigler recalled:

> Invariably, he would get around to the subject of baptism. And somebody asked him one time, "Why is it that at every funeral you seem to feel that you must say something about baptism?" And he said, "Well, it's the only time I can talk to the Mennonites."[6]

Zeigler recounted another episode when a Brethren evangelist departed from his prepared comments to preach a rousing sermon on baptism. After the service, Zeigler asked why he had changed topics. "And he said, 'I recognized [Mennonite] Bishop Ebersole, Jake Ebersole, in there and I thought I have to put in the right interpretation.'"[7]

They Learned It in Sunday School

But just as Brethren views of the world were evolving by the early 1900s, so were their attitudes toward other Christians. While the entire process stretched out over decades, the Brethren conversion from separation to cooperation began with the church's newfound zeal for evangelism and overseas missions. Growing Brethren interest in social causes, such as temperance and world peace, further hastened their conversion to ecumenicity.

Sunday schools, which Brethren resisted at first, gained wide acceptance in the Brotherhood by 1900, but Annual Conference frowned upon frivolous Sunday school celebrations or conventions sponsored by other groups.[8] In 1905, Conference cautiously permitted Brethren to attend such events, but urged participants to take care "so as not to compromise our principles."[9] The Elizabethtown congregation in 1907 hosted the Lancaster County Sunday School Convention.[10]

While Annual Conference only reluctantly was allowing limited association with other groups, overseas Brethren missionaries at the turn of the century routinely established Sunday schools with other Christians. Brethren in 1902 had joined the India Sunday-school Union, three years before Annual Conference had sanctioned such cooperation at home. In short, cooperation on overseas fields helped pave the way for ecumenism at home.[11]

Premature Ecumenism

While sentiments for ecumenical work were increasing during the early years of the century, denominational leaders in 1920 overestimated the church's commitment to cooperation. Annual Conference

A Sunday school class in the Conestoga congregation, ca. 1922. Teachers Addie Myer (left) and Leah (Myer) Stehman (right). Brethren participation in cross-denominational Sunday school events hastened their conversion from separation to cooperation with other Christian groups. Conestoga Congregational Archives.

in 1919 inaugurated an ambitious Five-Year Forward Movement, with specific financial goals to further evangelism, missions, Sunday schools, and other forms of outreach. In fall 1919, the Federal Council of Churches and other ecumenical agencies launched the Interchurch World Movement (IWM), a large-scale effort with similar goals to the Forward Movement. Leaders of the various Brethren boards in September 1919 endorsed the movement and committed a percentage of funds raised in the Forward Movement campaign to the ecumenical effort.[12]

Eastern District moved quickly to oppose this unprecedented entanglement with other persuasions. Meeting at the Schuylkill meetinghouse, Pine Grove, in April 1920, Eastern District drafted a query to Annual Conference, calling for the severing of all ties with the IWM.[13] The petition stated:

> We regard the fact of our General Church Boards having united with the Interchurch World Movement, as not in harmony with our long-established rule of faith and practice as a Brotherhood; therefore we request that our General Church Boards operate the Five-Year Forward Movement independent of any outside organization.[14]

Annual Conference delegates severed ties with the IWM by a decisive vote of 356 to 128. Their premature participation in the Interchurch World Movement ruled out Brethren ecumenical efforts on the policy level for more than 20 years.[15] Not until 1941 did Brethren affiliate with another ecumenical organization of the scope of the IWM.[16]

Cooperating Congregations

While Eastern District led the charge against *denominational* ecumenical involvements, some Eastern and Southeastern district *congregations* during the 1910s and 1920s courted cooperation at home. Philadelphia-area churches, some led by pastors attending non-Brethren seminaries, already were joining hands with other groups by the early 1910s. Philadelphia First church in 1913 took part in a Union Thanksgiving service with congregations of The Brethren Church and Dutch Reformed Church.[17]Also in 1913, Southeastern District ministers invited a non-Brethren representative of the Pennsylvania Arbitration and Peace Society to speak at an upcoming meeting.[18]

Not surprisingly, Eastern District churches were less eager to work with "other persuasions." The Mountville congregation in 1907 prohibited non-Brethren Sunday school workers from speaking in the Mountville church.[19] In 1916, a Mountville couple confessed that they had erred in attending services of another denomination. At the same meeting a sister repented of singing in the nearby Evangelical Church's choir.[20] Members of the East Fairview congregation in 1920 were instructed "to refrain from fellowshipping with people of other faiths in the study of the Bible."[21]

By the mid-1920s, association with other churches was a pressing issue in Eastern District. Popular elder I. W. Taylor, speaking at a 1927 Ministerial Meeting, cited the following reason for what he perceived as the church's lack of unity and vitality: "Too many regard our church as *a* church and not *the* church."[22] Among topics for discussion at the 1928 Eastern District Ministerial Meeting was, "How much should a minister associate with the local ministerium, or religious activities of other churches in the community?"[23]

Eastern District Brethren during the 1920s generally appeared ambivalent toward cooperation. Michael Kurtz, the conscientious elder of the Richland congregation, in Lebanon County, was tormented by pangs of guilt after he had preached in a non-Brethren church for the first time. His son Earl recalls, "I can remember him coming home and saying, 'I wonder if I did the right thing. I wonder whether I should have done that.'"[24]

During the 1920s, Dunkers were torn between two conflicting visions of the church. The older generation of leaders remained committed to a peculiar Church of the Brethren that stood apart. Their "foreign policy" in relating to the world and other churches was strictly isolationist. Plain dress served as an appropriate flag to represent their position.

The new generation of Brethren, burdened by the yoke of separatism, longed to work with other Christians to further Christ's kingdom. As more of them attended high school, college, and even seminary, they rubbed shoulders with other Christians and saw that they had much in common. A young man who graduated from a Lebanon County high school in 1927 was angered by his home church's stubborn separatism:

> I always felt badly when I was in high school. All the
> churches in Annville would close their service on a
> Sunday night of the high school baccalaureate. The
> Brethren never would. My heart used to burn. My par-
> ents were greatly upset when I graduated and (the Breth-
> ren) wouldn't close the service.[25]

By the 1930s, this new generation of ecumenically-minded Brethren—some of them embarrassed by their peculiar past—was assuming leadership posts in Eastern District. By then, the vision of a
cooperative Church of the Brethren—at least on a local level—was
supplanting the separatist stance of the past. The arrival of the first
large wave of seminary-trained pastors in Eastern District during the
1930s further eroded the traditional beachhead of separation.

The Lititz congregation, which hired its first full-time pastor in
September 1935, is a case in point. Less than a month later, Lititz
Brethren voted to cooperate with "other churches in the town of
Lititz" for a community Thanksgiving service—evidently their first
ecumenical endeavor. The following year, Lititz pastor James M.
Moore participated in a pulpit exchange. Moore preached in the
Lutheran church, while a minister from the United Brethren
church preached for the Brethren.[26]

By the late 1930s and 1940s, urban congregations with pastors
were formalizing ties with other denominations through local min-
isteriums and area councils of churches.[27] Ross D. Murphy, pastor
of the Philadelphia First church, became vice-president of the Philadelphia Federation of Churches in 1939, and then served as president from 1941 to 1943.[28]

While most cooperation was with Protestant bodies, a few congregations cultivated relationships in broader circles. When the
Elizabethtown church moved into a spacious new building in 1956,
the local Catholic parish purchased the old meetinghouse to use
as a parochial school. According to Nevin Zuck, ecumenical cooperation in Elizabethtown "reached its climax" when Brethren and
Catholics held a joint worship service to celebrate the transfer of
the building. The former Elizabethtown pastor recalls:

> We had an ecumenical service in our new building in
> which the Catholic priest preached the sermon and our

choir sang part of the mass in Latin. The [Catholic] Sisters that were there nearly were transported to the other world. They couldn't believe it![29]

The Harrisburg congregation, which was at the forefront of ecumenical involvements in Eastern District, went beyond cooperation with Catholics. The congregation in 1956 helped purchase an organ for the Dauphin County Prison as part of an "interfaith project," and several Harrisburg Brethren were later involved with the Harrisburg Peace Center, an interfaith organization whose executive committee included Brethren, Jewish, Quaker, and Unitarian representation.[30]

While it was mostly pastor-led, urban congregations that spearheaded the Brethren push toward cooperation, a few more progressive free ministers also favored such interaction. Rufus Bucher, elder of the Mechanic Grove church near Quarryville frequently conducted Quaker funerals and preached at Methodist camp meetings as early as the 1920s.[31]

During the 1940s, Bucher, Mountville elder Norman Musser, and Musser's son-in-law Nevin Zuck attended popular Presbyterian Bible conferences near Harrisonburg, Virginia. Zuck recalls:

> [It was a] very ecumenical gathering in its day. And we'd go down for three or four days, or a week, and we'd have a wonderful time. These men like Bucher and Musser, they'd rub shoulders with the great and the near great.
>
> Q: But they would still have their plain dress on?
>
> Oh yes. They were all called bishops.
>
> Q: Is that right?
>
> Oh yes, Bishop Musser and Bishop Bucher, because Presbyterians as a whole wore ties, . . . but these fellas were "clerically dressed."[32]

While Brethren such as Bucher and Musser enjoyed rubbing shoulders with prominent Presbyterians, cooperation in the 1940s had its limits. None of their Presbyterian friends could have communed in

Bucher's or Musser's churches, and, had they wished to join Mountville or Mechanic Grove, they would have needed to be rebaptized. Such were the paradoxes of an era of transition from isolation to ecumenism.

District Debates

Cooperation at the local level helped to open the door for ecumenical ties at the district and denominational levels. Southeastern District elders in 1929 for the first time discussed "going in with the State Council of Churches," but agreed to put the matter on hold.[33] The issue didn't resurface until 1937, when the District Conference appointed a committee to explore affiliation with the Pennsylvania Council of Churches (PCC). District Conference delegates approved affiliation the following year, Paul M. Robinson was chosen as the district's first representative, and a 10-dollar contribution was earmarked for the Council's work.[34]

Two years later, in response to a query from the Harrisburg congregation, Eastern District appointed a committee of its own to explore affiliation with the PCC.[35] The committee in 1941 recommended joining the Council, but some churches hedged. James M. Moore was appointed representative for one year to observe the Council's work.[36] Eastern District continued to send representatives over the next few years, but gave only token financial support. Meanwhile, proponents persuaded doubters of the Council's merits. In a 1946 District Conference report, Nevin Zuck noted:

> As we consider our relation to the council, it would seem that two things should govern our thinking: first, there are other Christians in the world. The kingdom of God is greater than the Church of the Brethren; and second, it is the Lord's will that Christians should live together in a courteous manner and in cooperation with one another.

> The Pennsylvania Council of Churches is the only organization in our state which offers us an opportunity to accomplish Christian tasks together. It will bring benefit to us, in so far as we allow it to do so. On the other hand, it gives us an opportunity to make our contribution to the life of the church of Jesus Christ in our state.[37]

Harrisburg First church's Jesse Reber (right), pictured here with regional secretary Roy Forney, was longtime general secretary of the Pennsylvania Council of Churches. Reber was instrumental in the construction of the Pennsylvania United Church Center (background), which houses judicatory offices of various denominations. BHLA.

With men such as Zuck and Harrisburg First church's Jesse Reber serving as advocates, suspicions toward the work of the Pennsylvania Council gradually subsided. By 1953, 11 Eastern District Brethren served in various positions with the PCC, and the district paid its quota of two cents per member.[38]

Reber, who served as associate secretary from 1947 to 1953 and as general secretary from 1953 to 1968,[39] promoted the construction of a United Church Center in Harrisburg to serve as headquarters for the Pennsylvania Council and district and state judicatories of various denominations.[40] Brethren in 1964 established an office for tri-district executive Joseph Long in the Center, taking their place alongside Lutherans, Methodists, and Presbyterians, and symbolizing a maturing commitment to cooperation.[41]

Controversial Councils

Far more controversial than cooperation with the Pennsylvania Council was the denomination's association with the Federal (later National) and World Councils of Churches, beginning in the 1940s. Rebuffed by Annual Conference delegates in 1920 for their unauthorized involvement in the Interchurch World Movement, denominational leaders for a time maintained a low profile in

*Brethren Service worker Helena Kruger, from the Annville church, with M.
R. Zigler (1891-1985) at the World Council of Churches headquarters in
Geneva, Switzerland in 1948. Zigler was a leading Brethren figure in the
ecumenical movement.* Martha Gibbel Collection, photo by J. Henry Long.

ecumenical affairs. Leaders such as M. R. Zigler during the 1930s
quietly related to committees of the Federal Council of Churches
(FCC), a U.S. ecumenical organization that had been founded in
1908. Zigler also participated in discussions with international
church leaders during the 1930s that eventually resulted in the
formation of the World Council of Churches (WCC).

The denomination's Council of Boards in 1938 approved a policy
of limited cooperation with both the Federal Council and the bud-
ding World Council of Churches. Three years later, the Council of
Boards recommended to the 1941 Annual Conference in La Verne,
California, that the Church of the Brethren officially join both the
FCC and the WCC.[42]

Perhaps anticipating a conservative challenge, the Conference
proposal plainly stated:

It is understood that the Church of the Brethren shall
not be bound by any action of these Councils and in no

way compromises its doctrinal position by this action. This authorization is made out of a desire to share in the larger fellowship of the Protestant world and to be a more effective comrade of other Christian groups in those great movements for peace and world reconciliation to which we all in Christ owe a common loyalty.[43]

Delegates meeting in La Verne approved affiliation with both organizations, but appointed delegates only to the FCC, since the WCC was still in the process of formation. When the WCC was officially organized in 1948, the Church of the Brethren was among its founding members.[44] The Federal Council of Churches in 1950 merged with other Christian agencies to become the National Council of Churches of Christ in the USA (NCC).[45]

Conservative Backlash

The 1941 decision ignited more than four decades of sometimes bitter controversy. Anti-ecumenical eastern Brethren charged that

Brethren delegates in the processional march at the Cleveland Constituting Convention of the National Council of Churches in 1951. BHLA, NCC and WCC File.

denominational leaders had maneuvered to have the issue of FCC/WCC affiliation decided at La Verne, where fewer conservative easterners would be present. Further, they charged, the issue was sprung intentionally upon unwitting delegates because proponents feared that, if the facts were known, affiliation would be rejected.

In deference to such charges, the issue was revisited at the 1942 Conference in Asheville, North Carolina. Delegates reaffirmed affiliation, but the matter continued to fester. Philadelphia First church's Roland Howe, who claimed neutrality on the issue, penned a resolution to the 1944 Standing Committee, asking for an intensive educational effort. Howe noted:

> . . . I cannot escape the thought that a very large majority of our members, both ministry and laity, are in the dark on this question . . .

> Would it not seem reasonable. . . that the La Verne Conference might have performed a greater service three years ago had more time and thought been given to possible reaction before hastening to register its seal of approval?[46]

In response to inquiries such as Howe's, the 1944 Annual Conference appointed a committee "to study the facts concerning the Federal Council, together with the general attitude of the brotherhood to it, to the end that our people may have dependable information, and that the unity of the church may be maintained."[47] The committee reported the following year that attitudes toward the Council varied widely "from active interest and support, through more or less indifference, to active opposition:"

> Some of the opposition arises from a misunderstanding of the purpose and the activities of the Federal Council of Churches of Christ in America; some from a fear that co-operation on our part will lead to a loss of denominational identity or of our distinctive principles; some to criticism of past activities of the Federal Council of Churches; some because of theological views of certain men who are members of churches constituting the Federal Council of Churches; some is obviously due to prejudice.[48]

After assuring delegates that the FCC "disavows any intention or effort to dictate the doctrinal beliefs of its constituent members," the report detailed the FCC's stated purposes: expressing fellowship and unity of the Christian church; united Christian service; encouraging "devotional fellowship and mutual council [sic] concerning spiritual life and religious activities;" and exerting "a large combined influence" on moral and social issues. At the committee's recommendation, delegates voted to continue affiliation.[49]

As the committee noted, opposition to the FCC stemmed from several sources, all of which were represented in eastern Pennsylvania. A number of congregations, influenced by fundamentalist thought, were infuriated by alleged pro-communist leanings in the FCC and WCC, and by key leaders associated with the movement who denied cardinal doctrines, such as the virgin birth and deity of Christ.

The Quakertown church in 1945 filed a protest against Brethren affiliation, objecting specifically to the modernistic views of FCC leaders.[50] The Hatfield congregation registered its opposition to the FCC at the 1947 Eastern District Conference, citing the traditional Brethren position that the church should not be "unequally yoked with unbelievers."[51] The White Oak congregation, near Manheim, in 1948 petitioned District Conference "in the name of unity" to ask Annual Conference to sever relations with the FCC.[52] The Spring Grove (later Blue Ball) congregation added its voice to the anti-Council chorus at the 1951 District Conference.[53]

At a Special Council Meeting in March 1962, the Indian Creek congregation stated its opposition to the NCC and WCC, citing these reasons:

> I. Many National Council Leaders deny cardinal doctrines.

> II. National Council is operating as a political group rather than a Spiritual Body.

> III. Our "Liberal" brethren leadership is eroding basic christian beliefs.

> IV. Ecumenical Movement is influencing Brethren Literature.

Noon meal at a 1950s District Conference at the Indian Creek meetinghouse near Harleysville. Many conservative Brethren opposed affiliation with the National and World Councils of Churches. BHLA, *Brethren Encyclopedia* Collection.

V.   World Council wants to unite with Rome.

VI.   Practically all leading denominations have had a battle over affiliation with National Council.

VII.   John 17, does not mean Organic Union, but a Spiritual Fellowship.

VIII.   Expression of opinion is partially suppressed in our Literature and at our Conferences.

IX.   There is considerable evidence of sympathy with Atheistic Communism on the part of some National Council Leaders.

X.   Elgin [i.e., denominational leadership] is willing to compromise in order to gain status.

XI.   During the last four years there has been a dramatic reversal of teaching in our Literature.[54]

In September 1962, newly hired tri-district Christian education director Virginia Fisher wrote of the unrest caused by ecumenical affiliations:

> There is a lessening of the "ties that bind" many people to the Church of the Brethren . . . The affiliation of our Church with the National Council of Churches and the World Council is causing much unrest, especially in those churches where there are no employed and trained pastors.[55]

In several congregations, opposition went beyond words of protest. During the 1940s, under the leadership of pastor Donald Martin, the Shamokin congregation had grown from a small mission to a church of nearly 200. Word of trouble at Shamokin reached Eastern District's Elders Body in 1948, and a committee was appointed to win back Martin, who was becoming increasingly antagonistic toward the church because of his disagreement with ecumenical liaisons and liberal trends. By 1949, Martin was withholding all financial support from the district and Brotherhood program.

After several unsuccessful attempts at reconciliation, at a special session in May 1950, elders issued an ultimatum that Martin either be reconciled to church program or resign. He refused to do either and was relieved of his ministry in November 1950.[56] Martin and nearly 50 members left to form Grace Independent Chapel.[57]

Similar troubles were brewing in the Big Swatara congregation, north of Hershey, where two free ministers and two deacons eventually left the Church of the Brethren for a more conservative body.[58] District elders reacted to the disquiet by appointing a committee to inform congregations of the good work that the FCC was doing.

Church of the Brethren general secretary Norman J. Baugher tried to quell the unrest with a February 1965 *Messenger* article explaining "What the National Council of Churches Means to Us." Baugher, who served at high levels within the NCC and WCC, argued, "In reality it [the NCC] is an extension of the Church of the Brethren." The NCC, Baugher argued, enabled Brethren and other denominations to achieve much more together than they could separately. He pointed to several areas of cooperation, including

joint curriculum efforts, sharing of information on new church design and salary structures for pastors, a united witness in Washington, cooperative relief work, and more. He concluded:

> The council is no more of a perfect organization than
> are our several denominations. But the council is making
> it possible for the Church of the Brethren to take advan-
> tage of expanding opportunities and to meet the chal-
> lenges of increased Christian responsibilities. It is not an
> entity separate from us. Rather, it is an agency through
> which we can do these things together.[59]

Despite denominational and district interpretation efforts,
Brethren affiliation with the NCC and WCC and liberal theological
trends continued to raise hackles at the Hatfield church. The congregation split in 1965, when 63 members (among them several
deacons) formed Penn Valley Grace Brethren Church.[60]

In Philadelphia, the fundamentalist Calvary congregation withdrew from the Church of the Brethren in December 1967. A letter
to the denomination's general offices listed three reasons for leaving: 1) "the increasing tendency toward embracing a liberal, modernistic theology;" 2) "denominational affiliation with the National
Council of Churches. . . ;" and 3) the use of higher criticism in
Sunday School curriculum."[61]

Although fundamentalist voices often portrayed their opposition
to the NCC and WCC as an effort to rescue the historic Church of
the Brethren from the liberal mainstream, those voices were, in
fact, as influenced by outside forces as their more ecumenically
minded fellow members. Both the liberal push for ecumenical cooperation and the fundamentalist opposition were indications that
the church was being shaped by outside currents, albeit from opposite ends of the theological spectrum.[62]

While fundamentalist Brethren were the most bitter critics of the
church's ecumenical stance, others raised concerns that the NCC
and WCC were enticing Brethren away from their distinctive beliefs
and practices—such as the love feast, trine immersion baptism,
and peace. Tradition-minded Brethren were alarmed by what they
saw as a growing tendency to mimic mainline denominations.

Others, however, argued that distinctiveness was passé. In a

1963 *Messenger* article, Inez Long, a member of the Lancaster church, pooh-poohed proponents of peculiarity:

> While many lament that we are not much different from other denominations, the idea that we must be different in order to justify our existence exposes the shallowness of our concept of what it means to be the church. Sects and splinter groups trying desperately to be a saving remnant within the church, and a pure breed preaching the whole truth, have strained the unity of the church to the breaking point.
>
> Is it not enough that a denomination is a part of the Christian church, its members linked with every other Christian to form the body of Christ alive in the world? [63]

Long and others believed that distinctive Dunkers had had their day. Rather than impede the ecumenical mainstream with sectarian beliefs and practices, Brethren needed to "go with the flow." Being Christian was uniqueness enough.

Baby Blessing and Believers Baptism

Consecrating babies was early evidence of such accommodation to the mainstream. Perhaps no issue had been more central to the early Brethren than believers baptism. Alexander Mack and his followers declared:

> . . . we have left all sects because of the misuses concerning infant baptism, communion, and church system, and unanimously profess that these are rather man's statutes and commandments, and therefore do not baptize our children, and testify that we were not really baptized.[64]

But as urban Brethren rubbed shoulders with other Christians during the first decades of the 20th century, a rite of inclusion for infants somehow seemed more acceptable. As early as 1914, Southeastern Pennsylvania ministers discussed the matter of "child consecration" and appointed a committee "to work out a plan for child's catechism."[65] The 1928 Eastern District Ministerial Meeting, in addition to discussing how much Brethren ministers should interact with other religious groups, addressed the question, "Should a minister have dedicatory services for blessing children?"[66]

By then, a few congregations had begun to dedicate infants. In the Ambler congregation, pastor Henry K. Garman in 1927 dedicated children in services conducted in their homes. The following year the congregation included child consecration in Sunday worship.[67] In 1930, Southeastern District's Brooklyn First congregation petitioned Annual Conference to develop a suitable order of worship and appropriate certificates for newly dedicated infants. The Brooklyn query noted "that there is a growing demand among the members of our churches, particularly the city congregations, for some kind of Consecration Service to be used in consecrating young children to the Lord."[68]

The following year, Conference approved such a service. The report's introductory comments included a recommendation that churches consecrating children "emphasize the idea of the consecration of parents as well as the consecration of the congregation to the interests of its childhood," likely to make clear the difference between infant consecration and infant baptism.[69] Writing in 1932, Brethren sociologist Frederick Dove observed:

> It would seem evident that the Brethren, who by tradition have so strongly opposed infant baptism, have sanctioned this practice of infant consecration as a form of compromise with those members who are favorably impressed with the practices of other churches in baptizing infants into their religious groups. It is significant, too, to note that this practice is observed most generally in those congregations which are located in the midst of the great culture currents of society.[70]

Despite some resemblance to infant baptism, infant consecration had become widely accepted by the late 1950s, even in some traditional congregations in Eastern District.[71] While few opposed an innocent ceremony of inclusion for infants, baby dedications foreshadowed an even more radical departure from traditional baptism practices. But first, Brethren altered another important ordinance—the love feast.

Is Not the Table the Lord's?

Brethren traditionally had practiced close communion,[72] in which only members in good standing could participate. For communion to be profitable, Brethren believed, communicants needed to share common beliefs and practices. But growing interaction with other Christians soon called such views into question.

First in eastern Pennsylvania to experience dissonance between cooperation with other churches and the practice of close communion were the Ambler and Philadelphia First congregations. The Ambler church voted in 1927 to "open the communion to any who professed faith in Christ"; Philadelphia First followed suit in April 1930.[73] Philadelphia First church's Roland Howe, in a 1933 letter, provided rationale for open communion:

> Is not the table the Lord's? Is not man a guest, not the host? Would not any church leader be exceeding his authority in a very presumptuous way by attempting to deprive any one from communion at His table, if that is the time and place the communicant feels at heart he ought to be? On the other hand, I cannot bring myself to believe that the Lord would look with disfavor on an invitation to others to join in such a fellowship even though their christian faith and practice might not be in strict keeping with the forms of ours.[74]

During the 1930s, most Brethren *could* bring themselves to believe what Howe could not. Eastern District elders in 1935, in response to a query asking whether members of The Brethren Church could commune with the Church of the Brethren, flatly ruled, "Our policy is close communion."[75] Two years later, an elder asked for an opinion on open communion, noting that the practice was becoming more common in the Church of the Brethren. In response, Eastern District elders cited an 1849 Annual Conference minute, which stated that the Lord's Supper is "a divine and sacred ordinance. . . and should be eaten by the members only."[76]

But by 1950, close communion was becoming untenable. While Brethren in former days routinely excluded people from their love feasts—even out-of-order *members*—by 1950, some Brethren hesitated to exclude anyone who professed Christ. Both sides of the open communion/close communion line supported their views with appeals to church unity.

The old Brethren believed that the presence of other Christians who were not committed to distinctive Brethren doctrines and practices disturbed unity. To commune was to be in agreement. How could outsiders, who obviously didn't meet Brethren standards, be allowed to participate? Advocates of open communion, on the other hand, argued that close communion violated the unity that Brethren shared with all Christians. What right had they to exclude other Christians from the *Lord's* table? Close communion, they believed, was an unbrotherly barrier to cooperation.

The latter view carried the day in 1951 when Annual Conference sanctioned open communion. The report stated in part:

> Some of our congregations permit those of other evangelical denominations to participate in the Love Feast, thus recognizing them as members of the family of Christ.

> We, therefore, would recommend. . . that local churches, where they so desire, may extend to evangelical Christians the privilege of participating in the Love Feast.[77]

An infant dedication in the Spring Creek congregation in 1946. A sign of accommodation to mainline Protestantism? Spring Creek Congregational Archives.

This 1978 love feast in the Middle Creek sanctuary was for Brethren only. Not until 1984 did the congregation open its communion to other Christians, one of the later Brethren congregations to make the transition from close to open communion. Middle Creek Congregational Archives.

With Conference permission, congregations gradually adopted open communion. By 1989, only six of 66 (nine percent) Atlantic Northeast District congregations practiced close communion. Of those adopting open communion, four percent adopted open communion prior to 1950, 31 percent during the 1950s, 25 percent during the 1960s, 23 percent during the 1970s, and the remaining 17 percent during the 1980s.[78]

But another hurdle for other Christians remained in place—the Brethren baptismal requirement.

Rebaptism Reconsidered

Trine immersion baptism by a Brethren minister was an absolute membership requirement at the turn of the century. Annual Conference had ruled in 1883 that even those who previously had been baptized in other denominations *by trine immersion* needed to be rebaptized by "an authorized administrator of the German Baptist brethren" in order to join the Brethren.[79] Attempts to soften that stance failed in 1905 and 1912, but the 1915 Annual Conference eliminated the rebaptism requirement for those previously baptized by trine immersion.[80] Later that year, the Lancaster congregation, in accordance with the new ruling, received a former

United Zion Church member based on his former baptism.[81]

Rebaptism didn't resurface at Annual Conference until 1949. By then, Brethren church planters, working closely with local Councils of Churches, were entering into comity agreements. In essence, these pacts between Protestants eliminated competition by dividing up the "mission field." But Brethren engaging in such cooperative church planting felt responsible to minister to the needs of all Christians within their area. New congregations (and some long established ones) found that the trine immersion requirement prevented other Christians from joining.

Thus, a 1949 Annual Conference query requested a study of the basis of membership in the Church of the Brethren "in order that we may move forward more effectively in the fields of evangelism and home missions," and a study committee was appointed.[82] Under the subheading "Some Practical Issues of Church Membership," the committee's 1950 report recommended that congregations decide for themselves whether to retain the trine immersion baptism requirement "as the Holy Spirit would direct, always being concerned for harmony in the congregation." Due to the report's controversial nature, the 1950 Annual Conference deferred action. A year later, delegates tabled it indefinitely.[83]

The issue resurfaced at the 1957 Conference in a statement on church extension from the General Brotherhood Board. In a section titled "Philosophy of Church Extension," the paper established "'oneness in Christ' with other Christian bodies who share the main stream of our Protestant faith" as the guiding principle for Brethren church-planting efforts. Further, the paper asserted, "This oneness foresees the end of exclusive religion in which the Jews as the chosen people, or the Brethren as the peculiar people, possess either a preferential or an exclusive gospel." Fleshed out in specifics, this new philosophy ruled out unbrotherly rebaptism requirements. (In addition, the paper urged Brethren to supplement semi-annual love feasts with Protestant "bread and cup communions.")[84]

Delegates balked at such a radical shift and instructed the General Brotherhood Board to rework the statement's most controversial provisions. The paper returned to the 1958 Annual Conference in Des Moines, Iowa, with two minor changes, making the provisions on rebaptism and bread and cup communion permissive rather than obligatory. After lengthy and heated debate, the statement was approved. Though Brethren would continue to practice trine immersion, new members could be received based on former baptisms.[85]

Reactions in the East were mixed. Traditional Brethren were outraged by the church's unwillingness to defend what they viewed as the biblical mode of baptism. The 1958 decision, as they saw it, was ample evidence that ecumenical involvements were leading Brethren to abandon their priceless heritage. Conservatives bristled at the insinuation that peculiarity was un-Christian. For 250 years, Brethren apologists had laboriously defended trine immersion. Suddenly, they were told, mode didn't matter. In fact, those who defended a particular mode actually were perpetuating unbiblical "exclusive religion." That the 1958 paper failed even to distinguish between infant baptism and believers' baptism added insult to injury.

Alarmed by the church's liberal direction, a number of conservative Brethren, many from Eastern and Southern Pennsylvania districts, met at the 1959 Annual Conference to form the Brethren Revival Fellowship (BRF). According to Linford Rotenberger, former pastor of the Quakertown congregation and the group's first chairman, the 1958 decision "had everything to do with the BRF being founded."[86]

The BRF believed that ecumenical involvements and related trends were symptoms of the church's drift from scriptural authority. Among concerns voiced at a 1964 BRF meeting were:

> Our disregard of the authority of the Scriptures as our rule of faith and practice; the pressure exerted to break down anything distinctive in our practices to make an ecumenical church work more smoothly; the continual stream of liberal speakers presented at our conferences both local and on the national level; our church school literature does not uphold the Bible as the inspired Word of God but is subjected constantly to the judgment of men . . .[87]

Other eastern Brethren thought the 1958 decision was long overdue. Caleb Bucher, pastor of the Royersford congregation during the 1950s, was reluctant to rebaptize Christians, but was pressured by an influential deacon. In Bucher's words,

Bob and Virginia Garland joined the Royersford church. Bob was the photography editor for the *Saturday Evening Post.* They were Episcopalians. I had to rebaptize them. [An influential deacon] said, "Yes sir, we'd be glad to have them, but they come our way."

Q: But you had some mixed feelings about that?

Oh yes, I never felt comfortable about [rebaptizing] . . . I always felt that we were emphasizing method instead of message. So it was important to get straightened out on that.[88]

As more Brethren married outside the church, many congregations faced growing numbers of couples in which one partner was a member, but the other refused to be rebaptized. Carl W. Zeigler, who pastored the Lebanon congregation during the 1950s, recalled:

Elder Rufus P. Bucher, assisted by Lester Schreiber, baptizes Anita Frey in the pond on the George Bucher farm near Mechanic Grove on August 10, 1946. The photo appeared in Holiday *magazine in June 1947. A 1958 Annual Conference decision permitted accepting members from other denominations without trine immersion baptism.* J. Kenneth Kreider Collection.

I baptized a Lutheran lady one time and when she came up out of the water she said, "I still don't think that this is necessary." She did it to reunite her family.[89]

In the Lititz congregation, mixed marriages spurred a "Resolution on the Question of Rebaptism" at the April 1956 Council Meeting:

Whereas the local church through the years has sustained serious membership losses due to our own members joining the denomination of the spouse, and

Whereas the local church has failed frequently to add prospective members because of the requirement of re-baptism, and

Whereas the requirement of re-baptism represents a denial of the validity and religious experience of other groups, and

Whereas in the Church of the Brethren nationally over half of its churches no longer require re-baptism,

Be it resolved:

1. That the local church continue to teach and practice Trine Immersion as the historic initiatory rite of entrance into the church.

2. That in receiving into membership those from other evangelical bodies, if they are satisfied with the method of their previous baptism and if their manner of life indicates genuine religious experience, we accept such persons on their confession of faith.

The resolution was discussed at length in April and narrowly rejected in October 1956. Finally, in October 1958, with Annual Conference permission, Lititz adopted the new policy.[90]

Already prior to 1958, at least four congregations in Eastern and Southeastern districts accepted new members on reaffirmation of faith. Eight others adopted the new policy by 1960, with eight more switching prior to 1970. A steady stream of congregations continued to waive the rebaptism requirement throughout the 1970s and 1980s. By the late 1980s, 62 percent of congregations accepted members baptized as *infants* without requiring rebaptism.[91] Those who rejected infant baptism drew lines at different points. A few continued to require trine immersion. Others accepted any form of immersion, while still others accepted all believers baptisms, regardless of mode.

COCU: From Unity to Union

With conservatives still smarting over the 1958 rebaptism decision, Brethren ecumenical involvements in the early 1960s took another controversial turn. While ecumenism during the 1940s and 1950s stressed unity through cooperative ministry, by the 1960s, emphasis was shifting from *unity* to *union*. In response to a call from Presbyterian Eugene Carson Blake and Episcopalian Bishop James A. Pike, a Consultation on Church Union (COCU) was organized during the early 1960s. The goal of the COCU was to merge several major denominations to form a new church, "truly evangelical, truly reformed, and truly catholic."[92] By 1966, eight mainline Protestant denominations, totalling about 24 million members, were full participants in the COCU.

Brethren, who since 1962 had monitored the COCU conversations through observer-consultants, broached the question of becoming full participants at the 1965 Annual Conference, but delayed a decision until the following year. The church's Fraternal Relations Committee recommended in 1966 that Brethren continue as observer-consultants.

While the committee lauded aspects of the COCU's work, the report acknowledged that the gulf between Brethren and other participants was too great. Among incompatibilities cited were understandings of the ordinances (sacraments), such as baptism and the love feast; "the sharp cleavage between clergy and laity" which seemed to be at odds with the Brethren concept of the priesthood of all believers; the "deep concern" over losing the historic Brethren peace position; and the "considerable risk of. . . disunity within the Brotherhood."[93]

The intense COCU debate at the 1966 Conference lasted six

hours, as respected Brethren lined up on opposite sides of the issue. Fraternal Relations Committee chairman Nevin Zuck, an Eastern District pastor who favored full participation in COCU, summarized the committee's report as a step toward greater cooperation. The report, he noted, was against full participation *at this time,* but didn't necessarily rule out future cooperation. He concluded:

> . . . We have said that we ought to pursue possible merger. We believe the Church of the Brethren needs to come to grip with this issue, that we can't avoid it.

> . . . I submit to you that the report comes out of long agonizing search and struggle. We believe it represents a direction we can go, a distance that we can travel in our pilgrimage toward the reunion of our Lord's church.[94]

Other Eastern District figures opposed participation in the COCU for the present and the future. Harrisburg First church pastor Wayne Zunkel argued that the Brethren concept of a church based on radical discipleship would be lost in merger. Said Zunkel:

> Basically we face one question and one question only. Does this concept that the essence of Christianity is radical discipleship still have value? . . . Or, has this concept outlived its usefulness, burned itself out? Shall we now head off for a coalition which does not accept this basic concept, taking with us whatever fragments of our ideals remain to see them assimilated, blunted, and, over a period of generations, lost?[95]

The answers to the questions Zunkel posed were clear to James F. Myer, a free minister in Lancaster County's White Oak congregation. Questioning the genuineness of COCU advocates' concern for unity, Myer stated:

> Now here we are assembled today, saying we are interested in unity when we know from the very beginning that if we were to join the Consultation on Church

Union, there would be a line of division go right down
through the Brotherhood causing unprecedented division and confusion among us.

Some of us do not need to join consultations for us to
decide whether we want to merge. We have already made
up our minds . . . We believe the Church of the Brethren
can fulfill her greatest role in this troubled age by preserving a New Testament church witness and this can be
done best alone.[96]

In the end, delegates decisively rejected full participation, approving the Fraternal Relations Committee recommendation to
continue as observer-consultants by a vote of 881 to 220.[97]

COCU supporters obviously were not pleased with the decision.
Inez Long, a freelance writer from the suburban Lancaster church,
penned a biting account of the proceedings for the liberal *Christian
Century,* in which she referred to Brethren COCU opponents as "parochial planners and scriptural literalists" who, rather than moving
toward merger, "assumed their historic defensive stance." The COCU
decision, Long wrote, demonstrated that the narrow, sectarian
Church of the Brethren remained "a denomination that takes to the
hills in extremism and returns to the alleys with parochialism."[98]

The Identity Crisis

As Brethren debated the COCU, in reality they were considering
the much more basic issue of the identity of their own church. By
the 1960s, ecumenical involvements had contributed to a Brethren
identity crisis. A denomination that always had identified itself in
terms of peculiar practices during the 1950s and 1960s traded
symbols of distinctiveness for those of mainstream Protestantism.
Pastor and historian Elmer Q. Gleim recalls:

We began to argue, "Who are the Brethren?" . . . And we
had a problem with identity . . . We weren't any longer
thinking of ourselves in terms of the old-fashioned distinctive doctrines and practices. And the result of that
switchover or change led us to a confusion because we just
didn't know what kind of a church we were.[99]

By the turbulent 1960s, declining membership statistics were a symptom of the Brethren identity crisis. Denominational membership peaked in 1963 and began a steady decline that continued into the 1990s. Eastern District during the 1960s and 1970s continued to lose members who disagreed with the larger church's ecumenical involvements and related liberal trends. One Eastern District observer notes:

> I know of individual cases where people felt the Brotherhood had become too liberal over the years. People left and went to more conservative churches. There were very few people who left and went to more liberal churches. There's significance in that. Perhaps we haven't given that enough consideration.[100]

During the years that the COCU polarized the church, significant numbers of Church of the Brethren members moved to more fundamentalist Grace Brethren congregations. Having split from The Brethren Church in 1939, the Fellowship of Grace Brethren Churches made rapid inroads in eastern Pennsylvania during the 1960s. Grace Brethren congregations begun in Lancaster (1960), Elizabethtown (1965), Myerstown (1967), and Lititz (1970) attracted disenchanted Church of the Brethren members, who contributed to Grace Brethren growth.[101] The Grace Brethren, who mixed love feast and trine immersion baptism with a fundamentalist theology, were an attractive alternative for dissatisfied Church of the Brethren members. Others joined conservative independent congregations, such as Lancaster's Calvary Independent Church which, according to one observer, drew heavily from the Brethren and Mennonites.[102]

Membership losses due to dissatisfaction with the Church of the Brethren's ecumenical affiliations continued into the 1980s. In 1989, 40 congregations reported that members had left "during the last ten years or so" because they disagreed with beliefs or positions of the church. Asked to list what beliefs or positions drove members away, 25 percent (10 congregations) specifically cited Brethren involvement with the NCC or WCC and the related liberal drift.[103]

While some disaffected Brethren voted with their feet, others expressed themselves at the offering plate. The Atlantic Northeast District Board, in a January 1971 letter to Church of the Brethren General Secretary S. Loren Bowman, voiced concern over "a decline of approximately $25,000 in congregational giving to the Brotherhood Fund this past year just from our district," while giving to other outreach areas increased. Noting that this was the first such decrease "in our area in our memory," the letter detailed some sources of dissatisfaction, including reduced Brethren evangelism efforts, lack of distinctively Brethren mission work, and production of fewer Brethren publications. The letter concluded:

> Finally, we feel that much of the criticism would subside if the church could move out boldly to *reaffirm its heritage* in ways appropriate to the new day in which we live. We pledge our continuing support to work with you toward that end.[104]

Reaffirming the Heritage

Beginning with Annual Conference's decisive rejection of full participation in the Consultation on Church Union in 1966, the headlong Brethren flight away from their peculiar past slowly ground to a halt. Having rejected union with mainline church bodies, certain voices within the church resurrected Anabaptist and Pietist themes. During the 1970s, groups such as the Brethren Revival Fellowship and Brethren Peace Fellowship gained wider respectability and gradually nudged the church out of the ecumenical mainstream into a less controversial position along the ecumenical edge, where Brethren could have some exchange with other churches without losing their Anabaptist and Pietist footing.

While the Church of the Brethren continued work with the NCC and WCC, it also cultivated relationships with other Anabaptist groups during the 1970s and 1980s. At the initiative of Brethren M. R. Zigler, representatives of the five largest Brethren groups came together in June 1973, beginning a process that culminated in the production of *The Brethren Encyclopedia* in 1983.[105] Brethren, Mennonites, and Quakers joined hands in the mid-1970s in a cooperative effort known as New Call to Peacemaking.[106] New Sunday school curriculum, *The Foundation Series,* produced cooperatively by Brethren, Mennonites, and Mennonite Brethren was introduced in 1977.[107]

Beginning in the early 1970s, Brethren, Mennonites, and Brethren in Christ in eastern Pennsylvania sponsored Keystone Bible Institutes, providing instruction for ministers and lay leaders in the Anabaptist tradition. A similar cooperative effort is Mennonite and Brethren Marriage Encounter, a program to strengthen marriages, sponsored since 1988 by eastern Pennsylvania Brethren, Mennonites, and Brethren in Christ. During the 1980s, the Church of the Brethren, the Mennonite Church, and the General Conference Mennonite Church began the arduous task of producing a joint hymnal. *Hymnal: A Worship Book* was released in June 1992, with booming pre-publication sales exceeding publishers' expectations.[108] Within Atlantic Northeast District, Elizabethtown College's Young Center for the Study of Anabaptist and Pietist Groups, dedicated in 1989, sparked renewed interest in Brethren heritage.[109]

As the 1990s approached, Brethren heritage was given higher priority in the denomination through a grassroots-focused goals process. A "Scripture and Heritage" goal, approved by delegates at the 1989 Annual Conference and reaffirmed by the 1989 Atlantic Northeast District Conference, called on Brethren to "celebrate Brethren identity as informed by scriptures," while maintaining a commitment to "give and receive gifts within the wider body of Christ."[110] By 1990, the church seemed to be moving toward a more balanced ecumenical stance that didn't sacrifice unity *within* the Church of the Brethren for a broader unity with other bodies. Ecumenical affiliations remained controversial, however, and occasional flare-ups reminded the church of the divisiveness of unity.[111]

10.

Going to Church

Changes in Brethren meetinghouses and worship practices during the 20th century mirrored the move into the mainstream that was evident in other areas of the church's life. As Brethren employed seminary-trained pastors and rubbed shoulders with other Christians, their buildings and worship patterns evolved from quaint to contemporary, from peculiar to Protestant.

Sprawling "church plants" crowned with steeples replaced plain meetinghouses. Stately sanctuaries, long and narrow, supplanted squarish auditoriums, and preachers tables gave way to elevated pulpits and divided chancels. Acolytes and offerings, preludes and postludes, organs and robed choirs, gradually found their way into Brethren worship, while traditional practices such as kneeling for prayer and *a cappella* congregational singing faded. Even the love feast service—once a two-day celebration at the center of the church's life—dwindled in significance. By the 1990s, the setting and style of Brethren worship communicated mainstream Protestant commitments.

"The Beauty of Holiness"

Brethren buildings and worship at the turn of the century were expressions of a peculiar people who valued separation, simplicity, and community. Describing traditional Brethren worship, Nancy Kettering Frye observes:

> Ministers and members of the congregation sat on the same level; all wore the same plain garb. Gone were the clerical robes, the elevated altar, the ecclesiastical music and liturgical mystery, and the sensual stimulation of incense, candles, flowers, statues, stained glass, intricate

carvings, bells and musical instruments. These Brethren were consciously choosing to emphasize *the beauty of holiness rather than the holiness of beauty.*[1]

A description of the Pricetown meetinghouse, penned just prior to the turn of the century by a newspaper reporter, epitomized Dunker meetinghouse architecture and theology:

> The interior consists of a plain room. The walls are entirely free of paper, paintings, fresco or kalsomine [a whitewash]. The windows are without ornament or decoration of any kind. The seats are plain, wooden benches with a straight board for a back. There is no pulpit or pulpit furniture. The preacher is not even given the prominence of having a raised platform on which to stand while addressing his audience. His bench is no softer than that of any of his hearers. He has a long table in front of him, on which is placed his Bible and hymn book. Back of the table stands a long bench. His bench and desk face the audience, and this is the only distinction that his office affords.[2]

The Heidelberg meetinghouse, located in Lebanon County, was built in 1867 and enlarged in 1900. It is pictured here ca. 1915. Elizabethtown College Archives.

In addition, benches on all sides of the auditorium faced toward the center, placing the focus not on an altar or platform "up front," but on the gathered congregation. The long "preachers bench" and "preachers table," located on the same level as the congregation, symbolized equality and shared leadership.[3] In short, "Brethren meetinghouses were buildings of the people, by the people, and for the people; democracy embodied in masonry and wood."[4]

While the worship diet in other churches included more exotic fare, served attractively by polished preachers and musicians, Brethren worship was strictly meat and potatoes, presented without garnish. Typically, worship began with an unaccompanied hymn. The song leader, often a minister or deacon, would read a line or two of the hymn, which the congregation then would sing at a deliberate pace.[5]

Next, a minister made some introductory remarks and invited the congregation to kneel for prayer. Instead of facing an ornate altar where a priest made intercession, worshippers turned and knelt around the "congregational altar," with elbows propped on benches. Prayers were long and unrehearsed and always ended with the Lord's Prayer.

A minister then would rise from behind the preachers table to read the scripture text for the morning. Many congregations read one "rotation chapter" each week, covering the entire New Testament over several years and thus buttressing the Brethren claim that the entire New Testament was their only creed. Little, if any, attention was paid to the liturgical calendar or special holidays.[6]

In many congregations, the preacher of the morning was selected on the spot through a ritual of polite mutual submission. A second minister would preach a shorter sermon, underscoring—or repeating—the thoughts of the first, and deacons sometimes were permitted to "bear testimony" after that. The service concluded with another prayer (with the congregation kneeling), an unaccompanied hymn, announcements, and dismissal.[7]

Sectarian Ordinances

In their observance of the ordinances, Brethren paid scrupulous attention to scriptural detail, with practical considerations taking a backseat to literal obedience. Normally held at midweek, the traditional Brethren love feast was a two-day pageant of preaching, preparation, and re-enacting the events in the upper room. This high, holy event included a morning preaching service, lunch, the afternoon "self-examination service," the evening love feast, and a second day of preaching and a noon meal. Patterned as closely as possible after the events in the upper room, the hours-long love feast proper included feetwashing, the Lord's supper, the passing of the holy kiss, and culminated with communion. At the conclusion, communicants "sang a song and went out into the night," following the example of Jesus's disciples.[8]

Brethren also sought to be faithful to Scripture in their baptism practices. In addition to their rigorous defense of trine immersion, they insisted on baptism in running water, since artificial pool baptism appears nowhere in Scripture.[9] Eventually, in 1902, Annual Conference allowed indoor baptisteries, "when absolutely necessary," but reiterated that "we always prefer that baptism be performed in a running stream."[10] Most churches in Eastern District shared that preference. At times, even the maverick Philadelphia First church—which baptized indoors without Conference permission—showed respect for biblical authenticity by letting the faucet run during baptism.[11]

In the early 1900s, new converts typically joined the church through revival meetings. In response to an invitation to accept Christ, converts stood. After "making a start" in this way, they received brief instruction, promised to uphold the peculiar doctrines of the Brethren, and were baptized.[12] Held once or twice a year, revival meetings routinely ran for two weeks, and sometimes longer when the Spirit seemed to be moving. An evangelist in the Tulpehocken congregation, for example, preached 28 sermons "full of sound doctrine" between January 31 and February 22, 1903.[13]

A Philadelphia First: Hiring an Architect

Even though most eastern Pennsylvania Brethren in 1900 worshipped according to traditional patterns in plain meetinghouses, a few had begun to embellish their buildings and worship. As with many changes, the Philadelphia First church took the lead.

Preparing to construct a new building in 1890, Philadelphia Brethren took an unusual step: They hired an architect. Benjamin D. Price evidently was more accustomed to designing churches than meetinghouses, because his plans included a steeple. In Roland

Built in 1891 on Carlisle and Dauphin streets, the Philadelphia First church stood in sharp contrast to traditional Brethren meetinghouses. The building is pictured here as it looked after the tower was added in 1905. Elizabethtown College Archives.

Howe's words:

> This [the steeple] was strenuously opposed. A modi-
> fied steeple was then drawn which met equal opposition,
> and the architect was asked to make an additional
> drawing for a tower without a steeple. This he positively
> refused, saying "No money could tempt me to spoil my
> own work by making any change in my original draw-
> ing—if you want a plan of a plain Dunker church for
> $75.00 or more, I will give you one."

Finally, a compromise was reached. The building was built without
an "elevation," but with an adequate foundation to add a steeple later.
A 1905 addition included the tower provided for in the original plan.
    But even without a tower, the Carlisle and Dauphin streets build-
ing stretched the definition of "meetinghouse." Though the Phila-

delphia Brethren early in the building process had stated their preference for "neatness and plainness" and against "vanity and extravagance," the finished product was far from plain, at least by Eastern District standards. Most noticeable were the ornate stained glass windows, installed in memory of longtime members of the church. As the architect had observed, the overall outside appearance with arched doors and windows was that of a proper Protestant church, not a plain Dunker meetinghouse.[14]

By the turn of the century, other Philadelphia-area congregations were incorporating churchly features into their meetinghouses. The Green Tree meetinghouse, built in 1845 near Oaks, was a rectangular stone building, free of stained glass and steeple. Inside, the auditorium was laid out along a horizontal axis, with preachers table and entrances along the long side of the building. In these respects it resembled a traditional meetinghouse.

But in 1890, Green Tree moved the entrance to the gable end, where a vestibule was added. Inside, aisles were carpeted and walls papered, and a central pulpit, positioned at the gable end opposite the new entrance, replaced the preachers table. A writer in 1915 observed, "As thus remodeled the cosy country church along the road at Green Tree gives a feeling of satisfaction to the most cultured aesthetic taste."[15]

By the 1920s and 1930s, rural Brethren were altering their meetinghouses—and their meetinghouse theology—in similar fashion.[16] Some congregations adopted the term "sanctuary" to describe their new interior designs, replacing the plainer term "auditorium." The raised pulpit, which symbolized the centrality of the Word, also elevated the preacher above the people. Before long, Brethren began to call buildings "churches," and to "go to church" instead of gathering *as the church* in plain meetinghouses.[17]

Learning the "Rudiments of Musick"

Few aspects of early Brethren worship were as out of tune with the times as their music. Brethren argued vehemently at the turn of the century that only *a cappella* congregational singing could please God. One writer pointed out that "Neither Christ nor the apostles ever authorized the use of musical instruments in worship either by precept or example." Moreover, he concluded:

Musical instruments are the usual accompaniment of wars. They are found at feastings and revelings. Even to-day our saloon-keepers take advantage of musical instruments to allure the young into the saloon.[18]

Through some creative exegesis of Amos 6, a Brethren tract argued that God even condemned David's use of the harp: "While David did much that is praiseworthy, yet he made some mistakes, and the prophet plainly names his use of musical instruments as one of them." The same tract traced the origin of instruments to the family line of Cain.[19]

Instrumental music, Brethren were convinced, did more to entertain than edify and ruined rather than reinforced spirit-filled singing. "Soul-less" instruments, they believed, could not express true worship. "Special music" by small groups or soloists similarly was condemned as a vain personal display that did more to titillate than illuminate.

But as they remodeled their meetinghouses, Brethren also borrowed mainstream worship practices. The Philadelphia First church began using a small organ in Sunday school services as

Early music instruction at Elizabethtown College fueled the evolution of musical tastes among Eastern District Brethren. Elizabethtown College Archives.

early as 1872, and a year later placed a larger organ in a basement Sunday school room. The new church, built in 1891, included a new organ. Special music was introduced in 1882, choirs were organized during the early 1890s, and, by 1900, a salaried organist and choir director led the church music program. By the time Annual Conference approved musical instruments in worship in 1920 (and then only in congregations where they would not disturb the peace), Philadelphia First church was about to purchase its *fourth* organ![20]

Meanwhile, singing schools, a new hymnal, and formal music training were preparing other eastern Pennsylvania congregations for a slower evolution of musical practices. Brethren initially had frowned upon singing schools, but, by the late 1800s, congregations were hiring trained teachers to hold weekly classes in a meetinghouse or public building.[21] Early Eastern District congregations to sponsor such schools were Lancaster (1892), Spring Creek (1896), and Lititz (1901). Cautious rural congregations waited somewhat longer before joining the trend. The Chiques congregation approved its first singing school in 1922 to teach the "rudiments of musick," presumably to include the modern spelling of the word. Singing schools remained popular into the 1930s, as Brethren learned to sing more in tune with the times.[22]

Spurred by shifting musical tastes, Annual Conference in 1900 authorized a new hymnal that would include the best of old Brethren songs, as well as faster-paced gospel songs for Sunday schools and revival meetings. In addition to new songs, the 1901 *Brethren Hymnal* included another novelty— musical notation.[23]

Along with a new hymnal and popular singing schools, Elizabethtown College also helped to fill in the chords as Brethren music modulated into the modern era. Founded in 1899, the college by 1904 offered instruction in piano and organ, even though the use of such instruments was prohibited in Brethren worship.[24] Professor B. F. Wampler started a college chorus in 1905 and began performing dramatic cantatas in a town auditorium. By 1910, students and faculty were forming popular quartets and trios. During its first 20 years, the college offered a music teachers course, a class in voice culture, and private music lessons, training the choristers and choir directors who would help transform Eastern District's musical tastes.[25]

Benedictions and Basket Collections

By the 1920s and 1930s, Brethren were increasingly open to new worship practices. Brethren ministers traditionally had dismissed services with announcements and a few words, such as "Let us depart in peace and the Lord willing we'll meet the next Lord's day."[26] Brethren thought it improper for ministers who were "as needy of blessings as their hearers" to pronounce a blessing upon the congregation.[27] But in a 1920 action deleting minutes that had been "made obsolete by common practice and consent," Annual Conference repealed the ban on benedictions.[28]

Before long, Eastern District churches followed the lead of the larger church, but not always without controversy.[29] Benedictions were discussed several times during the mid-1920s before gaining acceptance in the Annville congregation. Elder Carl Zeigler recalled, "I remember the Council Meeting when we decided to have a benediction and I think half of them were surprised that those benedictions were quotations from the Bible."[30]

In another peculiar practice, Brethren customarily cared for finances outside of worship. Unable to find gospel support for collections during worship, traditionalists argued that worship should not be mingled with finance. Besides, offerings inappropriately obligated visitors and non-members to help pay church expenses.[31] Rather than passing plates, many congregations assessed each household a percentage of their net worth and collected this "church tax" during the annual deacon visit or at Council Meeting. Members who refused to pay their share faced discipline.[32]

But after several decades of sporadic debate, the 1895 Annual Conference finally permitted "lifting a public collection when churches think it expedient to do so."[33] As was often the case, progressive urban congregations had already proceeded without permission, some driven by their need to pay professional pastors. The Ambler congregation in 1885 agreed to lift offerings immediately after services for that purpose and, before long, collected offerings during worship. In December 1915, the Lancaster church also approved weekly offerings.[34] By the 1930s, even cautious conservative churches were adopting this practical new method of collecting finances.[35]

"How Dignified Should a Minister Be?"

Preaching among the Brethren was a serious matter, designed to edify, not entertain. A 1920 admonition in the Elizabethtown Council Meeting minutes warned: "Members should guard against laughing during the preaching service when the minister says something that sounds a little amusing."[36]

In earlier years, the morning's preacher and hymns often were selected on the spot, with ministers relying rather directly on the inspiration of the Holy Spirit; but by the 1920s, many churches were establishing preaching schedules so that ministers could prepare sermons in advance.[37]

In general, Brethren were coming to prefer more polished preaching, as indicated by several questions raised at the 1932 Eastern District Ministers' Meeting: "Where should the minister spend more time in the preparation of his sermon; in the secret chamber or in his study?" "What reading course should be followed by ministers, especially our younger ministers who have not had the opportunity of a college training?" "Can a farmer preacher study?" "Is the ability of a minister to express his thought important?" "How dignified should a minister be?"[38] All these questions implied shifting expectations, with more emphasis on education, sermon preparation, and proper delivery.

By the 1930s, many urban congregations—especially those with professional pastors—had eliminated the second sermon and bearing of testimony by deacons. This trend gradually spread into other congregations.[39] But even where the second sermon persisted, the style of preaching was changing.

A longtime pastor recalls that, during the 1940s, older ministers in the Conewago congregation preached from scant notes or no notes at all, but a younger minister, who was a college graduate, used more extensive notes. Ministers in the East Fairview congregation by the 1940s no longer used the rotation chapter and preached mostly from notes or detailed outlines. A minister licensed in the mid-1940s was the first to preach from a manuscript.[40]

While new practices were gaining acceptance, traditional ones—including the ancient seating patterns that segregated men and women—gradually fell into neglect.[41] A longtime member of the Lititz church remembered how separate seating initially was tested during the late 1920s:

A young man would come to the ladies' side and sit with his girlfriend . . . Everybody stared at them and made them feel uncomfortable, but I don't think anything was done about it. And after somebody broke the ice, then it escalated.[42]

In the Richland congregation, practical considerations brought on the change, as one member recalls it:

There was a couple there who had four children. And they had trouble. The sons would of course be on the one side, and the mother on the other side, and here the children were going back and forth, you know, and there was a fuss. Finally somebody says, "Why in the world can't they at least let them sit together?"[43]

Practical considerations also began to change the way Brethren prayed. Patterned after their Savior in Gethsemane, the Brethren preferred kneeling as their posture for corporate prayer, even two or three times in the same service. Each prayer concluded with the Lord's Prayer. But while the old Brethren prayed repeatedly after the manner commanded by the Lord, more modern Brethren tired of the repetition. By the 1920s, congregations were omitting the Lord's Prayer at least once per Sunday service, but most continued to kneel.[44]

A Chorus or a Choir?

Annual Conference decisions in 1910 and 1920 cleared the way for special music and instruments in worship, respectively. Given the green light, Southeastern District churches quickly added instruments, soloists, and choirs to their worship. In the Green Tree church, singing schools at the turn of the century blossomed into a church choir by 1917. In 1923, the church organized a full *orchestra* to play during Sunday school, and, by the late 1920s, a band played at church functions.[45] The Ambler congregation also enjoyed an orchestra during Sunday school, beginning in the 1920s.[46]

Eastern District churches proceeded more cautiously. By 1920, a few had introduced occasional special music, and, before long,

The Green Tree Church of the Brethren Marching Band, June 1928. While progressive Southeastern District congregations organized bands and orchestras during the late 1920s, most Eastern District Brethren continued to oppose musical instruments in worship. Green Tree Congregational Archives.

others organized trios, quartets, and, informal choruses.[47] By 1930, Eastern District Conference programs occasionally included special music, but not everyone was happy about it. The White Oak church requested in 1930 that only congregational singing be included at District Conference. Delegates diplomatically responded: "While we would not prohibit special music when reverently sung to the glory of God, we do urge the value of congregational singing in our District gatherings."[48]

By the 1930s, choruses and choirs were becoming increasingly popular, although in the early years it was important to distinguish between the two. A sister from Lebanon County recalls:

> We called the chorus the Heidelberg choir one time and [Elder] Henry King told us it's not a choir, it's a chorus. You don't call it a choir!

> Q: And what was the difference he was perceiving?

> Well. . . , I guess "choir" is too fancy . . . And, you know,
> Lutheran and Reformed and all those churches had a
> choir. We had a chorus.[49]

But as congregations drifted closer to mainstream currents, choruses became choirs, replacing familiar songs with more complicated cantatas and chorales. As one brother remembers, the educated members of the Spring Creek congregation in Hershey, who favored a more cultured choir, "ran the chorus out" around 1940.[50]

Along with choirs came a push for instrumental accompaniment. While Southeastern District churches had embraced instruments by the early 1900s, Eastern District continued to resist. In 1914, the Harrisburg First church, at the advice of district elders, closed down an urban mission post because its leader had introduced musical instruments. Ten years later, instruments were still too controversial to be discussed in Harrisburg.[51] At a 1930 Eastern District Ministerial Meeting instrumental music was listed among "things that need discouraging" in our churches.[52]

By then, however, opponents of instruments were fighting a losing battle. As Table 10.1 shows, pianos began to appear in Eastern District churches during the 1930s and would become common by the 1960s. Organs followed a similar pattern, beginning in the 1940s. Of course, seldom were instruments welcomed overnight. Pianos and organs gained gradual acceptance as they were promoted through use by choirs, youth groups, and at church weddings, which were becoming common by the 1940s.[53]

The Lititz church is a case in point. In January 1939, Lititz permitted a harp at a wedding, on a one-time-only basis. Three years later, blanket approval was given for instruments at weddings, but they still were taboo in Sunday worship. In 1944, Lititz youth placed a piano in the basement, and a short time later an organ was added, but instruments still were prohibited in the main auditorium.

The church in 1946 approved a piano in the sanctuary to accompany the choir singing a cantata, but all congregational singing and most choir numbers continued to be rendered *a cappella*. A Lititz member recalls that at one point the piano was wheeled into the sanctuary only when the choir planned to use it:

(Top) The Lititz Church of the Brethren Men's Chorus, ca. 1935. During the 1920s and 1930s Eastern District elders such as Henry F. King (1877-1955) (bottom) were careful to distinguish between informal choruses and choirs.
Lititz Congregational Archives and Midway Congregational Archives.

Al Keller was janitor at that time and. . . he'd be pushing this thing in and out. When the choir didn't use it, well, then we had to push the piano out. Al said he was getting tired of doing that and we should either leave the piano in or out. So we left it in.

Shortly after the janitor settled the piano issue, the congregation in April 1951 approved installation of a pipe organ and the purchase of choir gowns. In less than 10 years, Lititz moved from an informal chorus that sang all *a cappella* songs to a robed choir singing anthems and cantatas, backed by a pipe organ. Before long, the congregation also sang with organ accompaniment.[54]

Condensed Love Feast

By the 1930s, congregations were accommodating the traditional two-day love feast to modern ways by shifting love feast to the weekend and eliminating some of the services.[55] The East Fairview congregation, for example, faced with fewer members who were self-employed

Table 10.1

Number of Atlantic Northeast District Congregations* Adding Worship Features by Decade

Innovation	pre-1930s	'30s-'40s	'50s-'60s	'70s-'80s	Uncertain	Total
Special Music	11	12	10	4	23	60
Piano in sanctuary	6	14	18	11	10	59
Organ in sanctuary	4	16	25	8	7	60
Paid organist	2	4	15	8	2	31
Acolyte	0	0	10	18	3	31
Choir	8	16	14	6	6	50
Choir robes	1	5	19	3	5	33
Bell choir	0	0	1	8	0	9
Bread and cup	0	1	9	29	4	43
Individual cups	5	11	21	7	18	62

*Out of a total of 66 congregations
Source: *Congregational Profile*

in agriculture, moved love feast from Tuesday and Wednesday to the weekend in 1936. Four years later they reduced the two-day event to one. The Elizabethtown church voted in November 1935 to "dispense with" the second day of the feast,[56] and, by the 1940s, churches were eliminating the afternoon self-examination service, as well. As the century progressed, most congregations would replace the traditional two-day event with a convenient evening service.[57]

Meanwhile, congregations began to shorten the love-feast service proper. Communicants traditionally had drunk communion juice from two "common cups," one passed among the brothers and another among the sisters. Many Brethren also ate the supper from common bowls, as they believed Jesus and the disciples did. Beginning in the 1910s, however, congregations began to shift toward individual communion cups and bowls, although at times years passed before such radical change was approved.

The issue was broached for the first time in the Elizabethtown congregation in 1918. After further discussion in 1925, 1926, 1934, and 1935, individual cups finally were approved in March 1936. Reasons for the change cited in Council Meeting minutes included a concern for "sanitation and cleanliness" and the fact that neighboring congregations already had made the change.[58] By the 1970s, most Brethren had shifted to individual cups and bowls. (See Table 10.1.) As congregations converted to individual communion cups, they also streamlined the bread-breaking process. Instead of passing strips of unleavened bread through the entire body, bread was placed on tables and broken in unison with partners across the table or seated next to each other. This new, more efficient method gradually became the norm in all but a few congregations. By the middle decades of the century, the process of speeding up the love feast was well underway.

Along with the abbreviated observance of the bread and cup, congregations began to eliminate the passing of the Holy Kiss. This greeting traditionally had been used twice during the love feast, once at the time of feetwashing, and again between the fellowship meal and communion. After some years of debate over this repetitive kissing, Annual Conference in 1913 permitted congregations to eliminate the second kiss "when it can be done in harmony." Eastern District churches gradually fell in line with the Conference action, although a few continued the second kiss into the 1990s.[59]

Preparation for a 1963 love feast in the Conestoga congregation. (Left) Elder S. Clyde Weaver (1901-1983) fills individual communion cups, while (right) deaconness Lizzie Buckwalter cuts the unleavened communion bread. Conestoga Congregational Archives.

From Meetinghouse to Church Plant

Meanwhile, Brethren meetinghouses continued to evolve along with worship practices. Although most congregations made incremental changes, reflecting a gradually evolving identity, the Spring Creek congregation underwent a radical transformation "virtually overnight," thanks in part to Milton S. Hershey. In 1935, the chocolate magnate gave each Protestant church in the town of Hershey a substantial gift for "general improvement of the church." The Brethren used some of the money to construct a parsonage for their recently hired pastor and the rest to remodel the meetinghouse. The writer of Spring Creek's congregational history described the new building after the 1936 renovation:

> There was a single entrance into the sanctuary from the rear. Many men and women still sat on separate sides, but it was the beginning of breaking away from

this custom. Upon entering the sanctuary (heretofore called an auditorium) the worshipper's eyes caught a beautiful and inspirational stained glass window of Christ praying. There was carpet on the floor, much quieter than hardwood. There were curtains on the windows. Now, instead of a speakers table seven inches high, there was a pulpit a few feet above the main floor, from which a pastor spoke . . . The church had taken a step, and a giant one at that, toward becoming "mainline."[60]

The building's most mainline feature was a stained glass window, framed by a divided chancel, with the pulpit moved to one side and a lectern added on the other. While such a layout was common in Presbyterian churches, a divided chancel was unprecedented in Eastern District. Convinced that the Hershey Brethren had abandoned the faith, at least one deacon left for a more traditional congregation down the road.[61]

Four years after Spring Creek built its stately "church," the Lebanon congregation in 1940 dedicated an impressive stone building of its own, with arched windows and a tower that compared favorably to other Protestant churches in the city. Carl W. Zeigler, who pastored the Lebanon congregation from 1940 to 1959, recalled:

> There was a strong push when the new church was built [that] we don't want to be different . . . We want to be recognized, we want to be accepted; we don't want to be like the little Dunkard Church down here on South Ninth Street . . . They wanted to say with the building that we're just [like everybody else]. They didn't use the term—we're not "sectarian," but this was really the base of it.[62]

Although Brethren buildings and worship had evolved significantly prior to 1950, especially in urban and small-town congregations, the mainstreaming process reached its zenith during the 1950s and 1960s, precisely the period when Brethren ecumenical interest was peaking.[63] Following the lead of Hershey and Lebanon, one congregation after another renovated or replaced Dunker meetinghouses with mainstream Protestant "churches," some with divided chancels and prominent steeples.[64]

A 1951 Annual Conference query, observing "considerable confusion" surrounding worship practices and chancel arrangements, requested a study to "define the function of the minister in worship in the light of the New Testament doctrine of the priesthood of believers" and "recommend appropriate chancel arrangements and church architecture." Conference appointed a three-member committee, which included Elizabethtown pastor Nevin Zuck. Citing the many changes that had taken place in Brethren worship, the committee's 1952 report concluded:

> The church can scarcely be said to have had a "historic position" on the matter of form and arrangements in worship except that of making changes from time to time . . . when it was felt that such changes would better serve the church . . .

Symbols of mainstream identity in the Palmyra congregation in 1959:
Divided chancel, an altar with cross and candles, and robed choirs.
Palmyra Congregational Archives.

The report observed that there were good reasons to favor a divided chancel and a central pulpit, and both were appropriate for Brethren, so long as they have a "sound doctrinal and practical basis." Rationale in favor of a central pulpit included: 1) it had been the prevailing pattern in the church; 2) it emphasized the spoken Word; 3) it tended to promote informality; and 4) it was more economical since no lectern or altar were needed.

On the other hand, the report said, some preferred the divided chancel because: 1) the altar in the center emphasized worship of God instead of just the spoken Word; 2) moving the barrier of pulpit and preacher to the side suggested direct access to God; 3) it provided greater variety in worship without moving furniture; 4) it is more convenient for weddings, funerals, dedications, and baptisms; 5) "it enhances the proportions of the sanctuary by giving it greater length;" and 6) "it allows for better use of symbolism in architectural design."[65] Of course, the committee's assertion that Brethren theology was neutral on chancel arrangements was dubious. A divided chancel required an altar to visually fill the space between pulpit and lectern. While altars suited mainline architectural understandings,[66] they were utterly foreign to the Brethren. God was present in the gathered congregation, Brethren believed, and not in the chancel of a church.

By the 1950s, however, they were losing sight of this distinction. Contributing to the confusion were non-Brethren architects who were designing new buildings. An informant remembers how the architect promoted the divided chancel in Richland's new sanctuary in 1961:

> We discussed it, and theological implications are such that the divided pulpit of course emphasized the altar more than what it should.
>
> Q: What do you mean, "More than what it should?"
>
> Well, more than what we did still . . . The architect was there and said that's what we're doing.[67]

The new Richland church also included stained glass windows, a steeple, and an indoor baptismal pool, all symbols of solidarity with mainline Christianity.

The Elizabethtown and Mountville congregations turned to a Lutheran architect to design new churches in 1956 and 1962, respectively.[68] Predictably, both featured prominent steeples and divided chancels. Nevin Zuck, who pastored the Elizabethtown church during the building project, explains:

> I think many of us said, Let us build a more formal chancel in which we can hold meaningful worship, preserve reverence, and yet have it usable for choirs, for plays, for weddings . . . Now we overdid it in Elizabethtown, I'll be the first to admit it, but we didn't know quite how to handle it. And therefore, I think, it was partly the architectural leadership we had plus the feeling that we ought to be a little more ordered in our worship . . .[69]

Even *Brethren* architects tended to follow mainline models. During the 1950s and 1960s, Arthur L. Dean served as building coun-

selor for the Church of the Brethren. Dean's resume included a
stint with the U.S. government during World War II and membership in the National Council of Churches' Department of Church
Building and Architecture.[70] Dean articulated his architectural per-
spective in an article titled "Pointing the Way" on a bulletin cover
used by Brethren during the 1950s:

> For generations our church spires have dotted the
> countryside, "pointing the way," as depicted on the bulletin
> cover . . . Church architecture today should suggest more
> than the church as a retreat from a busy world . . . Our
> buildings should suggest advance and not retreat; work,
> not idleness, and victory instead of defeat. They should be
> friendly, not austere and foreboding. We should work with
> people, not dominate them. Our buildings can be silent
> witnesses with loud voices proclaiming the never-dying love
> of an everlasting God.[71]

Dean's comments showed little appreciation for "austere" meetinghouses that suggest "retreat from a busy world." And his assertion that "our church spires" had dotted the countryside for
generations would have seemed ludicrous to most Brethren.[72]

Distressed by mainline trends, Arthur Gish, Isaac Clarence
Kulp, and John L. Ruth—three self-described "spiritual descendants of Anabaptists seeking to recover New Testament Community"—in 1973 called a meeting of like-minded souls. The invitation
included a biting critique of denominational leaders and trends in
church architecture:

> The profound and serious message of our Apostolic-
> Anabaptist Tradition is being dismissed by spokesmen
> eager to lead us to "relevance" and "Protestant" conform-
> ity . . . We have more important advances to make than
> to set steeples on our meetinghouses and chancels inside
> them, under the leadership of those who see bondage
> rather than Christ in our heritage.[73]

A former pastor in the Elizabethtown and Harrisburg First congregations during the 1950s and 1960s argued:

If we really had found out who we were we probably would have been building churches in the round, which celebrated our community of believers concept, rather than long, narrow churches with the preacher far away and high and lifted up. But I saw this so often in the 20 years I was in the district, that we built these beautiful structures, many times without realizing what we were doing. And I think part of it was—I wouldn't say self-hatred—but we were ashamed that we somehow weren't with it yet . . . And so they would go from a plain meetinghouse to suddenly something that was almost Lutheran in the way it was built.[74]

Of course, proponents of mainline buildings could list a number of practical reasons for building as they did. Steeples improved visibility and clearly identified the building as a church. As noted above, divided chancels were more flexible. Further, meetinghouses usually had inadequate space for organs, pianos, and choirs. Most of the new buildings in the 1950s and 1960s also included Christian education wings and ample office space for growing salaried staffs. In fact, these

Table 10.2

Number of Atlantic Northeast District Congregations*
Adding Building Features by Decade

Innovation	pre-1930s	'30s-'40s	'50s-'60s	'70s-'80s	Uncertain	Total
Stained glass	4	5	7	1	0	17
Steeple or tower	1	1	16	9	0	27
Parsonage	6	10	13	7	0	36
Church office	1	3	22	22	7	55
Padded pews	1	0	5	22	3	31
Divided chancel	1	2	12	6	0	21
Indoor baptistery	9	11	20	7	4	51
Pew Bibles	0	3	12	17	13	45
Gymnasium	0	0	2	10	0	12

*Out of a total of 66 congregations
Source: *Congregational Profile*

new buildings gave birth to a new term for the church building—"church plant."

In a 1964 report, Lititz pastor Olden Mitchell boasted that "our denominational church building counselor has described our building as possibly the most adequate total *church plant* in the Brotherhood." More than 50 churches had sent representatives of their building committees to admire the sprawling Lititz church.[75]

Another common feature of the new churches of the 1950s and 1960s was an indoor baptistery. Some urban and small-town churches, in fact, had added baptisteries well before then, but seldom without controversy. When aging elder J. H. Longenecker learned in the mid-1930s that a baptistery was being slipped surreptitiously into the Palmyra church, he dashed off a letter of caution to elder Frank Carper:

> Since pools in churches have been a debatable question through the years, and since there is still a question mark placed over it by many good and honest people. . . I am wondering in all seriousness why this question was handled so quietly, if not stealthily, so that neither the church nor even the church board was apprized [*sic*] of it . . .
>
> If the report goes out, as it will, that the Palmyra church has placed a pool in its house of worship I for one would have to say it was done by individuals, without the knowledge of the church.[76]

Despite such cautions, the Palmyra baptistery was there to stay. By the 1960s, indoor baptisteries were common in eastern Pennsylvania, as shown in Table 10.2.

Mastering the Art of Worship

Not surprisingly, as Brethren erected mainstream buildings with formal sanctuaries, their worship evolved accordingly. New "churches," built to reflect an emerging mainline identity, in turn shaped and molded Brethren theology and practice. The writer of a 1958 journal article observed:

From meetinghouse to church plant. Three buildings of the Lititz Church of the Brethren depict changes in Brethren architecture and identity: (Top) The 1887 meetinghouse on Willow Street; (bottom) a "churchhouse" constructed in 1926 on Center Street; and (right) the 1962 "church plant" on Orange Street. Lititz Congregational Archives.

. . . great changes are appearing in our church architecture. The plain structure is rapidly giving way to the
elaborate temple-like pattern, with steeple or tower, chancel, choir loft, and stately pews. The thought-provoking
congregational hymn singing is being replaced with classical
music rendered by robed choirs, directed by trained and (in
some places) paid directors, accompanied by expensive
pianos or electronic or pipe organs. We are rapidly moving
away from the free, simple worship to the elaborate liturgical
type. It is not uncommon to see the divided chancel and an
altar with lighted candles, and in a few places the plain
minister of the gospel has turned out to be a robed priest
conducting the service with pomp and dignity.[77]

Seminary-trained pastors were key proponents of more formal
worship, but an increasingly educated laity willingly collaborated.

Free minister James F. Myer argues:

> A lot of this [formal worship] was brought on by people who had been way up in those Yale and Harvard places, and they learned how to do it. And they came back and instructed our leaders how to do it . . .

> So they are . . . getting their education from outside sources and then they come and teach the Brethren pastors. And then those people come down to the congregations and they say, "Now here's what Tillich and so on and everybody says about these texts and how we ought to have worship."[78]

By the middle decades of the century, pastors followed a lectionary instead of rotation chapters, planned worship weeks or months in advance, and carefully coordinated sermons with choir anthems and worship centers. Churches paid increasing attention to the liturgical calendar, with a few dutifully displaying the proper colors for each season. Beginning in the mid-1950s, robed acolytes processed and recessed in many congregations, carrying the Christlight to and from the altar.

Formal choir gowns were further evidence of the Brethren move into the mainstream. Replacing plain dress of years past was more formal, less peculiar Protestant garb. To direct their choirs and play their pipe organs Brethren paid professionally trained musicians. (See Table 10.1.) While the early Brethren were concerned mostly with the quality of life fostered by their *a cappella* singing, by the 1960s, they were giving more consideration to the quality of the music itself.

As congregations adopted mainstream worship practices, traditional ones faded. A rite of humility such as kneeling for prayer made sense for plain-dressed Dunkers, but it was more "suitable" for mainstream Brethren, some dressed smartly in Sunday finery, to remain comfortably seated. By the 1950s and 1960s, the majority of eastern Pennsylvania congregations had given up kneeling, some nudged in that direction by newly hired pastors.[79] Replacing traditional patterns and postures of prayer were carefully crafted written prayers, litanies, and responsive readings.

Revival meetings were still another traditional practice facing decline. A 1954 Eastern District survey found that every congregation held at least one week of revival meetings per year, and that 75 percent of baptisms followed on the heels of revivals.[80] But by then a number of churches had instituted standard membership classes for children or youth. Similar to catechism in other churches, such classes contributed to the diminishing role of revival meetings, providing an alternative, more rational way of gaining church members. As membership classes came into vogue and the church competed with other social institutions for members' time, many congregations shortened or discontinued their revival services during the 1950s and beyond.[81]

The Love Feast Meal: "Let It Be Something!"

By mid-century, the process of abbreviating the love feast was accelerating. Many congregations already had reduced a two-day event to an evening service, and most had shortened the love feast itself by using individual communion cups and breaking bread in pairs. With the eucharist pared down to a few minutes, some congregations skimped on the traditional "fellowship meal" of meat and sop.[82] In his 1943 history of Philadelphia First church, Roland Howe lamented:

> I regret to record the fact that our Philadelphia church serves nothing more than unbuttered rolls, bits of diced cheese, and water . . . The menu would doubtless embarrass many devout elderly brethren and sisters, and others not so devout and elderly, who are accustomed to a "full supper" . . .

Howe went on to argue that the level of fellowship at love feast couldn't be expected to "rise above the quantity and quality of [the] meal." Rebutting those who defended the abbreviated meal, he concluded, "True, 'it is not what we eat'; that is clear, but for the sake of consistency, let it be something!"[83]

A number of other congregations followed Philadelphia First's lead during the 1950s and 1960s, serving sandwiches on styrofoam plates or cheese and crackers and fruit for the "fellowship meal." While Brethren meetinghouses were built to accommodate love feast, many of the buildings constructed after World War II were not. The 1962 Lititz church plant, for example, described as one of the most "adequate" in the denomination, amazingly had no place where the entire congregation could gather around tables for the traditional love feast.

Lititz's first meetinghouse, a "love feast house," had included benches that converted to tables, and their second churchhouse included shelf-like tables that were added to the backs of benches. The new building, however, had mainstream Protestant pews and a fellowship hall too small to accommodate the entire congregation. As a result, Lititz adapted their age-old love feast to fit their new building, first holding it in two shifts in the fellowship hall, and later serving cheese and crackers in the sanctuary. The problem was corrected in 1969 with the addition of a large gymnasium/fellowship hall provided for in the original plans.[84]

Love feast in Protestant-style sanctuaries also necessitated going to other rooms for feetwashing. Those who were squeamish about this embarrassing sectarian rite could remain seated in the sanctuary while others washed feet. By the 1960s, the love feast in

Deaconesses in the Middle Creek congregation prepare the traditional meal for a 1980 love feast. A few congregations abbreviated the fellowship meal during the mid-1900s, and more than two-thirds supplement the traditional love feast with periodic observance of the Eucharist alone. Middle Creek Congregational Archives.

many congregations had shrunk from two days to little more than an hour. A few congregations had gone to an abbreviated meal and essentially made feetwashing optional.

Protestant Communion

Despite the many changes taking place in love feasts, Brethren had maintained a strong consensus during the first half of the century against Sunday morning "pew communion," that did not include the other components of the love feast. Prior to the 1950s, anything less than the full love feast was considered unbiblical, un-Brethren, and unthinkable.[85]

Eastern District broached the issue for the first time at the 1955 District Conference, when Elizabethtown College trustees reported that they had approved a bread and cup communion at students' request. The report said in part:

> . . . since the college does not ask Church of the Brethren affiliation for admission; and in recognition of the fact that the college cannot rightly function as a congregation in which the observance of the church ordinances is regulated. . . therefore the board granted permission for a service in which the bread and the cup are carefully administered by the college administration . . .[86]

By the mid-1950s, with the Church of the Brethren drinking ever deeper from the ecumenical mainstream, Brethren were growing hesitant to insist dogmatically upon traditional practices. Recognizing that much of Protestantism observed just the Eucharist, Annual Conference in 1958 commended bread and cup communion.[87] Beginning in 1960, but especially in the 1970s and 1980s, congregations in eastern Pennsylvania acted on that commendation. By 1989, two-thirds of congregations supplemented love feast with additional bread and cup communions. (See Tables 10.1 and 10.3.)

Opponents of bread and cup communion argued that it would erode support for the love feast by providing an alternative for those who were uncomfortable with feetwashing or too busy to attend a special evening service. While other factors also came into play, bread and cup communion evidently was linked to such a decline. In the Lititz church, for example, love feast attendance peaked in

1962, the same year bread and cup communion was introduced. Love feast attendance began to slide in 1964—when bread and cup communion was stepped up to twice a year—and declined steadily after that. By 1988, average love feast attendance had decreased by 31 percent, and only a third of church members attended.[88]

From 1960 to 1989, average love feast attendance across the district plummeted from 228 to 123 per congregation.[89] While average congregational membership from 1960 to 1989 declined by 15 percent (314 to 266) and worship attendance dropped by 22 percent (211 to 165), love feast attendance plunged by 46 percent.[90] In 1960,

---

Table 10.3

Current Worship Practices in Atlantic Northeast District Congregations, by Percent*

Weekly benedictions	100%
Weekly offerings during worship**	98
Individual communion cups	94
Organs	91
Regular special music	91
Pianos	89
Adult choir	76
Worship planned a month or more in advance	70
Bread and cup communion	65
Children's or youth choir	64
Choir sings twice a month or more	62
Choir gowns	50
Revival once a year or more	50
Paid organist	47
Acolytes	47
Paid choir director	33
Sing *a cappella* once a month or more	21
Kneeling prayer weekly or usually	12
Separate seating for men and women	0

*Out of a total of 66 congregations
**The White Oak church takes offerings during worship on about 75% of the Sundays.
Source: *Congregational Profile*

more than two-thirds of the membership attended love feast (in earlier years the percentage surely was higher), but, by 1989, fewer than half the church members attended.[91]

Charismatic Controversies

By the 1970s, mainstream practices continued to filter into congregations, but stronger winds of change blew from a different direction. An experience in the Midway church, just outside Lebanon, in 1957 was a portent of things to come. Having attended Pentecostal tent meetings in the area, a minister and three deacons from Midway decided to share their ecstatic experience with the home congregation. One informant remembers:

> One Sunday morning they put on this thing after church. The men's choir was up there in the choir loft, and one of the men stood there like this, and he started speaking in tongues. And some of the younger women would lay on the bench and were speaking in tongues . . . Nobody knew anything about it. Nobody ever heard of speaking in tongues. It was so foreign. And they predicted that this was going to take over the whole Midway church . . .

> Well, that was awful. Our daughter, she would have been seven, and she was sitting up front, and she started crying.[92]

The charismatic Brethren soon began tent meetings in a field next to the church building.

Flabbergasted Midway leaders summoned district elders, who in November 1959 silenced the charismatic minister until reconciliation could take place. Noting his "insistence to follow his own interpretation of not only the Scriptures, but also on the matters of Church Administration," the elders in October 1960 reaffirmed their earlier decision, and a year later revoked his ministerial credentials. The minister and about 10 families left Midway to form a separate church.[93]

Midway's experience was an anomaly in 1957, but, by the 1960s, Protestants across the country were becoming familiar with charismatic gifts. On April 3, 1960, Episcopal pastor Dennis Bennett announced that he had received the baptism of the Holy Spirit and the gift of speaking in tongues. While adherents of Pentecostal groups—like the ones the Midway Brethren encountered—had exercised such gifts for decades, Bennett's experience marked the beginning of a new movement within mainline churches in North America.[94]

The charismatic movement soon was sweeping through Protestant and Catholic churches, including the Church of the Brethren. Pastor Russell Bixler, who was baptized in the spirit in 1967, established himself as the leading Brethren charismatic figure. From his home base in Pittsburgh, he traveled widely, helping ignite fires of Holy Spirit renewal and divisive controversy. By the early 1970s, the movement simultaneously was causing elation and alarm.[95]

In response, Standing Committee presented a statement of guidance to the 1972 Annual Conference, which was reprinted in the Atlantic Northeast District newsletter. It said, in part:

> While some members welcome [the charismatic movement] as meeting spiritual needs, others have concerns and even apprehension about actions which are considered "harmful" and "detrimental" to the unity of local churches.

> We urge our churches to review the experience of the church at Corinth in 1 Corinthians 12, 13, 14 where Paul gives instructions concerning the Charismatic gifts and how they need to be administered. It is no accident that 1 Corinthians 13 is in the middle of this discourse . . .[96]

Despite such counsel, differing views of charismatic gifts contributed to several splits in eastern Pennsylvania congregations. The district intervened in the divided Jennersville church in the mid-1970s and dismissed a charismatic pastor. He started a new congregation, and up to 80 members left—more than half the membership—crippling the southwestern Chester County congregation for years to come.[97]

About the same time, the Hatfield church lost several dissatisfied charismatic families, and similar concerns arose in the Mohrsville and Conewago churches.[98] Alarmed Brethren pastors in the Har-

Table 10.4
Current Building Features in Atlantic
Northeast District Congregations, by Percent*

Indoor baptistery **	77%
Parsonage	55
Padded pews	47
Steeple or tower	41
Divided chancel	32
Stained glass	26
Air conditioning	21
Gym/fellowship hall	18
Preachers' table	0

*Out of a total of 66 congregations
**Some congregations without indoor baptisteries of their own baptize in other church's facilities. Few baptize outdoors.
Source: *Congregational Profile*

risburg area in 1978 asked the district Ministry Commission to speak out against the Farr Family, a charismatic group that was leading worship in Brethren churches. The Commission instead told the pastors that "Brethren are inclusive enough" to permit a charismatic group to express themselves.[99]

Despite such claims of inclusiveness, divisions continued. After more than a decade of struggle, over two dozen members left the Middle Creek congregation to join charismatic Dove Christian Fellowship in 1984.[100] The Lititz and Mount Zion Road congregations suffered significant membership losses in 1985 after years of struggle,[101] and a number of other congregations lost smaller numbers of members to charismatic churches.

Typically, controversies centered on the style of music and worship and on leadership. Charismatics sought informal, Spirit-directed worship, often preferring modern praise choruses over traditional hymns. At times, when pastors failed to provide such worship, proponents of change questioned their spirituality. By the 1990s, not one congregation had successfully changed from a traditional to a charismatic worship style.[102] The growing acceptance of "praise choruses" during the 1970s and 1980s was perhaps the movement's only visible influence, as some Brethren supplemented hymnals with modern chorus booklets or projected lyrics on the sanctuary wall.[103]

Brethren Buildings and Worship Today

While the 20th century transformation of Brethren meeting-houses and worship styles is evident in every congregation, the extent of that transformation varied widely, as shown in Tables 10.3 and 10.4. Worship practices once considered worldly—weekly offerings and benedictions, instrumental and special music, and individual communion cups—became nearly universal. At the same time, some traditional practices—outdoor stream baptism, kneeling for prayer, and a *cappella* singing—once rigorously defended on scriptural grounds, were the exception to the rule.

Congregations were more selective when it came to some mainstream methods. Acolytes, gowned choirs, paid organists, and bread and cup communion were accepted by some, but resisted by others. Similarly, some traditional meetinghouse features—preachers tables

---

Table 10.5

Architectural Style by Ecumenical Attitudes, by Percent*

Attitude Toward Affiliation with the NCC and WCC

	Favor	Neutral	Oppose
Divided chancel	71% (10)	33% (11)	0% (0)
Central pulpit	29 (4)	67 (22)	100 (17)
Total	100% (14)	100% (33)	100% (17)

*Out of a total of 64 congregations. Two congregations did not respond.
Source: *Congregational Profile*

The Little Swatara congregation's Merkey meetinghouse (top), built in 1848 near Bethel, depicts a different identity than does the present Little Swatara church (bottom), completed in 1964. Sandra Kauffman Collection.

and squarish auditoriums—almost universally were replaced by pulpits and Protestant sanctuaries, but only a minority of churches erected steeples and divided their chancels.[104]

The most radical exchange of traditional Brethren practices for mainline ones took place in churches who were open to ecumenical cooperation. A divided chancel is a key symbol of mainstream identity, while a congregation's attitude toward the National and World Councils of Churches reveals general views toward cooperating with other denominations. Table 10.5 shows a striking relationship between attitudes toward ecumenicity and architectural features. Of 14 congregations who generally favor affiliation with the NCC and WCC, 71 percent have divided chancels. None of the 17 congregations who oppose such involvements have divided their chancels. Conversely, not one of the churches with divided chancels opposes ecumenical cooperation.

In short, those most favorably disposed to ecumenical cooperation were most likely to emulate mainline architecture. Those who opposed ecumenicity rejected the most radical departures from traditional Brethren practices.

"The Holiness of Beauty"

By the 1990s, most Brethren had embraced many of the same worship practices that they intentionally had rejected in earlier years. Instead of gathering *as the church* in plain meetinghouses, Brethren *went to church*, where they worshipped much like other Christians. An evolving self-understanding, a trained ministry, and ecumenical cooperation all played a part in the transition from peculiar to Protestant worship.

Unconcerned with ecclesiastical aesthetics, Brethren of old knelt on hardwood floors in austere meetinghouses, sang unaccompanied hymns to traditional tunes, and listened to exhortation from untrained elders. Today, the quality of the choir, the professionalism of the pastor, and the stylishness of the sanctuary all are thought to contribute to a "meaningful worship experience." A people who once worshipped in the "beauty of holiness" increasingly have sought the "holiness of beauty," as well.

11.

A Kaleidoscope of Congregations

The Brethren of eastern Pennsylvania have undergone a sweeping transformation during the 20th century. A church that once placed a premium on peculiarity gradually has embraced many of the beliefs, practices, and cultural traits of mainstream Protestant churches. Yet, the extent of that transformation varies widely from congregation to congregation. While some Brethren fully immersed themselves in mainstream currents and others drifted along, a few carefully navigated the eddies of traditional Brethrenism. In fact, the following true tale of two churches illustrates one of the most striking features of Brethren today—a wide diversity of thought and practice.

A Tale of Two Churches

The White Oak and Lancaster congregations are located less than 20 miles apart, but in many ways the distance that separates them is far greater. They share common roots in the Conestoga church, Lancaster County's first congregation, yet today White Oak and Lancaster live in starkly contrasting cultural worlds. Although both are progeny of the same mother church and both call themselves Brethren, today it is difficult to detect much family resemblance.

Formed in the city of Lancaster in 1891 with 50 members from the West Conestoga congregation (which had divided from Conestoga some years earlier), the Lancaster church from its beginning was open to new methods and ideas. Rather than call free ministers, Lancaster hired a part-time pastor, and in 1901 was the first Lancaster County congregation to employ a full-time pastor. The

Lancaster Brethren met in buildings bought from other denominations until 1897, when they built a new "churchhouse" on Charlotte Street. Although the building was simple in design and decor, the interior layout was more Protestant than peculiar.

During the 1920s, the Lancaster Brethren accepted special music, formed a choir, and built an outdoor baptistery on the lawn next to the church building. By the 1940s, the congregation clearly was moving toward the mainstream. In 1943, Lancaster Brethren remodeled their sanctuary, adding a choir loft and organ to the piano that had been placed there during the 1930s. Choir robes were purchased in 1944. During World War II, an American flag was placed in the sanctuary and the names of soldiers from the congregation were placed on an honor roll. When the Lancaster County Council of Churches was formed in 1946, the Lancaster Brethren were among the first to join.

Many of the mainstream tendencies of the 1940s and early 1950s became more pronounced during the late 1950s. The congregation opened its communion to all believers in 1955, replaced the Official Board with a lay-led Church Board in 1957, and a short time later decided to accept transferring members on their former bap-

Pastor Tobias F. Imler (1851-1917) and the Lancaster Young Ladies Sunday school class, 1902. BHLA, *Brethren Encyclopedia* Collection.

The Lancaster Church of the Brethren, built in 1959. Lancaster Congregational Archives.

tisms—even those who had been baptized as infants. Beginning in 1957, deacons were elected for specific terms instead of for life, and the elder-in-charge position, renamed "moderator," was opened to the laity.

In 1959, the Lancaster Brethren completed a colonial-style brick church in a suburban development, which featured a prominent steeple on the outside and a stylish sanctuary inside. A remote altar, in the center of a wide divided chancel, provided a focal point for worshippers, and an indoor baptistery replaced the outdoor pool next to the Charlotte Street building.

During the 1960s, the congregation added bread and cup communion, started a Scouting program, and became more active in community ministries and peace and justice concerns. Over the years, the Lancaster Brethren have combatted racism, provided low-income housing, carried out peace ministries, settled refugees, and supported a number of community service programs in the city of Lancaster, often in cooperation with the Lancaster County Council of Churches.[1]

Worship at Lancaster is decidedly mainline. A robed acolyte

carries the Christlight to the tapers on the altar. On any given Sunday, one of the congregation's robed adult or children's choirs, and sometimes one of several bell choirs, provides music. Salaried musicians direct the choirs, play the organ and other instruments, and provide leadership for the church's highly respected music program. Using *Hymnal: A Worship Book*, the newest Brethren/Mennonite hymnal, the congregation seldom sings *a cappella*.

Salaried staff plan worship themes and musical selections up to nine months in advance, and a detailed order of worship is printed each week with unison prayers, responsive readings, and titles of choir anthems. All told, the congregation employs two full-time and 10 part-time staff. When time comes for the sermon, a robed pastor—a doctor of ministry—takes his place in the prominent pulpit, where he is elevated a few feet above the congregation. Kneeling for prayer disappeared decades ago, along with prayer coverings for women.

Revival meetings at Lancaster were discontinued during the 1960s. Instead of responding to an invitation to accept Christ during a worship service, young people at a certain age are encouraged to attend a membership class—resembling catechism in mainline denominations—after which they can declare their intention to join the church and be baptized in the indoor baptistery.[2]

Corporate discipline no longer functions, and although nobody

Lancaster Brethren at worship in the 1990s. Lancaster Congregational Archives.

has been *asked* to leave the fellowship since 1960, some have *chosen* to go elsewhere. The Lancaster church grew dramatically during the middle decades of this century, peaking at 951 members in 1979. From there, membership plummeted, dipping below 600 in the early 1990s, before beginning to rebound. Despite ongoing efforts to remove inactive members from the roll, Sunday morning worship attendance in 1994 averaged half of total membership, and just over a third of members attend any given love feast. A few who do attend love feast refuse to wash feet.[3]

In short, the Lancaster congregation epitomizes the Brethren move toward the mainstream, providing a case study of significant social change. To be sure, the Lancaster Brethren perpetuate some Anabaptist themes, are conscious of their Brethren identity, and support Church of the Brethren institutions and programs. But symbols of accommodation to mainstream religion are more readily apparent than ties to traditional Brethren understandings.

White Oak, however, is a different story. More than any other congregation in the district, White Oak has staunchly resisted change. Modernity has had an impact there, but generally the strands of continuity with traditional Brethren thought and practice are more readily observable at White Oak than in other Brethren congregations.

White Oak divided from the Conestoga congregation in 1772 and originally comprised all of Lancaster County west of Lititz and Lancaster and part of southern Lebanon County. The congregation met in homes until 1859, when its first building, the Kreider meetinghouse south of Manheim, was constructed. By the 1880s, White Oak had ceded territory to the south and west to form the Chiques and Mountville congregations and the Lebanon County area to the Tulpehocken congregation, leaving White Oak's membership centered north and east of Manheim.[4]

White Oak differed little from other Lancaster County Brethren during the 19th century, but as changes swept across the denomination after 1900, White Oak dug in its heels. Sunday schools were almost universally accepted in eastern Pennsylvania by the turn of the century, but when White Oak started a Sunday school in 1902, it died quickly because of opposition in the congregation. Finally, in 1912, the White Oak Brethren accepted Sunday school.[5]

Frequently, the White Oak name has appeared in district and denominational minutes, protesting official actions that the congre-

The White Oak congregation's new building, built in 1981, is a modern expression of meetinghouse values. John Minnich Collection.

gation viewed as departures from the faith. An 1897 White Oak query asked Annual Conference to prohibit photography on Conference grounds, out of concern that Brethren were making graven images.[6] The congregation opposed the use of special music at District Conference in 1930 and ring ceremonies in Brethren weddings in 1944.[7]

In 1948, White Oak petitioned Annual Conference to discontinue affiliation with the Federal Council of Churches,[8] and, after the 1958 denominational decision to accept members from other churches without requiring rebaptism, White Oak petitioned Conference to at least require deacons and ministers to be baptized by trine immersion.[9] White Oak leaders have been closely linked with the Brethren Revival Fellowship, which has opposed many 20th century developments in the Church of the Brethren. Although White Oak has had little success in thwarting change in the denomination, its own congregational life has maintained remarkable continuity with traditional Brethrenism, despite some changes.

Perhaps the most visible change came in 1981, when White Oak completed an impressive new building on a hill outside of Manheim. Until then, the congregation rotated worship among three meetinghouses, one of the last two congregations in the district to worship in multiple places. Despite creature comforts, including padded pews and air conditioning, the new building is a recognizable attempt to express meetinghouse values. Although it is a quantum leap from White Oak's earlier buildings, the overall effect of the auditorium is plain, with no artwork, altar, or candles. Pews are arranged in a sloping semi-circle, expressing a commitment to the community of believers concept of the church. Ministers preach from a central pulpit located on a raised platform, but those seated in the rear of the auditorium are actually elevated above the ministers, which is reminiscent of raised side benches in traditional Brethren meetinghouses. The building has no steeple, stained glass, or divided chancel.[10]

As the plain-coated White Oak free ministers gather for worship on Sunday, they pause to greet one another with a holy kiss. Ministers and deacons and some laymen wear plain suits on Sundays and for church events, but wear no distinctive garb during the week. Neckties are discouraged, and the congregation has an unwritten expectation that guest ministers should not wear a necktie into the pulpit.[11]

Sisters are required to wear the prayer covering seven days a week, and all but a few comply. Although caped dresses are no longer common, sisters generally wear dresses, skirts, and culottes instead of shorts or slacks. Both men and women are encouraged to dress modestly and not wear jewelry. The congregation has lost a significant number of members to neighboring Brethren congregations who are less strict on the prayer covering and other issues.[12]

Sunday morning worship begins with several *a cappella* hymns—some shouted out as requests from the congregation— sung either from the 1901 *Brethren Hymnal* or a more recent nondenominational hymnal. Musical instruments are forbidden in worship, although, beginning in the 1980s, recorded music was allowed at

The White Oak congregation kneels for prayer in their plainly decorated auditorium during a 1995 worship service. John Minnich Collection.

church weddings, and special music was used occasionally. The 630-member congregation has no choir or chorus, no organ or piano.

The traditional worship pattern at White Oak varies little from week to week, with no printed order in the church bulletin. After the opening hymns, one of the congregation's eight ministers welcomes worshippers and leads a devotional period, ending with the first of two kneeling prayers. The ministers continue the long-held practice of preaching through the New Testament, one "rotation chapter" at a time. Leadership is provided by an Official Board composed of deacons and ministers called from within the congregation to serve for life. The congregation employs no salaried staff.[13]

Invitations to accept Christ are given several times a year during Sunday morning worship, and the congregation continues to hold semi-annual, 10-day-long revival meetings, during which the majority of new members express their desire to join the church. After receiving a home visit from two ministers, the applicant agrees to abide by church teachings and is baptized in an outdoor baptistery. Matthew 18 is read prior to baptism, and new members later receive additional instruction on the meaning of membership.[14]

Commitment to the church remains strong, as evidenced by average worship attendance of more than 90 percent of membership. Attendance at the two- to two-and-one-half-hour, semi-annual love feast averages more than two-thirds of membership.[15]

During love feast, communion bread is passed in strips, according to the traditional pattern, but individual communion cups replaced common cups in 1994, after a several-year debate centering on the health risks of common cups. To minimize the impact of this innovation on the length of the love feast, individual cups are passed through the congregation on trays, much like common cups were passed.[16]

The theme of self-examination is addressed the Sunday prior to love feast and also at a special self-examination service Saturday afternoon preceding the love feast. The two-day love feast concludes with Sunday worship, the second day meal having been discontinued some years ago because facilities cannot accommodate the entire congregation. The congregation does not observe bread and cup communion apart from the full love feast.[17]

Although the frequency of public confessions has decreased in recent years, White Oak continues to practice corporate discipline and public confession, mostly for sexual immorality. Traditional means of accountability—the annual deacon visit and close communion—remain in place, and trine immersion baptism is a membership requirement. Divorced and remarried people cannot join the church.[18]

White Oak, like Lancaster, has sponsored a number of refugees. In recent years the congregation has been increasingly active in evangelism and service ministries beyond its doors. During the 1980s, White Oak provided leadership and resources to plant two new churches in Lewiston and Brunswick, Maine, and provides volunteers for the Brethren Revival Fellowship's arm of Brethren Volunteer Service, which maintains strict standards of belief and conduct for its volunteers.

Of course, even White Oak is not immune to outside influences. Its central pulpit and revival services are adaptations from revivalism, a conservative mainstream influence of an earlier era. Although the congregation staunchly opposes the denomination's affiliation with the National and World Councils of Churches, White Oak supports several nondenominational ministries with volunteers and finances. One minister even holds an individual membership in the National Association of Evangelicals.[19]

Moreover, the congregation's evangelical hymnal not only includes favorite hymns about Christ's shed blood, but also nationalistic numbers that speak approvingly of the shedding of blood by Christian soldiers. And while White Oak avoids what it views as liberal theology in Brethren Sunday school curriculum, their more conservative materials from Union Gospel Press also are a significant outside influence.

Even so, White Oak has preserved many traditional Brethren understandings and practices. Were turn-of-the-century Dunkers to pay a visit to today's White Oak church, they likely would detect that they were among "Brethren." At Lancaster, they would strain to see strands of continuity with the church for which they labored.

Manifestations of Modern Brethrenism

As great as the gulf between White Oak and Lancaster is, a comparison of the two only begins to describe the breadth of diversity that has emerged among Atlantic Northeast District churches. To be sure, if one were to place White Oak and Lancaster on a continuum of social change, many more congregations would lean toward Lancaster than toward White Oak. (Elizabethtown, Lititz, Palmyra, Reading, and some others have followed a path similar to Lancaster's, and in some respects may be even more mainstream.) But other congregations simply would not fit on such a scale. Brethren evolution in this century has not been unidirectional, as a continuum would imply, but has proceeded in many directions at once, producing a colorful kaleidoscope of congregations.

Among the myriad manifestations of modern Brethrenism is the historic Germantown congregation, where membership peaked in 1934 with 463 members, before entering an eventually fatal decline. Prompted by a racially changing neighborhood, the mostly white congregation in 1964 disbanded and merged with Philadelphia First Church of the Brethren. Ronald and Ila Lutz in 1965 began operating community ministries—including a day care center—out of the Germantown building, but the congregation was dead.[20]

With district support, the Germantown congregation was resurrected during the 1980s, and today the 1770 "Mother Church" building not only houses a small heritage center, but also is home for an urban, mostly African-American congregation. In addition to the many pilgrims who visit the grave of Brethren founder Alexander Mack in the church cemetery each year, more than 80 worshippers gather each Sunday for two to three hours of spirited, contemporary worship in a remodeled sanctuary. In conjunction with other Brethren congregations and the district, Germantown provides counseling services to the community and actively ministers to homeless people.[21] The vibrant African-American congregation worshipping in the "Mother Church" today is indicative of the Brethren transformation.

The historic Philadelphia First church also has changed dramatically. Faced with a racial transition in the neighborhood at Carlisle and Dauphin streets, Philadelphia First relocated to the city's northern suburbs in 1957. In recent years, beset by leadership struggles, the congregation that once was a progressive trendsetter has dwindled to about 80 members, with worship attendance in the 50s.[22]

Pastor Richard Kyerematen with the Germantown church building in background. The African-American congregation worshipping in the "Mother Church" is indicative of the Brethren transformation. Messenger Collection, photo by Kenneth Bomberger.

Since 1990 Philadelphia First has shared its facilities with the Philadelphia Korean Fellowship of the Church of the Brethren, one of three Korean groups begun in the district during the early 1990s.[23]

In the city of Lancaster, the Hispanic Alpha and Omega church, planted in 1987, now worships in a building purchased from another denomination. The theologically evangelical congregation serves the Hispanic community with counseling services and on-going ministry to prisoners and their families.[24] Across town, the charismatic ACTS Covenant Fellowship gathers for weekly celebration in the Lancaster Recreation Center, having intentionally chosen not to purchase a building for worship. Worship includes periods of singing and silence to allow for prophetic words from God and the exercise of spiritual gifts. The more than 100 members gather during the week in cell groups, which are the heart of the congregation's structure and the setting where much of the pastoral care takes place.[25]

In northern Lancaster County, the East Cocalico congregation was born on Easter 1991, using an innovative telemarketing approach called "The Phone's for You." It has since grown to more than 80 members with worship attendance well over 100. With a strong commitment to evangelical theology, East Cocalico draws on insights from the church growth movement to reach out to "baby boomers" in one of the fastest growing townships in Lancaster County.[26]

A few miles away, the rural 210-member Mohler congregation has experienced rapid change during the 1980s. Formed in 1959 when the Springville congregation divided, Mohler evolved slowly until the 1980s when a flurry of significant changes were accepted almost overnight. Within five years of hiring its first full-time pastor in 1983, the two-day love feast was reduced to an evening service, week-long revival meetings were discontinued, the congregation voted to accept believers baptism by means other than trine immersion, a Christmas Eve bread and cup communion service was added, a church secretary hired, and a steeple affixed to the meetinghouse.

During the 1980s, the number of women wearing prayer coverings at Mohler declined dramatically. Today, about a quarter of sisters wear the covering to worship services, which remain relatively simple, without acolytes, robes, or divided chancel. The congregation continues to require believers baptism and has practiced occasional corporate discipline in recent years.[27] Although changes have been recent and in quick succession, Mohler today is typical of many evangelically-oriented Brethren congregations that fall somewhere between White Oak and Lancaster on the continuum of social change.

In contrast, the Ridgeway Community church is decidedly mainline Protestant. Founded in 1961 in the eastern suburbs of Harrisburg, Ridgeway, from its beginning, intentionally incorporated the worship practices of the many denominations represented in its membership. More than 60 percent of its members were formerly part of other denominations. The congregation observes love feast once a year instead of the more typical two times. They observe bread and cup communion bi-monthly, practicing it in two different ways, including the pastor serving the elements to kneeling communicants in priestly fashion.

Acolytes, choir robes, and stained glass have been present since the congregation's beginning, and many traditional Brethren practices—prayer coverings, kneeling for prayer, corporate discipline—have not. The inclusive congregation is one of few in the district led by a female pastor and is recognized for its willingness to open its facilities to many community groups.[28]

Although the Geiger Memorial Church in Philadelphia shares some common practices with Ridgeway, including stained glass windows and frequent bread and cup communion (observed monthly at Geiger), the Fundamentalist Geiger Brethren have entered the mainstream from the other shore. Founded in 1907 as an offspring of Philadelphia First, Geiger is a mostly white congregation located in a mostly black neighborhood. Once a congregation of more than 300 members, Geiger's membership and attendance today hover around 45.

In contrast to the inclusive Ridgeway congregation, Geiger is adamantly opposed to women in ministry and affiliation with the National and World Councils of Churches. New members are required to accept a doctrinal statement. Consistent with this statement, the congregation's pastor of nearly 30 years, teaches that pacifism is not biblical. An American flag graces the sanctuary.

The congregation views affiliation with the Church of the Brethren as a voluntary association and has had little involvement with the district for many years. The Geiger Brethren did reinstate an annual love feast in 1986 after a 35-year lapse and, interestingly, nearly half of the women wear prayer coverings to Sunday morning worship. Nearly all wear coverings to love feast.[29]

These brief congregational vignettes offer a glimpse of the diversity among Atlantic Northeast District Brethren in the 1990s. German Baptist Brethren at the turn of the century sought—and to a large extent achieved—uniformity in faith and practice, but Brethren in the 1990s display much greater diversity in ethnicity, theology, and practice. That diversity is reflected even in the terms churches use to describe themselves. Asked to choose one or more of five labels to describe their congregations' "primary theological or religious orientation," pastors and lay leaders responding to the *Congregational Profile* provided a wide variety of answers.[30] (See Table 11.1.)

As one might expect of a denomination that from its beginning adopted an Anabaptist vision of the church, Anabaptist was the most frequently used label, selected by 65 percent of congregations (42). But only 18 percent said that Anabaptist was sufficient *by itself* to describe their orientation. Most who selected Anabaptist also added one or two other labels, and more than a third (23) of the congregations did not choose Anabaptist at all! Nearly half included Evangelical in their self-description, nearly a third Mainstream Protestant, and more than 15 percent Fundamentalist. Only one congregation selected Charismatic.

That 82 percent of congregations included labels other than Anabaptist in their self-descriptions is indicative of the Brethren move toward the mainstream. That Brethren variously describe themselves as Anabaptist, Fundamentalist, Evangelical, Mainstream, Charismatic, and many combinations of these terms attests to the breadth of diversity in the Church of the Brethren.

Interpreting Change: Two Churches Revisited

The differences among Atlantic Northeast District congregations did not appear overnight. Like a gorge gradually carved out of solid rock by a rushing stream, the chasm between White Oak and Lancaster was created over many decades. A second look at these two congregations reveals how mainstream currents cut more deeply into some congregations than others. Key factors include location, boundary markers, education, leadership, and ecumenical alliances.

Location. Although one of the meetinghouses used by White Oak until 1981 was located in the borough of Manheim, the congregation is decidedly rural. Today, nearly a quarter of the congregation's families continue to earn their living by farming—more than any other congregation in the district except one—and other White Oak members work in farm-related occupations. By contrast, the mean percentage of farmers per congregation across the churches of the district is less than four percent, and virtually zero percent in the Lancaster church.[31]

In its early days, Lancaster was a "city church," eager to minister in the city, but also open to urban influences. The immersion in urban, and more recently suburban, culture exposed Lancaster

Table 11.1

Primary Theological or Religious Orientation of Atlantic Northeast District Congregations

Anabaptist and Evangelical	26%	(17)
Anabaptist	18	(12)
Evangelical	15	(10)
Mainstream Protestant	14	(9)
Anabaptist and Mainstream Protestant	8	(5)
Fundamentalist/Anabaptist/ Mainstream Protestant	8	(5)
Fundamentalist	3	(2)
Fundamentalist/Evangelical/Anabaptist	3	(2)
Fundamentalist and Anabaptist	1.5	(1)
Fundamentalist and Evangelical	1.5	(1)
Charismatic	1.5	(1)
Total	100%	(65)

Source: *Congregational Profile*

and other city churches in the district to winds of change that blew more gently in the country. Nearly all the significant changes among Atlantic Northeast District Brethren took root in urban and small-town churches, before branching out into the countryside. As they explore urban mission fields in the 21st century, Brethren will find it increasingly difficult to maintain vestiges of a unique identity.

Boundary Markers. Lancaster was more open to outside influences in other ways as well. The congregation in its early years dressed plainly and practiced corporate discipline, but, after the early 1930s, when Annual Conference relaxed the grasp of districts over congregations, Lancaster gradually discarded symbols of separation. Plain dress and the prayer covering fell by the wayside; the congregation opened its communion to all believers and accepted members from other denominations without rebaptism. All of these adaptations made it easier for outsiders to join. Today, as many as 40 percent of Lancaster members trace their roots to other denominations, bringing with them an openness to various expressions of Christian faith.[32]

In contrast, White Oak's insistence upon plain dress— especially the prayer covering for sisters—corporate discipline, close communion, and trine immersion has tended to limit the number of members joining from other churches. As few as 10 percent of White Oak members hail from another denomination, and many of those came from Anabaptist groups with even stricter standards than White Oak.[33] Thus, even this "outside" influence tends to discourage rather than encourage change at White Oak.

While some Brethren balk at the notion of intentionally making it difficult for new people to join the church, White Oak and several other congregations have shown that it is possible to sustain strong membership figures along with strict standards. Maintaining clear boundaries between church and world not only helps to preserve identity, but may in some cases be more of a boon than a barrier to growth.

Education. Higher education is yet another important promoter of cultural change. College carries members away from the congregational culture. Students return with a variety of experiences, new modes of critical thinking, and an openness to fresh ideas. While an estimated five percent of White Oak members have completed a college education, in Lancaster the number swells to more than 30 percent. In the district as a whole the percentage of college-educated members per congregation ranges from near zero to more than 60 percent, with a mean of 18 percent.[34]As the level of education among Brethren rises, maintaining traditional beliefs and practices becomes increasingly difficult.

The educational level of congregational leaders is especially significant. While Lancaster is led by seminary-trained pastors—some of whom have achieved the highest degree in their field—White Oak is led by eight self-educated free ministers, none of whom has attended college or seminary. Rather than exporting its ministers to faraway seminaries to learn ideas that may be foreign to the congregation, White Oak ministers learn on the job with the help of a district-sponsored reading course. While even White Oak's ministers might admit some benefits of seminary education, such training also is a source of innovation, importing ideas from outside of the Brethren tradition. The 20th century transition toward seminary-trained professional pastors was a key factor that opened congregations to mainstream influences.

Leadership. An additional difference between White Oak and Lancaster, and among other churches of the district, is how leaders are chosen and how long they serve. During its first 100 years, the Lancaster church was served by approximately 20 pastors and associate pastors, most of whom were called from outside the congregation. Their length of service ranged from two years to more than 20 years.[35] Each new pastor brought his own interests and emphases, some of which found their way into congregational life. By the same token, Lancaster's decision during the late 1950s to call term deacons and lay leaders to a Church Board further accelerated social change by ensuring turnover of the board at least every six years.[36]

On the other hand, White Oak's practice of calling ministers and deacons to serve for life provides continuity as one generation of leaders gradually replaces the previous one. Conservative ministers and deacons set the tone for congregational life, and members continue to call leaders that they believe will hold the line against harmful changes.[37]White Oak's refusal to accept volunteers to the ministry further guards against progressive individuals who might promote changes in the congregation. Of course, congregations who choose leaders from their own ranks to serve for life not only are better able to resist undesirable change, but also may reject helpful innovations.

Ecumenical Alliances. A final distinction between White Oak and Lancaster is their differing postures toward other Christians. Having joined the Lancaster County Council of Churches as a founding member, Lancaster was in the vanguard of ecumenical cooperation. The congregation works closely with the Lancaster County Council of Churches and has supplied three LCCC presidents from its ranks.[38] While attitudes toward the Church of the Brethren's cooperation with the National and World Councils of Churches vary among Lancaster members, they generally are positive, and over the years some have been outspoken supporters of such liaisons.

In contrast, White Oak consistently has opposed such involvements at the denominational level and seldom has cooperated with

White Oak's pattern of calling free ministers from within the congregation slows the rate of change. Plain-coated ministers in the early 1980s: (From left, seated) Samuel M. Cassel, Graybill Hershey, Caleb A. Kreider, Milton L. Hershey, Rufus G. Fahnestock, (standing) James F. Myer, J. Mervin Keller, Luther R. Patches, and J. Marvin Shenk. John Minnich Collection.

other communions on the local level. In fact, as the Church of the Brethren has evolved further from its historic positions, White Oak has been selective even in its interaction with other Brethren. Necktie-wearing ministers, for instance, are not invited to preach in the White Oak pulpit. White Oak youth do not participate in district and denominational youth activities, and the congregation carefully designates its financial support of denominational programs. While Lancaster interacts freely with other denominations, White Oak stands apart not only from other denominations, but even from other Brethren. By cooperating only with Brethren who share a common conservative vision, White Oak shields itself from change.

Even Annual Conference has been a key outside influence among the churches of eastern Pennsylvania. At the turn of the century, conservative churches tended to scrupulously observe Annual Conference edicts, and progressives tended to be less loyal to some of the church's rulings. But as Annual Conference reinterpreted traditional understandings, conservative congregations increasingly found themselves at odds with the larger church. In short, churches that faithfully followed Annual Conference rulings often were carried further toward the mainstream—some willingly, some not. White Oak, and other congregations that have chosen to dissent from some of the larger church's official actions, have more effectively preserved traditional understandings.

All of these interlocking factors—location, boundary markers, education, leadership, ecumenical alliances—are tied to the unevenness of change in the churches of eastern Pennsylvania. As congregations negotiated their way into the modern era, a combination of influences rendered them more or less able, more or less willing, to preserve traditional beliefs and practices.

What Does It Mean to Be Brethren?

Like the proverbial blind men who each grasped a different part of an elephant and arrived at competing conceptions of what an elephant was, the way in which one defines today's Church of the Brethren depends largely on which Brethren one observes. Lancaster, White Oak, and the kaleidoscope of congregations that form the Atlantic Northeast District all call themselves Brethren, but they define the essentials of Brethrenism in dramatically different ways.

Many questions remain. Is such diversity to be celebrated or lamented? Have Brethren merely updated an ancient vision, retaining essential kernels of truth while offering the chaff to the winds of change? Or has the vision itself become blurred, even lost? Is the Brethren transformation a tale of liberation from narrow parochialism, or of capitulation to the world? Have Brethren heeded the guidance of the Holy Spirit, or been led astray by the spirit of the age?

Indeed, many 20th century changes were promoted as promptings of the Holy Spirit, as necessary steps for Brethren to be faithful to their divine calling. Plain dress, some argued, hindered evangelism. Traditional nonresistance, which focused on purity in the church but said little about world events, was lampooned as quietistic and irresponsible. Rebaptism requirements and close communion were said to be unbrotherly barriers. But has abandoning such positions really enhanced the Brethren witness?

When the old Brethren gathered for love feast, nonmembers came to observe the spectacle of a peculiar people washing feet. Today, when all Christians are welcome in most congregations,

Sisters husking corn at the Neffsville Brethren Home in 1952 evoke an earlier era of Brethren life. Have Brethren heeded the Holy Spirit's guidance or been led astray by the spirit of the age? Elizabethtown College Archives.

many *members* do not attend. Modern Brethren champion peace and reconciliation among nations, but is their testimony really greater than that of the old Brethren, who seldom divorced their spouses and almost universally refrained from military service? Were the Brethren of old who witnessed by their simple and set-apart lifestyle really less evangelistic than Brethren who eagerly implement the latest "church growth" techniques?

On the other hand, from their beginning Brethren sought to be open to the Holy Spirit, whom they believed would guide the gathered church to a deeper understanding of its New Testament creed. In their zeal to preserve the past, have traditional Brethren been blind to the Spirit's new light? Perhaps Brethren who perpetuate prayer coverings and patriarchal patterns of leadership have confused culturally-bound means and methods with eternal mandates. Are Brethren who continue strict membership requirements and corporate discipline promoting costly discipleship or elevating law over love?

Lurking behind these many unresolved questions is an even greater one: What does it mean to be Brethren? It seems likely that unless Brethren can come to agreement on this basic question of identity, they will be further fragmented by the fickle currents of mainstream culture. The future of the Church of the Brethren may well depend on its willingness to honestly evaluate the past and forge a unique identity that is both consistent with its New Testament heritage and relevant for a new century.

Appendix A

Congregational Profile

A 12-page *Congregational Profile,* designed by the author, was mailed to pastors or moderators of the 67 congregations and fellowships of Atlantic Northeast District in January 1989. The survey included about 175 questions concerning leadership, worship, music, facilities, administration, membership, heritage, and distinctive beliefs. Partial or complete responses were received from 66 of the 67 congregations, a return rate of nearly 100 percent.

Pastors and/or informed members of congregations provided data on present practices, along with dates of important historical changes. In cases where exact dates of specific changes could not be found, respondents were urged to provide educated estimates. These dates were used to trace general trends in the churches of the district. While not all dates provided by respondents are completely reliable, they nonetheless provide a general picture of the decades during which important changes took place.

The *Congregational Profile* was modeled after a similar instrument used by Donald B. Kraybill and Donald R. Fitzkee in a comparative study of Church of the Brethren, Lancaster Conference Mennonite, and Old Order Amish congregations in Lancaster County, in 1986. Results of that study can be found in Donald B. Kraybill and Donald R. Fitzkee, "Amish, Mennonites, and Brethren in the Modern Era," *Pennsylvania Mennonite Heritage* 10 (April 1987): 2-11.

Appendix B

Present and Former Congregations and Fellowships of Atlantic Northeast District and Forerunner Districts*

Present Congregations and Fellowships

Name of Congregation	Date Founded **	County	Membership as of 12/31/94 ****
ACTS Covenant	1987	Lancaster	158
Akron	1913	Lancaster (E)	184
Alpha and Omega	1987	Lancaster	60
Ambler (Upper Dublin)*****	1840	Montgomery (NA)	112
Amwell	1733	Hunterdon, NJ (NA)	124
Annville	1912	Lebanon (E)	358
Bethany	1910	Philadelphia (NA)	38
Big Swatara	ca. 1798		
Hanoverdale		Dauphin (E)	186
Paxton		Dauphin (E)	44
Blue Ball (Spring Grove)	1897	Lancaster (E)	151
Brooklyn First	1899	New York City (NA)	183
Brooklyn Korean*	1992	New York City	15
Brunswick*	1986	Cumberland, ME	25
Chiques	1868	Lancaster (E)	549
Cocalico	1959	Lancaster (E)	103
Conestoga	1724	Lancaster (E)	305
Conewago	1912	Dauphin (E)	203
Coventry	1724	Chester (NA)	318
Drexel Hill	1953	Delaware (NA)	123
East Cocalico	1991	Lancaster	110

The present Atlantic Northeast District territory was divided between two districts from 1911 to 1970. Letters in parentheses after the county indicate whether congregations belonged to Eastern District (E) or North Atlantic District (NA) during this time period.

Name of Congregation	Date Founded	County	Membership as of 12/31/94
East Fairview	1902	Lancaster (E)	416
Elizabethtown	1902	Lancaster (E)	587
Ephrata	1864	Lancaster (E)	743
Florin	1954	Lancaster (E)	351
Geiger Memorial	1906	Philadelphia (NA)	42
Germantown +	1723	Philadelphia (NA)	62
Green Tree	1845	Montgomery (NA)	253
Haitian First of New York***	1992	New York City	84
Harmonyville	1913	Chester (NA)	72
Harrisburg First	1896	Dauphin (E)	233
Hatfield	1864	Montgomery (E)	103
Heidelberg	1919	Lebanon (E)	150
Hempfield	1974	Lancaster	586
Indian Creek	1785	Montgomery (E)	260
Jennersville	1929	Chester (E)	48
Lampeter	1978	Lancaster	235
Lancaster	1891	Lancaster (E)	644
Lebanon	1933	Lebanon (E)	279
Lewiston	1982	Androcoggin, ME	49
Liberty Tabernacle***	1992	Philadelphia	12
Lititz	1914	Lancaster (E)	627
Little Swatara	ca. 1798	Berks (E)	405
Long Run	1932	Carbon (E)	44
Mechanic Grove	1897	Lancaster (E)	483
Middle Creek (W. Conestoga)	1864	Lancaster (E)	460
Midway	1902	Lebanon (E)	406
Mohler (Springville)	1899	Lancaster (E)	231
Mohrsville (Maiden Creek)	1866	Berks (E)	127
Mt. Wilson	1979	Lebanon (E)	125
Mt. Zion Road (Fredericksburg)	1919	Lebanon (E)	117
Mountville	1882	Lancaster (E)	251
Myerstown	1919	Lebanon (E)	335
Open Door (Sunlin)***	1991	New York City	51
Palmyra	1921	Lebanon (E)	646
Parker Ford	1898	Chester (NA)	135
Philadelphia First	1813	Montgomery (NA)	72
Philadelphia Korean***	1991	Montgomery	45
Pottstown	1918	Montgomery (NA)	128
Providence	1994	Montgomery	167
Puerta Del Cielo***	1991	Berks	29

Name of Congregation	Date Founded	County	Membership as of 12/31/94
Quakertown	1936	Bucks (NA)	108
Reading	1898	Berks (E)	345
Richland	1919	Lebanon (E)	111
Ridgeway Community	1962	Dauphin (E)	214
Schuylkill	1877	Schuylkill (E)	234
Skippack	1957	Montgomery (E)	58
Spring Creek (Hershey)	1868	Dauphin (E)	406
Springfield	1868	Bucks (E/NA)	105
Stevens Hill Community***	1990	Lancaster	46
Swatara Hill	1960	Dauphin (E)	60
West Green Tree	1902	Lancaster (E)	199
White Oak	1772	Lancaster (E)	627
Wilmington ++	1916	New Castle, DE (NA)	116

Former Congregations and Fellowships

Name of Congregation	Date Founded	County	Outcome
Allentown	1938	Lehigh (E)	Disorganized in 1964
Bethel	1876	Hunterdon, NJ	Merged with Sand Brook in 1896 to form Union
Brooklyn Calvary (Brooklyn Italian)	ca. 1922	New York City (NA)	Merged into Brooklyn First in 1968
Denton	1909	Caroline, MD	Transferred to Eastern District of Maryland ca. 1911
East Petersburg	1918	Lancaster (E)	Merged with Salunga in 1974 to form Hempfield
Freeville	ca. 1922	Tompkins, NY (E)	Disorganized in 1926
Great Swamp	ca. 1735	Bucks	Disorganized after 1770
Lake Ridge	1915	Cayuga, NY (E)	Disorganized in 1977
Mingo	1869	Montgomery (E)	Merged with Royersford in 1994 to form Providence
Montreal, Canada	1900		Transferred to The Brethren Church in 1902
Norristown	1901	Montgomery (E/NA)	Disorganized in 1973
Paoli Immanuel	1963	Chester (NA)	Disorganized in 1983
Peach Blossom	1881	Talbot, MD	Transferred in 1944 to Mardela District

Name of Congregation	Date Founded	County	Outcome
Peach Blossom **Colored Church of Rising Light**	1898	Talbot, MD (E)	Disorganized by 1938
Pequea Valley (Gap)	1984	Lancaster	Disorganized in 1990
Philadelphia Calvary	1923	Philadelphia (NA)	Withdrew from the Church of the Brethren in 1972
Ridgely	1884	Caroline, MD (E)	Transferred in 1944 to Mardela District
Royersford	1901	Montgomery (NA)	Merged with Mingo in 1994 to form Providence
Salunga	1948	Lancaster (E)	Merged with East Petersburg in 1974 to form Hempfield
Sand Brook +++	1849	Hunterdon, NJ	Merged with Bethel in 1896 to form Union Church
Shamokin (Tower City)	1889	Northumberland (E)	Disorganized in 1967
Stevens Hill ++++	1965	Lancaster (E)	Disorganized in 1990
Swatara	1772	Multiple	Divided into Big/Little Swatara ca. 1798
Templo El Aposento	1992	Lancaster	Disorganized in 1993
Tulpehocken	1841	Multiple (E)	Divided into Heidelberg, Myerstown, and Richland in 1919
Union Church	1896	Hunterdon, NJ (NA)	Merged into Amwell in 1912

*This is intended to be an exhaustive list of congregations located in the territory of the present Atlantic Northeast District, or that once were member congregations of Atlantic Northeast or its forerunner districts.

**"Date founded" for congregations begun during the 1970s and after refers to the year fellowship status was granted by the district.

***Indicates fellowship status. New bodies in the Church of the Brethren are recognized as fellowships until they are strong enough to become full-fledged congregations.

****Membership statistics are taken from the 1995 Atlantic Northeast District Directory.

*****A name in parentheses is an earlier name for the same congregation.

+The Germantown congregation was disbanded in 1964 and reorganized as a fellowship in 1985.

++Wilmington was granted "misson status" in 1916 and became a full-fledged congregation in 1926.

+++Sand Brook withdrew from the Church of the Brethren in 1849 and rejoined in 1880.

++++Stevens Hill was disorganized in August 1990. Stevens Hill Community, which meets in the same location, was recognized as a fellowship in October 1990.

Endnotes

Endnotes for Chapter 1

1. Donald R. Fitzkee, *The Transformation of the Lititz Church of the Brethren, 1914-1989* (Lancaster, Pa.: Lititz Church of the Brethren, 1990), 17-18.

2. Donald F. Durnbaugh, ed. , *Church of the Brethren Yesterday and Today* (Elgin, Ill.: Brethren Press, 1986), 4.

3. Ibid., 6-7. For a translation of the open letter see William R. Eberly, ed., *The Complete Writings of Alexander Mack* (Winona Lake, Ind.: BMH Books, 1991), 9-14. For more information on Mack and the beginning of the Brethren movement see William G. Willoughby, *The Life of Alexander Mack: Counting the Cost* (Elgin, Ill.: Brethren Press, 1979).

4. Durnbaugh, ed. (1986:4). See also Donald F. Durnbaugh, ed., *The Brethren Encyclopedia* (Philadelphia and Oak Brook, Ill.: The Brethren Encyclopedia, Inc., 1983), s. v. "Anabaptism," by Cornelius J. Dyck and "Radical German Pietism," by C. David Ensign.

5. Dale Rupert Stoffer, *The Background and Development of Thought and Practice in the German Baptist Brethren (Dunker) and the Brethren (Progressive) Churches* (Ann Arbor, Mich.: University Microfilms International, 1980), 212. See also Durnbaugh (1986:8-9). Stoffer's work was subsequently published in the Brethren Encyclopedia Monograph Series. See Dale R. Stoffer, *The Background and Development of Brethren Doctrines, 1650-1987* (Philadelphia and Oak Brook, Ill.: The Brethren Encyclopedia, Inc., 1989).

6. Durnbaugh (1986:11).

7. Morgan Edwards, *Materials Towards a History of the American Baptists* (Philadelphia: Crukshank and Collins, 1770), 68; quoted in Martin Grove Brumbaugh, *A History of the German Baptist Brethren in Europe and America*, 2nd ed. (Elgin, Ill.: Brethren Publishing House, 1907), 189.

8. For an excellent description of some of the early meetinghouses within the Atlantic Northeast District, see Nancy Kettering Frye, "The Meetinghouse Connection: Plain Living in the Gilded Age," *Pennsylvania Folklife* 41 (Winter 1991-92): 50-82.

9. Eastern District of Pennsylvania Historical Committee, *History of the Church of the Brethren of the Eastern District of Pennsylvania* (Lancaster, Pa.: Historical Committee, 1915), 328-329. Subsequently cited as *History of the Church. . .* (1915).

10. *History of the Church of the Brethren, Eastern Pennsylvania, 1915-1965* (Lancaster, Pa.: Eastern District of Pennyslvania, 1965): 59. Subsequently cited as *History of the Church. . .* (1965). See also A. G. Breidenstine, "The Growth of a Rural Church," *Gospel Messenger*, 5 November 1938, 13.

11. Durnbaugh (1986:13-14).

12. Carl Frederick Bowman, "Beyond Plainness: Cultural Transformation in the Church of the Brethren from 1850 to the Present" (Ph. D. diss., University of Virginia, 1989), 179. Much of Bowman's dissertation, along with new material, can be found in his recently released *Brethren Society: The Cultural Transformation of a "Peculiar People"* (Baltimore: Johns Hopkins University Press, 1995).

13. Durnbaugh (1986:13).

14. *History of the Church. . .* (1915:564). In early years Annual Conference was commonly known as "Annual Meeting" or the "Big Meeting." Annual Conference Minutes before 1917 use the "Annual Meeting" designation. For clarity's sake, "Annual Conference" is used consistently in the text.

15. Ibid., 565.

16. Stoffer (1980:329).

17. *History of the Church. . .* (1915:586-587).

18. Ibid., 587-588. The earlier terminology for "District Conference" was "District Meeting. " For clarity's sake, "District Conference" is used consistently in the text.

19. C. Bowman (1989:142).

20. *History of the Church. . .* (1915:123).

21. *Minutes of the Annual Meetings of the Church of the Brethren, Containing All Available Minutes from 1778 to 1909* (Elgin, Ill.: Brethren Publishing House, 1909), 341-342.

This compilation of minutes before 1910 uses continuous pagination. Annual Meeting and Annual Conference Minutes after 1909 have been bound in several volumes, without continuous pagination. Subsequent references to Annual Meeting decisions before 1910 will include the publication date (1909) and page. References to Annual Conference decisions after 1909 will give the year of the Conference and the page in the minutes.

22. *Annual Meeting Minutes* (1909:341-342). For a more detailed account of this confrontation between Annual Conference and Philadelphia First Church, see C. Bowman (1989:142-147).

23. Donald F. Durnbaugh, ed., *Meet the Brethren* (Elgin, Ill.: Brethren Press for the Brethren Encyclopedia, Inc., 1984), 23.

24. *Annual Meeting Minutes* (1909:67).

25. See Floyd E. Mallott, *Studies in Brethren History* (Elgin, Ill.: Brethren Publishing House, 1954), 221; and Durnbaugh, ed., 1983, s. v. "Sunday School Movement," by R. Jan Thompson and Donald F. Durnbaugh.

26. See Durnbaugh, ed., 1983, s. v. "Sunday School Movement," by R. Jan Thompson and Donald F. Durnbaugh; and *History of the Church. . .* (1915:119-120).

27. *Annual Meeting Minutes* (1909:163).

28. *Eastern District Meeting Minutes*, May 10-11, 1905. These minutes provide no page numbers for the years 1897-1910.

29. See Stoffer (1980:436); and Durnbaugh (1986:29).

30. *History of the Church. . .* (1915:442).

31. Elmer Q. Gleim, *From These Roots: A History of the North Atlantic District* (Lancaster, Pa.: Atlantic Northeast District Historical Committee, 1975), 263, 299.

32. See (1871:21) in *Minutes of District Meetings of the German Baptist Brethren of the Eastern District of Pennsylvania from 1867 to 1896*. The minutes from these years have been compiled in this single volume with continuous

pagination, but without a date of publication. Subsequent references are to *Eastern District Meeting Minutes*, with the year of the meeting and the page number.

33. *History of the Church. . .* (1915:593).

34. *Eastern District Meeting Minutes* (1885:67).

35. *History of the Church. . .* (1965:140). The Eastern Shore congregations became part of the Mardela District in 1944. See also *History of the Church. . .* (1915:596-599).

36. Durnbaugh (1984:23-24).

37. Durnbaugh (1986:25).

38. C. Bowman (1989:227).

39. *Eastern District Meeting Minutes* (1870:16).

40. Gleim (1975:96).

41. *History of the Church. . .* (1965:188).

42. *Eastern District Meeting Minutes* (1887:75; 1893:109; April 27-28, 1898).

43. Durnbaugh, ed., 1983, s. v. "Lancaster Old German Baptist Brethren Church, PA," by Charles M. Hackman. Some individuals did identify with the Old Orders—among them well-known Elder George Bucher, founder of the Mechanic Grove congregation, near Quarryville, Pa. The Lancaster Old German Baptist Brethren congregation, near Lincoln, was organized in Lancaster County in 1909.

44. Ibid., s. v. "Philadelphia, PA, First Brethren Church," by Roger L. Wambold and Donald F. Durnbaugh.

45. This discussion of the division of Eastern District closely follows C. Bowman (1989:450-454). See also Gleim (1975:18-28).

46. *History of the Church. . .* (1915:586-587).

47. *Eastern District Meeting Minutes* (1882:54).

48. Ibid., April 20-21, 1904.

49. Standing Committee delegates at this time were always chosen from among elders. Eastern District was entitled to two delegates each year.

50. *Eastern District Meeting Minutes*, April 28-29, 1909.

51. C. Bowman (1989:451). Italics in original.

52. *Eastern District Meeting Minutes*, April 13-14, 1910.

53. *Full Report of the Proceedings of the Annual Meeting of the Church of the Brethren held at Winona Lake, Ind., June 7-9, 1910* (Elgin, Ill.: Brethren Publishing House, 1910), 173. From 1876 to 1930 a complete transcript of Annual Conference proceedings was published each year. Subsequent references will be noted as *COB Full Report*.

54. Ibid., 173-178; and C. Bowman (1989: 452-453).

55. Ibid., 175-176.

56. *Special Eastern District Meeting Minutes*, September 21, 1910.

57. The district name was changed to "District of Southeastern Pennsylvania, New Jersey, Eastern New York and Northern Delaware" in 1936 to reflect the addition of the Wilmington church. In 1954 the name "North Atlantic District" was adopted. See Gleim (1975:28). Hereafter, the new district will be referred to as "Southeastern District" when the point of reference is prior to 1954 or "North Atlantic District" when after 1954.

58. *COB Full Report* (1911:51).

59. C. Bowman (1989:453-454).

60. *Eastern District Meeting Minutes* (1911:2).

61. The founding of these institutions is discussed briefly in Chapter Four.

62. Leona List interview. A list of interviews and the date they were conducted is located in the Bibliography. Unless otherwise noted, interviews were conducted by the author.

63. Caleb W. Bucher interview. Ironically, the Mingo and Royersford congregations merged on January 1, 1994, to form the Providence Church of the Brethren. See *Atlantic Northeast District Conference Minutes* (1993:5).

64. For a thorough discussion of modernism, see William R. Hutchison, *The Modernist Impulse in American Protestantism* (New York: Oxford University Press, 1976).

65. Winthrop S. Hudson, *Religion in America*, 4th ed. (New York: Macmillan Publishers, 1987), 262-265, 337-343. See also Gleim (1975:78).

66. See Earl C. Kaylor, Jr., *Truth Sets Free: A Centennial History of Juniata College, 1876-1976* (South Brunswick and New York: A. S. Barnes and Co., 1977), 187-190; Kaylor, *Out of the Wilderness: The Brethren and Two Centuries of Life in Central Pennsylvania (1780-1980)* (New York: Cornwall Books, 1981), 256-265; Durnbaugh, ed., 1983, s. v. "School of Theology, Juniata College," by Earl C. Kaylor, Jr.; and Herbert Hogan, "The Intellectual Impact of the 20th Century on the Church of the Brethren" (Ph. D. diss., Claremont Graduate School, 1958), 377-399.

67. *Southeastern District Meeting Minutes* (1922:6-7).

68. See Ministerial Questionnaire, attached to Eastern District Ministerial Board Minutes, 1933.

69. Joseph M. Long interview. Nevin H. Zuck also observed several plain-dressed elders whose theology was more liberal than their garb may have indicated. Nevin H. Zuck interview.

70. Caleb W. Bucher speaking about his father Rufus P. Bucher in an interview with Donald B. Kraybill and Carl F. Bowman.

71. W. Dean Crouse interview.

72. Durnbaugh, ed., 1983, s. v. "Fraternity of German Baptists" and "German Baptist Brethren," by Donald F. Durnbaugh.

73. *Annual Meeting Minutes* (1909:479).

74. Harrisburg First Council Meeting Minutes, April 25, 1905.

75. *Eastern District Meeting Minutes*, May 10-11, 1905.

76. C. Bowman (1989:390).

77. *Annual Meeting Minutes* (1909:873).

78. C. Bowman (1989:396).

79. *Yearbook of the Church of the Brethren* (Elgin, Ill.: Brethren Publishing House, 1931), 48. Subsequent references are cited as *COB Yearbook*.

80. *Congregational Profile*. For a description of the *Congregational Profile* see Appendix A. In 1990 the Big Swatara congregation officially consisted of Brethren at two meetinghouses—Hanoverdale and Paxton. While the two congregations maintain some ties, they essentially function as separate entities. The last two congregations to abandon the multiple meetinghouse model—White Oak and Blue Ball—did so in 1981 and 1982, respectively.

81. *COB Yearbook* (1969:90-91). Palmyra's membership peaked in 1,048 in 1974.

82. Ibid. (1944:60).

83. Ibid. (1969:146).

84. *Atlantic Northeast District Directory* (1991:65).

85. For an overview of membership trends and possible causes, see the 1981 Annual Conference report on "Diminishing Membership in the Church of the Brethren" in *Minutes of the Annual Conference, 1980-1984* (1985:214-234).

Endnotes for Chapter 2

1. Other important Scriptures often cited by Brethren to support nonconformity were 1 Timothy 2:9, 1 Peter 3:3, 1 Thessalonians 5:22, 1 John 2:15, and 2 Corinthians 6:14.

2. Roger E. Sappington, ed., *The Brethren in Industrial America: A Source Book on the Development of the Church of the Brethren, 1865-1910* (Elgin, Ill.: Brethren Press, 1985), 94.

3. J. H. Moore, "Querist's Department," *Gospel Messenger*, 19 February 1898, 121.

4. *Revised Minutes of the Annual Meetings of the German Baptist Brethren* (Elgin, Ill.: Brethren Publishing House, 1908), 123. This decision reaffirmed an 1866 decree. *Revised Minutes* arranges Annual Meeting minutes topically.

5. *Annual Meeting Minutes* (1909:670).

6. *Eastern District Elders Body Minutes*, May 2, 1900. District Elders bodies met annually, just prior to the District Conference. Among other tasks, the Standing Committee served as the church's judicial body and frequently appointed committees to deal with difficulties in churches. See Durnbaugh, ed., 1983, s. v. "Standing Committee," by Roger W. Eberly.

7. Gleim (1975:21), quoting a report to the Annual Meeting.

8. Council Meeting Minutes of the Lancaster, Chiques, and Mountville congregations, 1898-1902.

9. See Annual Meeting Statements of 1863, 1864, 1865 in *Revised Minutes* (1908:134-135).

10. See 1852 and 1857 statements in *Revised Minutes* (1908:167-168).

11. See 1891 and 1893 statements in *Revised Minutes* (1908:169).

12. See 1866 statement in *Revised Minutes* (1908:166).

13. Examples of all of the above can be found in the Chiques, Lancaster, and Mountville Council Meeting Minutes around 1900.

14. *A Synodical [sic] Report of the Proceedings of the Brethren's Second Ministerial Meeting, of Eastern Pennsylvania* (1895:8-9).

15. *Revised Minutes* (1908:153).

16. Chiques Council Meeting Minutes, January 24, 1898; and Lancaster Council Meeting Minutes, July 11, 1900.

17. Rufus P. Bucher to George Bucher, 17 January 1904, reporting on a sermon delivered by a guest preacher at Elizabethtown College, George Bucher file, High Library, Elizabethtown College.

18. Members of the Lancaster congregation became quite exercised over the baptism issue in 1901, when Mennonite A. S. Wenger asserted that pouring was the early Christian mode and offered to debate publicly the issue with the Brethren. Feeling the need to "stand in defence of the truth," the Lancaster Brethren agreed to host the event. Wenger, apparently due to disapproval from other Mennonites, bowed out and the debate never took place. Lancaster Council Meeting Minutes, July 10, 1901. See R. H. Miller, *The Doctrine of the Brethren Defended* (Elgin, Ill.: Brethren Publishing House, 1903), 45-150, for a lengthy defense of Brethren baptism practices.

19. See 1894 and 1887 actions in *Revised Minutes* (1908:21-24).

20. W. B. Stover, "Why the Brethren Hold to Strict Communion," *Gospel Messenger*, 9 July 1898, 428.

21. *Revised Minutes* (1908:88).

22. Lancaster Council Meeting Minutes, February 1, 1899.

23. Chiques Council Meeting Minutes, March 8, 1924.

24. Mountville Council Meeting Minutes, March 21, 1906.

25. Members of the Chiques congregation in 1878 were admonished not to extend the right hand of fellowship and kiss of charity to "worldlings" after services. Chiques Council Meeting Minutes, March 25, 1878.

26. Chiques Council Meeting Minutes, April 10, 1882, include this item: "Is it considered according to the Gospel and order of the Brethren to call such as were expelled and joined another church, brother or sister? Ans. Improper and ought not to be done. "

27. *Synodical [sic] Report of the. . . Second Ministerial Meeting* (1895:49).

28. H. B. Brumbaugh, *The Church Manual*, rev. ed. (Elgin, Ill.: The Brethren's Publishing Company, 1893), 18. Italics in original.

29. J. H. Longenecker diary, in Jacob H. Longenecker file, High Library, Elizabethtown College. C. Bowman (1989:842) duplicates the format of the diary page, including page numbers referencing appropriate Annual Conference minutes for each of the areas under nonconformity.

30. H. B. Brumbaugh (1893:18-19).

31. A March 27, 1901, Mountville Council Meeting handled 34 items of business, 17 of which dealt in some way with discipline.

32. Mountville Council Meeting Minutes, March 27, 1901.

33. Chiques Council Meeting Minutes, March 11, 1901.

34. Ibid.

35. Ibid.

36. Mountville Council Meeting Minutes, March 23, 1904.

37. Ibid.

38. Elizabethtown Council Meeting Minutes, March 16, 1906.

39. Lancaster Council Meeting Minutes, December 18, 1901.

40. The Chiques congregation paid visiting evangelists "a dollar per day and fare and expense." Chiques Council Meeting Minutes, March 10, 1901.

41. H. B. Brumbaugh (1893:24-31).

42. Chiques, Mountville, and Lancaster Council Meeting Minutes provide examples of turn-of-the-century elections with varied outcomes.

43. *Report of the Brethren's Third Ministerial Meeting of Eastern Pennsylvania* (1896:2-3).

44. *Synodical [sic] Report of the . . . Second Ministerial Meeting* (1895:4-6).

45. For descriptions of Sunday morning worship services, see George L. Moore, "Dunkard Life in Lebanon Valley Sixty Years Ago," *Pennsylvania Folklife* 12 (Spring 1961): 10-23; and James Brubaker, ed., *Middle Creek Church of the Brethren Commemorates 125 Years of Worship, Fellowship and Service 1864-1989* (n. p., [1989]), 7-8.

46. "Notes from Our Correspondents," *Gospel Messenger*, 26 December 1903, 829.

47. See Chiques and Mountville Council Meeting Minutes; and Brubaker, ed. ([1989]:7-8).

48. Mary Schaeffer interview.

49. *Annual Meeting Minutes* (1909:341-342).

50. Many congregations continued to hold

scruples against taking offerings during services, even though Annual Meeting had granted the privilege to do so in 1895. See *Revised Minutes* (1908:178).

51. Chiques Council Meeting Minutes, February 25, 1922.

52. See Brubaker, ed. ([1989]:3) and G. Moore (1961) for descriptions of the Middle Creek and Hanoverdale meetinghouses around the turn of the century. Frye (Winter 1991-92) describes in detail the Germantown, Pricetown, Klein, Kreider, Long, and Bucher meetinghouses, all located within the bounds of Atlantic Northeast District.

53. Frye (Winter 1991-92:69). Adapted with permission.

54. Prior to the spring love feast, deacons also conducted an annual visit of all members to resolve differences within the congregation before members came to the tables. It appears that in earlier days the visit was conducted before each love feast, rather than just once a year. The Harrisburg First church conducted a "semi-annual visit" as late as 1915, when the practice evidently was discontinued. See Harrisburg First Council Meeting Minutes, June 1, 1905; September 23, 1915.

55. The mode of feetwashing was a controversial issue among Brethren prior to 1900. The "double mode," in which one person washed and another dried the feet of several others, was the accepted practice of the Brotherhood. The "single mode," where one person washed and dried the feet of the next, grew in popularity. Annual Meeting ruled in 1879 that either mode was acceptable. See *Revised Minutes* (1908:96-97). The Chiques congregation debated the issue for nearly four years before adopting the single mode in 1900. See Chiques Council Meeting Minutes, 1896-1900. The single mode generally was practiced in Eastern District by 1900.

56. Mary Schaeffer interview.

57. The 1910 Annual Meeting finally allowed women to break bread. For the Annual Meeting discussion and decision, see *COB Full Report* (1910:101-114). Examples of eastern Pennsylvania congregations adopting this new method include Elizabethtown, Chiques, Lancaster, and Mountville in 1910; Harrisburg First, 1911; East Fairview, 1912; Norristown, 1916; Big Swatara, 1919; Midway, 1921; and Richland, 1929. For a thorough discussion of women and bread breaking, see Pamela Brubaker, *She Hath Done What She Could* (Elgin, Ill.: Brethren Press, 1985), 45-60.

58. Many congregations at the turn of the century continued to use wine for communion, although temperance concerns would soon lead them to switch to grape juice. By 1920, few or no congregations in eastern Pennsylvania communed with wine. Examples of congregations switching from wine to grape juice are Mohler, 1911; Chiques 1913; and East Fairview, 1914. See *History of the Church . . .* (1965:17, 32); and Forrest Collier, Norman Harsh, Mary Weaver, eds., *East Fairview Church of the Brethren Seventy-fifth Anniversary History* (n. p., 1977), 9.

59. For more detailed descriptions of love feast practices, see Carl W. Zeigler Sr., "The Week-end Love Feast," *Gospel Messenger*, 4 February 1956, 12-15; and G. Moore (1961).

60. "Notes from Our Correspondents," *Gospel Messenger*, 26 March 1898, 201, 205; 30 April 1898, 285.

61. Mary Schaeffer interview.

Endnotes for Chapter 3

1. The church's earlier style of plural, nonsalaried ministry was commonly known as "free ministry," the term that will be used most frequently in this chapter. Paradoxically, while churches in what today is Atlantic Northeast District (AND) were among the earliest in the denomination to hire salaried pastors, AND also includes some of the few remaining Brethren free ministry congregations.

2. For a discussion of the relationship between foreign missions and the salaried ministry, see Elgin S. Moyer, *Missions in the Church of the Brethren: Their Development and Effect Upon the Denomination* (Elgin,Ill.: Brethren Publishing House, 1931), 237.

3. *Annual Meeting Minutes* (1909:257).

4. *Eastern District Meeting Minutes* (1892:100).

5. *COB Full Report* (1912:71ff.). The report discouraged setting apart one minister as pastor "to the exclusion of others," but during the debate it became clear it was the practice of excluding other ministers, and not salaried ministry *per se*, that the report disapproved. In essence, the report was calling for sensitivity to all ministers in the congregation when hiring a pastor. See C. Bowman (1989:369-370).

6. Mallott (1954:278).

7. They were Coventry, Germantown, Green Tree, Ambler, Amwell, Parker Ford, Geiger Memorial, Lancaster, and Harrisburg First. Many of these "paid pastors" were part-time, received no set salary, and still functioned within a system of plural leadership. Payment sometimes came directly from a few private members. Thus, to say that 10 congregations had "paid pastors" by 1900 really overstates the degree to which churches had progressed toward a salaried, professional ministry.

8. John S. Breidenstine, *A History of the Spring Creek Church of the Brethren 1848-1988* (n. p., [1988]), 15.

9. See Fitzkee (1990:13-15) for a description of the process in the Lititz congregation.

10. *COB Yearbook* (1930:48-49).

11. Data on when particular congregations hired pastors for the first time was obtained from three prior district histories, district directories, congregational histories, and the *Congregational Profile*.

12. They are Chiques, White Oak, Middle Creek, Heidelberg, Blue Ball, and Cocalico. Of those, five are located in Lancaster County and one in Lebanon County.

13. C. Bowman (1989:253).

14. Gleim (1975:113, 167-170).

15. Norman J. Baugher, "An Evaluation of the Free Ministry" (B. D. Thesis, Bethany Biblical Seminary, 1943), 17, points to this factor as one reason pastoral ministry came relatively late to the rural churches of Eastern District.

16. Floyd E. Mallott, "What is the Future System of Our Ministry," *Gospel Messenger*, 22 January 1938, 5-6. Mallott cites "the existence of a paid pastorate in the adjoining congregation" as a factor promoting change.

17. Dale W. Brown, in his article, "Shaping the Ministry: Some Candid Reflections on Bethany's Role," *Brethren Life and Thought* 25 (Winter

1980): 25, states that in later years "the professional ministry became so doctrinaire that free ministers who found their way to [the Church of the Brethren's] Bethany [Seminary] were advised strongly not to return to the local congregations which had laid hands on them." Pastoral ministry, viewed as the wave of the future, was promoted by denominational institutions.

18. J. Stanley Earhart interview.

19. Robert E. Faus, "Ministering to the Brethren," *Messenger*, July 1990, 25-26. Faus interviewed 210 people from 22 congregations—many from Atlantic Northeast District—that had recently switched from free ministry to pastoral ministry.

20. Jesse K. Hoffman interview. Italics added.

21. A congregational study of the East Fairview congregation near Manheim, conducted by J. Stanley Earhart in 1954, reveals that, out of 33 employed respondents, four were farmers. Out of the 29 who were not farmers, 11 of them previously had been farmers but moved into other occupations. Two-thirds of the respondents indicated that their fathers had been farmers. These numbers are indicative of the trend away from the farm that impacted the Brethren ministry. This informal survey covered about half of the heads of households in the congregation. See J. Stanley Earhart, "The East Fairview Church of the Brethren," May 21, 1954, TMs [photocopy].

In 1989, of 65 AND congregations reporting, 38% (25) said they had no men who earned their living by farming, while a full 80% (52) had 3% or fewer farmers. Only 4 congregations (6%) reported having 20% or more men in the congregation who earned their living by farming. *Congregational Profile*.

22. Baugher (1943:15).

23. Mallott (January 22, 1938:5-6).

24. Faus (1990:25-26).

25. See Fitzkee (1990:13). Also, the Palmyra and Mechanic Grove congregations seem to fit this pattern. Exceptional elders Frank S. Carper and Rufus P. Bucher prepared their congregations for pastoral ministry by assuming the role of pastor late in their lives.

26. *Eastern District Ministerial Meeting Minutes*, November 3-5, 1931.

27. Baugher (1943:15-16) cites this "'inherent desire to be like other denominations'" as a key factor in the transition from free to salaried ministry.

28. Ibid., 42.

29. Ibid., 40.

30. Regional secretary Levi K. Ziegler, who was charged with placing pastors in the Pennsylvania districts during the 1940s and 1950s, in July 1949 felt the need to remind his constituent churches that "The traditional salutation among Brethren. . . is 'brother' and 'sister.' It is in the interest of maintaining the simple Brethren dignity that your Secretaries endeavor to avoid the over-use of 'Reverend.'" See *Eastern Region Letter*, July 1949.

31. David W. Lehigh, "A Profession or a Calling?" *Gospel Messenger*, 14 May 1938, 9.

32. Baugher (1943:43).

33. *COB Full Report* (1912:79).

34. *Eastern District Ministerial Meeting Minutes*, November 10-11, 1915.

35. *COB Full Report* (1917:42).

36. Carl W. Zeigler, Sr. interviewed by Donald B. Kraybill.

37. Harold Z. Bomberger interview.

38. J. Stanley Earhart interview.

39. *Congregational Profile*. Chiques is the one congregation.

40. Most of the congregations who have called one or two ministers since 1960 called them in the 1960s and 1970s before making the transition to paid pastors.

41. *Congregational Profile*.

42. Ibid.

43. Robert E. Faus and Richard B. Gardner, "Issues in Ministry," *Messenger*, March 1987, 28.

44. Brown (1980:26).

45. Baugher (1943:44) points out that while it would be wrong to say that pastors caused a breakdown in community, it may not be going too far to say that pastors are evidence of this breakdown and continue to be more a part of the problem than the solution.

46. *Congregational Profile*.

47. ACTS Covenant Fellowship, a charismatic Brethren/Mennonite congregation in Lancaster city, is perhaps the best example. For a description of ACTS Covenant see Carla Boyers and Don Fitzkee, "Some plantings that rooted," *Messenger*, May 1991, 37-38.

48. *Congregational Profile*.

Endnotes for Chapter 4

1. H. B. Brumbaugh (1893:24-26).

2. See *Eastern District Elders Body Minutes*, 1897-1918, for examples of these functions.

3. Describing J. H. Longenecker, an elder of the Palmyra congregation at the turn of the century, a colleague noted: "Many times on his return from the Conference he would state that some decision was not according to his point of view, but he would always remind the church that this is now our Conference ruling and it becomes binding on the whole Brotherhood. . . " See Frank S. Carper, "70th Anniversary," *The Church Monthly*, October 1962, 4-6, newsletter of the Palmyra Church of the Brethren.

4. In 1885 the Brethren's Book and Tract Committee began, and in 1895 these two merged to form the General Mission Board and Tract Committee. A General Sunday School Board was founded in 1911, and in 1928 was combined with the General Welfare Board and Music Committee to form the Board of Religious Education. The General Ministerial Board, organized in 1921, was charged with developing a system of pastoral placement. See Mallott (1954:Chapter 20).

5. Albert C. Wieand, J. J. Yoder, and Edward Frantz, eds., *Pastor's Manual*, authorized by General Conference of the Church of the Brethren, (Elgin, Ill.: Brethren Publishing House, 1923), 37-42.

6. Wieand, et. al. (1923:34). Italics added.

7. H. L. Hartsough, Raymond R. Peters, M. R. Zigler, and Foster B. Statler, eds., *Brethren Minister's Manual*, authorized by General Ministerial Board (Elgin, Ill.: Brethren Publishing House, 1946). For a brief description of the factors that led Brethren to reorganization and resulted in the formation of the Church of the Brethren General Board, see Don Fitzkee, "Overcoming the Topsy syndrome: The making of the General Board," *Messenger*, March 1987, 12-14. For an overview of the growth and development of denominational polity and organization, see S. Loren Bowman, *Power and Polity among the Brethren* (Elgin, Ill.:

Brethren Press, 1987).

8. *Annual Conference Minutes* (1945:7).

9. Ibid. (1946:6-7).

10. I am indebted to Carl Bowman's extensive treatment of the decline of the authority of elders. See C. Bowman (1989:545-558).

11. *Annual Conference Minutes* (1947:4-16).

12. Ibid. (1968:82-86). Twenty years later, organizational concerns similar to those in 1968 resurfaced. The 1987 Annual Conference referred four separate queries dealing with organizational issues to a seven-member "Denominational Structure Committee." The committee brought to the 1989 Conference a report recommending sweeping changes, aimed at simplifying denominational structures and improving their responsiveness to "grassroots" members of the church. While many delegates seemed to resonate with the committee's diagnosis of structural ills, they rejected the proposed cure and elected a new committee. Having spent more than $30,000 over a four-year period, Annual Conference approved the 1991 report, which left structures intact. See *Annual Conference Minutes* (1989:834-852; 1991:262-283).

13. The home relocated at Neffsville in 1907 and changed its name to Brethren Village in 1972. Two more district-related retirement homes—Peter Becker Community, Harleysville, and the Lebanon Valley Brethren Home, Palmyra—opened their doors in 1971 and 1979, respectively. See *Atlantic Northeast District Conference Minutes* (1971:44; 1979:33).

14. After the district split in 1911, the two districts continued to cooperatively sponsor these agencies. The Home for Orphan and Friendless Children cared for nearly 1,000 children and young people from 1914 to 1962. The children's home was sold to the Brethren Home in 1963 because other agencies had taken over child welfare work and because of the growing expenses associated with complying with state welfare requirements. See Durnbaugh, ed., 1983, s. v. "Brethren Village," by Raymond R. Peters; and "Home for Orphans and Friendless Children," by Donald F. Durnbaugh. A new district ministry to children and youth—Church of the Brethren Youth Services (COBYS)—came into being at the 1979 Atlantic Northeast District Conference. See *Atlantic Northeast District Conference Minutes* (1979:60-66). The name was changed in 1992 to COBYS Family Services to reflect the broadened scope of the organization's work.

15. Durnbaugh, ed., 1983, s. v. "Elizabethtown College," by Carl W. Zeigler, Sr. Southeastern Pennsylvania District, which had developed strong ties to Juniata College voted not to assume partial control of the college. See *Southeastern District Meeting Minutes* (1917:7).

16. *History of the Church. . .* (1965:146). The name was changed the following year to Board of Christian Education.

17. See *Eastern District Meeting Minutes* (1911: 6; 1914:9-10; 1919:9; 1926:11; 1939:4-5).

18. *Annual Conference Minutes* (1917:6).

19. C. Bowman (1989:546).

20. *Annual Conference Minutes* (1927:5-6).

21. *COB Full Report* (1927:36-37). Remarks by S. H. Hertzler, quoted from C. Bowman (1989:547).

22. Caleb W. Bucher interviewed by Donald B. Kraybill and Carl F. Bowman.

23. Ibid.; and Mayno Hershey interview.

24. *Eastern District Meeting Minutes*, 1913-1929.

25. *Eastern District Elders Body Minutes* (1905:37).

26. Earl H. Kurtz interview.

27. *History of the Church. . .* (1965:143). For an overview of the Ministerial Board's work see *Eastern District Ministerial Board Minutes*, 1928-1934.

28. "Report to Elder's Body" from Nevin H. Zuck, District Ministerial Board secretary, *Eastern District Elders Body Minutes*, November 2, 1955.

29. *Eastern District Conference Minutes* (1949: 6-10). For more information on Camp Swatara, see Jon C. Wenger, *History of Camp Swatara: The First Fifty Years* (Manheim, Pa.: Privately printed, 1993).

30. *Southeastern District Meeting Minutes* (May 11, 1911:1; September 28, 1911:2; 1917:8; 1921:7-8; 1922:6; 1925:6-8).

31. Ibid. (1929:8).

32. Ibid. (1933:8; 1934:8).

33. *Southeastern District Conference Minutes* (1948:10; 1954:7).

34. *Annual Conference Minutes* (1947:4-16).

35. *Eastern District Conference Minutes* (1953: 50-56).

36. Ibid.

37. Eastern District elders voted not to enforce Annual Conference's call for a six-year term limitation on moderators of congregations. See *Eastern District Elders Body Minutes*, November 6, 1957.

38. Ibid.

39. *Southeastern District Elders Body Minutes*, November 2, 1948.

40. Eastern District approved the new plan at the 1957 District Conference and the new board began to function January 1, 1958. See *Eastern District Conference Minutes* (1957:59-66). North Atlantic District approved a revised constitution at its 1958 Conference and the new board began to function October 18, 1958. See *North Atlantic District Conference Minutes* (1958:2, 21).

41. In 1965 the North Atlantic District reorganized its board into four commissions—Nurture, Witness, Ministry, and Stewardship. *North Atlantic District Conference Minutes* (1965:21).

42. For a description of the new Board of Administration's responsibilities see the by-laws in *Eastern District Conference Minutes* (1957:60-65).

43. *Annual Conference Minutes* (1967:43-52).

44. *Eastern District Conference Minutes* (1967: 53); *Eastern District Elders Body Minutes*, October 28, 1967. In North Atlantic District the Elders Body was less important and less active. Strong pastors and lay leaders had been the primary players from the early days of the district. The District Elders Body appears to have faded away on its own. As of 1965, the Elders Council and Elders, Moderators, and Pastors Council were no longer listed as part of the district's organization. See *North Atlantic District Conference Minutes* (1965:23). No District Conference action appears to have been taken to officially discontinue the office.

45. Southeastern District had appointed a committee to look into hiring a part-time district staff person as early as 1940. After two years of study, the matter was dropped, likely due to the prohibitive expense. See *Southeastern District Conference Minutes* (1940:12; 1942:3).

46. *Annual Conference Minutes* (1960:21-25).

47. Virginia Fisher began work as full-time Tri-

District Director of Christian Education, October 1, 1961, working out of an office at Elizabethtown College. See *Eastern District Conference Minutes* (1970:12-14).

48. For a thorough discussion of the regional program in the Church of the Brethren see Harold Z. Bomberger, "The Regional Program in the Church of the Brethren," *Brethren Life and Thought* 27 (Summer 1982): 157-64.

49. Virginia Fisher continued as staff for Christian Education. Her office was relocated from Elizabethtown College to the United Church Center in 1967. See *Eastern District Conference Minutes* (1970:12-14).

50. *Minutes* of Joint Meeting of Tri-District Committee and District Boards of Administration of Eastern District, North Atlantic District, and Southern District, September 10, 1966.

51. *Southern Pennsylvania Special District Conference Minutes* (April 30, 1968:55).

52. Joseph M. Long and Virginia Fisher resigned August 30, 1971, and were replaced by new executive secretary Harold Z. Bomberger and associate executive secretary Henry H. Rist III. *Atlantic Northeast District Conference Minutes* (October 10-11, 1970:11; 1971:26-27; 1971:30).

53. Ibid. (April 4, 1970:49-50).

54. Ibid. (1986:57-61).

55. *Annual Conference Minutes* (1976:199-204).

56. *Atlantic Northeast District Conference Minutes* (1980:11).

57. J. Stanley Earhart interview.

58. Carl W. Zeigler, Sr. interviewed by Donald B. Kraybill.

59. Nevin H. Zuck interview.

60. Ibid.

61. *Atlantic Northeast District Board Minutes*, April 6, 1991.

62. J. Harry Enders interview.

63. H. B. Brumbaugh (1893:31).

64. Carl W. Zeigler, Sr. interviewed by Donald B. Kraybill.

65. Thus, when a denominational Temperance Committee was formed in 1908, districts and congregations soon formed committees to relate to the national body. The Temperance Committee reported at the 1911 Annual Meeting that 26 of 43 districts had organized temperance committees. *Annual Meeting Minutes* (1911:11).

66. Breidenstine ([1988]:31).

67. Lititz (1926), Spring Creek (1934), and Chiques (1935) are examples. See Fitzkee (1990:12); Breidenstine ([1988]:37); and *History of the Church. . .* (1965:18).

68. Lititz (1934) and Chiques (1941) are examples. See Fitzkee (1990:14); and *History of the Church. . .* (1965:16).

69. *Congregational Profile*.

70. See Chapter Six for a description of the annual visit's decline.

71. Nevin H. Zuck interview.

72. E. Miller Peterman interview.

73. Elizabethtown Council Meeting Minutes, July 6, 1944.

74. E. Floyd McDowell interview.

75. Nevin H. Zuck interview. Another church leader notes, "The reason the change [to a Board of Administration] came about is that Official Boards became stagnant and lacked the dynamic that was needed." J. Stanley Earhart interview.

76. The 1947 Annual Conference had

recommended that lay-led boards be elected, but did not prescribe a set pattern.

77. E. Floyd McDowell interview.

78. Earl K. Ziegler interview.

79. *Congregational Profile*. Some congregations have hybrid structures, combining an Official Board composed of ministers and deacons, with lay-led commissions and committees.

80. Nevin H. Zuck interview.

81. Ray A. Kurtz Interview.

82. See Fitzkee (1990:31). The Lititz congregation adopted a new plan of organization in 1955. By 1961, decreasing Council Meeting attendance was a concern. In September 1964, the congregation waived the requirement of a 10 percent quorum of members from its by-laws. During the 1980s, the congregation reduced the number of regular Council Meetings from four to two per year. Similarly, only 19 of more than 200 members attended a 1971 Council Meeting at the Mountville church. See Mountville Council Meeting Minutes, October 20, 1971.

83. Abram M. Hess interviewed by Donald B. Kraybill and Carl F. Bowman.

84. *Congregational Profile*.

85. J. Stanley Earhart interview.

86. A 1956 Annual Conference decision permitted "churches which desire to" to elect deacons for a specific term of service, rather than for life. *Annual Conference Minutes* (1956:12-14).

87. *Congregational Profile*.

88. June A. Gibble and Fred W. Swartz, eds., *Called to Caregiving: A Resource for Equipping Deacons in the Believers Church* (Elgin, Ill.: Brethren Press, 1987).

89. The Midway, Green Tree, and Richland congregations are examples.

90. Stevens Hill Community Church of the Brethren By-Laws.

91. *Atlantic Northeast District Directory*, 1991.

92. The 1955 Annual Conference recommended the name change. *Annual Conference Minutes* (1955:9).

93. Carl W. Zeigler, Sr. interviewed by Donald B. Kraybill.

94. Earl K. Ziegler interview.

95. J. Stanley Earhart interview.

96. J. Harry Enders interview.

97. Ibid. Italics added.

98. The Harrisburg First and Lititz congregations are examples.

Endnotes for Chapter 5

1. *History of the Church. . .* (1915:586-587).

2. Gleim (1975:250).

3. *History of the Church. . .* (1915:230).

4. Ibid., 494.

5. *History of the Church. . .* (1965:58).

6. Durnbaugh, ed., 1983, s. v. "Language Shift," by Fred W. Benedict.

7. Text of a speech delivered December 14, 1930, by A. L. B. Martin at a re-dedication service of the Harrisburg First church. Harrisburg First church archives.

8. The Lancaster City church voted in 1913 to have German preaching one Sunday a quarter, which they evidently did until 1926, when the action was repealed. The Richland congregation in Lebanon County discontinued German preaching in 1923, except for special occasions, while the

nearby Midway church decided in 1915 to have one German and one English sermon at each service. In the Chiques congregation, the transition began in the 1890s. English was in general use at Chiques by 1917, although a request for a German sermon was granted as late as 1936. See Lancaster Council Meeting Minutes, April 16, 1913; March 10, 1926; *History of the Church. . .* (1965:119, 103); and Chiques Council Meeting Minutes.

9. According to Eastern District Ministerial Meeting Programs, 1926 was the last year for a German sermon.

10. See *Eastern District Ministerial Board Minutes,* November 20, 1933; Carl W. Zeigler, Sr. interviewed by Donald B. Kraybill; and Luke H. Brandt interview.

11. Indian Creek is a notable exception to the general language trend. While, in general, the language transition moved from east to west, Indian Creek was at the center of a cluster of traditional congregations north of Philadelphia that were outside of the influence of the city.

12. *History of the Church. . .* (1965:65-67). Some evidence suggests that even after 1953 an occasional German sermon was preached at Indian Creek by minister Elmer Moyer.

13. J. H. Longenecker Diary, in Jacob H. Longenecker file, High Library, Elizabethtown College.

14. West Conestoga (later Middle Creek) Council Meeting Minutes, March 14, 1910. It is unclear what happened to this query. No further mention of it is made in West Conestoga, district, or Annual Meeting minutes.

15. Mountville Council Meeting Minutes, March 10, 1909.

16. Frederick Lewis Allen, *The Big Change: America Transforms Itself, 1900-1950* (New York: Harper & Brothers Publishers, 1952), 109-130.

17. Chiques Council Meeting Minutes, August 25, 1915.

18. Levi K. Ziegler, "Two Weeks in the Mechanic Grove Church, Pa.," *Gospel Messenger,* 6 July 1918, 427.

19. Breidenstine ([1988]:15).

20. Paul M. Grubb, Sr., interviewed by Donald B. Kraybill.

21. Abram M. Hess interviewed by Donald B. Kraybill and Carl F. Bowman.

22. Fitzkee (1990:12).

23. Mallott (1954:264).

24. Stevenson Whitcomb Fletcher, *Pennsylvania Agriculture and Country Life, 1840-1940* (Harrisburg: Pennsylvania Historical and Museum Commission, 1965), 62-65, 490-491.

25. Chiques Council Meeting Minutes, September 10, 1900. The Elizabethtown meetinghouse was a part of the Chiques congregation until 1902.

26. Roland L. Howe, *The History of a Church (Dunker) with comments featuring The First Church of the Brethren of Philadelphia, Pa., 1813-1943* (Philadelphia: By the author, 1943), 12; Frank Carper Notes, in Frank Carper file, High Library, Elizabethtown College; Mountville Council Meeting Minutes, December 26, 1911; and Mary Jane Kulp, ed., *History of the Coventry Church of the Brethren, 1724-1974* (n. p., [1974]), 53.

27. Paul M. Grubb, Sr., interviewed by Donald B. Kraybill. The Midway congregation added electric lights in 1924, followed by the East Fairview

congregation in 1925. See *History of the Church. . .* (1965:104); and Collier, et. al., eds. (1977:5).

28. Delbert C. Miller, "Radio and Television," in John F. Cuber, ed., *Technology and Social Change* (New York: Appleton-Century-Crofts, Inc., 1957), 157.

29. Gleim (1974:338).

30. Jack Brubaker, "The Scribbler," *Lancaster New Era,* 11 June 1991, A-14.

31. J. Stanley Earhart interview.

32. For a discussion on the effects of automobiles and radio see Francis R. Allen, "The Automobile" and Delbert C. Miller, "Radio and Television," in Cuber, ed. (1957:107-132, 157-186).

33. A congregational study of the East Fairview congregation near Manheim, conducted by J. Stanley Earhart in 1954, reveals that about half of the households owned televisions. This informal survey covered about half of the heads of households in the congregation. See Earhart, May 21, 1954, TMs [photocopy].

34. *Annual Meeting Minutes* (1910:5).

35. Ibid., 6. Italics added.

36. C. Bowman (1989:410).

37. *Annual Meeting Minutes* (1911:5). Italics added.

38. My discussion of the 1911 dress decision and the debate surrounding the issue of dress in the Brotherhood closely follows C. Bowman (1989:396-428).

39. It appears that for a brief time the district did maintain some dress standards for its leaders. The District Elders Body in 1913 refused to ordain D. W. Kurtz, when a brother "advised against the ordination of brethren, whose wives were not in order." The following year Kurtz was ordained after his wife had promised "she will not be in the way of her husband's ordination." *Southeastern District Elders Body Meetings,* August 28-29, 1913; April 22-23, 1914.

40. The tone of Eastern District Meeting Minutes and Southeastern District Meeting Minutes during the 1920s and 1930s stand in sharp contrast to each other. Eastern District Minutes every year include resolutions urging adherence to nonconforming principles and the simple life, while Southeastern District Minutes make virtually no mention of such issues.

41. *Eastern District Meeting Minutes* (1912:10).

42. C. Bowman (1989:417) notes that if the 1911 Annual Meeting had been held in the more conservative East, the landmark dress report may not have been approved in the first place. The 1915 Annual Meeting did actually strengthen the wording of the 1911 ruling to say "disorderly members should be dealt with as disorderly members." But the action was too little, too late. See *COB Full Report* (1915:154-156).

43. "The Obstruction in Church," *Gospel Messenger,* 8 August 1903, 504.

44. Harrisburg First Council Meeting Minutes, March 24, 1911; June 30, 1916.

45. See Lancaster Council Meeting Minutes, January 13, 1915.

46. *Eastern District Elders Body Minutes,* April 30, 1919.

47. *Eastern District Meeting Minutes* (1920:11).

48. Ibid. (1921:9).

49. Ibid. (1925:10-11).

50. Harrisburg First Special Council Meeting Minutes, February 15, 1924. Italics added.

51. *Petition to Annual Meeting, Through Standing Committee.* Calgary, Alta., June, 1923, and accompanying letter, in Harrisburg First church archives.

52. May 9, 1924, letter from Standing Committee to Petitioners of the Harrisburg Church and Vicinity, in Harrisburg First church archives.

53. *Eastern District Elders Body Minutes,* April 27, 1927.

54. Statement from Eastern District Ministerial Meeting, December 26, 1928. Italics added.

55. For a thorough discussion of the certificate question, see Chapter Six.

56. Harrisburg First Council Meeting Minutes, October 2, 1930.

57. *Eastern District Ministerial Board Minutes,* March 7, 1931.

58. *Eastern District Meeting Minutes* (1932:3-4).

59. Durnbaugh, ed., 1983, s. v. "Dunkard Brethren," by Nedra Ann Pike, Howard Surbey, and Jacob C. Ness.

60. *Eastern District Meeting Minutes* (1926:13). A similar petition came from the Southern Pennsylvania District.

61. V. F. Schwalm, *Otho Winger* (Elgin, Ill., Brethren Publishing House, 1952), 134-135.

62. *Annual Conference Minutes* (1926:11-12).

63. Durnbaugh, ed., 1983, s. v. "Dunkard Brethren. "

64. Eastern District Ministerial Board letter to churches of the the district, Summer 1926. Quoted from Schwalm (1952:135-136).

65. See *History of the Church. . .* (1965:143); and Carl W. Zeigler, Sr. interviewed by Donald B. Kraybill. Dunkard Brethren congregations eventually were established in Berks and Lancaster counties, and a few members left the Church of the Brethren for the Dunkard Brethren. Six members of the Reading congregation joined the Dunkards in 1926, according to Jerome Crowther, "History of the Church of the Brethren in Reading, 1898-1965," 1965 (?), TMs [photocopy], p. 9, Reading congregational file, High Library, Elizabethtown College. Arlene Keller recalls that "at least five or six families" from the Midway congregation joined the Dunkard Brethren some years after the initial division. Arlene Keller interview.

66. See C. Bowman (1989:397-398).

67. *Annual Meeting Minutes* (1911:5).

68. Congregational minutes make virtually no mention of beards for laymen in the early years of the 20th century. The Mountville Council Meeting Minutes, March 10, 1915, are an exception: They include a single admonition against brethren not wearing the beard.

69. Mountville Council Meeting Minutes, December 17, 1902; November 2, 1910.

70. Chiques Council Meeting Minutes, March 14, 1904; February 24, 1906; February 28, 1910; February 25, 1911; May 27, 1911; February 24, 1912; February 24, 1923.

71. Harrisburg First Council Meeting Minutes, February 19, 1906.

72. E. Miller Peterman interview.

73. Carl W. Zeigler, Sr. interviewed by Donald B. Kraybill.

74. Text of speech delivered by A. L. B. Martin at a re-dedication service of the Harrisburg First church, December 14, 1930. Harrisburg First church archives.

75. *Eastern District Elders Body Minutes,*

1923-1926. See also Lititz Council Meeting Minutes, October 12, 1927.

76. Conversation with Anna Carper.

77. October 1, 1929, letter from R. W. Schlosser to Frank Carper. Frank Carper file, High Library, Elizabethtown College. Schlosser is said to have received much ridicule for his meager beard. Carl W. Zeigler, Sr. interviewed by Donald B. Kraybill.

78. J. Harry Enders interview.

79. Earl K. Ziegler interview.

80. J. Harry Enders interview.

81. J. Stanley Earhart interview.

82. Nevin H. Zuck interview.

83. Harold Z. Bomberger interview.

84. In a January 6, 1904, letter to Elder George Bucher, Elder J. Y. King questioned why Bucher intended to participate in a Bible Institute at Elizabethtown College. King noted, "As a rule in these schools the order of the church is not so fully carried out. While there are some good, earnest, and loyal members there, there are such there too that are *not* loyal and not a few either. " George Bucher file, High Library, Elizabethtown College. Italics in original.

85. Harold Z. Bomberger interview.

86. Robert O. Hess interview.

87. Carl W. Zeigler, Sr. interviewed by Donald B. Kraybill. Ministers in three free ministry churches continued to wear plain suits into the 1990s.

88. Mountville Council Meeting Minutes, March 19, 1902. Prayer veils at the turn of the century had been fashioned from two pieces of light cotton net, large enough to cover much of the woman's head. Cap strings hung at the sides or were tied under the chin to keep the veiling in place. See Esther F. Rupel, "The Dress of the Brethren," *Brethren Life and Thought* 31 (Summer 1986): 148.

89. Mountville Council Meeting Minutes, December 8, 1915.

90. Ibid., November 8, 1928. Italics added.

91. Probably slacks. The objection was based on Deuteronomy 22:5. Mountville Council Meeting Minutes, September 30, 1935; November 8, 1939; November 19, 1943.

92. *Congregational Profile.*

93. Margaret (Peggy) Cassel interview.

94. *Middle Creek Directory* (1987:6).

95. *Congregational Profile.*

96. Ibid.

97. Pauline Rosenberger interview.

98. For a discussion of the importance of distinctive dress for another Anabaptist group, see Donald B. Kraybill, *The Riddle of Amish Culture* (Baltimore: Johns Hopkins University Press, 1989), 49-51.

Endnotes for Chapter 6

1. Sexual sins were an exception to this rule. Until 1915, sexual sin brought automatic disowning. Those who repented eventually could be reinstated.

2. C. Bowman (1989:326-327) notes that, while churches did disfellowship as a last resort, confession and restoration were more common than disowning.

3. This common phrase appears in Lancaster Council Meeting Minutes, January 22, 1896.

4. For prohibitions against amusements, see

Annual Meeting Minutes (1909:139, 185, 251-252, 496-497, 560, 823).

5. J. H. Moore, *The New Testament Doctrines* (Elgin, Ill.: Brethren Publishing House, 1915), 162-163.

6. Lancaster Council Meeting Minutes, November 30, 1901.

7. Chiques Council Meeting Minutes, March 9, 1903; March 13, 1905; February 23, 1907.

8. Mountville Council Meeting Minutes, July 20, 1904; and Elizabethtown Council Meeting Minutes, June 21, 1906; November 4, 1909.

9. The following year the church disowned a brother who violated both proscriptions. See Chiques Council Meeting Minutes, February 25, 1911; August 26, 1911; May 16, 1912.

10. Elizabethtown Council Meeting Minutes, November 22, 1910; February 8, 1911.

11. See *Annual Meeting Minutes* (1909:541); Lancaster Council Meeting Minutes, April 20, 1892; September 13, 1908; January 27, 1909; January 12, 1910; Elizabethtown Council Meeting Minutes, June 30, 1904; and Mountville Council Meeting Minutes, March 13, 1907; March 9, 1910.

12. *Annual Meeting Minutes* (1909:763-764, 876).

13. *Eastern District Meeting Minutes*, May 12-13, 1897.

14. *Annual Meeting Minutes* (1909:791, 876).

15. See Lancaster Council Meeting Minutes, October 17, 1900; July 10, 1901; June 19, 1903; July 10, 1907; January 15, 1908; April 12, 1911. The Harrisburg First, Chiques, and Elizabethtown congregations also opposed lodges and life insurance around the turn of the century. See Chiques Council Meeting Minutes, March 9, 1896; March 8, 1897; April 13, 1900; September 10, 1900; Harrisburg First Council Meeting Minutes, June 6, 1904; and Elizabethtown Council Meeting Minutes, March 8, 1906; March 28, 1907.

16. Mountville Council Meeting Minutes, August 22, 1906; August 7, 1907. Similar cases were addressed by the Lancaster church. See Lancaster Council Meeting Minutes, November 16, 1907; October 8, 1913.

17. Mountville Council Meeting Minutes, March 9, 1910.

18. The Ambler Council Meeting minutes contain little evidence of confessions or disowning after 1875. See Peggy C. Cramer, comp., *Early Records of the Ambler Church of the Brethren* (Apollo, Pa.: Closson Press, 1990), 29-35.

19. For elaboration on this point, see C. Bowman (1989:494). In a 1920 Annual Conference discussion on the repeal of "obsolete" Conference minutes, Eastern District Elder J. H. Longenecker noted that "while some of these minutes may be considered obsolete in some sections of the Brotherhood, they are still in force in other sections because we held onto them." *COB Full Report* (1920:175-180).

20. See Mountville Council Meeting Minutes, March 19, 1902; July 20, 1904; November 2, 1910; August 29, 1917.

21. See *Annual Meeting Minutes* (1914:3-4); and *COB Full Report* (1914:67-81).

22. *COB Full Report* (1916:56-57).

23. The Elizabethtown and Lancaster churches, for example, disowned fornicators at the beginning of a Council Meeting and reclaimed them at the end of the same meeting! See Lancaster Council Meeting Minutes, February 7, 1915; and Elizabethtown

Council Meeting Minutes, March 5, 1914.

24. See *COB Full Report* (1915:157ff.); Chiques Council Meeting Minutes, January 1, 1919; and Mountville Council Meeting Minutes, April 5, 1923.

25. *Annual Meeting Minutes* (1912:3; 1915:7).

26. *Annual Conference Minutes* (1920:14).

27. Ibid., 7-10.

28. *COB Full Report* (1920:88-96). Eastern District elder Samuel H. Hertzler also opposed the statement, objecting specifically to the paper's permissiveness on suing.

29. *Annual Conference Minutes* (1920:11-12).

30. Fitzkee (1990:7-8). Italics added.

31. Mountville Council Meeting Minutes, November 8, 1933. Italics added.

32. See Ralph W. Schlosser, *History of Elizabethtown College, 1899-1970* (Elizabethtown, Pa.: Elizabethtown College, 1971), 58-60. Objections to intercollegiate athletics were raised at the 1929 District Meeting. See *Eastern District Meeting Minutes* (1929:6).

33. "Church News," *Gospel Messenger*, 24 December 1938, 30.

34. Examples include Ambler, Elizabethtown, Chiques, and Lititz. A notable exception is the Mountville church, which disowned a brother in 1932 for attending a circus. See Mountville Council Meeting Minutes, November 9, 1932.

35. *Eastern District Meeting Minutes* (1928:9).

36. Carl W. Zeigler, Sr. interviewed by Donald B. Kraybill.

37. Carl W. Ziegler [*sic*], "Baneful Effects of Worldly Amusements." Pamphlet from the 1920s.

38. Arlene Keller interview. Jesse K. Hoffman, a longtime minister in the Skippack congregation, also remembers a strong emphasis against movies during the 1940s. See Mountville Council Meeting Minutes, November 8, 1944, for an admonition against movies.

39. Amos A. Hummer, "Worldly Amusements," *Gospel Messenger*, 5 March 1938, 23-24.

40. See Mountville Council Meeting Minutes, March 6, 1923. Chiques, Mountville, and Elizabethtown Council Meeting Minutes show no decline during the 1920s in the number of cases involving the law. From 1911 to 1920, 10 examples of questions pertaining to law appear in the Council Minutes of these three churches. From 1921 to 1930, the number of such cases increases slightly to 12.

41. See Chiques Council Meeting Minutes, November 25, 1922; and Mountville Council Meeting Minutes, August 3, 1922. Eastern District Elders added their opposition to Farm Bureau membership in fall 1922. See *Eastern District Elders Body Minutes*, April 26, 1922.

42. Elizabethtown Council Meeting Minutes, January 3, 1929; May 3, 1933.

43. *Southeastern District Elders Body Minutes*, April 30, 1925; February 10, 1928.

44. I am indebted to Carl F. Bowman's careful research and cogent analysis of the issues at stake in the certificate question. See C. Bowman (1989:454-473).

45. *Annual Meeting Minutes* (1909:841).

46. In the early 1900s, some Brethren in Manheim who lived within three blocks of White Oak's Manheim meetinghouse were expected to travel three miles to East Fairview. See *History of the Church*. . . (1965:26). A 1901 Annual Meeting decision did allow those who lived close to a boundary line to hold membership in either con-

gregation, if both congregations agreed. See *Annual Meeting Minutes* (1909: 743). The Harrisburg First church during the 1910s made use of this concession. See Harrisburg First Council Meeting Minutes, October 7, 1914; September 23, 1915. Not all congregations were so flexible, however. Asked whether those who live near a boundary can join another congregation, a 1914 Mountville Council Meeting answered: "Decide that line shall be line." See Mountville Council Meeting Minutes, July 29, 1914.

47. This discussion of the 1926 certificate solution closely follows Carl F. Bowman's account. See C. Bowman (1989:457ff.).

48. See *Annual Conference Minutes* (1923:12); and *COB Full Report* (1924:83-91; 1926:56).

49. *COB Full Report* (1929:105-111). Italics added.

50. *Annual Conference Minutes* (1931:8-9).

51. Roland Howe noted in his congregational history, "The Philadelphia Church has had on its roll from time to time a number of members who came from a distance for communion because they were not free to fellowship in their home congregation." See Howe (1943:487). See also Carl W. Zeigler, Sr. interviewed by Donald B. Kraybill, and Elizabethtown Council Meeting Minutes, May 3, 1933, for references to Philadelphia First church. See E. Miller Peterman interview for data on Baltimore First.

52. See Silas Shoemaker and Nevin Zuck, *The Church of the Brethren in Ambler: A History of the One Hundred and Two Years of the Old Upper Dublin Church of the Brethren*, 1942, TMs [photocopy], 16; and Jesse K. and Hilda Hoffman interview.

53. *Eastern District Ministerial Board Minutes*, April 1934.

54. Nevin H. Zuck interview.

55. *Southeastern District Elders Body Minutes*, April 22, 1936.

56. Annual Conference in 1932 recognized this new category of Brethren, and, about the same time, the Ambler church removed inactives from the membership roll for the first time. See *Annual Conference Minutes* (1932:7); and Ambler Council Meeting Minutes, April 3, 1925; February 28, 1926; January 22, 1932; in Cramer, comp. (1990). In the few cases where Ambler did exercise discipline, it appeared to be severe. An April 3, 1925, minute recommended "dismemberment" of a brother!

57. See Howe (1943:662-663).

58. See Council Meeting minutes from respective congregations and Breidenstine ([1988]: 40-51).

59. *Annual Meeting Minutes* (1909:669, 762-763).

60. Frederick Denton Dove, *Cultural Changes in the Church of the Brethren* (Elgin, Ill.: Brethren Publishing House, 1932), 224.

61. *Annual Conference Minutes* (1933:10-11).

62. Of 23 congregations reporting, one accepted divorced and remarried persons for the first time during the 1930s, four during the 1940s, three during the 1950s, eight during the 1960s, and seven in the 1970s and beyond. In 1989, 61 of 66 congregations accepted divorced and remarried members, but many could not pinpoint a date when such acceptance began. See *Congregational Profile*.

63. Fitzkee (1990:17).

64. *Annual Conference Minutes* (1937:7-8).

65. Ibid., (1938:41).

66. Ibid., (1944:8).

67. Ibid., (1947:17-19).

68. Ibid., (1954:8-9).

69. Rufus D. Bowman, *Seventy Times Seven* (Elgin, Ill.: Brethren Publishing House, 1945), 132.

70. The *Congregational Profile* asked informed members to explain when and why the annual deacon visit was discontinued in their congregations.

71. "Pastoral visitation replaced the deacon visit. There's no doubt about that," says one longtime Brethren. See Ray A. Kurtz interview.

72. Lititz Council Meeting Minutes, January 3, 1918; March 21, 1923.

73. Fitzkee (1990:10).

74. See Lititz Council Meeting Minutes, January 29, 1940; March 13, 1940; and Lititz Official Board Meeting Minutes, February 3, 1936; March 17, 1937.

75. *Congregational Profile*. Some congregations attempted to update this traditional practice by beginning "Undershepherd Programs. " This friendlier version of the old visit assigned a specific "flock" of families to deacons for pastoral care and nurturing throughout the year. Instead of asking members whether they were keeping their commitments to the church, the emphasis shifted to how the church could be of better service in meeting the needs of members.

76. Ibid. Based on responses from 32 congregations.

77. Ibid.

78. Carl W. Zeigler, Sr. interviewed by Donald B. Kraybill. Rebuffed at Lebanon, one of the couples went to the Palmyra church's Frank Carper, who performed the ceremony. Carper was satisfied that the divorcee in the couple was the innocent party, and his Official Board did not stand in the way of the ceremony.

79. See Eugene F. Roop, "The Brethren and Church Discipline (II)," *Brethren Life and Thought* 14 (Summer 1969): 176.

80. *Annual Conference Minutes* (1962:58-59; 1963:16-17). Italics added.

81. Ibid. (1964:10-14).

82. Dale W. Brown, "Some Ecumenical Postures for Brethren," *Brethren Life and Thought* 3 (Autumn 1963): 50.

83. Richard A. Bollinger, *The Church in a Changing World*. A Report of the Second Theological Study Conference held at Oak Brook, Ill., from July 20 to July 24, 1964, on the theme, "The Meaning of Membership in the Body of Christ" (Elgin, Ill.: Brethren Press, 1965), 60-62.

84. Elizabethtown Council Meeting Minutes, March 16, 1938.

85. Ibid., June 4, 1952.

86. Ibid., December 10, 1953. Italics added. The matter was resolved without resorting to the law.

87. *Church News*, Elizabethtown Church of the Brethren Newsletter, June 1963, 3. Italics added.

88. "Letter to Deacons, Former Deacons, Ministers, Church Board Members, and Other Selected Persons," 1976, attached to Elizabethtown Council Meeting Minutes.

89. *Annual Conference Minutes* (1976:199ff). Italics in original.

90. C. Bowman (1989:662). Italics in original.

91. *Annual Conference Minutes* (1977:305). Italics added.

92. C. Bowman (1989:702).

93. District Executive's Report, *Atlantic*

Northeast District Conference Minutes (1981:27). Examples of congregations where pastors resigned as a result of divorce during the 1970s and 1980s include Elizabethtown, Germantown, and Philadelphia First.

94. J. Harry Enders interview. Former and present district executives Harold Z. Bomberger, Earl K. Ziegler, and Allen T. Hansell, who placed all pastors from 1970 onward, know of no other divorced and remarried pastors placed in AND churches. A pastor of a progressive Atlantic Northeast District congregation did divorce and remarry during the early 1970s and continued on as pastor, likely becoming the first divorced and remarried pastor in the district. Telephone conversations with Harold Z. Bomberger and Allen T. Hansell, April 20, 1994; Earl K. Ziegler, May 19, 1994. Personal correspondence from Harold Z. Bomberger, April 23, 1994.

95. *Congregational Profile*. Cases of removing inactives were not considered.

96. J. Harry Enders interview.

97. Carl W. Zeigler, Sr. interviewed by Donald B. Kraybill.

98. James F. Myer interview.

99. *Annual Conference Minutes* (1985:128-137).

100. See Boyers and Fitzkee, May 1991, 37-38.

101. March 4, 1991, letter from Lititz Deacon Board to members. "Separated member" was a new category recommended by the 1985 Conference paper on membership to replace the term "inactive member."

Endnotes for Chapter 7

1. See Roger E. Sappington, *Brethren Social Policy* (Elgin, Ill.: Brethren Press, 1961), 31.

2. Richard V. Pierard, "The Church of the Brethren and the Temperance Movement," *Brethren Life and Thought* 26 (Winter 1981): 39.

3. *Annual Meeting Minutes* (1909:431). Italics added.

4. Ibid., 497.

5. Sappington (1961:37); *Annual Meeting Minutes* (1909:719).

6. I. J. Rosenberger, "Other Societies," *Gospel Messenger*, 9 May 1903, 291-292.

7. *Annual Meeting Minutes* (1909:871).

8. Ibid., 871-872.

9. For a transcription of the debate, see *COB Full Report* (1908:58-75).

10. Ibid., 59.

11. I am indebted to Carl F. Bowman's interpretation of the 1908 Annual Meeting action and its impact. See C. Bowman (1989:349-354).

12. *Annual Meeting Minutes* (1912:9).

13. Ibid., 3. Italics added. My treatment of the 1912 Annual Meeting report on voting builds on Carl F. Bowman's fuller discussion. See C. Bowman (1989:354-360).

14. *COB Full Report* (1912:89-98).

15. Kulp, ed. ([1974]:25).

16. Carl W. Zeigler, Sr. interviewed by Donald B. Kraybill.

17. *Eastern District Meeting Minutes* (1914:10).

18. *Southeastern District Ministerial Meeting Minutes*, November 25, 1912.

19. Gleim (1975:78).

20. "Notes from Our Correspondents," *Gospel Messenger*, 15 June 1918, 379.

21. "Notes from Our Correspondents," *Gospel Messenger*, 11 May 1918, 304.

22. Chiques Council Meeting Minutes, August 26, 1916.

23. Harry K. Balsbaugh, "History of the Church of the Brethren, Harrisburg, Pa.," 1959, TMs [photocopy], pp. 100-101, Harrisburg First church archives.

24. *Annual Conference Minutes* (1926:76-77).

25. See Lawrence H. Fuchs, "Election of 1928," in *History of American Presidential Elections*, Vol. 3, Arthur M. Schlesinger, Jr., ed. (New York: McGraw-Hill, 1971), 2585-2704.

26. "The Messenger and the Candidates," *Gospel Messenger*, 27 October 1928, 677.

27. "Two Obligations That Will Remain," *Gospel Messenger*, 3 November 1928, 693.

28. "Brief History of the Richland Church of the Brethren," in Program of Golden Anniversary Services, September 19-21, 1969.

29. See J. Stanley Earhart interview; and Carl W. Zeigler, Sr. interviewed by Donald B. Kraybill. Among topics for discussion at the 1928 Eastern District Ministerial Meeting were "What should our ministers preach on the question of voting?" and "Should our ministers take part in politics?" This is further evidence that the 1928 presidential election was causing some Brethren to reevaluate attitudes toward voting. See Eastern District Ministerial Meeting Program, December 26, 1928.

30. Luke H. Brandt and Harold Z. Bomberger interviews.

31. Note from November 5, 1939, Ambler Church of the Brethren bulletin, in Cramer, comp. (1990:254).

32. *Eastern District Elders Body Minutes*, April 28, 1909.

33. This treatment of Martin Grove Brumbaugh builds on C. Bowman (1989:440-449).

34. For more information on Brumbaugh's educational career see Earl C. Kaylor, Jr. (1977:index). A comprehensive treatment of M. G. Brumbaugh by Kaylor is in process at this writing. The as yet untitled volume covers Brumbaugh's educational achievements, relationship with the Church of the Brethren, election to the governorship, and legislative accomplishments.

35. See Philip S. Klein and Ari Hoogenboom, *A History of Pennsylvania* (New York: McGraw-Hill Book Company, 1973), 382-383, 386; Earl C. Kaylor, Jr. (1981:319-322); and Durnbaugh, ed., 1983, s. v. "Martin Grove Brumbaugh," by Dennis L. Slabaugh.

36. C. Bowman (1989:442).

37. Gleim (1975:173 and index).

38. *COB Full Report* (1915:193).

39. *Eastern District Meeting Minutes* (1915:10). Italics added.

40. For the reactions of one Lancaster County minister to Governor Brumbaugh, see excerpt from Abram M. Hess interviewed by Donald B. Kraybill and Carl F. Bowman, in C. Bowman (1989:444-445).

41. Carl W. Zeigler, Sr. interviewed by Donald B. Kraybill.

42. Harold Z. Bomberger and Luke H. Brandt interviews.

43. Caleb W. Bucher interview.

44. "Election Results," *Intelligencer Journal* (Lancaster), 27 April 1932, 1, 7.

45. Elizabethtown Council Meeting Minutes,

May 12, 1932.

46. Carl W. Zeigler, Sr. interviewed by Donald B. Kraybill.

47. "Moderator," *Intelligencer Journal* (Lancaster), 29 April 1932, 1.

48. Alice Allen, ed., *The Pennsylvania Manual* (Harrisburg: Commonwealth of Pennsylvania, 1948), 388.

49. Carl W. Zeigler, Sr. interviewed by Donald B. Kraybill.

50. Leona List interview.

51. *Congregational Profile*.

52. *Southeastern District Ministerial Meeting Minutes*, November 25, 1912.

53. *Annual Conference Minutes* (1926:7).

54. Howe (1943:529).

55. See Gleim (1975:234, 269, 271, 294, 327).

56. *History of the Church. . .* (1965:62).

57. Program of the 50th Anniversary of Scouting in Elizabethtown.

58. "Protestant Churches Sponsor 42,633 Scout Packs, Troops, Posts," *Gospel Messenger*, 5 July 1958, 20.

59. Kulp, ed. ([1974]:87).

Endnotes for Chapter 8

1. *Annual Meeting Minutes* (1909:237).

2. For a thorough study of the peace churches' response to World War I, see Albert N. Keim and Grant M. Stoltzfus, *The Politics of Conscience: The Historic Peace Churches and America at War, 1917-1955* (Scottdale, Pa.: Herald Press, 1988), 32-55.

3. *Annual Meeting Minutes* (1910:15).

4. Ibid. (1911:7).

5. Ibid. (1916:12).

6. *Eastern District Elders Body Minutes* (1915: 89-90).

7. Rufus D. Bowman, *The Church of the Brethren and War, 1708-1941*, rev. ed. (New York: Garland Publishing, 1971), 171; and Keim and Stoltzfus (1988:32-36).

8. *Annual Conference Minutes* (1917:17). Italics added.

9. R. Bowman (1971:188).

10. See *Eastern District Meeting Minutes* (1918:10); and *Southeastern District Meeting Minutes* (1919:7).

11. I. W. Taylor, "A Visit to Camp Meade, Admiral, Md.," *Gospel Messenger*, 13 October 1917, 645. Ober and Taylor met only with those who refused all cooperation. Some Brethren evidently were participating in training at Camp Meade.

12. *Eastern District Meeting Minutes* (1918:11).

13. Informants who grew up in the Mechanic Grove and Conestoga congregations report that all or most of their young men received agricultural exemptions during World War I. See Caleb W. Bucher interviewed by Donald B. Kraybill and Carl F. Bowman; and Abram M. Hess interviewed by Donald B. Kraybill and Carl F. Bowman.

14. Carl W. Zeigler, Sr. interviewed by Donald B. Kraybill.

15. Mayno Hershey interview.

16. "Notes from Our Correspondents," *Gospel Messenger*, 25 May 1918, 333.

17. Gleim (1975:302).

18. "Notes from Our Correspondents," *Gospel Messenger*, 28 September 1918, 621.

19. R. Bowman (1971:179).

20. *Minutes of the Special General Conference* (January 9, 1918:3-6).

21. R. Bowman (1971:184-187).

22. Durnbaugh, ed., 1983, s. v. "World War I" and "World War II," by Donald F. Durnbaugh.

23. R. Bowman (1971:235).

24. *Annual Conference Minutes* (1919:34).

25. *Eastern District Meeting Minutes* (1920:11).

26. *Annual Conference Minutes* (1924:9-13).

27. The Mountville congregation, for example, in 1925 disowned a man who "was charged with fornication and having enlisted in the army." Mountville Council Meeting Minutes, November 11, 1925.

28. R. Bowman (1971:237).

29. *Annual Conference Minutes* (1931:45).

30. Lititz Council Meeting Minutes, August 3, 1924. See also Fitzkee (1990:11). The Elizabethtown congregation in July 1924 appointed a committee to distribute literature "discouraging this oncoming military demonstration." See Elizabethtown Council Meeting Minutes, July 23, 1924.

31. *Annual Conference Minutes* (1935:40-41).

32. Sappington (1961:51).

33. In addition, the BSC helped administer the Civilian Public Service program for conscientious objectors during World War II. See Durnbaugh, ed., 1983, s. v. "Spanish Civil War," by Donald F. Durnbaugh; and Donald F. Durnbaugh, ed., *To Serve the Present Age* (Elgin, Ill.: Brethren Press, 1975), 107-116.

34. For a thorough discussion of the creation of the CPS program, see Keim and Stoltzfus (1988). For a concise summary see Donald F. Durnbaugh "An experiment in church/state relations," *Messenger*, October 1990, 11, 14.

35. *Minutes of Special Eastern District Meeting* (February 22, 1941:23-24).

36. Durnbaugh, ed., 1983, s. v. "World War II," by Donald F. Durnbaugh.

37. Ambler had nearly 100 people in the armed forces during the war, while three men chose alternative service. See Gleim (1975:201); and Shoemaker and Zuck, 1942, TMs [photocopy]. According to Gleim (1975:255-256, 349), the Royersford congregation, totaling less than 135 members, sent 22 men and women into the armed forces, with few or no CPSers, while Philadelphia's Calvary church saw 69 out of 332 members enter the military. The Parker Ford congregation had only two conscientious objectors (Gleim 1975:216); and almost all of the draftees from the Philadelphia First congregation joined the military, as well. See W. Dean Crouse interview.

38. Gleim (1975:306). Gleim, who pastored the Bethany congregation during World War II, recalls that a number of members worked at the nearby Frankford Arsenal and the Philadelphia Navy Yard. Elmer Q. Gleim interview.

39. Gleim (1975:357).

40. Elmer Q. Gleim interview.

41. Caleb W. Bucher, "Pastor's Letter," in *Brethren Beacon*, October 1, 1944.

42. Don Fitzkee, "War Heroes," *Messenger*, October 1990, 18.

43. A longtime member of the Harrisburg First congregation estimates that about 85 percent of its draftees entered the military, including the pastor's son, who was an officer in the Navy. See E. Miller Peterman interview. Carl W. Zeigler, Sr., who

pastored the flag-flying Lebanon congregation during World War II, remembered only two conscientious objectors out of 25 or more draftees. "I must confess," said Zeigler, "that the two COs were not appreciated by the general run of the congregation." Carl W. Zeigler, Sr. interview by Donald B. Kraybill.

44. J. Stanley Earhart interview.

45. See James F. Myer and Luke H. Brandt interviews.

46. About a third of the draftees from the Fredericksburg (now Mount Zion Road) congregation north of Lebanon chose CPS. See *History of the Church. . .* (1965:46). A man who grew up in the Conewago congregation south of Hershey estimates that just under half of its young men were conscientious objectors. See Luke H. Brandt interview.

47. Explaining why most men from the Philadelphia First congregation chose the military, a former pastor notes:
"These men there in the Philadelphia First church, many of them were in high-powered, then high-tech industries. . . . They were captains of industry. That's what you have to remember. " W. Dean Crouse interview.

48. James F. Myer interview.

49. C. Bowman (1989:612-614; 642-644) also observes this link between nonconformity and nonresistance.

50. Carl W. Zeigler, Sr. interview by Donald B. Kraybill.

51. *Annual Conference Minutes* (1938:41).

52. *Southeastern District Meeting Minutes* (1941:5).

53. Durnbaugh, ed., 1983, s. v. "Civilian Public Service," by Kenneth I. Morse.

54. Gleim (1975:183).

55. Durnbaugh, ed., 1983, s. v. "Brethren Service Center, New Windsor, MD," by Kenneth I. Morse.

56. For an account of Ben Bushong's contributions in the early days of the Heifer Project see M. Rebecca Bushong, "Ben Bushong—Apostle of Mercy," *Brethren Life and Thought* 24 (Spring 1979): 71-88.

57. "Regional Youth Interested in Brethren Volunteer Service," *Eastern Region Letter*, July 1950, 1.

58. In the years 1954 through 1986, 95 men from the congregation joined the military, while 14 performed alternative service. Among Palmyra women who were never subject to a draft, four entered the military, while nine performed volunteer service. See Palmyra congregational directories, 1954-1986.

59. Kulp, ed. ([1974]:73-74).

60. *Eastern District Board Minutes*, Social Education and Action Commission Report, 1963. Italics added. Percentages were based on responses from 32 congregations. "Recently" was not defined in the minutes.

61. *Eastern District Conference Minutes* (1967:54).

62. C. Wayne Zunkel, "Brethren bidding for bolder peace action," *Messenger*, 14 March 1968, 17.

63. Inez Long, "Dare Brethren join step with marchers?" *Messenger*, 20 January 1966, 6-7.

64. "COs in full public view," *Messenger*, 27 June 1967, 15.

65. Harrisburg First Council Meeting Minutes, January 28, 1968.

66. *Annual Conference Minutes* (1970:66).

67. See Ronald E. Keener, "Campus recruitment for war and peace," *Messenger*, 1 May 1971, 2-3; "Score One for the Military," *Atlantic Northeast District Brethren Peace Fellowship Newsletter*, December 1970, 1-2; and Atlantic Northeast District Board Minutes, October 24, 1970.

68. J. Kenneth Kreider, "Readers Write," *Messenger*, 1 August 1971, inside cover-1. Kreider is also quoted in Keener, 1 May 1971.

69. *Atlantic Northeast District Conference Minutes* (1971:51).

70. Ibid. (1972:54).

71. "Troublers of Israel," *Atlantic Northeast District Brethren Peace Fellowship Newsletter*, May 1972, 2.

72. David C. Ogren, "Readers Write," *Messenger*, 16 September 1965, inside cover, reacting to Kenneth I. Morse, editorial, "Let's listen to the loyal opposition," *Messenger*, 24 June 1965, 32.

73. *Annual Conference Minutes* (1948:62-64).

74. Ibid. (1957:13-19).

75. Ibid. (1967:64-67).

76. Ibid. (1968:87-90).

77. Ibid. (1969:61-64).

78. Ibid. (1970:63-67). See also "Annual Conference '70," *Messenger*, 30 July 1970, 2.

79. "Annual Conference Report: Love in Deed and Truth, in Work and Worship," *Messenger*, 15 August 1971, 9-14.

80. For the committee's final report, see *Annual Conference Minutes* (1973:63-65).

81. See "Annual Conference Report," *Messenger*, 31 July 1969, 5.

82. Luella Reinhold Harris, "Readers Write," *Messenger*, 14 August 1969, inside cover.

83. J. Kenneth Kreider, "Readers Write," *Messenger*, 25 September 1969, inside cover.

84. Paul A. Gish, "Readers Write," *Messenger*, 15 January 1970, 1, 29.

85. Ernest L. Reisinger, "Readers Write," *Messenger*, 12 March 1970, 1.

86. For a summary and defense of Glick's actions see an article by Ted Glick's father, G. Wayne Glick, an ordained minister and college professor from the Lancaster congregation, "The Laws of Men and the Law of God," *Messenger*, 15 October 1971, 9-11, 25. Ted Glick wrote letters to *Messenger* interpreting his actions. See 12 February 1970: inside cover; and 1 November 1972:1, 21. Glick eventually was tried separately from the rest of the "Harrisburg Seven." See "Judge Severs Glick's Trial," *Intelligencer Journal* (Lancaster), 18 January 1972, 6.

87. "Concern Is Shown For Harrisburg 7," *Intelligencer Journal* (Lancaster), 27 January 1972, 52.

88. "Thanks be to God for a Successful '89 Relief Auction," *Brethren News*, November 1986, 4.

89. "Disaster Relief Auction," *Brethren News*, November 1989, 11.

90. For a short history of the auction see "From the Beginning," in the 1991 Brethren Disaster Auction tabloid.

Endnotes for Chapter 9

1. This chapter applies much of Bowman's analysis of church unity at the denominational level to the district and congregational levels. See C. Bowman (1989:664-678).

2. "Inviting Others to Preach," *Gospel Messenger*, 3 March 1906, 138.

3. J. Harry Enders interview.

4. West Conestoga Council Meeting Minutes, April 6, 1903.

5. Mountville Council Meeting Minutes, December 16, 1908.

6. Carl W. Zeigler, Sr. interviewed by Donald B. Kraybill.

7. Ibid.

8. Two such groups were the International Sunday School Convention and the American Sunday School Union—Christian agencies promoting Sunday school work during the nineteenth century. See Durnbaugh, ed., 1983, s. v. "American Sunday School Union," by R. Jan Thompson, and "International Sunday School Convention," by Hazel M. Kennedy.

9. *Annual Meeting Minutes* (1909:813).

10. *History of the Church. . .* (1965:32).

11. For a thorough description of the impact of missions on the Church of the Brethren, see Moyer (1931:229-257.) Also, Hogan (1958:314) points to foreign missions as a key factor leading Brethren toward ecumenical cooperation.

12. Durnbaugh, ed., 1983, s. v. "Interchurch World Movement," by Edward K. Ziegler.

13. *Eastern District Meeting Minutes* (1920:10).

14. *COB Full Report* (1920:134-135).

15. Sappington (1961:54).

16. Brethren did cooperate extensively with Mennonites and Friends between the World Wars to obtain legal provisions for conscientious objectors.

17. Howe (1943:208).

18. *Southeastern District Ministerial Meeting Minutes*, December 11, 1913.

19. Mountville Council Meeting Minutes, March 13, 1907.

20. Ibid.

21. Collier, et. al., eds. (1977:13).

22. *Eastern District Ministerial Meeting Minutes*, November 1-3, 1927. Italics added.

23. Eastern District Ministerial Meeting Program, November 4-6, 1930. Italics added.

24. Earl H. Kurtz interview.

25. Carl W. Zeigler, Sr. interviewed by Donald B. Kraybill.

26. Fitzkee (1990:15).

27. Examples include Harrisburg First, which voted in March 1944 to join the United Churches of Greater Harrisburg; Reading, which joined the Greater Reading Council of Churches as an original member in January 1947; and Lancaster, which joined the Lancaster County Council of Churches in 1947. See Harrisburg First Council Meeting Minutes, March 14, 1944; Crowther (1965 (?):16, 18); and C. John Bryer, *History of the Lancaster Church of the Brethren, 1891-1991* (n. p., [1991]), 9.

28. Gleim (1975:76).

29. Nevin H. Zuck interview.

30. See Harrisburg First Council Meeting Minutes, May 18, 1953; January 10, 1956; and "Growing Edges," *Messenger*, 6 January 1966, 18.

31. Caleb W. Bucher interview.

32. Nevin H. Zuck interview.

33. *Southeastern District Elders Body Minutes*, April 17, 1929.

34. *Southeastern District Meeting Minutes*, April 22, 1937; April 21, 1938.

35. *Eastern District Meeting Minutes* (1940:4).

36. Ibid. (1941:3-4).

37. Ibid. (1946:32).

38. Ibid. (1953:33-34).

39. Gleim (1975:295).

40. C. Wayne Zunkel interview.

41. *Atlantic Northeast District Conference Minutes* (October 10-11, 1970:13).

42. Sappington (1961:70-71).

43. *Annual Conference Minutes* (1941:50).

44. Durnbaugh, ed., 1983, s. v. "World Council of Churches," by Dale L. Ott.

45. Durnbaugh, ed., 1983, s. v. "Ecumenism" and "National Council of Churches of Christ in the USA," by Edward K. Ziegler.

46. "The Howe Resolutions," in I. N. H. Beahm, *Twenty Reasons* (n. d.:18). Prior to the 1945 Annual Conference Beahm wrote a lengthy tract, citing 20 reasons why the Church of the Brethren should withdraw from the FCC. He included Howe's resolution as a supplement.

47. *Annual Conference Minutes* (1944:50). Eastern District in fall 1944 referred to this committee queries from the White Oak and Indian Creek congregations, each requesting that the Church of the Brethren immediately withdraw from the FCC. See *Eastern District Meeting Minutes* (1944:4).

48. *Annual Conference Minutes* (1945:14).

49. *Annual Conference Minutes* (1945:15-16).

50. Hogan (1958:420).

51. *Eastern District Meeting Minutes* (1947:7). See 2 Corinthians 6:14-18.

52. Ibid. (1948:11). Delegates respectfully returned the paper.

53. *Eastern District Conference Minutes* (1951:5).

54. Indian Creek Special Council Meeting Minutes, March 27, 1962.

55. "First Annual Report," Tri-District Director of Christian Education Virginia Fisher, October 1, 1961-September 30, 1962.

56. *Eastern District Elders Body Minutes*, November 3, 1948; November 2, 1949; May 30, 1950; November 1, 1950.

57. After years of decline, the Shamokin church marked its 50th anniversary before closing its doors in November 1966. *Eastern District Conference Minutes* (1966:18-19).

58. See *Eastern District Elders Body Minutes*, November 1, 1950; *History of the Church. . .* (1965:14); and Hiram J. Frysinger interview.

59. Norman J. Baugher, "What the National Council of Churches Means to Us," *Messenger*, 18 February 1965, 10-12, 22.

60. Durnbaugh, ed., 1983, s. v. "Telford, PA, Penn Valley Grace Brethren Church," by William F. Tweeddale and Donald F. Durnbaugh.

61. After several years of legal wrangling over church property, Calvary church in 1972 purchased the building from the Atlantic Northeast District for $5,000 and became an independent congregation. See Gleim (1975:352-353).

62. Conversation with Steven Longenecker, professor of history at Bridgewater (Va.) College.

63. Inez G. Long, "Less Time on Yard Goods," *Messenger*, 26 October 1963, 15.

64. Eberly, ed. (1991:10-11).

65. *Southeastern District Ministerial Meeting Minutes*, November 9, 1914. Subsequent minutes give no evidence that the committee actually carried out its task.

66. Eastern District Ministerial Meeting Program, December 26, 1928.

67. Gleim (1975:197).

68. *Annual Conference Minutes* (1930:30).

69. Ibid. (1931:5-6).

70. Dove (1932:146).

71. Examples are Chiques (1957) and Middle Creek (1959). See Chiques Council Meeting Minutes, February 26, 1957; and *History of the Church. . .* (1965:135).

72. Though sometimes referred to as "closed" communion, the Brethren practice was "close" communion. The emphasis was on the close fellowship shared by participants.

73. See Gleim (1975:482); and Howe (1943:482).

74. Howe (1943:484-485).

75. *Eastern District Elders Body Minutes*, April 24, 1935.

76. See *Annual Meeting Minutes* (1909:108); and *Eastern District Elders Body Minutes*, April 28, 1937.

77. *Annual Conference Minutes* (1951:21).

78. *Congregational Profile*. Based on 48 congregations who reported dates.

79. *Annual Meeting Minutes* (1909:420).

80. *Annual Meeting Minutes* (1915:10).

81. Lancaster Council Meeting Minutes, October 30, 1915.

82. *Annual Conference Minutes* (1949:56).

83. Ibid. (1951:9).

84. Ibid. (1957:70-71).

85. Ibid. (1958:10-15).

86. Linford J. Rotenberger interview.

87. *Brethren Revival Fellowship Meeting Minutes*, July 16, 1964.

88. Caleb W. Bucher interview.

89. Carl W. Zeigler, Sr. interviewed by Donald B. Kraybill.

90. Fitzkee (1990:25-26).

91. *Congregational Profile*.

92. Durnbaugh, ed., 1983, s. v. "Consultation on Church Union," by Edward K. Zeigler.

93. *Annual Conference Minutes* (1966:45-51).

94. "The Big Debate of 1966: Excerpting the Views of Conference Delegates," *Messenger*, 1 September 1966, 16-19.

95. Ibid. In the months preceding the 1966 Annual Conference debate, Zunkel also expressed his views in "Readers Write," *Messenger*, 23 December 1965, inside cover; and 12 May 1966, inside cover.

96. "The Big Debate. . .," *Messenger*, 1 September 1966, 16-19.

97. For an account of the 1966 COCU debate, see "Report Urges Ecumenicity," *Messenger*, 23 June 1966, 12-13; and "Vignettes of an Annual Conference," *Messenger*, 4 August 1966, 1-2. The Winter 1966 issue of *Brethren Life and Thought* also focuses on the Consultation on Church Union.

98. See Inez Long, "Brethren Take to the Hills and Alleys," *Christian Century* 83 (July 20, 1966): 916-917. COCU advocates attempted at the 1968 Annual Conference to re-open the question of full participation, but delegates voted 607 to 349 not to reconsider. See *Annual Conference Minutes* (1968:86-87).

99. Elmer Q. Gleim interview.

100. Luke H. Brandt interview.

101. See Carl W. Zeigler, Sr. interview by Donald B. Kraybill and Carl F. Bowman; Abram M. Hess interview by Donald B. Kraybill and Carl F. Bow-

man; and J. Harry Enders interview. See also individual entries on these congregations in Durnbaugh, ed., 1983.

102. Carl W. Zeigler, Sr. interview by Donald B. Kraybill.

103. *Congregational Profile*.

104. January 9, 1971, letter from Atlantic Northeast District Board to Church of the Brethren General Board. Italics in original.

105. Durnbaugh, ed., 1983, "Introduction," by Donald F. Durnbaugh.

106. Durnbaugh, ed., 1983, s. v. "New Call to Peacemaking," by Robert J. Rumsey.

107. Durnbaugh, ed., 1983, s. v. "Sunday School Literature," by Hazel M. Kennedy.

108. "Sales of new hymnal are exceeding expectations," *Messenger*, March 1992, 8.

109. Kay Rohrer, "College dedicates new center," *Sunday News* (Lancaster), 8 October 1989.

110. *Annual Conference Minutes* (1989:880-881); *Atlantic Northeast District Conference Minutes* (1989:56-60).

111. As recently as 1981, in response to a query from the East Fairview congregation, Annual Conference reviewed and reaffirmed Brethren affiliation with the NCC and WCC. The 1982 Conference passed a statement from the General Board articulating a "Brethren vision of unity." See *Minutes of the Annual Conference, 1980-1984* (1985:254-269, 408-410).

Endnotes for Chapter 10

1. Frye (Winter 1991-1992:77). Italics added. I use Frye's distinction between the "beauty of holiness" and the "holiness of beauty" elsewhere in this chapter, as well.

2. *The Reading Eagle*, 18 August 1894, quoted in *History of the Church. . .* (1915:479-480).

3. See Dale W. Brown, "A People Without a Liturgy?" *Brethren Life and Thought* 21 (Winter 1986): 27.

4. Frye (Winter 1991-1992:77).

5. This practice of "lining" likely grew out of the days when most Brethren did not have hymnals or were unable to read. Hymnals used around 1900 provided words without notes, so the songleader "gave rise to the tune" and the congregation joined in. See Durnbaugh, ed., 1983, s. v. "Lining of Hymns," by Nancy Rosenberger Faus.

6. The Chiques congregation was so unconcerned with holidays that it held Council Meeting on Christmas Day. See Chiques Council Meeting Minutes, December 25, 1899.

7. For descriptions of Sunday morning worship services around 1900, see Brubaker, ed. ([1989]:7-8) and G. Moore (1961:10-23).

8. See Chapter Two for a fuller description of love feast.

9. Eastern District Brethren were scandalized in the mid-1870s when progressive Philadelphia First church built a wooden baptismal pool inside the meetinghouse. The matter came before the 1875 Annual Conference, where delegates flatly ruled, "As we have no authority in the Scriptures for baptizing in the house, we consider it wrong to do so. " Despite protests from Philadelphia minister J. P. Hetrick—including a graphic description of the nature of the mud in the Delaware River—Annual Conference refused to yield the following year. See *Annual Meeting Minutes*

(1909:323); and *COB Full Report* (1876:61ff.), quoted in C. Bowman (1989:145-147).

10. *Annual Meeting Minutes* (1909:765-766).

11. Howe (1943:137).

12. For a description of a Brethren baptism in Lebanon County in 1938, see Ann Hark, *Hex Marks the Spot* (Philadelphia: J. B. Lippincott Company, 1938), 158-171.

13. See "Notes from Our Correspondents," *Gospel Messenger,* 14 March 1903, 173. Revivals stretching into the third week remained common into the 1930s. According to "Church News," *Gospel Messenger,* 12 March 1938, 21, Elder Henry King preached into the third week at a Spring Creek revival meeting in 1938.

14. Howe (1943:86-87).

15. *History of the Church. . .* (1915:246-247).

16. Congregations reorienting their meetinghouses included Annville, 1917; Mingo, 1926; Elizabethtown, 1934; Akron, 1936; Skippack, 1937; and Hanoverdale, 1939. See Frye (Winter 1991-1992:73); *History of the Church. . .* (1965:3, 9, 32, 107-108, 130); and Hiram J. Frysinger and Jesse K. Hoffman interviews.

17. Both Lancaster and Harrisburg First Council Meeting Minutes by 1910 refer to the building as the "church." See Lancaster Council Meeting Minutes, April 8, 1896; August 12, 1908; and Harrisburg First Council Meeting Minutes, April 24, 1902; April 25, 1905.

18. Joseph Studebaker, "Vocal Versus Instrumental Music for Worship—No. 1," *Gospel Messenger,* 18 June 1898, 371-372.

19. "Vocal and Instrumental Music in Worship," General Missionary and Tract Committee, n. d.

20. See *Annual Conference Minutes* (1920:11-12); Gleim (1975:168); and Howe (1943:305-311).

21. While Annual Conference at first opposed singing schools, decisions in 1862 and 1874 cautiously permitted them. See *Annual Meeting Minutes* (1909:206, 317).

22. See Lancaster Council Meeting Minutes, October 19, 1892; November 20, 1893; Breidenstine ([1988]:55); West Conestoga Council Meeting Minutes, October 14, 1901; and Chiques Council Meeting Minutes, August 30, 1922. For a list of singing school leaders in Eastern District see *History of the Church. . .* (1965:151-52).

23. See *Annual Meeting Minutes* (1909:715). While a few Sunday school songbooks and less popular hymnals produced by Brethren prior to 1901 included notes, the "old black book", as the 1901 hymnal was affectionately called, was the first such hymnal to gain wide acceptance in the churches of eastern Pennsylvania. See Durnbaugh, ed., 1983, s. v. "Hymnals," by Hedwig R. Durnbaugh and Nevin W. Fisher. For a list of hymn- and songbooks used in Eastern District see *History of the Church. . .* (1965:149, 153).

24. Since the late 1800s, it had been common for Brethren to have musical instruments in their homes for personal use. An 1894 Annual Meeting decision in essence allowed instruments in homes, even though the statement said that the Conference "does not mean to justify or encourage the use of musical instruments in private houses." *Annual Meeting Minutes* (1909:599).

25. *History of the Church. . .* (1965:156-161).

26. Carl W. Zeigler, Sr. interview by Donald B. Kraybill.

27. Quotation from the 1851 *Annual Meeting Minutes* (1909:123). As late as 1919, Eastern District elders, citing Conference minutes, spoke against benedictions. See *Eastern District Elders Body Minutes,* April 30, 1919.

28. *Annual Conference Minutes* (1920:14).

29. Churches incorporating benedictions into their worship during the 1920s and 1930s include Chiques, 1923; Richland, 1928; Hatfield, 1929; and Mountville, 1930. See Chiques Council Meeting Minutes, August 29, 1923; "Brief History of the Richland Church. . .," September 19-21, 1969; *History of the Church. . .* (1965:58); and Mountville Council Meeting Minutes, November 12, 1930.

30. Carl W. Zeigler, Sr. interview by Donald B. Kraybill.

31. C. Bowman (1989:559); and Carl W. Zeigler, Sr. interview by Donald B. Kraybill.

32. The Ambler congregation in the 1880s collected "semi-annual dues" at Council Meeting. The Chiques church cared for finances on the annual visit. Faced with members who refused to contribute "their valuation," Chiques in April 1881 ruled that those who failed to pay up would "fall under the judgment of the church." See Ambler Council Meeting Minutes in Cramer, comp., (1990); and Chiques Council Meeting Minutes, April 1881.

33. *Annual Meeting Minutes* (1909:616).

34. See Ambler Council Meeting Minutes, February 28, 1885; February 27, 1897; February 26, 1898; in Cramer, comp. (1990: 38, 50-51); and Lancaster Council Meeting Minutes, December 1, 1915.

35. The Mountville congregation approved weekly offerings (and benedictions) in 1930, followed by Midway congregation in 1933. In the Chiques congregation, occasional offerings for specific causes were lifted as needed by the mid-1920s, but requests for regular offerings were rejected in 1933, 1942, and again in 1948. See Mountville Council Meeting Minutes, November 12, 1930; *History of the Church . . .* (1965:102); and Chiques Council Meeting Minutes, May 27, 1933; October 1, 1933; February 28, 1942; February 2, 1948; February 24, 1940; and November 29, 1941.

36. See Elizabethtown Council Meeting Minutes, March 23, 1920. In a similar vein, Elizabethtown elder Samuel H. Hertzler once confessed to a younger minister, "I fear I am sometimes too humorous for the pulpit." See Ralph W. Schlosser, "Fifty Years of Change," *Messenger,* 23 May 1968, 20-21.

37. At the 1927 Eastern District Ministerial Meeting, Martha Light noted that more study was required to preach today than in earlier days. At the same meeting, conservative elder J. H. Longenecker recommended making preaching assignments in advance, rather than selecting preachers on the spot. See *Eastern District Ministerial Meeting Minutes,* November 1-3, 1927.

38. Eastern District Ministerial Meeting Program, December 26, 1932.

39. A longtime member of the Mountville congregation recalls that bearing of testimony by deacons ceased in his congregation in 1931 when the last deacon of an earlier generation died. The East Fairview congregation in Lancaster County eliminated the second sermon by 1930. See J. Harry Enders and J. Stanley Earhart interviews.

40. Luke H. Brandt and J. Stanley Earhart interviews.

41. The Elizabethtown church in 1925 approved sitting together in "family groupings." See Elizabethtown Council Meeting Minutes, November 12, 1925. According to informants, men and women sat together in the East Fairview and Spring Creek churches by the 1930s, and in the Richland church by the 1940s. Joseph M. Long, J. Stanley Earhart, and Earl K. Ziegler interviews.

42. Fitzkee (1990:4-5).

43. Ray A. Kurtz interview.

44. For references to decreasing use of the Lord's Prayer in the Lititz, Elizabethtown, and Mountville congregations, see Fitzkee (1990:3); Elizabethtown Council Meeting Minutes, November 23, 1922; and Mountville Council Meeting Minutes, November 8, 1933.

45. See Gleim (1975:230-232); and Shoemaker and Zuck, 1942, TMs [photocopy].

46. See April 4, 1937 and October 17, 1937 bulletins in Cramer, comp. (1990:237, 240); and Gleim (1975:198).

47. According to *History of the Church. . .* (1965:91), the Little Swatara church granted permission for special music at revival meetings in 1919, provided the evangelist had no objections. Lititz and Elizabethtown approved "special singing" at regular services in the late 1920s. See Fitzkee (1990:11); and Elizabethtown Council Meeting Minutes, September 6, 1928.

48. See *Eastern District Meeting Minutes* (1930:4) and Eastern District Ministerial Meeting Programs. Not until 1937 was special music regularly featured at Eastern District Ministers' Meetings. The 1920 Ministers' Meeting did include a duet, but special music did not appear again until 1937.

49. Arlene Keller interview.

50. C. Bowman (1989:560).

51. See Harrisburg First Council Meeting Minutes, March 24, 1914; May 9, 1914; July 15, 1924; and *History of the Church. . .* (1965:51).

52. *Eastern District Ministerial Meeting Minutes*, November 4-6, 1930.

53. Prior to that, weddings were usually held in homes. See Durnbaugh, ed. 1983, s. v. "Wedding Customs," by Emmert F. Bittinger.

54. Fitzkee (1990:16, 19, 21). See also Breidenstine ([1988]:53-57) for a description of a similar transition in the Spring Creek congregation.

55. In fact, many congregations in the Greater Philadelphia Area apparently never observed the traditional two-day love feast. The demographic factors that led rural congregations to condense their love feasts to one day from the 1930s on may have prevented urban churches from ever beginning the practice.

56. Collier, et. al., eds. (1977:9); and Elizabethtown Council Meeting Minutes, November 14, 1935.

57. Only four of 73 congregations and fellowships in the 1994 Atlantic Northeast District Directory report a two-day love feast. A few others may still hold a version of the two-day feast, but only reported the date of the love feast service proper. See Chapter Six for more information on the self-examination service.

58. See Elizabethtown Council Meeting Minutes, March 20, 1918; November 5, 1925; January 8, 1926; May 3, 1934; November 14, 1935; and March 5, 1936. Individual soup bowls evidently were approved at another time. Other congregations accepting individual communion cups in the 1930s and 1940s include: Spring Creek, 1935; Lititz, 1938 (soup bowls in 1940); and Mountville, 1942. See Breidenstine ([1988]:61); Fitzkee (1990:16, 19); and Mountville Council Meeting Minutes, November 11, 1942.

59. See *Annual Meeting Minutes* (1913:4). Eliminating the second kiss from the love feast often generated controversy. The Lancaster church discussed the matter in 1916, before tabling it indefinitely. See Lancaster Council Meeting Minutes, April 18, 1916; September 27, 1916. The Harrisburg First and Mountville congregations also denied requests to eliminate the kiss in 1919 and 1938, respectively. See Harrisburg First Council Meeting Minutes, April 21, 1919; and Mountville Council Meeting Minutes, November 9, 1938. According to Breidenstine ([1988]: 61), the Spring Creek congregation eliminated the second kiss in 1932. Gradually the second kiss disappeared in most congregations, and in some the holy kiss was eliminated entirely, replaced by a hug or handshake.

60. Breidenstine ([1988]:24).

61. Luke H. Brandt interview.

62. Many at Lebanon pushed for a divided chancel in their new church, but Zeigler demanded a central pulpit. Less than a year after he concluded his pastorate, the congregation divided its chancel. See Carl W. Zeigler, Sr. interview by Donald B. Kraybill; and Carl W. Zeigler, Sr. interview by Donald B. Kraybill and Carl F. Bowman.

63. See Durnbaugh, ed., 1983, s. v. "Architecture," by Kenneth I. Morse, for an overview of Brethren architecture and for comment on the impact of ecumenical contacts.

64. Examples include Elizabethtown, 1956; Philadelphia First, 1957; Palmyra, 1957; Florin, 1958; Lancaster, 1959; Reading, 1959; Mechanic Grove, 1959; Richland, 1961; Mountville, 1962; Lititz, 1962; Little Swatara, 1964. See *Congregational Profile* and *History of the Church. . .* (1965).

65. *Annual Conference Minutes* (1952:17-18).

66. Technically, only Roman Catholics have altars. Protestants have "communion tables." For an explanation of the difference, see Durnbaugh, ed., 1983, s. v. "Communion Table," by Donald F. Durnbaugh. We use "altar" because it was the term commonly used by Brethren, albeit wrongly.

67. Ray A. Kurtz interview.

68. J. Harry Enders interview.

69. Nevin H. Zuck interview.

70. Ridgeway Community Church News Bulletin, March-April 1962, 9.

71. Cover of a church bulletin used by Brethren during the 1950s.

72. In an article describing the benefits of Brethren affiliation with the National Council of Churches, General Secretary Norman Baugher noted that Dean gained "invaluable professional information" from the NCC and that annual NCC-sponsored Conferences "made available to local congregations a wealth of material on new church design." See Norman J. Baugher, "What the National Council of Churches Means to Us," *Messenger*, 18 February 1965, 11-12. Clearly, ecumenical affiliations pushed the Brethren toward mainline church design.

73. See Gemeinschaft I invitation, Indian Creek Church of the Brethren file, High Library, Elizabethtown College. The Indian Creek church, Harleysville, hosted the meeting, and each of

the organizers gave an address. Gish and Kulp are Brethren, and Ruth is a Mennonite. For more information on the Gemeinschaft gathering see Joyce Shutt, "Listening to an echo," *Messenger,* October 1973, 8-9.

74. C. Wayne Zunkel interview.

75. See Fitzkee (1990:30). Italics added. Also, the Harrisburg First Council Meeting Minutes use the term "church plant" as early as 1941.

76. J. H. Longenecker to F. S. Carper, 3 January 1936, Frank S. Carper file, High Library, Elizabethtown College. Carper evidently made other changes rather quietly. Informant Harold Z. Bomberger was amazed to see a divided chancel—which he considered "too Lutheranish"—in the Palmyra sanctuary around 1950. When Bomberger asked how Carper "got away with it," Carper's wife said, "He didn't ask anyone. He just did it." See Harold Z. Bomberger interview.

77. John W. Lear, "The Brethren Past and Present," *Brethren Life and Thought* 3 (Winter 1958): 17.

78. James F. Myer interview. Carl W. Zeigler, Sr. made a similar observation, noting that Bethany Theological Seminary president Paul Robinson and many other Brethren leaders were trained in non-Brethren seminaries. See Carl W. Zeigler, Sr. interview by Donald B. Kraybill.

79. The Hatfield congregation, for example, agreed in 1948 to stay seated for the closing prayer, but continued to kneel for the main prayer each Sunday. Kneeling finally ceased altogether in the mid-1960s, coinciding with the arrival of the congregation's first pastor. See *History of the Church. . .* (1965:58). Similarly, the Conewago congregation hired its first pastor in 1965, and, by the late 1960s, kneeling was on its way out. Luke H. Brandt interview. The *Congregational Profile* provided additional data on the disappearance of kneeling.

80. "Report of Abundant Life Committee," in *Eastern District Conference Minutes* (1954:52-53).

81. In the Lititz church, the pastor initiated membership classes in 1953, and six years later the congregation discontinued the annual week-long revival series. See Fitzkee (1990: 23, 32). Half of Atlantic Northeast District congregations still hold revival services once or twice a year. See Table 10. 3.

82. Dove (1932:147) observed: "Modern industrial life of the urban communities has made certain cultural adjustments necessary. . . The busy worshipers in the modern urban churches must commemorate the Lord's supper with a conventional morsel of cheese and a cracker."

83. Howe (1943:450-451).

84. See Fitzkee (1990:30, 33-34) and interviews with Lititz members. The Elizabethtown Church adapted their love feast in the same manner during the 1960s. See *History of the Church. . .* (1965:38).

85. Even in Southeastern District, where other innovations were accepted with relative ease, a strong preference for the full love feast prevailed. Southeastern District elders were scandalized in 1929 when Philadelphia's Geiger Memorial church elected a Baptist pastor without requiring him to be rebaptized. Convinced that a pastor willing to disregard Brethren baptismal practices would be disloyal in other ways, elders ruled the election illegal.

On Easter 1930, the new pastor introduced bread and cup communion to the congregation. After several years of sometimes acrimonious negotiation between district and congregation, the pastor and monthly bread and cup communions won the day. The Fundamentalistic Geiger Brethren totally eliminated the love feast around 1951, but reinstated it in 1986. See *Southeastern District Elders Body Minutes,* 1929-31; and *Congregational Profile.*

86. Delegates appointed a committee to investigate this departure from Brethren practice at the college, and the following year the committee's innocuous report recommended that the church respect the college's "academic freedom and religious liberty" and that the college respect the church's desire that official practices of the Church of the Brethren be upheld. See *Eastern District Conference Minutes* (1955:44; 1956:64).

87. Annual Conference Minutes (1958:13). This was the same landmark decision that waived the trine immersion baptism requirement.

88. See Fitzkee (1990:31-32). Other informants agree that the introduction of the bread and cup communion has eroded support for the love feast. See J. Stanley Earhart and E. Miller Peterman interviews.

89. Based on 44 churches reporting statistics from 1960 and 62 churches reporting for 1988 on the *Congregational Profile.*

90. *Congregational Profile.* Fifty-four congregations provided membership and attendance data for 1960, and 63 for 1988. Informants were asked to estimate 1960 figures where exact numbers were not available.

91. In several large congregations with a clearly mainstream Protestant orientation, love feast attendance declined even more precipitously. In the 30-year period beginning in 1960, the Palmyra church's average love feast attendance decreased by 61 percent. Membership and Sunday worship attendance fell by five percent and 33 percent, respectively. In the Elizabethtown church, love feast attendance plummeted by about 66 percent during a similar time period.

On the other hand, congregations that have maintained a more distinctive Anabaptist identity and have not introduced bread and cup communion generally have seen love feast remain stronger. Love feast attendance in the White Oak and Middle Creek churches from 1960 to 1989 increased by 18 and 20 percent, respectively. See *Congregational Profile* and Elizabethtown Council Meeting Minutes, June 3, 1953.

92. Arlene Keller interview.

93. See *Eastern District Elders Body Minutes,* 1959-1961; and Arlene Keller interview.

94. Bennett wrote about his experience in Dennis J. Bennett, *9 O'clock in the Morning* (Plainfield, New Jersey: Logos International), 1973.

95. For a brief evaluation of the early charismatic movement among Brethren, see Matthew M. Meyer, "Speaking in Tongues—Glossolalia," *Brethren Life and Thought* 20 (Summer 1975): 133-152; and Russell Bixler's response "'Speaking in Tongues—Glossolalia': A Response," *Brethren Life and Thought* 21 (Winter 1976): 51-58. Bixler described his spiritual journey in a brief autobiography. See *It Can Happen to Anybody!* (Monroeville, Pa.: Whitaker Books, 1970). Fred W. Swartz, "The new Russell Bixler comes forward," *Messenger,* July 1973, 14-18, sympathetically pro-

files Bixler's ministry.

96. *Atlantic Northeast District Newsletter,* October 1972, 2.

97. See Atlantic Northeast District Ministry Commission Minutes, January 23, 1975; March 13, 1976; April 30, 1976; November 22, 1977; and *Congregational Profile.*

98. See Atlantic Northeast District Witness Commission Minutes, April 26, 1977; and March 29, 1978, and April 3, 1978, correspondence between Jeffrey L. Miller and James F. Myer, attached to 1978 Ministry Commission Minutes.

99. Atlantic Northeast District Ministry Commission Minutes, June 12, 1978.

100. See *Congregational Profile;* and Brubaker, ed. ([1989]:19-20).

101. Lititz resolved a decade-long identity struggle in 1985 by passing a statement affirming the Church of the Brethren and the congregation's leaders. As a result, about 35 charismatic members left. See Fitzkee (1990:36-37). After three years of controversy, a group of charismatic Brethren left the Mount Zion Road congregation in 1985. See *Congregational Profile.*

102. A new charismatic congregation was formed in 1987 in Lancaster. Dually affiliated with the Church of the Brethren and the Mennonite Church, ACTS Covenant Fellowship sought to integrate Anabaptist and Pentecostal understandings of the church. Several members of other Brethren churches helped establish ACTS. See Boyers and Fitzkee, May 1991, 37- 38.

103. *Congregational Profile.*

104. Many of the district's largest congregations were among the minority who erected steeples and divided chancels. This minority of congregations may actually have represented a majority of total members.

Endnotes for Chapter 11

1. Much of this short history of the Lancaster church is based on a recent congregational history by C. John Bryer. See Bryer (1991).

2. This description of the current Lancaster church is drawn largely from the *Congregational Profile* and telephone conversations with Lancaster pastors Guy Wampler and John David Bowman.

3. See Bryer (1991:10, 16) and *Atlantic Northeast District Directories.* Bryer describes Lancaster's decades of growth as "a time when the church was no longer a 'set-apart sect,' but it had not yet evolved into a main line denomination."

4. *History of the Church. . .* (1915:393-394).

5. *History of the Church. . .* (1965:138).

6. See *Eastern District Meeting Minutes,* May 12-13, 1897; and *Annual Meeting Minutes* (1909:656).

7. *Eastern District Meeting Minutes* (1930:4; 1944:4). District Meeting ruled, "It is not consistent for ministers to officiate at weddings using the ring ceremony."

8. Eastern District Meeting decided not to forward the 1948 query to Annual Conference. Ibid. (1948:11).

9. *Annual Conference Minutes* (1959:72-73).

10. *Congregational Profile.*

11. James F. Myer interview. One deacon wears a standard suit without a necktie.

12. *Congregational Profile.*

13. Ibid.

14. James F. Myer interview.

15. *Congregational Profile.*

16. Telephone conversation with James F. Myer. The shift to individual communion cups was prompted by healthcare professionals in the congregation who feared that they might transfer the deadly AIDS virus—which they could contract in their work—to other members of the congregation. During the transition from common to individual cups these healthcare professionals used individual cups while the rest of the congregation continued to use common cups.

17. James F. Myer interview.

18. *Congregational Profile.*

19. Ibid. and James F. Myer interview.

20. See Durnbaugh, ed., 1983, s. v. "Philadelphia, PA, Germantown Church of the Brethren," by Ronald G. Lutz; and Gleim (1974:120-128) for a history of Germantown prior to 1980.

21. For accounts of more recent developments in Germantown see "Germantown church gets another start," *Messenger,* October 1985, 6; Fitzkee, "New Life in Germantown," *Messenger,* December 1987, 17-21; "Germantown launches ministry to homeless," *Messenger,* August/September 1988, 4; and Fitzkee, "From Ghana to Germantown: An African missionary in America," *Messenger,* May 1991, cover, 38-39.

22. *Congregational Profile.*

23. See Boyers and Fitzkee, "Some plantings that rooted," *Messenger,* May 1991, 34, for an account of the beginnings of Philadelphia Korean. Other Korean congregations are Brooklyn Korean and Open Door Fellowship, both located in New York City. See *Atlantic Northeast District Directory* (1994:46, 62).

24. See "Fellowships received into five districts," *Messenger,* December 1987, 7.

25. See Boyers and Fitzkee, "Some plantings that rooted," *Messenger,* May 1991, 37-38.

26. See Don Fitzkee, "The Birth of a Church," *New Beginnings,* June 1991, 4-5.

27. *Congregational Profile.*

28. Ibid.; and telephone conversation with pastor Judith Kipp.

29. Ibid.

30. Choices provided on the *Congregational Profile* were Fundamentalist, Evangelical, Charismatic, Anabaptist, Mainstream Protestant, or a combination of these. Sixty-five congregations responded.

31. *Congregational Profile.* Pastors and informed lay leaders were asked to estimate the percentage of men in the congregation who earned their living by farming.

32. Ibid. and Bryer (1991:10).

33. *Congregational Profile.* White Oak has drawn members from conservative Mennonite groups and the Dunkard Brethren Church.

34. Ibid. Pastors and informed lay leaders were asked to estimate the percentage of members who had completed a college education.

35. Bryer (1991:31).

36. Bryer (1990:26) notes that the increase in community involvement coincided with Lancaster's move from an Official Board to a lay-led Church Board.

37. James F. Myer interview.

38. Bryer (1991:26-28).

Sources Consulted

Primary Sources
Denominational
Minutes of the Annual Meetings of the Church of the Brethren, Containing All Available Minutes from 1778 to 1909. Elgin, Ill.: Brethren Publishing House, 1909.

Minutes of the Annual Conference of the Church of the Brethren, 1910-1922.

Church of the Brethren Annual Conference Minutes, 1923-1979.

Minutes of the Annual Conference, Church of the Brethren, 1980-1984. Elgin, Ill.: Brethren Press, 1985.

Annual Conference Minutes, 1985-1992.

Full Report of the Proceedings of the Annual Conference of the Church of the Brethren, 1876-1930.

Classified Minutes of the Annual Meetings of the Brethren: A History of the General Councils of the Church from 1778 to 1885. Mt. Morris, Ill. and Huntingdon, Pa.: The Brethren's Publishing Company, 1886.

Revised Minutes of the Annual Meetings of the German Baptist Brethren. Elgin, Ill.: Brethren Publishing House, 1908.

Revised Minutes of the Annual Meetings of the Church of the Brethren from 1778 to 1922. Elgin, Ill.: Brethren Publishing House, 1922.

The Brethren Family Almanac. Elgin, Ill.: Brethren Publishing House, 1911-1916.

Church of the Brethren Yearbook. Elgin, Ill.: Brethren Press, 1918-1992.

District
Atlantic Northeast District Board Minutes, 1970-1992.

Church of the Brethren Districts, Atlantic Northeast, Minutes, 1970-1989.

Atlantic Northeast District Conference Minutes, 1990-1992.

Atlantic Northeast District Directories, 1970-1992.

Minutes of the District Meetings of the German Baptist Brethren of the Eastern District of Pennsylvania from 1867 to 1896.

Minutes, Eastern District of Pennsylvania, Church of the Brethren, 1867-1944.

Eastern District of Pennsylvania, Church of the Brethren, Minutes, 1945-1959.

Church of the Brethren Districts, Eastern Pa., Minutes, 1960-1970.

Eastern District Board Minutes, 1957-1970.

Eastern District Elders Body Minutes, 1897-1967.

Eastern District Ministerial Board Minutes, 1928-1934.

A Synodical [sic] Report of the Proceedings of the Brethren's Second Ministerial Meeting of Eastern Pennsylvania, November 26-28, 1895.

Eastern District Ministerial Meeting Minutes, 1924-1935.

Eastern District Ministerial Meeting Programs, 1893-1962.

Eastern Region Letter, 1947-1964.

Southeastern District Elders Body Minutes, 1913-1948.

Southeastern District Meeting Minutes, 1911-1954.

Southeastern District Ministerial Meeting Minutes, 1912-1921.

North Atlantic District Meeting Minutes, 1954-1970.

Southern Pennsylvania Special District Conference Minutes, April 30, 1968.

Minutes of Joint Meeting of Tri-District Committee and District Boards of Administration of Eastern District, North Atlantic District, and Southern District, September 10, 1966.

"First Annual Report." Tri-District Director of Christian Education Virginia Fisher, October 1, 1961- September 30, 1962.

Brethren Disaster Relief Auction tabloid, 1991.

Brethren Revival Fellowship Meeting Minutes, July 16, 1964.

Congregational
"Brief History of the Richland Church of the Brethren." In Program of Golden Anniversary Services, September 19-21, 1969.

Chiques Church of the Brethren Council Meeting Minutes, 1868-1990.

Church News. Elizabethtown Church of the Brethren Newsletter. June 1963.

Congregational Files, High Library, Elizabethtown College.

Congregational Profile. See Appendix A.

Cramer, Peggy C., comp. *Early Records of the Ambler Church of the Brethren, Ambler, Montgomery Co., PA.* Apollo, Pa.: Closson Press, 1990.

Elizabethtown Church of the Brethren Council Meeting Minutes, 1902-1986.

Harrisburg First Church of the Brethren archives.

Harrisburg First Church of the Brethren Council Meeting Minutes, 1896-1968.

Indian Creek Special Council Meeting Minutes, March 27, 1962.

Lancaster Church of the Brethren Council Meeting Minutes, 1891-1917.

Lititz Church of the Brethren Council Meeting Minutes, 1914-1989.

Middle Creek Congregational Directory, 1987.

Mountville Church of the Brethren Council Meeting Minutes, 1901-1979.

Palmyra Congregational Directories, 1954-1986.

Program of the 50th Anniversary of Scouting in Elizabethtown.

Ridgeway Community Church News Bulletin, March-April 1962.

Stevens Hill Community Church of the Brethren By-Laws.

West Conestoga (Middle Creek) Church of the Brethren Council Meeting Minutes, 1897-1914.

Files of Unpublished Papers

Beahm, I. N. H. Unpublished papers. High Library.
Elizabethtown College.
Bucher, George. Unpublished papers. High Library.
Elizabethtown College.
Carper, Frank S. Unpublished papers. High Library.
Elizabethtown College.
Longenecker, Jacob H. Unpublished papers.
High Library. Elizabethtown College.

Personal Interviews

Interviews were used as supplementary sources
throughout the book. Those interviewed have been
leaders in Atlantic Northeast District and its fore-
runners during the period covered by the study.
All the interviews were conducted between 1986
and 1991, with the majority in early 1991. Unless
otherwise noted, interviews were by the author.
Special thanks to Donald B. Kraybill and Carl F.
Bowman, who made available transcripts of interviews they had conducted.

Harold Z. Bomberger, January 15, 1991
Luke H. Brandt, February 2, 1991
Caleb W. Bucher, May 5, 1986;* January 21, 1991
Franklin K. and Margaret Cassel, January 31,
1989
W. Dean Crouse, January 24, 1991
J. Stanley Earhart, February 8, 1991
J. Harry Enders, March 20, 1990

Hiram J. Frysinger, February 5, 1991
Elmer Q. Gleim, January 31, 1991
Paul M. Grubb Sr., April 1, 1986**
Mayno Hershey, October 14, 1988
Abram M. Hess, May 5, 1986*
Robert O. and Floy Hess, January 9, 1991
Jesse K. and Hilda Hoffman, January 29, 1991
Clifford B. and Hazel Huffman, March 20, 1991
Arlene Keller, February 12, 1991
Earl H. Kurtz, January 14, 1991
Ray A. Kurtz, February 5, 1991
Leona List, January 24, 1991
Joseph M. Long, January 30, 1991
E. Floyd McDowell, January 30, 1989
Betty Malenke, January 29, 1991
Wilbur A. "Whip" Martin, May 3, 1991
James F. Myer, March 20, 1991
E. Miller Peterman, November 19, 1990
Pauline Rosenberger, January 21, 1991
Linford J. Rotenberger, January 24, 1991
Mary Schaeffer, November 23, 1990
Carl W. Zeigler, Sr., February 17, 1986;** February
20, 1986;** March 18, 1986;** June 6, 1986*
Earl K. Ziegler, February 1, 1991
Nevin H. Zuck, January 21, 1991
C. Wayne Zunkel, April 11, 1991

*Interviewed by Donald B. Kraybill and Carl F.
Bowman
**Interviewed by Donald B. Kraybill

Bibliography

Allen, Alice, ed. *The Pennsylvania Manual*. Harris-
burg: Commonwealth of Pennsylvania, 1948.
Allen, Frances R., "The Automobile," in *Technol-
ogy and Social Change*. John F. Cuber, ed. New
York: Appleton-Century-Crofts, Inc., 1957, 107-
132.
Allen, Frederick Lewis. *The Big Change: America
Transforms Itself, 1900-1950*. New York: Harper
& Brothers Publishers, 1952.
"Annual Conference '70." *Messenger*, 30 July
1970, 2-13.
"Annual Conference Report." *Messenger*, 31 July
1969, 2-9.
"Annual Conference Report: Love in Deed and
Truth, in Work and Worship." *Messenger*, 15 Au-
gust 1971, 9-14.
Balsbaugh, Harry K. "History of the Church of the
Brethren, Harrisburg, Pa," 1959, TMs [photo-
copy].
Baugher, Norman J. "An Evaluation of the Free
Ministry." B.D. Thesis, Bethany Biblical Semi-
nary, 1943.
⸺⸺⸺. "What the National Council of Churches
Means to Us." *Messenger*, 18 February 1965, 10-
12, 22.
Beahm, I. N. H. *Twenty Reasons*. n.d.
Bennett, J. Dennis. *9 O'clock in the Morning*.

Plainfield, N. J.: Logos International, 1973.
"The Big Debate of 1966: Excerpting the Views of
Conference Delegates." *Messenger*, 1 September
1966, 16-19.
Bixler, Russell. *It Can Happen to Anybody!* Mon-
roeville, Pa.: Whitaker Books, 1970.
⸺⸺⸺. "'Speaking in Tongues—Glossolalia:' A
Response." *Brethren Life and Thought* 21 (Win-
ter 1976): 51-58.
Bollinger, Richard A. *The Church in a Changing
World*. A Report of the Second Theological Study
Conference held at Oak Brook, Ill., from July 20
to July 24, 1964, on the theme, "The Meaning of
Membership in the Body of Christ." (Elgin, Ill.:
Brethren Press, 1965).
Bomberger, Harold Z. "The Regional Program in
the Church of the Brethren." *Brethren Life and
Thought* 27 (Summer 1982): 157-164.
Bowman, Carl Frederick. "Beyond Plainness: Cul-
tural Transformation in the Church of the Breth-
ren from 1850 to the Present." Ph.D. diss.,
University of Virginia, 1989.
⸺⸺⸺. *Brethren Society: The Cultural
Transformation of a "Peculiar People."* Balti-
more: Johns Hopkins University Press, 1995.
Bowman, Rufus D. *The Church of the Brethren
and War, 1708-1941*. Rev. ed. New York: Gar-

land Publishing, 1971.

_____. *Seventy Times Seven.* Elgin, Ill.: Brethren Publishing House, 1945.

Bowman, S. Loren. *Power and Polity among the Brethren.* Elgin, Ill.: Brethren Press, 1987.

Boyers, Karla and Don Fitzkee. "Some plantings that rooted." *Messenger,* May 1991, 37-38.

Breidenstine, A. G. "The Growth of a Rural Church." *Gospel Messenger,* 5 November 1938, 328-329.

Breidenstine, John S. *A History of the Spring Creek Church of the Brethren 1848-1988.* n.p., [1988].

Brown, Dale W. "A People Without a Liturgy?" *Brethren Life and Thought* 21 (Winter 1986): 24-32.

_____. "Shaping the Ministry: Some Candid Reflections on Bethany's Role." *Brethren Life and Thought* 25 (Winter 1980): 24-27.

_____. "Some Ecumenical Postures for Brethren." *Brethren Life and Thought* 3 (Autumn 1963): 49-56.

_____. "To Not to be or Really to be Brethren." Text of address at Atlantic Northeast District Conference, October 12, 1973.

Brubaker, Jack. "The Scribbler." *Lancaster New Era,* 11 June 1991, A-14.

Brubaker, James, ed. *Middle Creek Church of the Brethren Commemorates 125 Years of Worship, Fellowship and Service 1864-1989.* n.p., [1989].

Brubaker, Pamela. *She Hath Done What She Could.* Elgin, Ill.: Brethren Press, 1985.

Brumbaugh, H. B. *The Church Manual.* Rev. ed. Elgin, Ill.: The Brethren's Publishing Company, 1893.

Brumbaugh, Martin Grove. *A History of the German Baptist Brethren in Europe and America.* 2nd ed. Elgin, Ill.: Brethren Publishing House, 1907.

Bryer, C. John. *History of the Lancaster Church of the Brethren, 1891-1991.* n.p., [1991].

Bucher, Caleb W. "Pastor's Letter." *Brethren Beacon,* October 1, 1944.

Bushong, M. Rebecca. "Ben Bushong—Apostle of Mercy." *Brethren Life and Thought* 24 (Spring 1979): 71-88.

Carper, Frank S. "70th Anniversary." *The Church Monthly,* October 1962, 4-6.

"Church News." *Gospel Messenger,* 12 March 1938, 21; 24 December 1938, 30.

Collier, Forrest, Norman Harsh, Mary Weaver, eds. *East Fairview Church of the Brethren Seventy-fifth Anniversary History.* n.p., 1977.

"Concern Is Shown For Harrisburg 7." *Intelligencer Journal* (Lancaster), 27 January 1972, 52.

"COs in full public view." *Messenger,* 27 June 1967, 15.

Crowther, Jerome. "History of the Church of the Brethren in Reading, 1898-1965." 1965 (?), TMs [photocopy].

"Disaster Relief Auction." *Brethren News,* November 1989, 11.

Dove, Frederick Denton. *Cultural Changes in the Church of the Brethren.* Elgin, Ill.: Brethren Publishing House, 1932.

Durnbaugh, Donald F. "An experiment in church/state relations." *Messenger,* October 1990, 11, 14.

_____, ed. *The Brethren Encyclopedia.* Phila-
delphia and Oak Brook, Ill.: The Brethren Encyclopedia, Inc., 1983.

_____, ed. *Church of the Brethren Yesterday and Today.* Elgin, Ill.: Brethren Press, 1986.

_____, ed. *Meet the Brethren.* Elgin, Ill.: Brethren Press for the Brethren Encyclopedia, Inc., 1984.

_____, ed. *To Serve the Present Age.* Elgin, Ill.: Brethren Press, 1975.

_____. "Will the Brethren Prevail?" *Brethren Life and Thought* 10 (Winter 1965): 54-62.

Earhart, J. Stanley. "The East Fairview Church of the Brethren," May 21, 1954, TMs [photocopy].

Eastern District of Pennsylvania Historical Committee. *History of the Church of the Brethren of the Eastern District of Pennsylvania.* Lancaster, Pa.: Historical Committee, 1915.

Eberly, William R., ed. *The Complete Writings of Alexander Mack.* Winona Lake, Ind.: BMH Books, 1991.

Edwards, Morgan. *Materials Towards a History of the American Baptists.* Philadelphia: Crukshank and Collins, 1770.

"Election Results." *Intelligencer Journal* (Lancaster), 27 April 1932, 1, 7.

Eller, Geraldine Crill. "Adolescent Thinking—Blue Jeans and the Brethren." *Brethren Life and Thought* 3 (Winter 1958): 39-47.

Faus, Robert E. "Ministering to the Brethren." *Messenger,* July 1990, 25-26.

Faus, Robert E. and Richard B. Gardner. "Issues in Ministry." *Messenger,* March 1987, 28.

"Fellowships received into five districts." *Messenger,* December 1987, 7.

Fitzkee, Don. "The Birth of a Church." *New Beginnings,* June 1991, 4-5.

_____. "From Ghana to Germantown: An African missionary in America." *Messenger,* May 1991, cover, 38-39.

_____. "New Life in Germantown." *Messenger,* December 1987, 17-21.

_____. "Overcoming the Topsy syndrome: The making of the General Board." *Messenger,* March 1987, 12-14.

_____. "War Heroes." *Messenger,* October 1990, 18.

Fitzkee, Donald R. *The Transformation of the Lititz Church of the Brethren, 1914-1989.* Lancaster, Pa.: Lititz Church of the Brethren, 1990.

Fletcher, Stevenson Whitcomb. *Pennsylvania Agriculture and Country Life, 1840-1940.* Harrisburg: Pennsylvania Historical and Museum Commission, 1965.

Frye, Nancy Kettering. "The Meetinghouse Connection: Plain Living in the Gilded Age." *Pennsylvania Folklife* 41 (Winter 1991-92): 50-82.

Fuchs, Lawrence. "Election of 1928," in *History of American Presidential Elections.* Vol. 3. Arthur M. Schlesinger, Jr., ed. New York: McGraw-Hill, 1971, 2585-2704.

"Germantown church gets another start." *Messenger,* October 1985, 6.

"Germantown launches ministry to homeless." *Messenger,* August/September 1988, 4.

Gibble, June A. and Fred W. Swartz, eds. *Called to Caregiving: A Resource for Equipping Deacons in the Believers Church.* Elgin, Ill.: Brethren Press, 1987.

Gish, Paul A. "Readers Write." *Messenger,* 15 January 1970, 1, 29.

Gleim, Elmer Q. *From These Roots: A History of the North Atlantic District.* Lancaster, Pa.: Atlantic Northeast District Historical Committee, 1975.

Glick, G. Wayne. "The Laws of Men and the Law of God." *Messenger,* 15 October 1971, 9-11, 25.

Glick, Ted. "Readers Write." *Messenger,* 12 February 1970, inside cover.

_____. "Readers Write." *Messenger,* 1 November 1972, 1, 21.

"Growing Edges." *Messenger,* 6 January 1966, 18.

Hark, Ann. *Hex Marks the Spot.* Philadelphia: J. B. Lippincott Company, 1938.

Harris, Luella Reinhold. "Readers Write." *Messenger,* 14 August 1969, inside cover.

Hartsough, H. L., Raymond R. Peters, M. R. Zigler, and Foster B. Statler, eds. *Brethren Minister's Manual.* Authorized by General Ministerial Board. Elgin, Ill.: Brethren Publishing House, 1946.

History of the Church of the Brethren, Eastern Pennsylvania, 1915-1965. Lancaster, Pa.: Eastern District of Pennsylvania, 1965.

Hogan, Herbert. "The Intellectual Impact of the 20th Century on the Church of the Brethren." Ph.D. diss., Claremont Graduate School, 1958.

Howe, Roland L. *The History of a Church (Dunker) with comments featuring The First Church of the Brethren of Philadelphia, Pa., 1813-1943.* Philadelphia: By the author, 1943.

_____. "Love Feasts Here and There, Second Half." *Gospel Messenger,* 29 April 1933, 7-8, 20.

Hudson, Winthrop S. *The Great Tradition of the American Churches.* New York: Harper and Brothers, 1953.

_____. *Religion in America.* 4th ed. New York: Macmillan Publishers, 1987.

Hummer, Amos A. "Worldly Amusements." *Gospel Messenger,* 5 March 1938, 23-24.

Hutchison, William R. *The Modernist Impulse in American Protestantism.* New York: Oxford University Press, 1976.

"Inviting Others to Preach." *Gospel Messenger,* 3 March 1906, 138.

"Judge Severs Glick's Trial." *Intelligencer Journal* (Lancaster), 18 January 1972, 6.

Kaylor, Earl C., Jr. *Out of the Wilderness: The Brethren and Two Centuries of Life in Central Pennsylvania (1780-1980).* New York: Cornwall Books, 1981.

_____. *Truth Sets Free: A Centennial History of Juniata College, 1876-1976.* South Brunswick and New York: A. S. Barnes and Co., 1977.

Keener, Ronald E. "Campus recruitment for war and peace." *Messenger,* 1 May 1971, 2-3.

Keim, Albert N. and Grant M. Stoltzfus. *The Politics of Conscience: The Historic Peace Churches and America at War, 1917-1955.* Scottdale, Pa.: Herald Press, 1988.

Klein, Philip S. and Ari Hoogenboom. *A History of Pennsylvania.* New York: McGraw-Hill Book Company, 1973.

Kraybill, Donald B. *The Riddle of Amish Culture.* Baltimore: Johns Hopkins University Press, 1989.

_____ and Donald R. Fitzkee. "Amish, Mennonites, and Brethren in the Modern Era." *Pennsylvania Mennonite Heritage* 10 (April 1987): 2-11.

Kreider, J. Kenneth. "Readers Write." *Messenger,* 25 September 1969, inside cover.

_____. "Readers Write." *Messenger,* 1 August 1971, inside cover-1.

Kulp, Mary Jane, ed. *History of the Coventry Church of the Brethren, 1724-1974.* n.p., [1974].

Lear, John W. "The Brethren Past and Present." *Brethren Life and Thought* 3 (Winter 1958): 15-21.

Lehigh, David W. "A Profession or a Calling?" *Gospel Messenger,* 14 May 1938, 9.

Long, Inez G. "Brethren Take to the Hills and Alleys." *Christian Century* 83 (July 20, 1966): 916-917.

_____. "Dare Brethren join step with marchers?" *Messenger,* 20 January 1966, 6-7.

_____. "Less Time on Yard Goods." *Messenger,* 26 October 1963, 15.

Mallott, Floyd E. *Studies in Brethren History.* Elgin, Ill.: Brethren Publishing House, 1954.

_____. "What is the Future System of Our Ministry?" *Gospel Messenger,* 22 January 1938, 5-6.

Marty, Martin E. *Righteous Empire: The Protestant Experience in America.* New York: Dial Press, 1970.

"The Messenger and the Candidates." *Gospel Messenger,* 27 October 1928, 677.

Meyer, Matthew M. "Speaking in Tongues—Glossalalia." *Brethren Life and Thought* 20 (Summer 1975): 133-152.

Miller, Delbert C. "Radio and Television," in *Technology and Social Change.* John F. Cuber, ed. New York: Appleton-Century-Crofts, Inc., 1957, 157-186.

Miller, R. H. *The Doctrine of the Brethren Defended.* Elgin, Ill.: Brethren Publishing House, 1903.

"Moderator." *Intelligencer Journal* (Lancaster), 29 April 1932, 1.

Moore, George L. "Dunkard Life in Lebanon Valley Sixty Years Ago." *Pennsylvania Folklife* 12 (Spring 1961): 10-23.

Moore, J. H. *The New Testament Doctrines.* Elgin, Ill.: Brethren Publishing House, 1915.

_____. "Querist's Department." *Gospel Messenger,* 19 February 1898, 121.

Moore, R. Laurence. *Religious Outsiders and the Making of Americans.* New York: Oxford University Press, 1986.

Morse, Kenneth I. "Let's listen to the loyal opposition." *Messenger,* 24 June 1965, 32.

Moyer, Elgin S. *Missions in the Church of the Brethren: Their Development and Effect Upon the Denomination.* Elgin, Ill.: Brethren Publishing House, 1931.

Niebuhr, H. Richard. *Christ and Culture.* New York: Harper and Brothers, 1951.

_____. *The Social Sources of Denominationalism.* Cleveland and New York: The Word Publishing Company, 1929.

"Notes From Our Correspondents." *Gospel Messenger,* 26 March 1898, 201, 205; 30 April 1898, 285.

"Notes From Our Correspondents." *Gospel Messenger,* 14 March 1903, 173; 26 December 1903, 829.

"Notes From Our Correspondents." *Gospel Messenger,* 11 May 1918, 304; 25 May 1918, 333; 15 June 1918, 379; 28 September 1918, 621.

"The Obstruction in Church." *Gospel Messenger,* 8 August 1903, 504.

Ogren, David C. "Readers Write." *Messenger*, 16 September 1965, inside cover.

Pierard, Richard V. "The Church of the Brethren and the Temperance Movement." *Brethren Life and Thought* 26 (Winter 1981): 36-44.

"Protestant Churches Sponsor 42,633 Scout Packs, Troops, Posts." *Gospel Messenger*, 5 July 1958, 20.

"Regional Youth Interested in Brethren Volunteer Service." *Eastern Region Letter*, July 1950, 1.

Reisinger, Ernest L. "Readers Write." *Messenger*, 12 March 1970, 1.

"Report Urges Ecumenicity." *Messenger*, 23 June 1966, 1-2.

Rohrer, Kay. "College dedicates new center." *Sunday News* (Lancaster), 8 October, 1989.

Roop, Eugene F. "The Brethren and Church Discipline (I)." *Brethren Life and Thought* 14 (Spring 1969): 92-102.

_____. "The Brethren and Church Discipline (II)." *Brethren Life and Thought* 14 (Summer 1969): 168-182.

Rosenberger, I. J. "Other Societies." *Gospel Messenger*, 9 May 1903, 291-292.

Rupel, Esther F. "The Dress of the Brethren." *Brethren Life and Thought* 31 (Summer 1986): 135-150.

"Sales of new hymnal are exceeding expectations." *Messenger*, March 1992, 8.

Sappington, Roger E. *Brethren Social Policy*. Elgin, Ill.: Brethren Press, 1961.

_____, ed. *The Brethren in Industrial America: A Source Book on the Development of the Church of the Brethren, 1865-1910*. Elgin, Ill.: Brethren Press, 1985.

Schlosser, Ralph W. "Fifty Years of Change." *Gospel Messenger*, 23 May 1968, 20-21.

_____. *History of Elizabethtown College, 1899-1970*. Elizabethtown, Pa.: Elizabethtown College, 1971.

Schwalm, V. F. *Otho Winger*. Elgin, Ill.: Brethren Publishing House, 1952.

"Score One for the Military." *Atlantic Northeast District Brethren Peace Fellowship Newsletter*, December 1970, 1-2.

Shoemaker, Silas and Nevin Zuck. *The Church of the Brethren in Ambler: A History of the One Hundred and Two Years of the Old Upper Dublin Church of the Brethren*. 1942, TMs [photocopy].

Shutt, Joyce. "Listening to an echo." *Messenger*, October 1973, 8-9.

Stoffer, Dale Rupert. *The Background and Development of Brethren Doctrines, 1650-1987*. Philadelphia and Oak Brook, Ill.: *The Brethren Encyclopedia*, Inc., 1989.

_____. *The Background and Development of Thought and Practice in the German Baptist Brethren (Dunker) and the Brethren (Progressive) Churches*. Ann Arbor, Mich.: University Microfilms International, 1980.

Stover, W. B. "Why the Brethren Hold to Strict Communion." *Gospel Messenger*, 9 July 1898, 428.

Studebaker, Joseph. "Vocal Versus Instrumental Music for Worship—No. 1." *Gospel Messenger*, 18 June 1898, 371-372.

Swarr, Philip Cassel. "A Historical-Sociological Study of the Church of the Brethren." 1963 (?), TMs [photocopy].

Swartz, Fred W. "The new Russell Bixler comes forward." *Messenger*, July 1973, 14-18.

Taylor, I. W. "A Visit to Camp Meade, Admiral, Md." *Gospel Messenger*, 13 October 1917, 645.

"Thanks be to God for a Successful '89 Relief Auction." *Brethren News*, November 1986, 4.

"Troublers of Israel." *Atlantic Northeast District Brethren Peace Fellowship Newsletter*, May 1972, 2.

"Two Obligations That Will Remain." *Gospel Messenger*, 3 November 1928, 693.

"Vignettes of an Annual Conference." *Messenger*, 4 August 1966, 1-2.

"Vocal and Instrumental Music in Worship." General Missionary and Tract Committee, n.d.

Wenger, Jon C. *History of Camp Swatara: The First Fifty Years*. Manheim, Pa.: Privately printed, 1993.

Wieand, Albert C., J. J. Yoder, and Edward Frantz, eds. *Pastor's Manual*. Authorized by General Conference of the Church of the Brethren. Elgin, Ill.: Brethren Publishing House, 1923.

Willoughby, William G. *The Life of Alexander Mack: Counting the Cost*. Elgin, Ill.: Brethren Press, 1979.

Zeigler, Carl W. Sr. "The Week-end Love Feast." *Gospel Messenger*, 4 February 1956, 12-15.

Ziegler [sic], Carl W. "Baneful Effects of Worldly Amusements." Pamphlet from the 1920s.

Ziegler, Jesse H. *The Broken Cup: Three Generations of Dunkers*. Elgin, Ill.: Brethren Publishing House, 1942.

Ziegler, Levi K. "Two Weeks in the Mechanic Grove Church, Pa." *Gospel Messenger*, 6 July 1918, 427.

Zunkel, C. Wayne. "Brethren bidding for bolder peace action." *Messenger*, 14 March 1968, 17.

_____. "Readers Write." *Messenger*, 23 December 1965, inside cover.

_____. "Readers Write." *Messenger*, 12 May 1966, inside cover.

Index

Page numbers in italics indicate illustrations.

About the Author

Donald R. Fitzkee is an ordained minister in the Chiques Church of the Brethren, near Manheim, Pennsylvania. A graduate of Elizabethtown College and Eastern Baptist Theological Seminary, he has written extensively for the Church of the Brethren denominational magazine, *Messenger*, and for other Brethren publications. Donald lives with his wife Carolyn in Rheems, Pennsylvania.